# Microsoft®
# Visual Basic® .NET
# Programming

### for the
## absolute
## beginner

# Microsoft® Visual Basic® .NET Programming

## for the absolute beginner

Premier
Press

JONATHAN S. HARBOUR

The Premier Press logo and related trade dress are trademarks of Premier Press, Inc. and may not be used without written permission.

Microsoft, the .NET logo, Visual Basic, and/or other Microsoft products referenced herein are either registered trademarks or trademarks of Microsoft Corporation in the U.S. and/or other countries.

All other trademarks are the property of their respective owners.

*Important:* Premier Press cannot provide software support. Please contact the appropriate software manufacturer's technical support line or Web site for assistance.

Premier Press and the author have attempted throughout this book to distinguish proprietary trademarks from descriptive terms by following the capitalization style used by the manufacturer.

Information contained in this book has been obtained by Premier Press from sources believed to be reliable. However, because of the possibility of human or mechanical error by our sources, Premier Press, or others, the Publisher does not guarantee the accuracy, adequacy, or completeness of any information and is not responsible for any errors or omissions or the results obtained from use of such information. Readers should be particularly aware of the fact that the Internet is an ever-changing entity. Some facts may have changed since this book went to press.

ISBN: 1-59200-002-9

Library of Congress Catalog Card Number: 2002106530

Printed in the United States of America

02 03 04 05 BH 10 9 8 7 6 5 4 3 2 1

Premier Press, a division of Course Technology
2645 Erie Avenue, Suite 41
Cincinnati, Ohio 45208

**Publisher:**
Stacy L. Hiquet

**Marketing Manager:**
Heather Hurley

**Managing Editor:**
Sandy Doell

**Acquisitions Editor:**
Todd Jensen

**Senior Project Editor:**
Heather Talbot

**Editorial Assistants:**
Margaret Bauer
Elizabeth Barrett

**Technical Reviewer:**
Greg Perry

**Copyeditor:**
Jenny Davidson

**Interior Layout:**
Shawn Morningstar

**Cover Designer:**
Mike Tanamachi

**CD-ROM Producer:**
Keith Davenport

**Indexer:**
Sherry Massey

**Proofreader:**
Kim Benbow

*This book is dedicated to my sister, Joy.*
*May you find happiness and contentment.*

# Acknowledgments

I would like to thank everyone who helped make this book a reality. First, I thank God for giving me a talent for expressing my thoughts in writing. Thanks to my family and friends for their support. To my wife, Jennifer, for hanging in there during my hectic schedule the past few months. To Jeremiah and Kayleigh, for causing so many welcome and needed distractions while I'm writing. To fellow lan party campers: Justin Galloway, John Striker, Chris Henson, and Gerald Winkler. To some great people with whom I've had the pleasure of working: Steve Myers, Todd Schuett, Tom Biermann, Randy Smith, Long Nguyen, Maria Maldonado, Matt Klein, Matt Hamby, and the rest of the Phoenix staff at ValueOptions.

I owe a debt of gratitude to everyone at Premier Press who helped to create this book. I am amazed with the amount of creative freedom I'm given, and appreciate their trust. To Emi Smith, who got the idea after several of my proposals that I wanted to do something other than a game development book—thanks for being supportive. To Mitzi Foster, for cheerfulness and lending an ear from time to time. To Todd Jensen, for your energy and passion for getting things done! Thank you for keeping me on schedule and for putting up with the many changes this book went through before it was completed. To Heather Talbot for managing the project and putting in all the finishing touches. To Andy Harris, series editor, for input that helped guide the direction of this book. He was right; it is surprisingly difficult to write a beginner's book. To Greg Perry, technical editor, for some very helpful suggestions.

To the developers of Paint Shop Pro at Jasc Software for a truly excellent program that has gotten me through several books now. To the developers of WinAmp and the following musicians for keeping me inspired: Enya, The Cranberries, U2, Paula Cole, Enigma, Heather Nova, Faith Hill, John Williams, Shania Twain, and Creed. Finally, to Microsoft for developing products that not only provide many with a living, but also with a great deal of entertainment. Okay, back to another round of *HALO*...

# About the Author

**J**onathan S. Harbour has been fascinated with computers since his first experience with a Commodore PET in 1979. He's been programming for 15 years, having started with Microsoft BASIC and Turbo Pascal on a Tandy 1000. Jonathan graduated from DeVry Institute of Technology with a degree in computer information systems in 1997. He has since worked on information systems for cellular, aerospace, pharmaceutical, education, medical research, and healthcare companies. He is currently employed with ValueOptions in Phoenix, Arizona.

In his spare time, Jonathan enjoys learning new coding tricks in Visual Basic, C++, and other languages. He regularly hosts HALO LAN parties with friends and fellow Xbox fans. He also reads programming and science fiction books. Jonathan authored *Visual Basic Game Programming with DirectX* and *Pocket PC Game Programming*. He is currently working on a game programming book based on the DarkBASIC language.

# Contents

Introduction . . . . . . . . . . . . . . . . . . . . . . . . . . . . . . . xviii

**PART 1**

**Introduction to
Visual Basic .NET . . . . . . . . . . . . . 1**

Chapter 1: **Getting Started with
Visual Basic .NET . . . . . . . . . . . . . . . . . .3**

Project Preview—Guessing Game . . . . . . . . . . . . . . . . . . . 4
What Is Visual Basic? . . . . . . . . . . . . . . . . . . . . . . . . . . . . 4
    Programming Languages . . . . . . . . . . . . . . . . . . . . . . . 5
    Rapid Application Development . . . . . . . . . . . . . . . . . . 5
    Database Development . . . . . . . . . . . . . . . . . . . . . . . . 5
    The Graphical User Interface. . . . . . . . . . . . . . . . . . . . 6
    Introduction to VB.NET . . . . . . . . . . . . . . . . . . . . . . . 7
Writing Code . . . . . . . . . . . . . . . . . . . . . . . . . . . . . . . . . . 7
    Greetings to the World . . . . . . . . . . . . . . . . . . . . . . . 9
Chapter Project—Guessing Game . . . . . . . . . . . . . . . . . . 20
    Creating the New Project. . . . . . . . . . . . . . . . . . . . . . 20
    Understanding Windows Forms . . . . . . . . . . . . . . . . . 23
    Using the Control Toolbox. . . . . . . . . . . . . . . . . . . . . 23
Summary. . . . . . . . . . . . . . . . . . . . . . . . . . . . . . . . . . . . 39

Chapter 2: **Overview of Visual Studio .NET . . . . . .41**

The Languages Spoken by Visual Studio .NET . . . . . . . . . 42
    Visual Basic .NET . . . . . . . . . . . . . . . . . . . . . . . . . . . 44
    Visual C# .NET . . . . . . . . . . . . . . . . . . . . . . . . . . . . . 46
    Visual C++ .NET . . . . . . . . . . . . . . . . . . . . . . . . . . . . 47
    Visual J# .NET . . . . . . . . . . . . . . . . . . . . . . . . . . . . . 47
    Support Libraries . . . . . . . . . . . . . . . . . . . . . . . . . . . 47

Introduction to the .NET Framework . . . . . . . . . . . . . . . . . . 48
   The Importance of Software Standards . . . . . . . . . . . . . 48
   Emerging Technologies . . . . . . . . . . . . . . . . . . . . . . . . 48
   Writing "Really" Reusable Code . . . . . . . . . . . . . . . . . . 49
   Object-Oriented Standards . . . . . . . . . . . . . . . . . . . . . 49
The Visual Studio .NET Development Environment . . . . . . 50
   The Visual Studio .NET User Interface . . . . . . . . . . . . . 50
   Customizing the User Interface . . . . . . . . . . . . . . . . . . 65
Summary . . . . . . . . . . . . . . . . . . . . . . . . . . . . . . . . . . . . 67

Chapter 3: **The Basics of a
            Graphical User Interface** . . . . . . . . . . .**69**

Project Preview—Tic-Tac-Toe . . . . . . . . . . . . . . . . . . . . . 70
Graphical User Interfaces—The Big Picture . . . . . . . . . . . 70
   Multi-Tasking and Multi-Processing . . . . . . . . . . . . . . . 72
Forms and Controls . . . . . . . . . . . . . . . . . . . . . . . . . . . . 75
   Adding and Removing Controls . . . . . . . . . . . . . . . . . . 76
   Naming Controls . . . . . . . . . . . . . . . . . . . . . . . . . . . . . 79
   Moving and Resizing Controls . . . . . . . . . . . . . . . . . . . 80
   Setting Control Properties . . . . . . . . . . . . . . . . . . . . . . 80
The Standard Dialogs . . . . . . . . . . . . . . . . . . . . . . . . . . . 80
   Using the MsgBox Function . . . . . . . . . . . . . . . . . . . . . 82
   Using the InputBox Function . . . . . . . . . . . . . . . . . . . . 90
Chapter Project—The Tic-Tac-Toe Game . . . . . . . . . . . . . 92
   Creating the New Project . . . . . . . . . . . . . . . . . . . . . . . 94
   The Main Form . . . . . . . . . . . . . . . . . . . . . . . . . . . . . . . 94
   Building the User Interface . . . . . . . . . . . . . . . . . . . . . . 97
   Writing the Source Code . . . . . . . . . . . . . . . . . . . . . . 101
Summary . . . . . . . . . . . . . . . . . . . . . . . . . . . . . . . . . . . 109

Chapter 4: **Forms and Toolbox Controls** . . . . . . .**111**

Introduction to Windows Forms . . . . . . . . . . . . . . . . . . . 112
   Understanding the Windows Forms Engine . . . . . . . . 113
   Windows Messages and Event Procedures . . . . . . . . . 117
Programming the Toolbox Controls . . . . . . . . . . . . . . . . 118
   Basic Controls . . . . . . . . . . . . . . . . . . . . . . . . . . . . . . 118
   Slider Controls . . . . . . . . . . . . . . . . . . . . . . . . . . . . . . 127
   Listing Controls . . . . . . . . . . . . . . . . . . . . . . . . . . . . . 130
   Container Controls . . . . . . . . . . . . . . . . . . . . . . . . . . . 134
Summary . . . . . . . . . . . . . . . . . . . . . . . . . . . . . . . . . . . 136

**Programming Fundamentals in Visual Basic .NET . . . . . . . . 139**

Chapter 5: **Variables and Data Types** . . . . . . . . .141

Project Preview—Typing Tutor . . . . . . . . . . . . . . . . . . . . 142
Variables of All Types . . . . . . . . . . . . . . . . . . . . . . . . . . . 142
    What Is a Variable?. . . . . . . . . . . . . . . . . . . . . . . . . . 142
    Using Variables . . . . . . . . . . . . . . . . . . . . . . . . . . . . 143
Learning the Data Types . . . . . . . . . . . . . . . . . . . . . . . . 144
    Listing of Data Types . . . . . . . . . . . . . . . . . . . . . . . 145
    Choosing a Data Type . . . . . . . . . . . . . . . . . . . . . . 146
    The Variables Program. . . . . . . . . . . . . . . . . . . . . . 146
    Assigning Values at Declaration . . . . . . . . . . . . . . . 150
    Variable Objects . . . . . . . . . . . . . . . . . . . . . . . . . . . 152
What's So Special about Strings?. . . . . . . . . . . . . . . . . . 155
    Declaring and Using Strings . . . . . . . . . . . . . . . . . . 156
    Modifying Strings. . . . . . . . . . . . . . . . . . . . . . . . . . . 156
Chapter Project—The Typing Tutor Program . . . . . . . . . . 160
    Creating the Project . . . . . . . . . . . . . . . . . . . . . . . . 161
    Building the User Interface . . . . . . . . . . . . . . . . . . . 161
Summary. . . . . . . . . . . . . . . . . . . . . . . . . . . . . . . . . . . . 171

Chapter 6: **Branching Statements and Program Logic** . . . . . . . . . . . . . . . .173

Project Preview—The DiceWar Program . . . . . . . . . . . . . 174
Learning about Program Logic . . . . . . . . . . . . . . . . . . . . 174
    What Is a Branching Statement? . . . . . . . . . . . . . . . 175
    The If...Then Statement. . . . . . . . . . . . . . . . . . . . . . 175
    The Select...Case Statement . . . . . . . . . . . . . . . . . . 178
Understanding Subroutines . . . . . . . . . . . . . . . . . . . . . . 179
    Using Subs and Functions. . . . . . . . . . . . . . . . . . . . 180
    Returning Values with Functions . . . . . . . . . . . . . . . 180
Chapter Project—The DiceWar Program. . . . . . . . . . . . . 181
    Running the Program. . . . . . . . . . . . . . . . . . . . . . . . 181
    Designing the Project. . . . . . . . . . . . . . . . . . . . . . . . 184
    Writing the Source Code . . . . . . . . . . . . . . . . . . . . . 188
Summary. . . . . . . . . . . . . . . . . . . . . . . . . . . . . . . . . . . . 194

xii

Table of Contents

Chapter 7: **Number Crunching: Mathematical and Relational Operations** . . . . . . . . . **197**

Project Preview—The Math Quiz Program . . . . . . . . . . . . 198
Mathematical Operators . . . . . . . . . . . . . . . . . . . . . . . 198
   Basic Number Crunching . . . . . . . . . . . . . . . . . . . . . 199
   The Simple Math Program . . . . . . . . . . . . . . . . . . . . 203
   Advanced Number Crunching . . . . . . . . . . . . . . . . . . 203
Random Numbers . . . . . . . . . . . . . . . . . . . . . . . . . . . 205
   Creating Random Numbers . . . . . . . . . . . . . . . . . . . . 206
Relational Operators . . . . . . . . . . . . . . . . . . . . . . . . . 206
   Object Relationships . . . . . . . . . . . . . . . . . . . . . . . . 207
   Relational Operators . . . . . . . . . . . . . . . . . . . . . . . . 207
Chapter Project—The Math Quiz Program . . . . . . . . . . . 210
   Designing the Project . . . . . . . . . . . . . . . . . . . . . . . 210
   Writing the Source Code . . . . . . . . . . . . . . . . . . . . . 214
Summary . . . . . . . . . . . . . . . . . . . . . . . . . . . . . . . . . 217

Chapter 8: **Loops, Arrays, and Structures** . . . . . . **219**

Introduction to Looping Commands . . . . . . . . . . . . . . . 220
   What Is a Loop? . . . . . . . . . . . . . . . . . . . . . . . . . . . 220
   Iteration and Repetition . . . . . . . . . . . . . . . . . . . . . . 222
   For...Next Loop . . . . . . . . . . . . . . . . . . . . . . . . . . . 222
   Do Loops . . . . . . . . . . . . . . . . . . . . . . . . . . . . . . . 223
Arrays . . . . . . . . . . . . . . . . . . . . . . . . . . . . . . . . . . . 225
   What Is an Array? . . . . . . . . . . . . . . . . . . . . . . . . . . 225
   Declaring a Variable Array . . . . . . . . . . . . . . . . . . . . 225
   Understanding Arrays . . . . . . . . . . . . . . . . . . . . . . . 226
Structures . . . . . . . . . . . . . . . . . . . . . . . . . . . . . . . . 227
   What Is a Structure? . . . . . . . . . . . . . . . . . . . . . . . . 228
   Filling a Structure with Variables . . . . . . . . . . . . . . . . 228
   Using Structure Arrays . . . . . . . . . . . . . . . . . . . . . . 228
Summary . . . . . . . . . . . . . . . . . . . . . . . . . . . . . . . . . 231

PART

# Object-Oriented Programming with Visual Basic .NET . . . . . . 233

Chapter 9: **The Basics of Object-Oriented Programming** . . . . . . . . . . . . . . . **235**

Project Preview—The Blocks Program . . . . . . . . . . . . . . . 236
Introduction to Object-Oriented Programming. . . . . . . . . 236
    Overview of OOP . . . . . . . . . . . . . . . . . . . . . . . . . . . . . 237
    OOP Fundamentals . . . . . . . . . . . . . . . . . . . . . . . . . . 238
The Extraordinary Property. . . . . . . . . . . . . . . . . . . . . . . 242
    What Is a Property? . . . . . . . . . . . . . . . . . . . . . . . . . . 242
    Creating Properties . . . . . . . . . . . . . . . . . . . . . . . . . . 242
    Using Properties. . . . . . . . . . . . . . . . . . . . . . . . . . . . . 243
    Automatic Data Validation . . . . . . . . . . . . . . . . . . . . . 243
Chapter Project—The Blocks Program . . . . . . . . . . . . . . . 244
    Designing the Project. . . . . . . . . . . . . . . . . . . . . . . . . . 245
    Writing the Source Code . . . . . . . . . . . . . . . . . . . . . . . 250
Summary. . . . . . . . . . . . . . . . . . . . . . . . . . . . . . . . . . . . 256

Chapter 10: **Understanding and Using Classes . . . 257**

Project Preview—The Pet Shop Program . . . . . . . . . . . . . 258
Introduction to Visual Basic Classes. . . . . . . . . . . . . . . . . 259
    What Is a Class? . . . . . . . . . . . . . . . . . . . . . . . . . . . . . 259
    Understanding Classes and OOP. . . . . . . . . . . . . . . . . 260
    Encapsulation. . . . . . . . . . . . . . . . . . . . . . . . . . . . . . . 262
    Inheritance . . . . . . . . . . . . . . . . . . . . . . . . . . . . . . . . . 262
    Polymorphism . . . . . . . . . . . . . . . . . . . . . . . . . . . . . . 263
    The Format of a Class . . . . . . . . . . . . . . . . . . . . . . . . . 264
Creating Visual Basic Classes . . . . . . . . . . . . . . . . . . . . . 266
    Real-World Example—The Animal Class. . . . . . . . . . . . 267
    The Dog Class . . . . . . . . . . . . . . . . . . . . . . . . . . . . . . 273
    The Cat Class . . . . . . . . . . . . . . . . . . . . . . . . . . . . . . . 277
    The Bird Class . . . . . . . . . . . . . . . . . . . . . . . . . . . . . . 280
Chapter Project—The Pet Shop Program . . . . . . . . . . . . . 283
    Running the Program. . . . . . . . . . . . . . . . . . . . . . . . . . 283
    Revisiting the Project . . . . . . . . . . . . . . . . . . . . . . . . . 284
    Finishing the Source Code. . . . . . . . . . . . . . . . . . . . . . 288
Summary. . . . . . . . . . . . . . . . . . . . . . . . . . . . . . . . . . . . 291

**xiv**

Table of Contents

Chapter 11: **Namespaces and
Visual Inheritance** . . . . . . . . . . . . . . .**293**

Using Namespaces . . . . . . . . . . . . . . . . . . . . . . . . . . . . 294
  Renaming the PetShop Project . . . . . . . . . . . . . . . . . 294
  What Is a Namespace? . . . . . . . . . . . . . . . . . . . . . . . 297
  Creating a Namespace . . . . . . . . . . . . . . . . . . . . . . . 297
  Completing the Pet Class . . . . . . . . . . . . . . . . . . . . . 300
  Moving the Animal Class into the Pets Namespace . . . 301
  Creating the Pets.Dogs Namespace . . . . . . . . . . . . . . 303
  Creating the Pets.Cats Namespace . . . . . . . . . . . . . . 307
  Creating the Pets.Birds Namespace . . . . . . . . . . . . . . 308
  Moving Form Code into a Module . . . . . . . . . . . . . . . 310
  Form1 Source Code . . . . . . . . . . . . . . . . . . . . . . . . . 314
  Completing the PetStore Project . . . . . . . . . . . . . . . . 315
  Adding New Functionality to PetStore . . . . . . . . . . . . 316
Visual Inheritance . . . . . . . . . . . . . . . . . . . . . . . . . . . . 318
  Creating a Reusable Form . . . . . . . . . . . . . . . . . . . . 318
  Reusing the Reusable Form . . . . . . . . . . . . . . . . . . . . 319
  Running the VisualInheritance Program . . . . . . . . . . . 321
Summary . . . . . . . . . . . . . . . . . . . . . . . . . . . . . . . . . . 321

PART 4 **Advanced Programming
Topics in Visual Basic .NET . . . 323**

Chapter 12: **Graphics Programming** . . . . . . . . . .**325**

Project Preview—The Paint Program . . . . . . . . . . . . . . 326
Graphics in Abundance! . . . . . . . . . . . . . . . . . . . . . . . 326
  Overview of Graphics Support . . . . . . . . . . . . . . . . . 328
  The Graphics Object . . . . . . . . . . . . . . . . . . . . . . . . . 328
Basic Graphics Programming . . . . . . . . . . . . . . . . . . . . 330
  The CreateGraphics Function . . . . . . . . . . . . . . . . . . 330
  Drawing Lines . . . . . . . . . . . . . . . . . . . . . . . . . . . . . 330
  Drawing Rectangles . . . . . . . . . . . . . . . . . . . . . . . . . 332
  Colors, Pens, and Brushes . . . . . . . . . . . . . . . . . . . . 333
Chapter Project—The Paint Program . . . . . . . . . . . . . . 333
  Creating the Project . . . . . . . . . . . . . . . . . . . . . . . . . 337
  Writing the Source Code . . . . . . . . . . . . . . . . . . . . . 338
Summary . . . . . . . . . . . . . . . . . . . . . . . . . . . . . . . . . . 343

Chapter 13: **Using Program Menus** . . . . . . . . . . .**345**

Creating a Main Menu. . . . . . . . . . . . . . . . . . . . . . . . . . . 346
The MainMenu Control . . . . . . . . . . . . . . . . . . . . . 346
Customizing the Main Menu . . . . . . . . . . . . . . . . . 348
Programming the Main Menu . . . . . . . . . . . . . . . . 352
Creating a Context Menu . . . . . . . . . . . . . . . . . . . . . . . . 354
The ContextMenu Control . . . . . . . . . . . . . . . . . . . 355
Customizing the Context Menu . . . . . . . . . . . . . . . 355
Programming Context Menus . . . . . . . . . . . . . . . . 357
Summary. . . . . . . . . . . . . . . . . . . . . . . . . . . . . . . . . . . . 362

Chapter 14: **Sequential and
Random-Access Files** . . . . . . . . . . . .**363**

Project Preview—The Trivia Program . . . . . . . . . . . . . . 364
Introduction to File Processing . . . . . . . . . . . . . . . . . . . 364
Reading and Writing Files . . . . . . . . . . . . . . . . . . . 365
File Access Modes . . . . . . . . . . . . . . . . . . . . . . . . . 365
Using Sequential Files. . . . . . . . . . . . . . . . . . . . . . . . . . 366
Understanding Sequential Files. . . . . . . . . . . . . . . 366
Reading and Writing Sequential Files . . . . . . . . . . 367
Sequential File I/O—The ReadWrite Program. . . . . . . . 368
Building the ReadWrite Program. . . . . . . . . . . . . . . 368
Writing the Source Code . . . . . . . . . . . . . . . . . . . . 369
Creating a Rich Text Editor—The ScratchPad Program . . . 372
Opening and Saving RichText Files . . . . . . . . . . . . . 373
Writing the Source Code . . . . . . . . . . . . . . . . . . . . 374
Using Random-Access Files . . . . . . . . . . . . . . . . . . . . . 377
Understanding Random-Access Files . . . . . . . . . . . 377
Structures—User-Defined Types . . . . . . . . . . . . . . . 377
The Seek Method. . . . . . . . . . . . . . . . . . . . . . . . . . . 379
Random-Access File I/O—The RandomTest Program . . . . 379
Building the RandomTest Program . . . . . . . . . . . . . 379
Writing the Source Code . . . . . . . . . . . . . . . . . . . . 380
Chapter Project—The Trivia Program . . . . . . . . . . . . . . 383
Creating the Project . . . . . . . . . . . . . . . . . . . . . . . . 384
Writing the Source Code . . . . . . . . . . . . . . . . . . . . 386
Summary. . . . . . . . . . . . . . . . . . . . . . . . . . . . . . . . . . . . 389

Chapter 15: **Structured Error Handling and Debugging** . . . . . . . . . . . . . . . . . . .391

Introduction to Error Handling . . . . . . . . . . . . . . . . . . . . . 392

Avoid the Dreaded Exception Error! . . . . . . . . . . . . . . 392

Trapping Program Errors . . . . . . . . . . . . . . . . . . . . . . . 392

Writing an Error Handler. . . . . . . . . . . . . . . . . . . . . . . . . 393

Try...Catch...Finally . . . . . . . . . . . . . . . . . . . . . . . . 393

Improved Error Handling . . . . . . . . . . . . . . . . . . . . . . 394

Debugging in VB.NET . . . . . . . . . . . . . . . . . . . . . . . . . . . 394

The ErrorTest Program. . . . . . . . . . . . . . . . . . . . . . . . 395

Running the ErrorTest Program. . . . . . . . . . . . . . . . . . 395

Changing Variables at Runtime . . . . . . . . . . . . . . . . . . 398

Summary. . . . . . . . . . . . . . . . . . . . . . . . . . . . . . . . . . . . 401


PART **5** **Appendices.** . . . . . . . . . . . . . . **403**


Appendix A: **Recommended Reading** . . . . . . . . . . .405


Appendix B: **Using the Book's CD-ROM** . . . . . . . . .409

Project Source Code Files . . . . . . . . . . . . . . . . . . . . . . . . 410

Ready-to-Run Sample Programs. . . . . . . . . . . . . . . . . . . 410


**Index.** . . . . . . . . . . . . . . . . . **411**

# Letter from the Series Editor

With the original release of the Visual Basic Programming language, Microsoft helped make programming much more accessible to those who didn't want to focus on arcane languages, such as C and Java. The language really was visual. Much of the work could be done by painting various objects on the screen, and then writing code in a simple language to make those objects interact.

This was such an appealing idea that VB became a hugely popular language for all levels of programmers. It wasn't long before advances in computing technology outpaced the original designs of VB. For example, the Internet was not a major factor when VB first appeared, and local networks were rare. Most people were running Windows 3.1, and database programs were considered something usually reserved for large corporations.

The programming world has gotten more complex, and programming languages have gotten more complicated as well. The .NET environment is one of the farthest-reaching initiatives in the history of computing. VB.NET, as a part of this system is vast and complex. Learning to program in such a powerful environment can be daunting. That's why you need this book.

Jonathan is an experienced programmer and an excellent teacher. He knows the territory, and he'll guide you through it. VB.NET retains the main elements of older-style VB, but adds the much more powerful .NET engine and full-blown object-oriented design. The things that make VB.NET a little scary for a beginner also make it a lot of fun to learn with skillful guidance, and that's what you'll have.

Games are fun to write. They are visual, you can see what's going on, they're fun to show off, and they are more inherently reinforcing than more practical applications. Even though this book demonstrates games, it's about "serious" programming as well. Throughout the book, you'll see examples of how the techniques described are applied in "real world" situations.

I think you'll really enjoy learning to write programs with this book. Best of luck to you as you begin.

Andy Harris

Series Editor, *For the Absolute Beginner* series

# Introduction

elcome to *Microsoft Visual Basic .NET Programming for the Absolute Beginner!* This book is one of many in the *For the Absolute Beginner* series by Premier Press. The goal of this series is to teach a language through part theory and part hands-on experience. The theory is presented with easy-to-understand terminology using analogies to the real world, while the hands-on experience is gained through practice writing sample programs and simple games.

What is Premier Press's *For the Absolute Beginner* series all about? Books in this series are geared for computer users and programmers who already have some computer experience, and would like to learn a new programming language. This goal allows this book and others to make a few assumptions about the reader, and then focus on the subject with zest, teaching the language more efficiently than books targeted for novice users. The nomenclature "Absolute Beginner" does not refer to the reader's overall experience with computers; on the contrary, it refers to the reader's experience with a specific language.

This book uses simple games to teach new programming topics relevant to Visual Basic .NET. Games are fantastic learning tools because if you make a mistake while writing a simple game, you will easily spot the error while the game is running, because games are visual in nature. The game will either look appealing and work as expected or it won't. Games are great learning tools for a new programming language. Regardless of your experience level as a programmer, you will be able to follow along with the step-by-step tutorials in this book as you learn how to write Visual Basic .NET programs.

## Reader's Expectations

Everyone has their own opinions, values, and expectations when reading a new book. It's my job to teach you how to program Visual Basic .NET with a pleasant and productive writing style. Unfortunately, it is difficult to cater to the needs of every reader; therefore, the end result is usually the lowest common denominator as far as the material being useful to everyone. I have attempted to cover the basics of this material as thoroughly as possible while using a fun and easy writing style.

Because you are likely to already have some computer experience, I will not explain the basics of using a computer or installing programs. If you are interested in writing Visual Basic .NET programs, then it may be that you are experienced with a previous version of Visual Basic or another language; perhaps you are a computer user and this is your first foray into computer programming; or perhaps you are a decision maker at your company, and want to keep abreast of the latest technology. As a computer-savvy user, you may know all about Windows, and you may be an expert with applications like Microsoft Office.

Therefore, you can expect to find chapters that come to the point clearly and concisely. You probably want to learn as much as possible in the least amount of time, whether you are an experienced programmer or not. Prior experience will help you to grasp new subjects more easily, but you will enjoy the casual treatment of new topics if you are new to programming.

## Author's Expectations

To get the most out of this book you will need Visual Studio .NET Professional, because this product includes all the advanced controls and components that are covered in this book. If you have a more advanced version, such as Visual Studio .NET Enterprise Developer or Visual Studio .NET Enterprise Architect, you will have no problem running the sample programs in this book. These latter editions are overkill for the purpose of learning, but there's no harm in having additional features that you may learn to use later.

These editions of Visual Studio .NET are extremely expensive. The Enterprise Architect edition costs several thousand dollars, because it comes with Visio, SQL Server 2000, and other advanced products.

However, there is an alternative to purchasing these expensive tools. Microsoft has provided an individual version of Visual Basic .NET that does not include C# or C++—just Visual Basic. It is called Visual Basic .NET Standard. This is a scaled-down version that allows you to write simple Visual Basic programs, and is intended for individual or educational use in which large-scale database connectivity is not needed. This version is very affordable—around $100—but does not allow you to create custom controls or DLLs.

There is yet another option that you might find useful. Microsoft provides a Trial Version of Visual Studio .NET that is fully functional for 60 days. After the trial, you must purchase the software or uninstall it. You can order the Visual Studio .NET Trial Version for only a few dollars (the cost of shipping & handling) from http://msdn.microsoft.com.

For the purposes of this book, I will assume that you have Visual Basic .NET Standard Edition. While there may be differences between this version and the one you are using, and the screenshots in this book may look *slightly* different from what you see on your screen, you should not have any trouble adapting to the version you are using. Most of the differences will be in the project dialogs that describe the languages and project types available in your copy of Visual Studio .NET. If you have the Professional Edition, it will show Visual C# and any other languages that you have installed. There are no functional limitations to the Standard Edition (aside from limited database connectivity), which is fully capable of running the projects in this book and compiling standalone executable programs.

The important fact here is that you can use this book to learn Visual Basic .NET with little or no initial cost for the compiler.

## System Requirements

The system requirements depend entirely on what it takes to run Visual Studio .NET—the environment that you will use to write Visual Basic .NET programs. This development tool requires Windows NT, 2000, or XP. It simply won't work on Windows 95, 98, or ME. The reason for this is that Windows 95, 98, and ME are based on the ANSI character set where each character represents one byte of memory. Windows NT, 2000, and XP, on the other hand, use the Unicode character set in which each character represents two bytes of memory. Because Visual Basic .NET uses Unicode exclusively, you will only be able to write programs under the Windows NT line of operating systems.

 **The screenshots used in this book will reflect the user interface of Windows 2000. If you are using Windows XP or Windows .NET, the sample programs will look different on your system.**

By personal experience, I can vouch for the fact that you will want the most powerful computer you can get to develop Visual Basic .NET programs. Here is a list of minimum requirements for Visual Studio .NET:

- Windows 2000, Windows XP, or Windows .NET
- Pentium III or Athlon 500MHz processor
- 160MB system memory
- 2GB free hard-drive space
- CD-ROM drive

For best results, I recommend at least a 1GHz processor and 512MB of RAM.

# Book Support on the Web

This book has a support site on the Web on which you can find additional information since the book was printed, such as reader reviews, online resources, an errata list (if necessary), and screenshots of the sample programs from the book. The support site is located at http://www.jharbour.com/vbnet.

# Join the Visual Basic Discussion List

Additional support for this book will primarily take place on the official discussion list at YahooGroups, a free Web service that provides newsgroup-like messages directly to your inbox. To join this discussion group, for sharing your ideas, comments, or questions, send an e-mail to Visual-Basic-Net-Programming@ YahooGroups.com to add your e-mail address to the list.

In case you are interested, I maintain similar discussion lists for my other books as well. Each list is a great place for readers to gather, share ideas, and code. Visit my Web site at http://www.jharbour.com for links to these other lists.

# Contacting the Author

If you have any comments or questions about the contents of this book, feel free to contact the author directly by sending an e-mail to jonathan@jharbour.com or by visiting the Web site for this book at http://www.jharbour.com/vbnet.

# Conventions Used in This Book

The following styles are used in the book to present additional information in the form of hints, traps, tricks, real-world subjects, definitions, and challenges. These sections help to make a chapter more interesting and easier to read.

 *Hint* sections highlight subjects that are important to remember.

 *Trap* sections warn of potential problems that you may encounter.

*Trick* sections show how to solve problems using special features of the language.

**IN THE REAL WORLD**

*In the Real World* sections step out of the general discussion and explain how a topic relates to real-world development.

**Definition**

*Definition* sections describe new terminology that was discussed in the chapter.

**CHALLENGES**

*Challenge* sections list several programming challenges that will enhance your understanding of the topics presented in a chapter.

## Summary

Visual Basic .NET is a challenging development language to master. The only way to truly understand a programming language is to start writing programs. The chapters of this book will teach you how to use the Visual Basic .NET environment and how to write complete programs.

# Part

# I

## Introduction to Visual Basic .NET

Chapter 1: **Getting Started with Visual Basic .NET**

Chapter 2: **Overview of Visual Studio .NET**

Chapter 3: **The Basics of a Graphical User Interface**

Chapter 4: **Forms and Toolbox Controls**

CHAPTER

# Getting Started with Visual Basic .NET

**W**elcome to the first chapter of *Microsoft Visual Basic .NET Programming for the Absolute Beginner*! This chapter is an overview of Visual Basic .NET— a little theory here, a little source code there, and a lot of new stuff throughout. I hope you like learning new things, because this chapter is full of new information! Visual Basic .NET is an exciting language, and it's absolutely a blast to use! As I'm sure you will find out soon enough, the learning curve for Visual Basic is short. You'll be up to speed and able to write your own programs in no time. I'll help you through the tough spots and introduce you to key topics. The rest is up to you! Software development is all about creativity, so put on your creative hat and stretch your fingers. When it comes to Visual Basic, the keyboard is your palette, the mouse is your brush, and infinite possibilities are your canvas. Here is a brief overview of the topics that are covered in this chapter:

- **Project preview—Guessing Game**

- **What is Visual Basic?**

- **The graphical user interface**

- **Introduction to Visual Basic .NET**

- **Writing code**

- **Chapter project—Guessing Game**

The foundation that develops while learning a new language is the most important part of the learning process. That is what this book strives to accomplish—to teach you the basics of Visual Basic .NET, the foundation that will allow you to immediately start writing Visual Basic .NET programs. Not only will the following pages teach you everything you need to know to start writing VB.NET programs, you will also gain a good level of exposure to actual working VB.NET programs, along with familiarity with the development environment.

Because this is the first chapter, I would like to jump right in and show you how to write your first VB.NET program to give you an idea what lies ahead in later chapters. This first program is simple enough that you will have no trouble understanding how it works; I will explain each step along the way. This chapter also includes a simple game that you will build from scratch, and you will learn all kinds of new things along the way.

## Project Preview—Guessing Game

This chapter features a complete project—a Guessing Game program that you will be able to build from scratch. Figure 1.1 shows a screenshot of Guessing Game.

## What Is Visual Basic?

Visual Basic is a graphical programming language and the top of the class in Rapid Application Development (RAD) tools for Windows. In fact, Visual Basic is the most popular Windows development tool in the world, with an estimated user base of over three million. To put it simply, Visual Basic is being used to solve business problems more than any other development tool. Every hour spent learning Visual Basic can be associated with potential future income because the demand for experienced Visual Basic developers is unmatched. There is simply no other development tool available for high-level projects that is better suited than Visual Basic.

FIGURE 1.1

The Guessing Game program demonstrates the topics covered in this chapter.

## Programming Languages

If you are approaching Visual Basic .NET from another field, and you are not a full-time computer programmer, you may be at a loss about what has made Visual Basic so popular. For starters, Visual Basic is a programming language. There are many ways to write a computer program because there are many programming languages.

## Rapid Application Development

I have mentioned Rapid Application Development already. In a nutshell, RAD is a technique for prototyping a computer program as quickly as possible so that end-users can see what the program will look like when finished. RAD prototypes may look completely functional, but usually lack any special features. For example, suppose a video store owner wants to inventory the videos in each of his stores and keep the data in a database. Rather than wait several weeks or months for a program to be written, RAD developers will build a prototype of the application so that the client (the video store owner) has a chance to see the program running and offer suggestions to improve the usability of the program.

Visual Basic is a powerful tool for prototyping and building complete software projects. Visual Basic is especially adept at handling databases, too.

## Database Development

That brings up an important point. What, you may be wondering, is a database? It's a term that is used quite a bit, but often not well understood. Basically, a database is a collection of information. The organization of the information is called the database design methodology. Whereas simple databases, like one that keeps track of telephone numbers, might be easy to design, larger databases can become unbelievably complicated. In fact, some database systems are so huge and complicated that the system must be programmed to organize itself because it is too complex for human intervention.

Depending on your background, databases might seem important or irrelevant. Let me emphasize an important point: databases are everywhere and store information about everything. Imagine the databases needed to keep track of vehicle registrations and driver's licenses alone. That is but one public service in an information sector that is truly mind-boggling.

Boring? Well, maybe. Databases are an important factor, but there are a lot of other things you can do with Visual Basic, such as graphics programs, educational programs, physics simulation programs, and even games. I am not exaggerating when I tell you that you are limited only by your imagination. As Kevin Costner and James Earl Jones discovered in the movie *Field of Dreams*—if you build it, they will come. I'm not sure who "they" are in this analogy, but if you build it... they will download it. Oh well, you get the idea.

## The Graphical User Interface

The key to the success of Visual Basic is a fantastic and easy-to-learn language that powers a drag-and-drop visual user-interface design tool. Visual Basic .NET shares this Windows Form engine with other .NET languages, therefore all the source code that you write with Visual Basic .NET is compatible with Visual C# and Visual C++. But what is a user interface?

The graphical user interface, or GUI as it has come to be known, is a visual method of using software, primarily with a mouse. In the old days of UNIX and MS-DOS, computer users were forced to memorize strange commands and had to type them into a command-line interface. Type a command, press Enter, and the computer spews out some information (or more commonly, it would beep with a rude error message).

Windows replaced MS-DOS, and along with it came even more complexity. Windows is not an easy operating system to program. Believe it or not, in the old days Windows programmers had to use Microsoft C, which ran under MS-DOS! Talk about ironic. Not only was Windows difficult to program, but the development tool didn't even run under Windows. As you can imagine, those were not the good old days. Most veteran Windows programmers have no fondness for the way things used to be.

Visual Basic was written to solve the problem and make Windows programming easier. The ability to drag controls onto a form and mold the controls to your liking using simple properties is a trademark feature of Visual Basic (as you will see in this chapter and those that follow). In a very real sense, the entire Visual Studio .NET suite—Visual C++, Visual C#, Visual J++—has given up its roots and now acts more like Visual Basic with RAD features.

## Introduction to VB.NET

Visual Basic .NET is the latest incarnation of the world's most popular computer programming language, and it brings a lot of new features to the table. This new thing called "dot net" is a revolutionary change from Visual Studio 6.0 (which included Visual Basic 6.0). Visual Studio .NET is not "Visual Studio 7.0" as you might think. On the contrary, it is a new product developed from scratch, not tied to the previous version (and not entirely compatible either). In a sense, you might think of this as a whole new product line starting at version 1.0—but that's only partially true. The people who created Visual Basic .NET took all of the favorite features of Visual Basic 6.0, and the features of a dozen other popular languages, and crammed all of this new goodness into a single new development tool. The result is a stellar programming language, and it has no equivalent in the computer world.

## Writing Code

Now that you have been introduced to the Visual Basic .NET development environment and have a basic idea what it's all about, I'll show you how to write a simple program to familiarize you with the development environment.

Unlike Visual Basic 6.0, VB.NET does not use a project workspace to keep track of the projects you are working on (which may be one or several projects). Instead of the concept of a workspace, VB.NET (and the rest of the .NET languages) uses a "solution" to solve programming problems. Most programs are written, after all, to process data in one way or another, and that data may not be in a suitable format that is useful—meaning, programs are written to *process* data and present it in a desired way, such as a report. Most programs are written just to solve a single problem, and many programs are used once and then discarded. For example, many of the perceived problems with Y2K involved writing run-once programs that corrected date problems in a database. Once run, such programs are no longer needed. Visual Studio .NET embodies the concept of solving programming problems by treating a project workspace as a solution. In fact, the solution file even has an extension of .sln.

As you can imagine, Visual Studio .NET solutions can be quite extravagant. Not only can you have multiple Visual Basic projects in the solution, you can also have multiple *languages* that are part of the solution. Isn't that amazing? In previous versions of Visual Studio, it was possible to create ActiveX components and share them between languages—in essence, these were component object model (COM) objects, which is what Visual Studio 6.0 was based upon. That is no longer an issue with Visual Studio .NET. Although you can still use COM and ActiveX, these technologies are now obsolete because it is possible to use .NET languages interchangeably. You can write a program using any combination of Visual Basic, C# (pronounced "See Sharp"), or C++ (pronounced "See Plus Plus").

In the past, it was difficult for managers to make use of programmers with varying skills in different languages. Visual Basic programmers and C++ programmers generally don't agree on how to solve programming problems. But with .NET, this is no longer an issue, because a solution can be created that includes both Visual Basic and C++ source code. Isn't that amazing? But if you think about it, this is how the real world works.

### Definition

*Components* are pieces of programs written in such a way that they can be used by more than one program. This is called "code reuse" and is a very important concept that is at the core of Microsoft's .NET strategy.

### IN THE REAL WORLD

Consider the construction of a new house as an analogy for writing software. To build the house as quickly and efficiently as possible, a contractor will hire carpenters, plumbers, electricians, masons, tile and carpet installers, window installers, and so on. Now imagine if a builder tries to construct a house by hiring only carpenters, or just plumbers? The house might get built, in time, but how inefficient would that be?

Likewise, bringing together various languages and technologies into a single software solution results in a more powerful application. Allowing Visual Basic and C++ programmers to share components and build upon each other's work is the key to efficient software development, especially on large projects. Further, projects based on Visual Basic alone benefit from true object-oriented component reuse because programmers can build upon each other's work more easily and efficiently than in the past.

Although it would be fun to create a sample program that demonstrates using multiple languages, I'm going to stick to Visual Basic. If you feel confident enough to try it on your own, feel free to experiment with Visual Studio .NET! There are a multitude of features that I will only be able to touch upon in these pages.

> **Definition**
>
> *Object-Oriented Programming (OOP)* is a methodology (or rather, way of doing things) in which information is stored together with the programs that use that information. In technical terms, the information is called *data* and the programs are called *methods*.

## Greetings to the World

Now it's time to get down to business. Are you tired of theory already? I'm not! This stuff is fun. But theory means nothing without practice. I've watched a lot of Jackie Chan movies, but I still don't know anything about kung fu. If you want to master something, you have got to practice and start with the basics.

 **TRICK** The key to becoming an expert programmer is to write tons of code!

Start Visual Studio .NET by selecting Start, Programs, Microsoft Visual Studio .NET, and then select the Microsoft Visual Studio .NET program from the pop-up list. The default Start Page should be the first thing that is displayed when Visual Studio .NET starts running. The Start Page shows all of the recent solutions that you have worked on (or it could be blank if this is the first time you have used it). There is a button on the Start Page called New Project that you will want to click in order to start a new project. If, for some reason, the Start Page does not show up by default when you run Visual Studio .NET, click the File menu at the top of the screen and select New, Project (as shown in Figure 1.2).

By using either method, the New Project dialog should appear (see Figure 1.3).

The New Project dialog needs to be discussed before going any farther because it is sort of complicated. On the left side of the dialog is a list of Project Types, which includes the following:

- Visual Basic Projects
- Visual C# Projects
- Visual C++ Projects
- Setup and Deployment Projects
- Other Projects
- Visual Studio Solutions

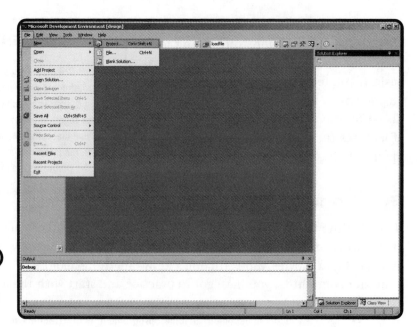

FIGURE 1.2

Creating a new
project with Visual
Basic .NET.

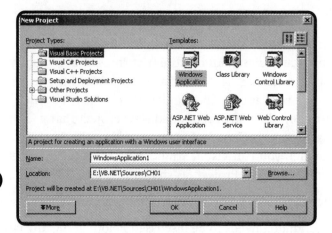

FIGURE 1.3

The New Project
dialog.

The first option in the list, Visual Basic Projects, should be selected by default. On
the right side of the dialog is the list of Templates for each project type.

**There are several versions of Visual Studio .NET, but the most common is the
Professional version, which is shown in the screenshots in this chapter. Another
common (and less expensive) version is Visual Basic .NET Standard, which
includes only Visual Basic and none of the other languages or tools.**

You will notice that each language has its own set of icons for these templates to make it easier to differentiate between them (usually when you have a large solution with multiple languages). Here is the list of templates for Visual Basic:

- Windows Application
- Class Library
- Windows Control Library
- ASP.NET Web Application
- ASP.NET Web Service
- Web Control Library
- Console Application
- Windows Service
- Empty Project
- Empty Web Project
- New Project In Existing Folder

If you look at the top-right corner of the New Project dialog, you should see two small buttons that affect the layout of the items in the template list (shown in Figure 1.4).

You can switch between Large Icons and Small Icons by pressing either of these two buttons. The Small Icons view is sometimes more convenient because you can see more items in the list than you can when Large Icons are displayed. Regardless of the view you settle on, for this program you will want to select a Console Application (see Figure 1.5).

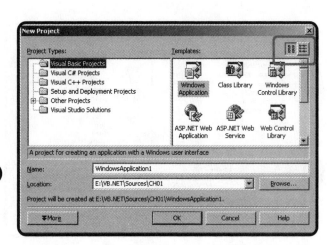

**FIGURE 1.4**

The Large Icons and Small Icons buttons.

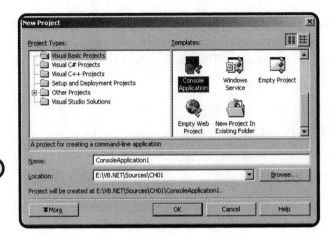

**FIGURE 1.5**

The Console
Application
project type.

Did you notice how the project name changed when you selected the Console Application template? The name was changed to ConsoleApplication1. Click on the Name field now and change the name of the program to Greeting, as shown in Figure 1.6.

The next thing that you might want to do is select where the new project files will be stored on your hard drive. Select the folder by typing it into the Location field, or locate an existing folder with the Browse button.

Pay no attention to the folder name in the screenshot, because that is the location where I stored the project. You can store the project anywhere you like, although it makes sense to organize your projects under a main folder. In this case, I stored my projects in E:\VB.NET\Sources. You will likely see this path in later sample programs as well.

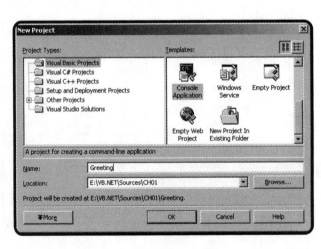

**FIGURE 1.6**

Changing the name
of the new
program.

**TRAP** Make sure you keep track of your folders because they will be strewn, seemingly, all over your hard drive if you don't set the location yourself.

You are now ready to create the new project by pressing the OK button. But first, take a look at the More button at the bottom-left corner of the dialog in Figure 1.6. When you press the More button, the dialog grows to display a hidden field and checkbox, as shown in Figure 1.7.

Because this is an option that is not often used, it can be hidden away with the More/Less button. Visual Studio .NET is replete with features like this, in which you can show or hide relevant information to suit your tastes. In this case, you can have Visual Studio create a new folder for you when the project is created. Because the New Project automatically creates a new folder for you, this option is only useful when you are creating a large-scale application; therefore, you should probably keep the option unchecked.

### Code Editor Window

When you click OK to close the New Project dialog, Visual Studio creates a new solution and a new project for you, as shown in Figure 1.8.

Because this is a console application, there's no form or controls available in this program. This is quite a bit different from Visual Basic 6.0, which did not have the ability to create a console application. What this means is that when you compile the program, you can actually run it from the Command Prompt (formerly called the DOS Prompt). When you run the program from within Visual Studio, a new Command Prompt window automatically appears. Go ahead and

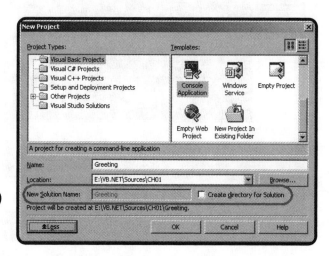

**FIGURE 1.7**

Additional options for the project.

run the empty program by pressing F5. You should see a screen like the one shown in Figure 1.9 for a moment, and then it disappears.

The program window is completely black because this program doesn't do anything. Soon I'll show you how to add some functionality to this program so the Command Prompt window will display something and even let you type something in

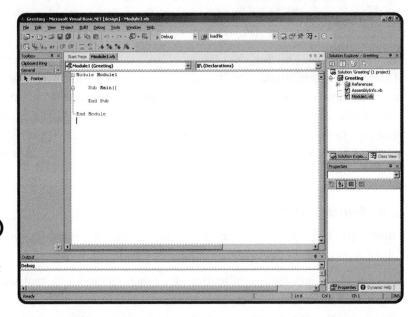

**FIGURE 1.8**

The new Console Application project is ready for your source code.

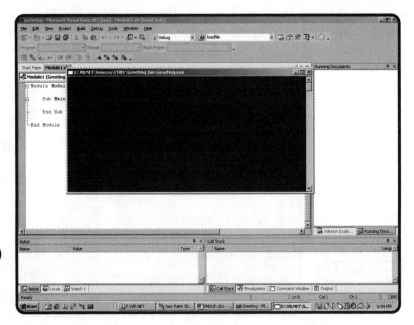

**FIGURE 1.9**

The Console Application doesn't do anything yet.

to the program. If you're a little turned off by this crude program, hang in there for a short while; soon I'll show you how to write a program with a form and some controls. Console applications are so simple, this is the best place to start.

## How About Something Useful?

Now, let's add some code to make this program actually do something useful. This program needs to display a line of text and then wait for the user to press Enter to continue. Add the following two lines of code inside Sub Main:

```
Console.WriteLine("Welcome to Visual Basic .NET!")
Console.ReadLine()
```

After you have typed in these two lines, the source code for the program should look like Figure 1.10.

It should be pretty obvious that the first line displays the message "Welcome to Visual Basic .NET!" But what about the second line? ReadLine is a Visual Basic command that reads a line of characters from the keyboard and ends with the Enter key.

 **You can start a program in Visual Basic .NET by pressing the F5 key.**

Now go ahead and run the program by pressing F5. The Greeting program is shown in Figure 1.11.

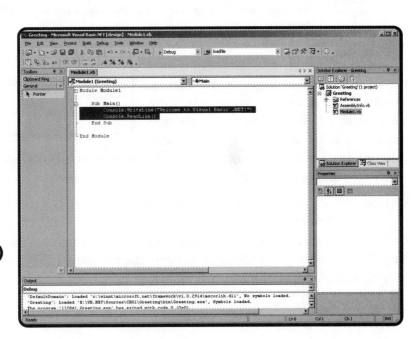

**FIGURE 1.10**

The Greeting program displays a message on the console.

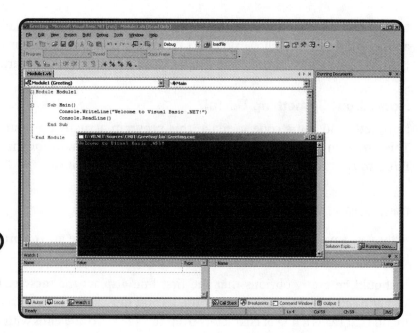

**FIGURE 1.11**

The Greeting
program displays a
message on the
console.

This short program waits for you to type in a line of characters, after which the
ReadLine command will grab them out of the console. You can actually see what
was typed in because ReadLine returns the characters as a string.

**HINT**

Visual Basic provides a huge list of commands—also called functions, subs, or
methods—that give your programs functionality. I will explain this topic more in
later chapters.

In order to receive the string, you need to copy
the value returned by ReadLine into a string
variable. I won't be explaining everything
about variables until Chapter 6, "Branching
Statements and Program Logic," but it's hard

**Definition**

A *string* is a collection of characters.

to write a program without them, therefore I'll provide a brief introduction right now.
A variable holds data that other parts of the program can use.

Variables must be declared before they are used in Visual Basic .NET. In Visual
Basic 6.0 and prior versions, you could get away with using variables without
declaring them first, and this led to a lot of buggy programs. The main reason
why Visual Basic .NET is different is because the programs have to be compiled so
they are compatible with the other .NET languages, like C# and C++. This is most

definitely not a bad thing, and there are so many advantages to Visual Basic .NET that prior versions of Visual Basic seem very limited in comparison.

To declare a new variable, you must use the `Dim` keyword, which is short for dimension, referring to the process of reserving memory for the new variable. The actual process no longer even remotely resembles the BASIC language, of which Visual Basic was derived, but `Dim` has been around for so long now that it would not be a Visual Basic program without it. Originally, `Dim` was used just to create an array, but Visual Basic uses `Dim` to create any variable.

As I mentioned a moment ago, `ReadLine` returns a string, therefore this program needs a string variable. Declare the variable like this:

```
Dim name As String
```

How about that? You can create any variable you need using the `Dim` command. Now, how about a new version of the Greeting program that does something with this new variable? The following lines of code add some new features to the Greeting program. Type the lines in bold between the two existing lines of the program.

```
Console.WriteLine("Welcome to Visual Basic .NET!")
Console.Write("Please type your name: ")
Dim name As String
name = Console.ReadLine()
Console.WriteLine("Hello, {0}!", name)
Console.WriteLine()
Console.WriteLine("Press Enter to quit...")
Console.ReadLine()
```

After you have made the changes to the source code, the program should look like Figure 1.12. (The new lines have been highlighted in the code editor window.)

After you type in the new code save the project by clicking File, Save All. You can also save the project by clicking the Save All icon on the toolbar (see Figure 1.13).

After saving the project, run the program by pressing F5. Figure 1.14 shows the output of the new version of the Greeting program.

There is one line of this program that displays the characters typed into the console (the user's name), and it looks kind of funny:

```
Console.WriteLine("Hello, {0}!", name)
```

It's probably obvious to you what this line of code does from looking at the output, but how does it work? The curly braces surround a number that refers to the variable that follows. This is a feature of the `WriteLine` command. `WriteLine`

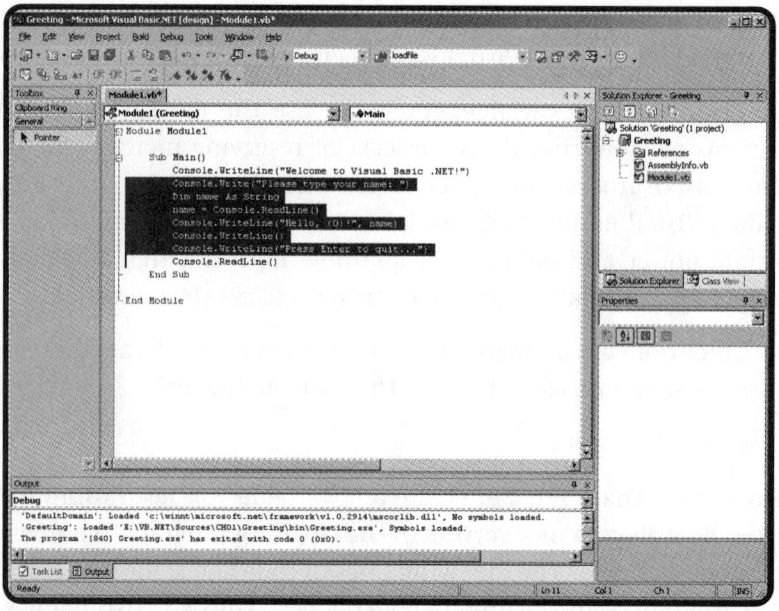

**FIGURE 1.12**

The new Greeting program in the Visual Basic .NET editor.

**FIGURE 1.13**

Click the Save All icon on the toolbar to save the entire project.

allows you to display the contents of variables in whatever order you want. Separate each variable by a comma and then refer to them as {0}, {1}, {2}, and so on. I'll cover WriteLine in more detail later, so don't worry if you don't understand it at this point.

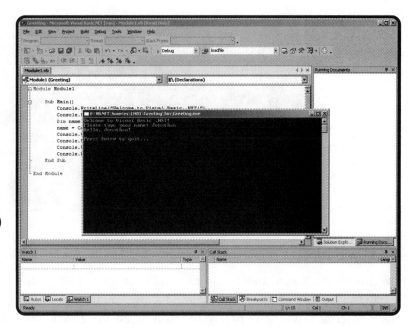

**FIGURE 1.14**

The new Greeting
program reads user
input and displays
the contents of the
string variable.

Before retiring the Greeting program and moving on, I would like to show you how
to run the program from the Command Prompt. After all, this is a console application, therefore you can run it from a console (as opposed to running a program
from the Start menu). The Command Prompt is usually found in the Start menu
under Accessories. You need to change to the folder containing the Greeting program. In my case, I typed the following command to change to the correct folder:

```
CD \VB.NET\Sources\CH01\Greeting\bin
```

Replace the pathname that I used with the pathname to the folder where you
stored the project, and remember to add \bin to the path. Then run the program
by typing the following command:

```
Greeting.exe
```

You first need to compile the program by pressing F5 in Visual Basic editor to create the Greeting.exe file. Assuming you did that in one of the previous steps, the
program should run directly inside the Command Prompt, as shown in Figure 1.15.

Congratulations, you have successfully run your first Visual Basic .NET program!
This program might be simple, but it helped to show you some key features of the
language and gave you some experience working with the Visual Basic editor.
Now, how about something a little more interesting? The next project is called
"Guessing Game" and uses a form with some controls instead of the console. You
can now close the Greeting program by selecting File, Close Solution.

**FIGURE 1.15**

Running the
Greeting program
directly from the
Command Prompt.

# Chapter Project—Guessing Game

Now that you've had a chance to write and compile a simple console application,
I'd like to take you to the next level and show you how to build a program with
a user interface—which is pretty much a given for a Windows program these
days. The program is called Guessing Game and will provide you with some experience with Windows Forms, controls, and events.

## Creating the New Project

If you don't have Visual Basic .NET running yet, fire it up. Open the New Project
dialog by clicking File, New, Project, as shown in Figure 1.16.

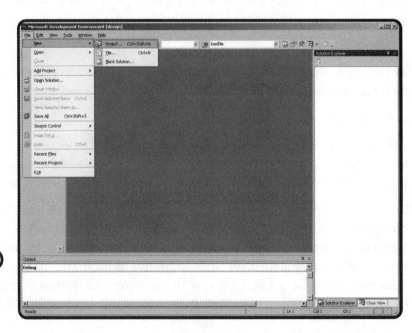

**FIGURE 1.16**

Opening the New
Project dialog with
the File menu.

The New Project dialog should appear with the Windows Application template selected (see Figure 1.17).

## Selecting the Project Type

The Guessing Game program will have a form, therefore it needs to be a Windows Application. If it is not already selected, choose the Visual Basic Projects (as shown in Figure 1.17) item at the top of the list of Project Types (this should be the default).

Next, select Windows Application from the list of templates on the right side of the New Project dialog.

## Naming the Project

Now replace the default project name of WindowsApplication1 with the name GuessingGame (see Figure 1.18).

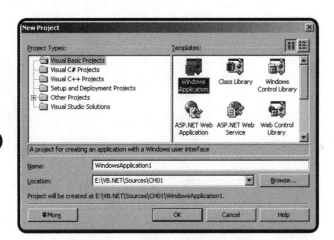

**FIGURE 1.17**

The New Project
dialog with the
Windows
Application
template selected.

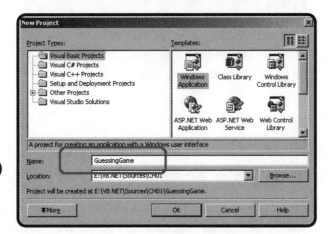

**FIGURE 1.18**

Change the name
of the project to
Guessing Game.

The Location field should still point to the folder you used for the previous program; therefore, you can leave it as is or type in a new folder in which you would like the GuessingGame project to be saved on your hard drive (see Figure 1.19).

Click OK on the New Project dialog to have the project created for you. The new project has a form called Form1.vb, and is shown in Figure 1.20.

### The Anatomy of a Windows Application

Whoa, look at that! This project looks a lot more like prior versions of Visual Basic, with a default form ready for user-interface controls. This is the Rapid

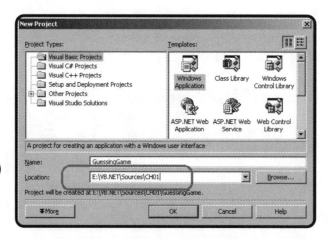

**FIGURE 1.19**

Setting the destination folder for the new project.

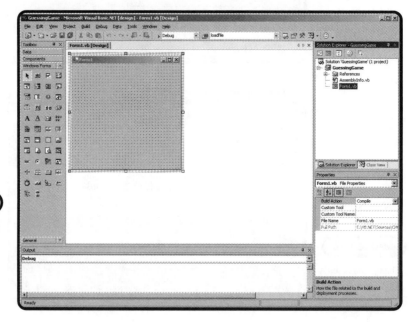

**FIGURE 1.20**

The new Guessing Game project has been generated and is ready for custom source code.

Application Development (RAD) feature that has made Visual Basic famous. Of course, you know that with the console application, Visual Basic .NET is capable of far more than previous versions of Visual Basic. But this new Windows Application project should look familiar to many Visual Basic 6.0 programmers.

As Figure 1.21 shows, the integrated development environment (IDE) is comprised of four main sections:

- The Toolbox
- The Editor window
- The Property window
- The Solution Explorer

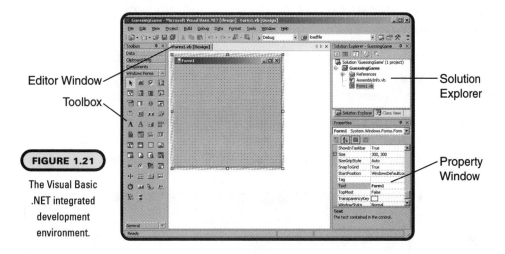

**FIGURE 1.21**

The Visual Basic .NET integrated development environment.

## Understanding Windows Forms

What are Windows Forms, you might ask? This is a new concept with Visual Basic .NET. In previous versions of Visual Studio, Visual Basic was the only language that had a form engine, or was based entirely on forms. Now, in Visual Studio .NET, all of the languages share this new Windows Form engine, which can be beneficial when you need to make use of features in C# or C++, for example.

## Using the Control Toolbox

The control Toolbox is located on the left side of the screen, and contains all of the controls you'll need to write a Visual Basic program. In fact, the cool thing about this Toolbox (and the Windows Form engine) is that all the .NET languages use the same controls! I will explain each of the controls in more detail in later chapters. For now, I'm going to focus on the Label control and TextBox control.

You can either double-click the Label control in the Toolbox to have a control placed on the form for you, or you can use the mouse to drag a Label onto the form with the size and position that you want (see Figure 1.22).

Use the resize blocks (the little white squares around the Label) to stretch the Label control across the top of the form. This Label will be the title for the game. See Figure 1.23 to see how it should look.

Now, change the message inside the Label to the name of this game. If the Label control isn't selected, click it once with the mouse to highlight the Label on the form. Take a look at the Property window at the bottom-right corner of the screen. There are a lot of properties for the Label control. The one that lets you change the text inside the Label is—surprise!—the Text property. Click the input field next to the Text property and change it so that it reads Guessing Game, as shown in Figure 1.24.

As soon as you press the Enter key after typing in **Guessing Game**, or as soon as you move the mouse cursor off the input field, look at the Label on the form. See, it has changed to Guessing Game like you told it to! (See Figure 1.25.)

Now, the Label shows the correct text, but it doesn't look very attractive. Let's make the font bigger, bolder, and also centered on the form. As you might have guessed, you can change all of these features using the Property window.

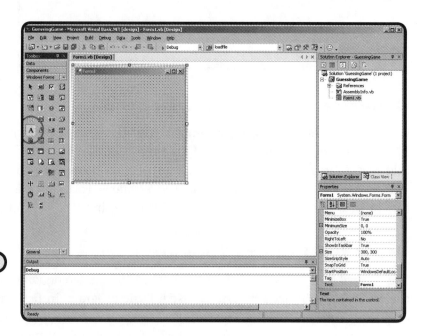

**FIGURE 1.22**

Selecting the Label control from the Toolbox.

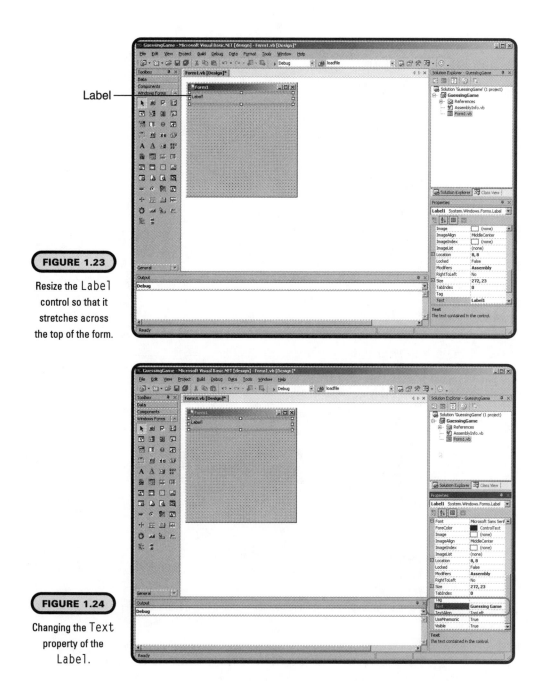

Label

**FIGURE 1.23**

Resize the Label
control so that it
stretches across
the top of the form.

**FIGURE 1.24**

Changing the Text
property of the
Label.

First change the font. Scroll down the list of properties until you find the Font
property. When you click the Font property, you will notice that a small ellipsis
button appears in the input field to the right. Click that button to bring up the
standard Font selection dialog (shown in Figure 1.26).

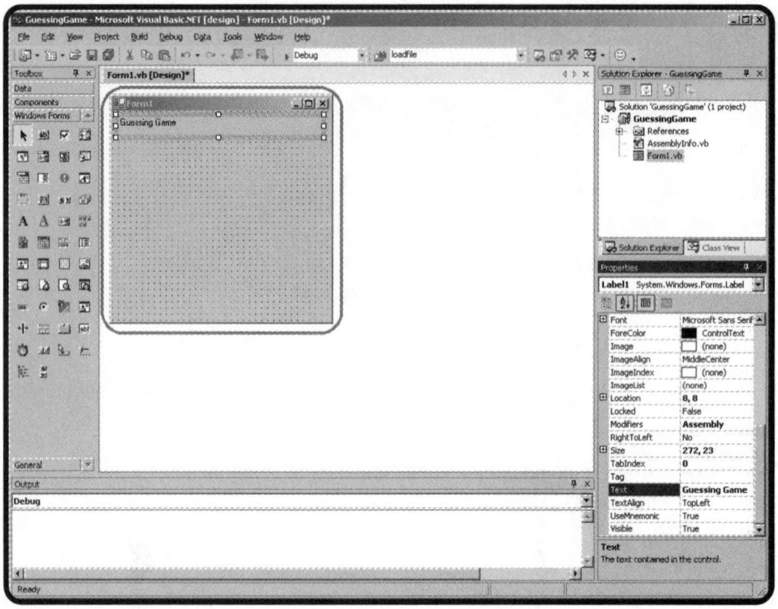

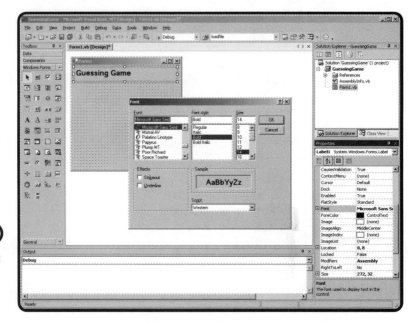

**FIGURE 1.25**

The Label on the form changes when you modify the Text property.

**FIGURE 1.26**

Use the Font dialog to change the appearance of a Label.

You can use this dialog to change the font however you like, and the Label will be changed to whatever you select. Change the font style to Bold and the size to 14, and then click OK. The Label is immediately updated to reflect your changes.

Now to center the Label. You can do this by changing the TextAlign property.

When you click the `TextAlign` property, a drop-down arrow button appears. Click the button to bring up the alignment selections (as shown in Figure 1.27). Choose the TopCenter alignment.

There, now the `Label` is finished, so it's time for the next control. The Guessing Game needs an input field in which you can type a number. The game reads this number and tells you if you guessed correctly or not. Along with the input field, there needs to be a `Label` that explains what to do. Add another `Label` to the form, and change the text as shown in Figure 1.28 so that it reads "Enter a number from 1 to 10:" Also make sure it is centered.

Now, let's add the input field to the form so the user can type in a number. The input field in Visual Basic is called a `TextBox`, and it is located in the control Toolbox (as shown in Figure 1.29). Drag a new `TextBox` control under the `Label` as shown.

Now, look at the properties for the new `TextBox` (which is called TextBox1). Scroll down to the `Text` property and delete the contents so that the `TextBox` is empty (see Figure 1.30). You don't want to have anything inside the `TextBox` when the game starts (because the user needs to type in a number).

Now, the Guessing Game project is starting to take shape. Only one more control is needed to finish the user interface: a `Button`! The user could probably just press Enter after typing in a number, but a `Button` is a lot more fun. Select the `Button` control from the Toolbox (as shown in Figure 1.31) and drag a new `Button` onto the form.

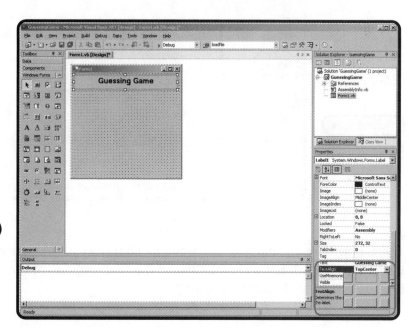

**FIGURE 1.27**

The `TextAlign` property determines how the `Label` is aligned on the form.

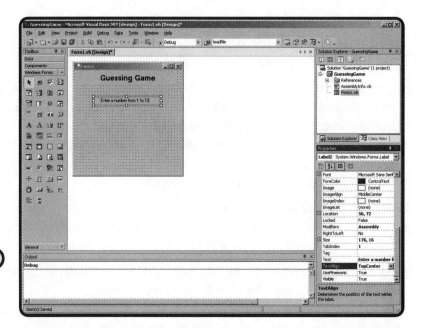

The next `Label`
describes what to
do in the game.

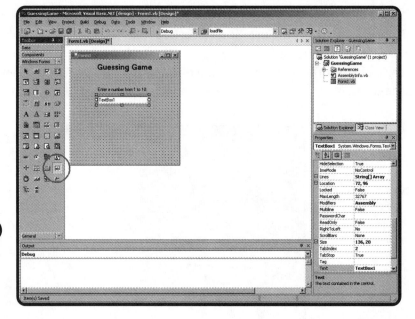

The second `Label`
describes what to
type into the
`TextBox`.

There, now the game has a `Button`. Good job! But the `Button` is currently showing
Button1 which will not do at all. Change the `Text` property of the `Button` so that
it reads GUESS, as shown in Figure 1.32.

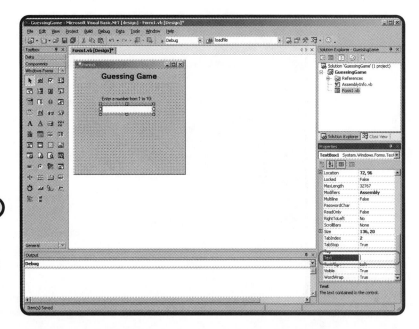

Remove the contents of the TextBox so it is empty when the program starts running.

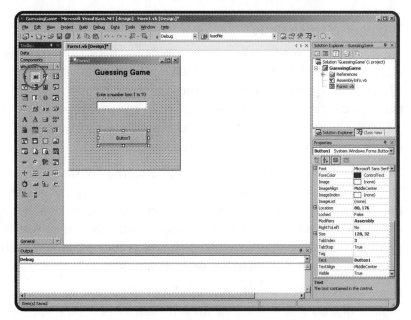

Add a new Button to the form using the Button control in the Toolbox.

Now the user interface for the Guessing Game is finished! You can run the program by pressing F5 if you want to see how it looks. The game doesn't do anything yet, because you haven't added any code to the user interface events. That is what I'll cover next, the real meat of the program.

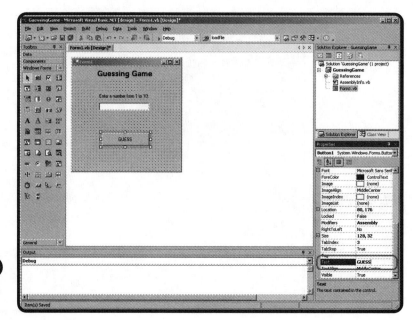

**FIGURE 1.32**

Changing the name of the Button.

## Typing in Source Code

The source code for Guessing Game needs to check the TextBox to make sure a number has been entered. It must then ensure that only a number between 1 and 10 has been entered. If either of these input validation tests fail, the program needs to display a warning message. When the user types in a number between 1 and 10 correctly, the game logic kicks in. I'll start with the first part of the program and then work on the logic after that is finished.

The controls on a form are directly tied to the source code, which is sort of "beneath" the form, if you can picture it as such. See for yourself: double-click the Button. The source code for the form appears, and a new event has been added for the Button_Click event, which is what you need (see Figure 1.33). An event is something that Visual Basic sends to your program to tell it that something has happened, such as a mouse-click or key-press.

Don't worry about the code surrounding the Button1_Click event because I will explain that code later. For now, all you need to focus on is Button1_Click. In fact, ignore the parameters as well (ByVal sender as System.Object, and so on). Type in the following lines of code inside the Button1_Click event. After you have typed in the code, it should look like Figure 1.34.

```
'make sure the TextBox contains a number
If IsNumeric(TextBox1.Text) = False Then
```

```
    MsgBox("Please enter a number between 1 and 10!")
    Exit Sub
End If


'make sure the number is between 1 and 10
If Val(TextBox1.Text) < 1 Or Val(TextBox1.Text) > 10 Then
    MsgBox("Please enter a number between 1 and 10!")
    Exit Sub
End If
```

After you type in the new source code, run the program by pressing F5. Figure 1.35 shows the Guessing Game program running. If you type in something other than a number, the first part of the validation code kicks in and displays the error message, "Please enter a number between 1 and 10!"

Likewise, if you type a number that is outside the range of 1 to 100, the program displays the same error message (see Figure 1.36).

However, if you enter a correct number (between 1 and 10), the program does nothing. That means it worked, and the logic for handling a correct number is not yet in place. So, let's add that logic to the program now. Quit the program by clicking the small X in the top-right corner of the program window.

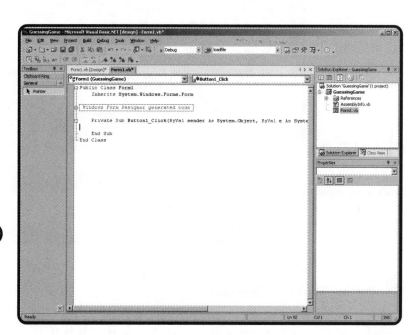

**FIGURE 1.33**

The source code
for the
`Button_Click`
event in the
Guessing Game.

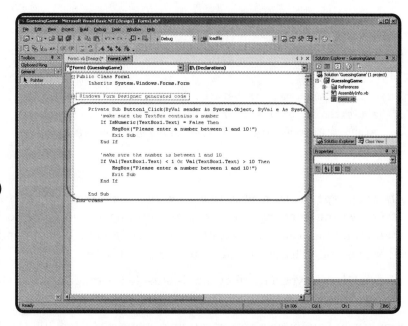

**FIGURE 1.34**

The validation code for the `Button1_Click` event makes sure a valid number was typed into the `TextBox`.

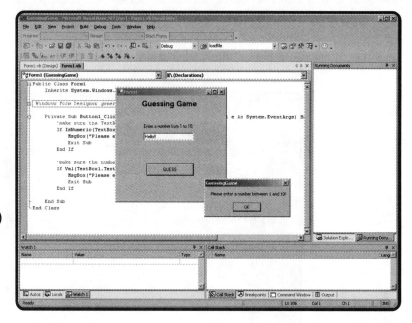

**FIGURE 1.35**

If you type in anything other than a number, the program displays an error message.

## Generating Random Numbers

Before the program can check the number, a random number must first be generated, and I haven't introduced you to the event that is first run when the program starts. This event is called `Form_Load`, and it runs before any other code in the program. In fact, it runs as soon as the form appears on the screen. So, that

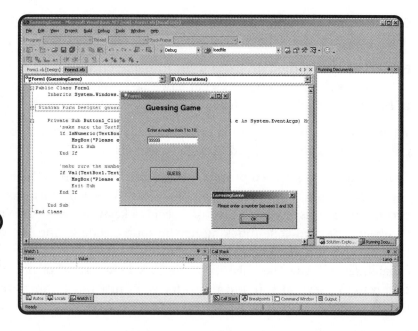

**FIGURE 1.36**

Typing in a number outside the correct range also results in an error message.

means Form_Load is a great place to insert source code to initialize anything that the program needs later on. For the purpose of this game, what is needed is a random number between 1 and 10. Let me show you how to do it.

Look at the top of the source code Editor window. There are two drop-down lists there (see Figure 1.37).

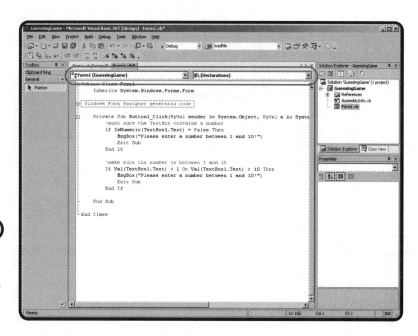

**FIGURE 1.37**

The Class list and Method list (highlighted) above the source code Editor window.

Click the Class drop-down list (the one on the left) to see the list of classes available to the program. Select the item called Base Class Events as shown in Figure 1.38.

Next, click the Method drop-down list (the one on the right) to see the list of methods for the form (which is what Base Class Events includes). Select the item in the menu called Load, as shown in Figure 1.39.

When you click the Load item, a new event is added to the source code for the program. This new event is called Form1_Load (see Figure 1.40).

That was quite an involved process just to add a new event to the form, wouldn't you agree? In the old days (for example, Visual Basic 6.0), this was much easier, because there was no main class, no Inherits keyword, and no Windows Form Designer-generated code mucking up the source code listing. As you will learn later on, this initial complexity reaps many rewards due to the immense new capabilities of Visual Basic .NET. For now, try to ignore all of the extra information being thrown at you and try to focus on just those things that I've highlighted for you.

Now that the Guessing Game program has a Form_Load event, you can type in some initialization code to generate the random number that the game needs. Type the following code inside the Form_Load event, so that the final result looks like Figure 1.41.

```
Randomize()
num = Int((Rnd() * 6) + 1)
```

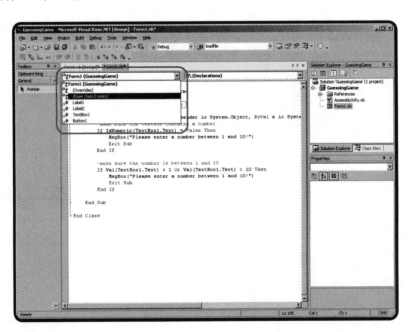

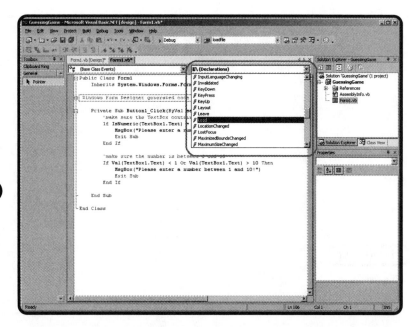

**FIGURE 1.39**

Select the Load event in the Method drop-down list to add the Form_Load event to the program.

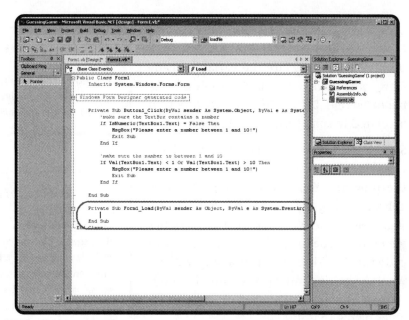

**FIGURE 1.40**

The new Form_Load event.

But wait, there's a problem! Look at the second line of code, which starts with num =. Notice the curvy line beneath the word num? That tells you something is wrong with that word. Visual Basic compiles source code on the fly, in the background. So it immediately picks up syntax errors. In this case, the num variable has not been declared yet, therefore you'll need to add the variable to the program.

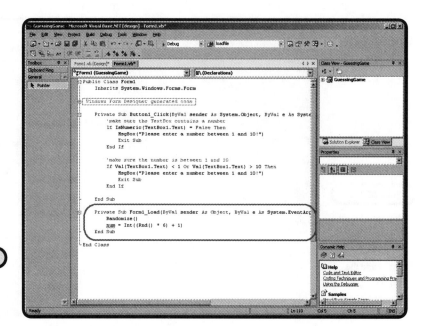

**FIGURE 1.41**

The completed
Form_Load
source code.

Because the variable, num, is needed by both Form_Load and Button1_Click, there's a problem. If you declare the variable inside Form_Load, then the variable won't be visible to Button1_Click. This is a problem that is related to something called scope.

So, the solution is to declare num as a global variable that is visible to all of the events in the program. You can declare global variables near the top of the source code listing, below the Windows Form Designer generated code line. This is a section of code that is hidden from view, and which I won't be getting into at this point. For now, remember that you can declare global variables below that line.

Add the following lines of code to the top of the program listing, as shown in Figure 1.42.

```
'declare the number variable
Dim num As Integer
```

> **Definition**
>
> A *syntax error* is a problem with source code, usually involving a misspelled word or undeclared variable.

> **Definition**
>
> *Variable Scope* refers to the visibility of a variable throughout a program. Variables that are visible to the entire program are known as global variables. Variables that are visible only to a specific part of the program, such as an event, subroutine, or function, are known as local variables.

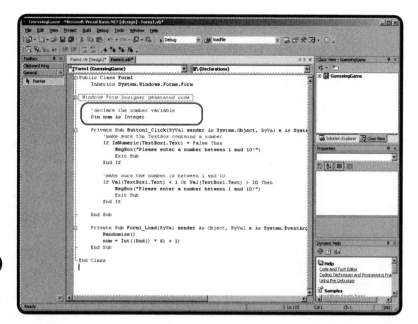

**FIGURE 1.42**

Declaring a global variable.

## Game Logic

Now for the game logic. Type in the following lines of code at the end of the Button1_Click event, so that it looks like Figure 1.43.

```
'check for high answer
If Val(TextBox1.Text) > num Then
    MsgBox("That number is too high")
ElseIf Val(TextBox1.Text) < num Then
    MsgBox("That number is too low")
Else
    MsgBox("That number is CORRECT!")
    End
End If
```

The game logic is handled by the If...Then conditional statement. A condition is a piece of logic that the program checks. If the condition is true, then the source code following the condition is followed. If the condition is false, then the program skips those lines of code. Now you see why I called this the "program logic." The first line (after the comment) checks to see if the entered number is greater than the random number. If it is, then a message is displayed telling the user that the number is too high. The ElseIf line checks to see whether the number was too low. Now here is where something interesting happens. You don't actually need to check for when the numbers are equal because that is assumed if the first two conditions failed. If the number is not greater, and not less, then it must be equal!

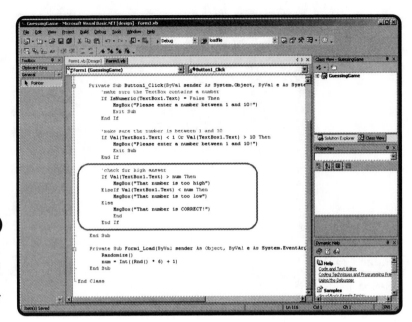

**FIGURE 1.43**

The game logic checks to see if the entered number is too high, too low, or right on target.

Go ahead and save the project now by clicking the Save All icon on the toolbar, or by selecting Save All from the File menu. Then run the game by pressing F5. It's now finished, so you can actually play it for the first time! (See Figure 1.44.)

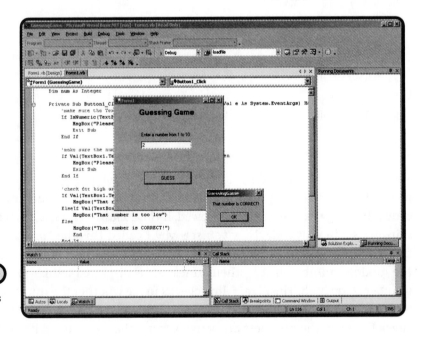

**FIGURE 1.44**

Guessing Game is ready to play!

# Summary

Congratulations on completing the first chapter on your quest to learn Visual Basic .NET. This chapter has covered a lot of material and jumped right into the action by covering two complete programs, which you were able to build from scratch. First, the Greeting program displayed output and read input using the console. Second, the Guessing Game program showed you how to program a real user interface with Visual Basic .NET.

You learned how to declare variables, how to use `Form1_Load`, and also how to program the events in a program. That's a considerable amount of new material for just the first chapter! If you enjoyed the programming so far, strap on your seat belt because even more surprises are waiting in the next chapter!

## CHALLENGES

The following challenges will help to reinforce the material you have learned in this chapter:

1. The Guessing Game is a simple introduction to Visual Basic .NET, and it was supposed to be as simple as possible to act as a learning tool. But the program is capable of much more! Try to modify the game so that it doesn't end when you get the correct answer. Instead, have the game generate a new random number and let the user try to guess it again without quitting.

2. The Guessing Game could be greatly improved by telling the player how many turns it took to get the right answer. Add a `Label` to the form that shows the number of times the player has pressed the GUESS button.

3. The range of numbers is kind of small. Modify the game so that it uses a larger range, such as 1 to 100, or even 1 to 1000!

# Overview of Visual Studio .NET

T he first chapter gave you a brief introduction to Visual Basic .NET and showed you how to write two sample programs to help provide a general feel for the capabilities of the language. This chapter is a little less practice and a little more theory, providing a general explanation of .NET and a detailed explanation of Visual Studio .NET. There is a lot more to .NET programming languages than is readily apparent. Therefore, this chapter is meant to give you a head start to understanding the basic premise: what is .NET, and why has Microsoft changed everything with this new version of Visual Studio? If you were a beginning or even seasoned Visual Studio 6.0 programmer, Visual Studio .NET was probably a shock to your sensibilities (as it was mine). Why change something that worked so well? The reason is not easy to answer in a single sentence, but you should have a good idea why Microsoft changed Visual Basic by the end of this chapter.

Here is a brief overview of the specific topics that are covered in this chapter:

- The languages spoken by Visual Studio .NET

- Introduction to the .NET Framework

- The Visual Basic .NET development environment

Visual Basic .NET is a graphical programming language that lets you build a complete application without writing any source code, although the capabilities are significantly limited if you do not write code. As a visual design tool, Visual Basic .NET allows you to develop applications quickly; this is called Rapid Application Development (RAD). Learning about the bigger concepts behind .NET is important for every developer to understand because the underlying foundation is key. Until you can grasp why Microsoft made so many changes, it will be difficult to grasp exactly what it is all about. Sure, Visual Basic has a lot of new features, but at the same time, it seems to have lost a lot of beloved features as well. Why?

As I will explain in this chapter, a new paradigm shift was needed to move Windows software development (based on user base, the largest platform for software development in the world today) to the next level of sophistication. Visual C++, Visual Basic, and Microsoft's Component Object Model (COM), which includes ActiveX components, have not been the resounding successes that they could have been. COM was a valiant attempt to promote code reuse and object-oriented systems development. But one of the failures of COM was its reliance upon the flawed and inefficient Windows registry to keep track of components. It was therefore impossible to distribute new ActiveX controls and code libraries without registering them first.

Microsoft .NET is a complete replacement for COM and a few other Microsoft technologies—paradigm shift! However, I should point out that Windows 2000 embraces COM+, and .NET fully supports it. I'll talk about COM more in the following pages.

## The Languages Spoken by Visual Studio .NET

The core features and capabilities of Visual Basic .NET (also called VB.NET) were the driving force behind the design of Visual Studio .NET, which is comprised of four primary languages:

- Visual Basic .NET
- Visual C# .NET
- Visual C++ .NET
- Visual J# .NET

In addition to the major languages, Visual Studio .NET provides the following two support libraries that are key to Web and database development:

- ASP.NET (Active Server Pages .NET)
- ADO.NET (ActiveX Data Objects .NET)

Visual Studio .NET is a large development environment that is completely self-contained, incorporating all three languages, numerous

**Definition**

The *.NET Framework* is the core architecture behind Visual Basic .NET and the other .NET languages, providing a common runtime, compatible code libraries, a fully integrated Windows API library, along with ASP.NET and ADO.NET.

libraries, and the huge .NET Framework library, which was designed to replace the aging Windows Application Programming Interface (API).

Visual Basic power users frequently use Windows API functions to enhance the functionality of Visual Basic programs. Now functionality of the entire Windows API is built into the class libraries in the .NET Framework. Figure 2.1 illustrates the inter-relationships present in Visual Studio .NET.

Experienced Visual Basic programmers will immediately note that Visual Studio .NET evolved more out of Visual Basic 6.0 than it did from Visual C++ 6.0. The Windows Forms engine is central to developing user interfaces with Visual Studio .NET languages. Visual C++ 6.0 is more of a low-level language and does not feature Visual Basic 6.0's awesome RAD features (such as a drag-drop Control Toolbox and simple control events).

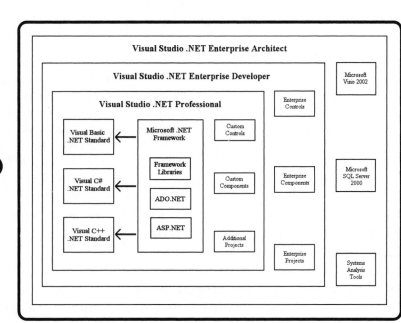

**FIGURE 2.1**

Visual Studio .NET was built upon the Microsoft .NET Framework and three primary languages: Visual Basic .NET, Visual C# .NET, and Visual C++ .NET.

> **IN THE REAL WORLD**
>
> Visual Studio .NET comes in a variety of versions. If you are unsure which version will best meet your needs, I recommend that you order the trial version, which is fully functional for a 60-day period, allowing you to gain some exposure to the complete product. If you are a student or faculty member at a college, university, or trade school, you may be eligible for the academic version. Browse to http://msdn.microsoft.com/vstudio/productinfo/trial.asp for more information.

Possibly the most important fact to consider when choosing which .NET language to focus on is that these languages all support the core .NET Framework. The exception is Visual C++, which has significantly more access to the Windows operating system and is clearly the language of choice for power users (and those of you who prefer `WinMain` and `WndProc` instead of `Form1_Load`).

> **Definition**
>
> `WinMain` and `WndProc` **are the core functions called any time a Windows program starts running. These low-level functions are built into the Common Language Runtime (CLR) and are not compiled into each Visual Basic .NET program directly.**

## Visual Basic .NET

Visual Basic .NET was based on Visual Basic 6.0, but makes no attempt to retain backward compatibility with projects developed with earlier versions. Visual Basic .NET, therefore, is significantly more than just the "next version" of Visual Basic. It is, for all practical purposes, a whole new product. Visual Basic 6.0 is the last version of traditional Visual Basic. Therefore, 6.0 is likely to be in continued use for years to come.

### Upgrade Path for Visual Basic 6.0

The vast number of development projects based on Visual Basic 6.0 will ensure its con-

> **Definition**
>
> *Intermediate Language (IL)* **is the binary format of programs compiled by Visual Studio .NET. All .NET-compliant languages (such as Visual Basic and Visual C#) must be compiled to the IL format, which is in turn executed by the** *Common Language Runtime (CLR)*. **CLR, in turn, is comprised of the distribution files required to run a .NET program on a destination PC, usually handled by an application's primary install program.**

tinued popularity even though Visual Basic .NET is being used for new development work. Due to the number of changes introduced in .NET, the two versions of Visual Basic are significantly incompatible, and it is not possible to write version-independent code due to the changes in the framework. Whereas Visual Basic 6.0

projects frequently called on Windows API subroutines to extend the basic functionality of the language, Visual Basic .NET has the rich and powerful .NET Framework at its disposal, which includes a huge assortment of class libraries.

### In the Real World

Visual Basic .NET Standard Edition retails for about $100 and is a fully-functional version of the compiler, complete with the .NET Framework and Visual Studio .NET documentation. The only limitation to this affordable version is that it does not compile custom controls or code libraries. I used the Standard Edition during most of the development of this book; it is an excellent alternative to the more expensive options (Professional, Enterprise Developer, and Enterprise Architect).

## Porting Visual Basic 6.0 Projects

I highly recommend that you avoid porting projects of significant size from Visual Basic 6.0 to Visual Basic .NET. The effort is just too counter-productive. There is really no need to upgrade existing projects to .NET. Rather, continue to promote the use of Visual Basic 6.0 for such projects and defend the language! Visual Basic 6.0 has not become obsolete with the release of .NET.

## Cross-Version Development

However, one thing that I would definitely recommend is cross-version development in large projects that do not need to share code or components. Specifically, if you are working on a project that uses Extensible Markup Language (XML) to share data between programs, then you should have no problem developing different programs within a specified project requirement using Visual Studio

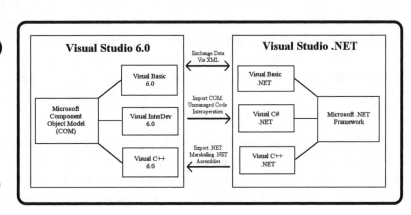

**FIGURE 2.2**

Inter-process communication between Visual Studio 6.0 and Visual Studio .NET is not a simple prospect unless a standard format like XML is used.

6.0 and Visual Studio .NET languages, interchangeably. Figure 2.2 shows an illustration of how Visual Studio 6.0 and Visual Studio .NET might communicate.

The problem of incompatibility will only start to cause problems if you or someone else wants to reuse code across versions. That simply will not work and should be avoided. Cross-version reuse introduces more problems than it solves, and you are better off rewriting parts of a project when necessary, or continuing to use the same version when code reuse is a high priority.

Most likely, in such a situation, there will be two significant camps:

- Those supporting Visual Studio 6.0 and COM.
- Those supporting Visual Studio .NET.

### Combining Visual Basic 6.0 and Visual Basic .NET Development

Because programmers are finicky people who vehemently defend their personal favorites when it comes to languages and technology, the best plan within a large development project is to decide which parts of the system need to be interchangeable and which parts don't. For those parts that are borderline interchangeable, consider using a standard like XML to communicate or share data (or better yet, use XML for all inter-process and inter-program data transfer).

I have witnessed programmers in the midst of XML overkill, using an XML parser inside every single subroutine so that parameters can be passed as XML strings. That idea is founded on sound theory but is ridiculous in practice. Just stick to the easiest and simplest solution and your code will be fast, efficient, and reusable, even in the midst of a multi-language project.

## Visual C# .NET

Visual C# .NET is a brand new language that was first released with Visual Studio .NET. Microsoft offers a Standard Edition of Visual C# (as well as for Visual C++ and Visual Basic) for a very affordable price, and is a great option if you want to experiment with the new language without committing to the expensive Visual Studio .NET Professional. Visual J#, which is a Java implementation for .NET, is available as a free download for Visual Studio .NET users. Numerous other languages are being developed for .NET, such as Perl.

The C# language is a descendant of C++, retaining most of the power of C++, while doing away with features that lead to buggy code (such as pointers). C# is a cousin to the Java language, sharing many similar features but diverging in most other areas. C# is the preferred .NET language for programmers with a background in C or C++ who may not be drawn to Visual Basic for whatever reason.

## Visual C++ .NET

Visual C++ .NET is the power-user's compiler of choice, capable of building stand-alone executable programs that do not need the .NET Framework and are capable of running on any native Windows operating system without a special installer. At the same time, Visual C++ .NET also supports .NET Framework development, like the other two languages. This duality of support ensures that component developers will continue to be able to use Visual C++ .NET to create custom controls and code libraries for non-.NET products.

Visual C++ source code that does not use .NET is called "unmanaged code" because it does not gain the advantages that .NET provides, such as garbage collection (the automatic removal of unused objects in memory). Visual C++ source code that supports .NET is called "managed code."

## Visual J# .NET

Visual J# .NET is an upgraded version of Visual J++ 6.0 that fully supports the .NET Framework. This language was not included with the retail Visual Studio .NET because it was apparently not completed in time and not considered a key language to warrant delaying the release. Visual J# .NET is available as a free add-on to Visual Studio .NET.

Visual J# .NET is Microsoft's own implementation of the Java language and includes Microsoft extensions, such as JavaCOM and JDirect. Unfortunately, J# is not compatible with Sun Microsystems' Java 2 language, the Java Development Kit (JDK), or the Java Virtual Machine (JVM).

## Support Libraries

In addition to the four main languages, Visual Studio .NET incorporates Active Server Pages .NET (ASP.NET) and ActiveX Data Objects .NET (ADO.NET).

### Active Server Pages .NET (ASP.NET)

ASP.NET is driven by the scripting languages, JScript and VBScript. Scripting is really completed within the source code for Web pages (Hypertext Markup Language, or HTML). You may freely mix JScript and VBScript code in the same Web page, as long as the scripting languages are in separate blocks of script code. Visual Studio .NET completely integrates Web functionality into the source code editor, fully supporting syntax highlighting and IntelliSense drop-down lists.

ASP.NET is the driving force behind Web Forms and Web development for Visual Studio .NET and is supported by all of the .NET languages.

# Introduction to the .NET Framework

There are cases in which the complexity of software is just too much for a single person to grasp. System maintenance is becoming more important as software continues to evolve. Businesses depend on software for day-to-day work. The days of custom-building monumental software systems are coming to an end because such systems are impossible to maintain. The latest generation of large-scale software systems handles all the low-level details for the programmers and analysts and allows them to use GUI tools to build applications.

## The Importance of Software Standards

One such example is Microsoft's .NET Framework, which brings a multitude of languages and design tools together into a seamless whole so that people can focus on gathering the requirements for a system, building prototypes, and then completing the applications—all without writing any low-level code.

**Low-level code is the source code that controls how user-interface controls work, how databases communicate, how a Web browser talks to a Web site, and so on. It is the underlying processes that create an architecture upon which your programs rely.**

Think of the low-level architecture as roads, highways, street lights, and road signs, and your application as a car. In the past, programmers had to build the roads as well as the cars, and the vast majority of development time was spent on building just the roads! That was one of the most frustrating parts of a programmer's job—not only was the underlying architecture not present, the tools to build that architecture were not standardized. Further complicating the problem was the fact that computers created by different companies were not able to communicate.

## Emerging Technologies

A whole host of new technologies have emerged in the last 10 to 15 years that have completely changed the landscape of software design. Different brands and scales of computers (for example, mainframes and PCs) can now communicate over the Internet using protocols that were invented for Web browsers, such as Hypertext Transport Protocol (HTTP) and Extensible Markup Language (XML).

Just as civilization is cultivated by a common language, so too is computing. In retrospect, the past is akin to barbarism.

## Writing "Really" Reusable Code

One of the most significant attempts by the software industry to attack the problems arising out of a lack of standards was the object-oriented programming (OOP) paradigm. OOP provides a means for programmers to write reusable classes that can be used for multiple projects. The structured programming paradigm that preceded OOP had a more limited form of code reuse, which involved copying and pasting source code from one program into another and then adapting the code to meet the requirements of the new system. OOP, on the other hand, was supposed to solve the problem by allowing programmers to write the code once and then reuse it across multiple projects.

Why is code reuse often so impractical, and why is OOP still considered state of the art after so many years? In a word: framework. The underlying architecture—the framework—has never been a standard that programmers could rely upon. One of the most significant proponents of the OOP framework was the Java language, developed by Sun Microsystems. Java attacked the standardization problem full-on by promising "write-once, read-anywhere" programs that could be compiled on any computer and then run on any computer or operating system (given that a Java runtime library is available for that computer system).

The concepts and innovations introduced with the Java language are significant and ultimately found in many of the advanced features of Microsoft's .NET Framework. Java, as a single language, was just too limited in scope, however, to single-handedly solve the problems of computing standards. But Java was a wake-up call for many software companies that had previously developed operating systems and programming languages that—even within such companies—were not standardized.

## Object-Oriented Standards

Microsoft, as well as many other software companies, has tried in earnest to come up with a standard for OOP and code reuse, such as the Component Object Model (COM). Microsoft's COM has allowed developers to build custom user-interface controls and code component libraries that are reusable across many languages (such as Microsoft Visual Basic and Visual C++, and Borland Delphi and C++Builder, all of which support COM). The ability to write source code using Visual Basic, and then reuse that same code in Borland Delphi is significant!

These two languages are utterly alien to each other! Visual Basic was originally based on the BASIC language, while Delphi was based on Pascal. Numerous other companies support COM as well, and this has only benefited their customers.

# The Visual Studio .NET Development Environment

Visual Studio .NET includes a powerful and feature-rich development environment, bringing together several languages into a seamless whole. This section will explore the development environment in detail, giving you an introduction to the main features of Visual Studio .NET.

## The Visual Studio .NET User Interface

The Visual Studio .NET user interface features a standard menu, toolbar, and multiple windows that can be docked and minimized. Auto-hide is a particularly nice feature of Visual Studio .NET, helping to reduce the number of open windows in the environment, while still keeping those windows handy when needed. Figure 2.3 shows the environment with a new project ready to go.

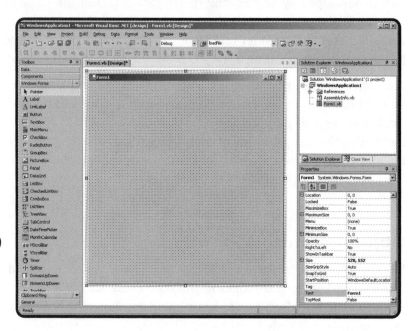

**FIGURE 2.3**

The integrated development environment for Visual Basic .NET.

## Menus

The main menu for Visual Studio .NET is the same for any .NET language that uses the Windows Forms Designer, so to learn one set of menus is to learn them all—a great time-saver. When an ASP.NET or HTML file is being edited, however, the menus will change to reflect the features of those files. This section will focus only on .NET-specific languages.

**File**. The File menu (shown in Figure 2.4) was designed to support the Solution Explorer with handling multiple projects at one time.

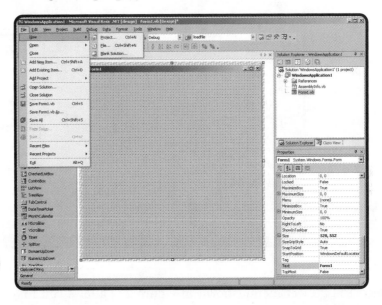

**FIGURE 2.4**

The File menu.

**Edit**. The Edit menu (shown in Figure 2.5) includes the standard text editing features, such as copy, cut, and paste, but also has some advanced features that you will find useful, such as outlining and commenting/uncommenting source code.

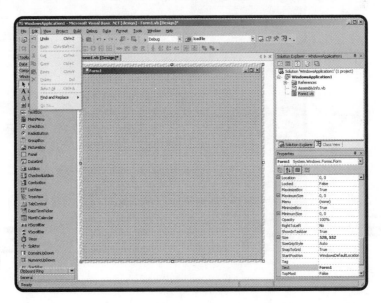

**FIGURE 2.5**

The Edit menu.

**View**. The View menu (shown in Figure 2.6) allows you to switch between the Source Code and Forms Designer edit windows, and also allows you to bring up dockable windows that have been closed.

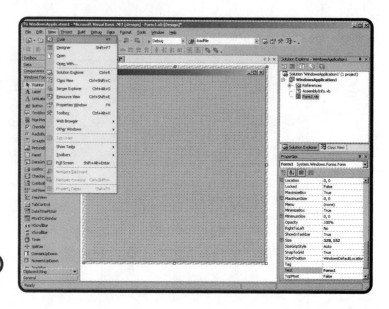

FIGURE 2.6

The View menu.

**Project**. The Project menu (shown in Figure 2.7) allows you to add new components and files to the project, such as a new form or control.

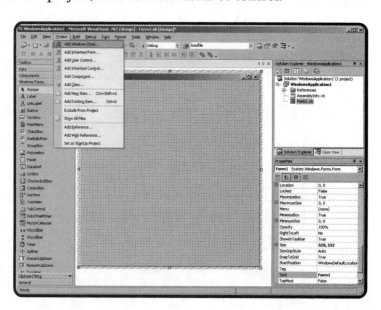

FIGURE 2.7

The Project menu.

**Build**. The Build menu (shown in Figure 2.8) includes the commands needed to compile or build a project or solution into an executable or redistributable file (such as a .DLL).

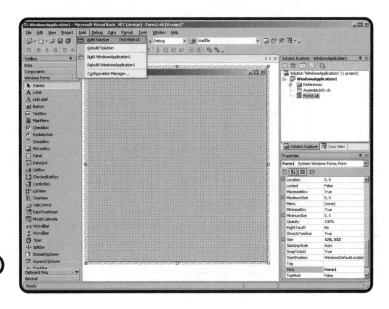

**FIGURE 2.8**

The Build menu.

**Debug**. The Debug menu (shown in Figure 2.9) is used when stepping through a program that has been stopped with a breakpoint or error condition.

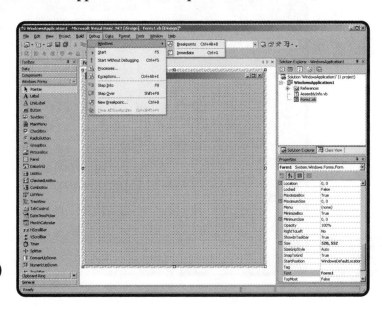

**FIGURE 2.9**

The Debug menu.

Microsoft Visual Basic .NET Programming for the Absolute Beginner

**Data**. The Data menu (shown in Figure 2.10) is useful when connecting controls to a database or when using an ADO.NET dataset.

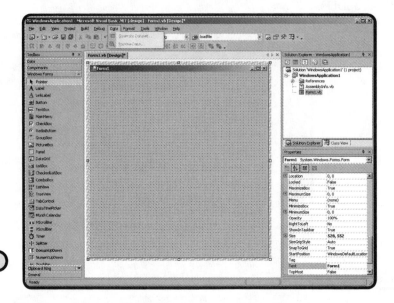

**FIGURE 2.10**

The Data menu.

**Format**. The Format menu (shown in Figure 2.11) is a user-interface menu that helps to align and format the position and size of controls.

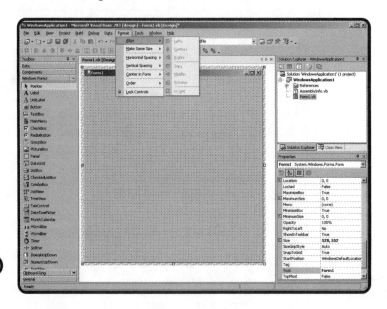

**FIGURE 2.11**

The Format menu.

**Tools**. The Tools menu (shown in Figure 2.12) includes numerous commands that may be needed during a development project. Most importantly however, is the last item in the Tools menu, called Options. Use this command to customize the user interface and settings of your projects.

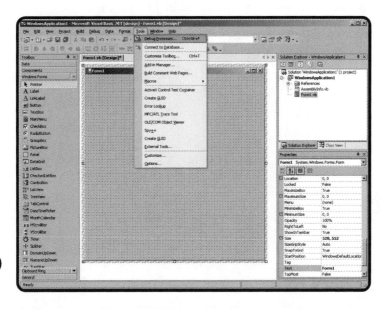

**FIGURE 2.12**

The Tools menu.

**Window**. The Window menu (shown in Figure 2.13) allows you to select among the open files loaded into Visual Studio .NET and arrange the windows on the screen.

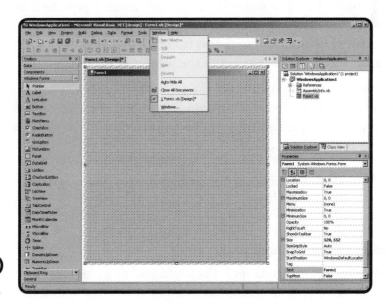

**FIGURE 2.13**

The Window menu.

**Help**. The Help menu (shown in Figure 2.14) includes numerous commands for searching the integrated help system that comes with Visual Studio .NET. If you are ever stuck on a strange error message or language feature, you can usually find help on the item using this menu. You can quickly bring up help on a selected control or word in the editor by pressing F1.

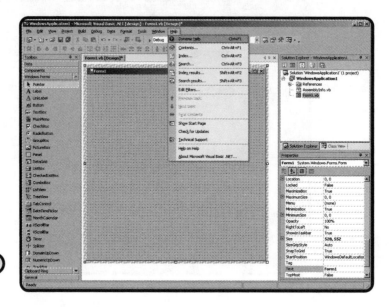

**FIGURE 2.14**

The Help menu.

## Toolbars

Visual Studio .NET features numerous toolbars that provide a means to quickly perform some action by pressing one of the icons on a toolbar (see Figure 2.15). There are over 20 toolbars to choose from, therefore you will want to display only those toolbars that are relevant to the project at hand.

You can use the View menu to display a list of toolbars, or you can right-click on any current toolbar to bring up a drop-down list of available toolbars (as shown in Figure 2.16). To arrange the toolbars, simply drag the left edge of the toolbar to a new location and release.

 **The toolbar will continue to move with the mouse as long as you hold down the mouse button.**

## Windows Forms Designer

The Windows Forms Designer is the key to building graphical user interfaces with Visual Studio .NET languages. Visual Basic was the first Windows tool to feature a graphical form editor with drag-drop control functionality. The Forms Designer is automatically configured for any type of file you are editing. For example, when working on an ASP.NET project, the Forms Designer will display controls in the Toolbox that are relevant to Web pages (see Figure 2.17).

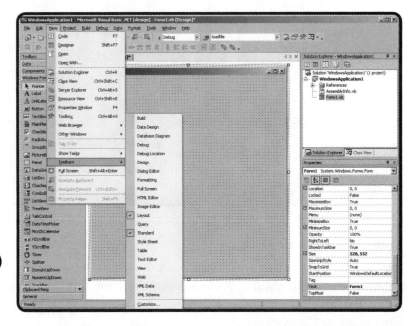

**FIGURE 2.15**

Displaying toolbars via the View menu.

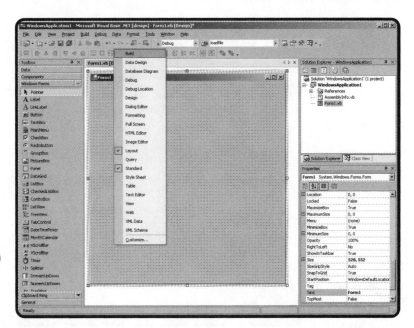

**FIGURE 2.16**

Displaying toolbars via the right-click Toolbar menu.

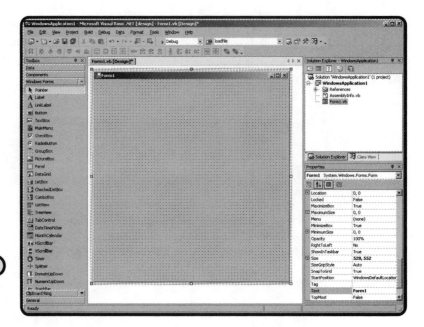

**FIGURE 2.17**

The Windows
Forms Designer.

## Code Editor Window

The source code editor for Visual Studio .NET is truly a magnificent tool to behold because it is absolutely loaded with functionality and supports numerous languages. This editor is capable of editing just about any type of file imaginable with ease (see Figure 2.18).

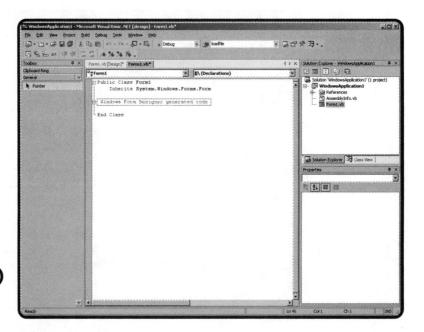

**FIGURE 2.18**

The Code Editor
window.

### *Editing HTML Files*

If you load an HTML file into the code editor, HTML code will be highlighted and formatted on the screen. (In fact, the formatting is mandatory, and the code editor will automatically format messy HTML files.) You are not required to set up an ASP.NET project just to edit an HTML page (as was usually the case with Visual InterDev 6.0, which is now integrated into Visual Studio .NET). Figure 2.19 shows a sample HTML file loaded into the editor.

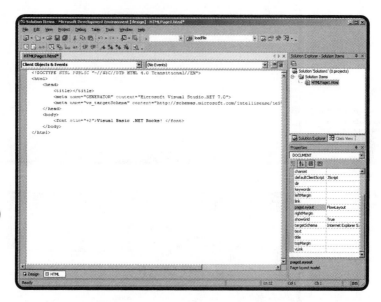

**FIGURE 2.19**

Editing an HTML
file with the code
editor is a piece
of cake.

In addition, the Windows Forms Designer is linked to the Code Editor window so that you can switch from source-code view to user-interface view with the touch of a button. With HTML files, the designer will show an actual representation of what the Web page will look like because Visual Studio .NET literally incorporates the Internet Explorer engine within. Figure 2.20 shows the output of the HTML page. Right-click the code editor and select View Design to see for yourself.

Imagine you are designing a guest book for an old Web site that you created several years ago. Instead of using a proprietary tool like Symantec Visual Page or Macromedia Dreamweaver, try using the Visual Studio .NET code editor! You will be amazed with the HTML editing features that are built in.

Here's an awesome feature of the code editor. Bring up the source code for the "Visual Basic .NET Rocks!" page again by right-clicking the display window and selecting View HTML Source (also available in the View menu). Add a blank line after <body> and type the "<" character, which is the start of an HTML tag. Check it out, an IntelliSense drop-down list of HTML tags! See Figure 2.21 and marvel.

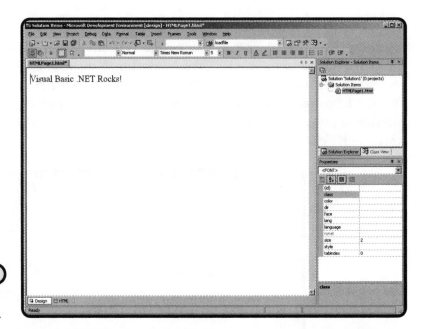

**FIGURE 2.20**

Output from the sample HTML file.

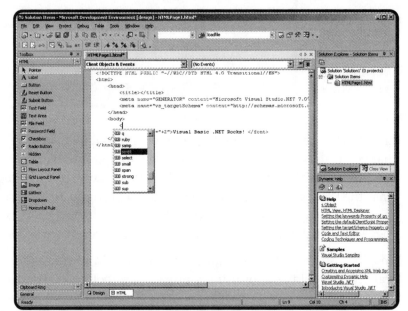

**FIGURE 2.21**

Never memorize an HTML tag again, thanks to IntelliSense and the awesome code editor built into Visual Studio .NET.

You might recall when IntelliSense was first introduced in Visual Basic 5.0. Now it's in all of Microsoft's products and development tools from nearly everyone else in the software industry. Yes, thank you Visual Basic. Intrigued? You will be pleased to find that everything in .NET supports IntelliSense, including XML, ADO.NET, and so on. Often you will not even need a reference book with IntelliSense available.

### Editing Binary Files

Before moving on to the next part of the Visual Studio .NET development environment, I want to show you another intriguing format supported by the editor. If you drag a binary file (such as COMMAND.COM) from the Windows Explorer to Visual Studio .NET, the code editor will transform itself into a binary hex editor, which may be useful any time you need to edit a binary file but don't have a hex editor handy (see Figure 2.22).

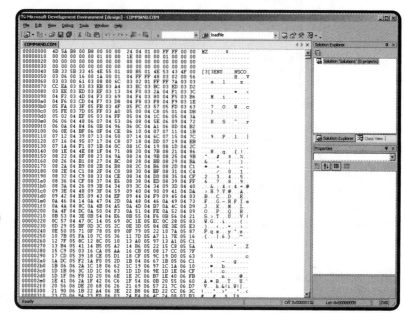

**FIGURE 2.22**

The Visual Studio .NET code editor features a hex editor for modifying binary files.

## Solution Explorer

The Solution Explorer contains the files and resources, as well as individual projects, that are used by your application. This window was called Project Explorer in earlier versions of Visual Basic (see Figure 2.23).

**FIGURE 2.23**

The Solution Explorer undocked from the right side of the environment window.

## Properties Window

The Properties window is part of the Windows Forms Designer and is useful for Windows Forms, as well as for Web Forms (ASP.NET). Properties are the key to designing a custom user interface with controls (see Figure 2.24).

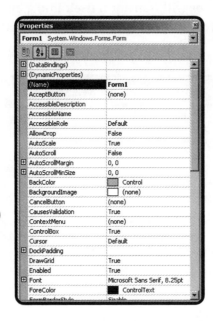

**FIGURE 2.24**

The Properties window undocked from the right side of the environment window.

## Output Window

The Output window is a valuable debugging tool that you can use while a program is running. You can send messages to the Output window using the `Debug.WriteLine` function. The `Debug` object has numerous other methods that you are free to use to assist in the development process (see Figure 2.25).

## Control Toolbox

The Control Toolbox holds all of the controls available to the project (depending on the project type, the list will show different controls). This is the primary means of adding `TextBox`, `Label`, `Button`, `ListBox`, and other controls to a form when the program is being created (see Figure 2.26).

In addition to the default list, you can change the Toolbox so that it displays a small icon for each control. This is useful because it shows all of the controls without the need to scroll down the list. To change the format of the display, right-click on the Toolbox and select or deselect List View from the drop-down menu (as shown in Figure 2.27).

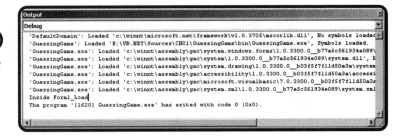

**FIGURE 2.25**

The Output window undocked from the bottom of the environment window.

**FIGURE 2.26**

The Control Toolbox displaying controls in a list.

Once changed, the Toolbox is easier to use, but may not be convenient if you are not familiar with the list of controls (as shown in Figure 2.28). If you are unsure, simply hover the mouse over an icon and the name of that control will appear in a ToolTip.

### The AutoDock Feature

The AutoDock feature is one of the new features of Visual Studio .NET that makes the development environment more intuitive and manageable. Simply click and hold the top of one of the windows in the environment (such as the Properties window) and drag the window to any edge inside Visual Studio .NET, and you will see the outline of a new position for the window. Figure 2.29 shows this feature in action.

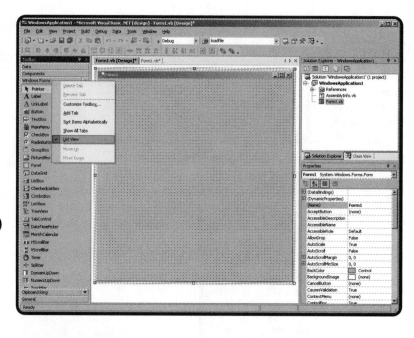

**FIGURE 2.27**

Changing the display of available controls in the Toolbox from a list to a group of icons.

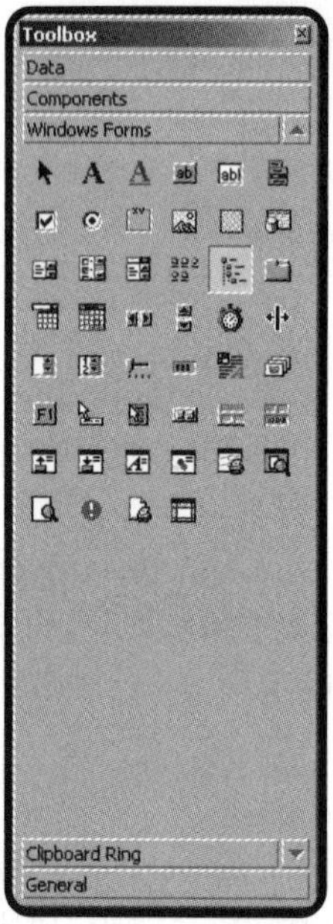

**FIGURE 2.28**

The Control Toolbox displaying the available controls as small icons.

After releasing the mouse on the AutoDock selection, the Toolbox window is repositioned back in its normal position at the left edge of the development environment (see Figure 2.30).

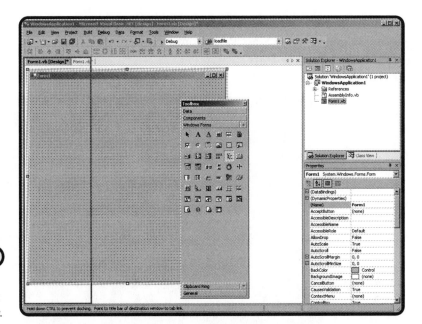

FIGURE 2.29

Docking the
Toolbox to the left
side of the window.

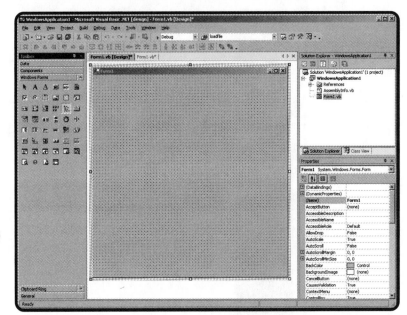

FIGURE 2.30

The result of
docking the Toolbox
at the left edge of
the window.

## Customizing the User Interface

Depending on your background, you may be comfortable with the development
environment of another tool besides Visual Basic. Visual Studio .NET makes it easy

for you to customize the environment to suit your tastes. Simply bring up the Start Page by selecting Show Start Page from the Help menu (as shown in Figure 2.31). Figure 2.32 shows the Start Page.

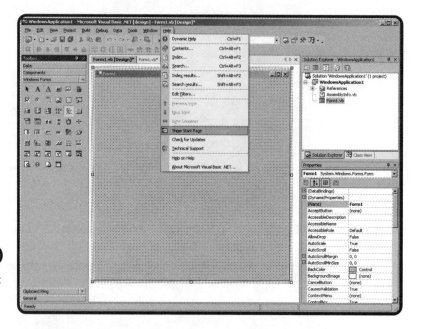

**FIGURE 2.31**

Displaying the Start Page using the Help menu.

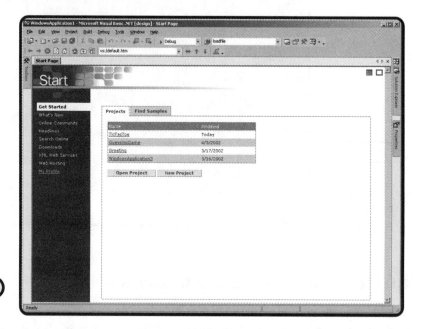

**FIGURE 2.32**

The Start Page.

From the Start Page, bring up the customization page by selecting My Profile on the left edge of the screen. The profile screen allows you to change the basic layout of Visual Studio .NET by selecting the options listed in Figure 2.33.

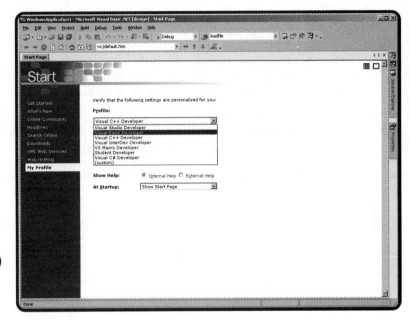

**FIGURE 2.33**

Changing the developer profile.

## Summary

This chapter provided an overview of Visual Studio .NET and covered the major features of the development environment, including the program menus, toolbars, and the various windows that make Visual Studio .NET a productive and efficient development tool. By learning to customize the environment to your tastes, you will become more comfortable with the user interface and will learn the new environment quicker. Your development work will also be more productive if you select an environment with which you are already skilled at using (such as Visual Basic 6.0).

# CHALLENGES

The following challenges will help to reinforce the material you have learned in this chapter.

1. Create a new Windows Application in Visual Studio .NET and familiarize yourself with the features available for each of the design windows.

2. Add a new project to the Solution Explorer to gain some familiarity with the method used to separate and organize multiple projects within a solution.

3. Try out several different profiles for Visual Studio .NET to find the one with which you are most comfortable, and note how Visual Studio .NET automatically configures the user interface for each profile.

# CHAPTER 3

# The Basics of a Graphical User Interface

Visual Basic .NET is a graphical programming language that lets you build a complete application with very little source code. As a visual design tool, Visual Basic .NET allows you to develop applications quickly; this is called Rapid Application Development (RAD). The key to building a good productivity application is the ease with which the user is able to learn and use the user interface.

This chapter covers the following topics:

- **Project preview—Tic-Tac-Toe**

- **User interfaces—The Big Picture**

- **Forms and controls**

- **The standard dialogs**

- **Chapter project—Tic-Tac-Toe**

By "productivity" I am referring to software that was designed to help a person accomplish something. Most software falls into the productivity group, although a lot of software lacks a user interface and simply does its job behind the scenes. For example, database servers and Web servers will run as a background service, and for the most part, seem to not really do anything. But rest assured, when a database request or Web page request comes in, these servers kick into high gear and deliver the goods.

That is why such programs are called "server programs," because they provide something to a client. Such is the essence of client/server computing: a single server program provides services to numerous client programs. The real benefit to the scheme is that when you need to make changes to the system, you need only change the server, not all the clients.

Why is this concept relevant in the context of a chapter about user interfaces? You can use Visual Basic .NET to build server programs as well as client programs, although client programs (also called applications) get most of the attention. Knowing how to create a visually appealing—as well as useful and ergonomic—user interface is a key skill that must be learned over time.

## Project Preview—Tic-Tac-Toe

This chapter builds a complete project based on the classic game of Tic-Tac-Toe that you will learn to write from scratch. Check out Figure 3.1 for a screenshot of the game.

## Graphical User Interfaces—
## The Big Picture

Before delving into the subject of actually creating user interfaces, I'd like you to ponder the question: What is a graphical user interface (GUI)? It is a term that you've probably heard many times before and you probably take it for granted. At the lowest level, a user interface is anything that lets a person communicate with a computer.

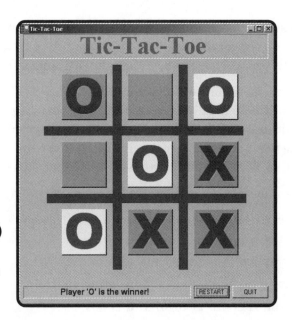

**FIGURE 3.1**

Get ready for Tic-Tac-Toe, the sample game developed in this chapter.

The keyboard and mouse are the most common user-interface devices, as well as joysticks for flight simulators and arcade games. Voice recognition is also a form of user interface serving the function of a keyboard. Perhaps some day, neural interfaces will let users control a computer by thought alone.

> **Definition**
>
> A *Graphical User Interface (GUI)* is the visual part of a program containing forms and controls.

Sound too far fetched? It's not as fictional an idea as you might suspect. The human brain can be measured with electrodes on the temples just like muscle reflexes.

> **IN THE REAL WORLD**
>
> I worked as a software engineer for a company called Noraxon USA, Inc. that specializes in muscle-recording instruments, a science called electromyography (EMG), serving rehabilitation and physical therapy clinics. I used a wireless measuring device called Telemyo, attached to my forearm, to control a game from across the room by simply moving my wrist left or right!

Although a user interface can be many things, it usually involves "objects" that work well with a mouse and keyboard because those are the primary input devices.

For example, the TextBox control was designed for keyboard input, whereas the Button control was designed for mouse input. These are two of the most common user-interface controls you will use in VB.NET (or any GUI language).

What, you might wonder, is a control? A user-interface control is a visual "object" placed on the screen that generally accepts user input and helps the program communicate with the user. Some controls, such as Timer, are visible during development, but not when the program is running. There are dozens of controls that you can use for your VB.NET programs. Here is a short list of such controls:

- Button: Accepts mouse clicks that trigger events in the program.
- TextBox: Accepts keyboard input and also displays text.
- Label: Displays text.
- Panel: Contains controls in manageable groups.
- PictureBox: Displays pictures and contains other controls.
- Timer: Triggers timed events at regular intervals.

Without controls, programs would not be very useful (except maybe as server programs). Most programs are designed to accomplish a specific task, with the vast majority keeping track of some sort of database. Database applications by far outnumber other custom-developed programs, and Visual Basic is the primary language used to build database applications. At the other side of the ravine, server programs are usually written with a language such as Visual C++, because it excels at doing things extremely fast.

> **Definition**
>
> A *control* is a visual object on the screen that helps the program to communicate with the user by accepting input or displaying output.

So, there are really two groups of programs in the business environment:

1. **Client programs:** developed with languages like Visual Basic—well-suited for building front-end programs with user interfaces.
2. **Server programs:** developed with languages like Visual C++—well suited for building back-end data processing programs that run at high speed.

## Multi-Tasking and Multi-Processing

When a program, such as a database server, runs in the "background," it is multi-tasking, leaving other programs free to run in the "foreground." A background program, then, is said to have no user interface, whereas a foreground program does have a user interface.

You can test this theory easily enough. Open up a Web browser, such as Microsoft Internet Explorer, and visit your favorite Web site. Before the page loads, minimize the Web browser so that it is no longer in the "foreground." What happens to the

> **Definition**
>
> *Multi-tasking* is the process of doing more than one thing at a time.

Web page? It's still there in the Web browser, waiting for you to browse it. But the Web browser is minimized, so you can't see it. If you wait a moment and then maximize the Web browser window again, the Web page should be loaded because after you minimized the browser window, the page continued to load "in the background."

## Foreground and Background Processes

That is the key to understanding the concepts of "front-end" and "back-end" programs. Clients usually run in the foreground, therefore they are called front-end programs. Servers usually run in the background, therefore they are called back-end programs.

Note also that server programs (such as Microsoft SQL Server 2000) are best used on a dedicated computer. What dedicated means in the context of computing is that a computer is set aside for a specific purpose. In the case of a database server, it usually takes more than one to handle all the clients connecting to it!

> **Definition**
>
> A *front-end program* is a client application that connects to a database or other server program.

Just imagine all the requests that eBay gets on an hourly basis. The auction site, http://www.ebay.com, hosts millions of auctions a day, and all the information is stored in a database. Not even a top of the line PC could hope to handle a fraction of the data

> **Definition**
>
> A *back-end program* is a server program that accepts connections from client applications.

processing that is required at the back end to keep eBay running. In the old days, before PCs became so cheap and readily available, and even before the Internet became popular, huge mainframe computers handled the data processing needs of a company. These processes usually supported sales, inventory, and payroll. Today, there are still mainframes, but the state of the art is in multi-processing systems (computers with more than one central processing unit—also called a "processor" or a "CPU").

## Multi-Processing

When a single PC can't handle all the "hits" that a server gets in a specific time period (such as a minute or hour), what is usually needed is a PC with more CPUs. Dual-CPU systems and Quad-CPU systems are easily built using off-the-shelf components. When you need more than four CPUs, you start to get into custom hardware systems. Most large manufacturers offer a line of high-end servers with support for common configurations of 8, 16, 24, and 32 CPUs. Any more processing power than that and you really need to move into a higher echelon of computing and go with a mainframe that can bring hundreds of CPUs online to handle server traffic.

## Server Clusters and Farms

However, when you ratchet up the computing scale to the mainframe level, the costs can go up significantly, and there is a lower-cost option. Rather than use a single, large, powerful mainframe, with a central failure point, it is more efficient and less error prone instead to set up a cluster of servers, often called a "server farm." If client "hits" start to tax a server too much, just add another PC and you have doubled the power of the server. Where you once had just one dedicated PC hosting a database server or Web server (or both), you now have two PCs. Most modern server programs, such as Microsoft SQL Server 2000, support clustering, and the process is automatic once set up.

> **Definition**
>
> *Multi-processing systems* are computers with more than one processor that are capable of handling more data-processing tasks than computers with just a single processor.

If your database server starts to run out of hard-drive space, don't panic—just add another PC! You can continue to add machines to the cluster whenever your server needs more processing power. The server software ensures that if one or two PCs fail, the server can continue to run. How does that work? As you can imagine, clustering is quite complicated. But server clusters are usually connected to backup systems; therefore, if part of the server fails, the backup system can restore the data that was lost.

> **Definition**
>
> A *mainframe computer* is a powerful, singular, data-processing computer system capable of handling an enormous amount of data very quickly and generally more powerful than any PC (because both mainframes and PCs undergo upgrades during their lifetimes).

## The Big Picture

Now, you might be wondering, what does all this have to do with user interfaces? Programmers are usually highly focused people who work earnestly on something—attacking it with vigor and compulsion until it is completed—and I include myself in this group. But we programmers often lose track of the bigger picture, which is probably why software and hardware gurus specialize. The two groups usually come from the same educational backgrounds but diverge into the software side or the hardware side. Hardware people are usually called LAN technicians or server administrators, whereas software people are usually called software developers or programmers. Consider the multitude of creative job titles in both professions as colorful mnemonics of the two basic groups of people.

But aside from that, the important point I am trying to make here is that you should be familiar with both specialties: software and hardware. Because programmers are quite often put into the role as analysts, who must determine how a new application will be designed and built and often find themselves performing the role of database administrator (DBA) on the project (which involves designing and creating the database tables), it is critical that programmers understand as much about the back end as they do about creating user interfaces for applications. Simply connecting to a database and then forgetting about the back end is a mistake. You never know how much your programs will be used, therefore you must be careful to design the program well from the start. Poorly written queries can overload a server unnecessarily, which might lead to additional costs for new hardware when a more efficiently written program might have prevented it.

# Forms and Controls

When it comes to programming a user interface, modern languages like VB.NET are as much a design tool as a language. Some popular application design tools like PowerBuilder focus entirely on the interface, and you connect components with connector lines using the mouse. (Although PowerBuilder fans will argue that VB.NET is no different!) When you connect a control to a database field, that field is literally

> **Definition**
>
> A *Database Management System*, also called a "database" or "DBMS," is a server program that provides data to clients. The program requests specific subsets of data using Structured Query Language (SQL). Relational databases are often called "RDBMSs."

linked to the database! You don't have to write any source code at all to bring up the data because the tool does that work for you.

VB.NET is like many other modern visual software design tools but also includes a powerful language behind the user interface. In previous versions of Visual Basic, the form file (with an extension of .frm) contained a list of controls and their Globally Unique Identifiers (GUIDs).

A *Globally Unique Identifier (GUID)* is a 128-bit pseudo-random number that is guaranteed to be unique. The odds of generating two identical GUIDs, even considering the millions of computers in the world, are so remote that you can count on each GUID being unique. For this reason, Microsoft SQL Server 2000 uses GUIDs for primary keys.

## Adding and Removing Controls

The subject of programming user-interface controls is quite complicated when taken in its entirety because each control has specific features (called properties) that must be accessed differently from the other controls. There are some consistencies, such as the Text property, that change the contents of a control. These controls also share a common set of events, for the most part. For example, most controls have a click event that is generated any time the user clicks the control with the mouse (for example, Button1_Click).

Figure 3.2 shows a simple project with basic user-interface controls on a form.

### The Control Toolbox

The Toolbox window holds all of the controls available to your VB.NET programs. The built-in controls are called "intrinsic controls" because you don't need to do anything special to use them—these controls are automatically included in each VB.NET project (see Figure 3.3).

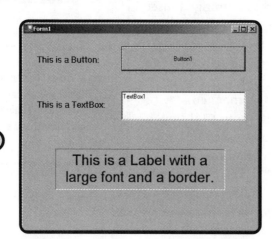

**FIGURE 3.2**

A simple user interface with a Button, a TextBox, and a Label.

FIGURE 3.3

The Toolbox
contains all the
user-interface
controls for a
VB.NET program.

Now, I'd like to formally introduce you to these three impetuous controls because
they are the foundation—and indeed, the cornerstones—of most VB.NET programs
that you are likely to write.

## The Label Control

The Label control can display a text string using any custom color or font that
you choose and can include a border. You can change the Text property of a Label
at design time and at runtime. Can you think of any immediate uses for the Label
control? Any time you have a data-entry form, such as for an inventory database
program, you will need to describe each field with a Label. Otherwise, the user
won't be able to figure out what to type into each field (and such a program
would be useless). Figure 3.4 shows the Label control highlighted in the Toolbox.

 **Design time describes the situation in which a project is being created inside
the VB.NET environment. Runtime, on the other hand, describes the situation
after the program has been compiled and is running.**

## The TextBox Control

The TextBox control is an input field in which the user can type in a text string or
make changes to an existing text string (as in the case of a database application).

**FIGURE 3.4**

The Label control
as it appears in the
Toolbox.

When it comes to data entry forms, the TextBox is the control of choice. You can customize the appearance of a TextBox by modifying its properties. Try setting the foreground and background colors (or the font) for some unique and intriguing data entry fields!

The TextBox control can be used for small fields or large fields. As an example, the familiar Windows Notepad program is a simple text editor that you have probably used many times. The main control in Notepad is a huge TextBox! Notepad wasn't written with Visual Basic, though. Like most Windows utility programs, Notepad was created with Visual C++. Figure 3.5 shows the TextBox control highlighted in the Toolbox.

## The Button Control

The Button control is an event notification control that passes events directly back to your program. This allows you to build functionality into the program that responds to button events. Buttons are general-purpose controls with a standard look and feel that Windows users expect in an application. However, you can change the font and color of the text that appears on a Button through the properties. Figure 3.6 shows the Button control highlighted in the Toolbox.

FIGURE 3.5

The TextBox
control as it
appears in the
Toolbox.

FIGURE 3.6

The Button
control as it
appears in the
Toolbox.

## Naming Controls

Some programmers are real sticklers when it comes to variable naming conventions, and several styles are commonly used. The most common convention is called *Hungarian Notation*, which calls for variable names that are preceded by the data type. For example, an `Integer` variable called `Number` should be called `intNumber`. A `String` variable called `Name` should be called `strName`. By simply glancing at the variable in the middle of a source code listing using this standard, you can easily tell what type of variable it is.

In general practice, it is a good idea to use this notation. But in the interest of readability and learning, I'll stick to using simple variable names without any notation throughout the book.

## Moving and Resizing Controls

When it comes to actually placing controls on the form, I can think of three ways to do it.

1. Drag the control from the Toolbox to the form.
2. Double-click the control in the Toolbox.
3. Select the control in the Toolbox and then "draw" the control on the form.

Go ahead and try out all three ways to add a control until you have found the method that you find most comfortable. After all, you will be doing this a lot!

## Setting Control Properties

The standard controls in VB.NET have a lot more functionality than is apparent just by looking at them. If you peruse the Properties window (see Figure 3.7), you will find a long list of properties for each user-interface control—as well as properties for the form itself. Click a control and the Properties window will change to reflect the new control that you selected (see Figure 3.8).

## The Standard Dialogs

Once in a while it is nice to be able to just pop up a message or ask the user to type in something without creating a whole user interface made up of controls on a form. As you have seen in the last few pages, quite a bit is involved in creating a user interface. Visual Basic makes the process easier than in some languages, such as Visual C++, because Visual Basic uses default values for all the properties for each control. To truly customize a user interface for a specific application, you will need to modify those default properties. Thankfully, it is easy to modify them right in the Properties window, and Visual Basic will remember those properties when you close the project and re-load it again later.

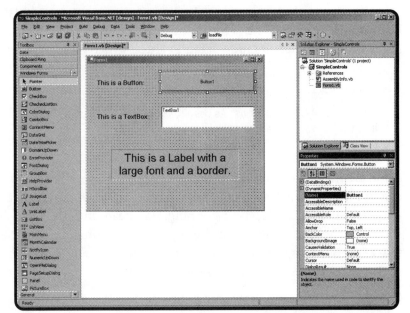

**FIGURE 3.7**

The Properties window lets you change the properties of a control or form.

**FIGURE 3.8**

Selecting different controls on the form will change the list of properties to reflect the highlighted control.

But often you will encounter a situation in which you need to display something quickly and easily without requiring a new form and a user interface. The standard dialogs are a great help in this regard.

**Does the word "dialog" conjure up a mental image of two people talking? When I hear the word, I think of a requirements meeting in which I have a dialog with the end users over what they need in a new application. Technology sure does a disservice to the English language when it comes to further polymorphing common words. The term "dialog box" is a crude analogy of a human talking directly with a computer by typing in something or pressing a button in response to an inquiry message.**

You can call up two simple dialogs at any time. The first one, MsgBox, displays a message in a pop-up window, and is often used to display error messages. The second one, InputBox, displays a prompt in which the user can type in something and is often used to quickly and easily get some input from the user. However, MsgBox and InputBox are not controls that you add to a form, like a TextBox or Label. On the contrary, MsgBox and InputBox are functions that you call inside the source code of your program.

## Using the MsgBox Function

You can change the appearance of a MsgBox with numerous button layouts and icons to choose from. Here is the definition for the MsgBox function. Note that the latter two parameters include default values, which I will explain later.

```
Public Function MsgBox(
    ByVal Prompt As Object,
    Optional ByVal Buttons As MsgBoxStyle = MsgBoxStyle.OKOnly,
    Optional ByVal Title As Object = Nothing
) As MsgBoxResult
```

If you are intimidated by the definition of MsgBox, don't be! It's amazingly easy to use, as I'll show you. Let's create a small program to demonstrate the MsgBox function. If Visual Basic .NET isn't running, go ahead and fire it up. The Start Page should be the first thing that comes up. You can either click the New Project button on the Start Page, or select File, New, Project to open the New Project dialog (as shown in Figure 3.9). You should be familiar with this dialog from the last chapter.

Call this new program MsgBox by typing it into the name field. Also, be sure to select an appropriate folder in which you would like the new project to be created. When the new project has been generated, double-click the form to open the Code window. As you can see from the listing that follows, Visual Basic has already written some source code for you!

```
Public Class Form1
    Inherits System.Windows.Forms.Form
```

```
+ Windows Form Designer generated code

    Private Sub Form1_Load(ByVal sender As System.Object, _
        ByVal e As System.EventArgs) Handles MyBase.Load

    End Sub
End Class
```

Now, I've massaged the code a little to prevent the lines from wrapping, which does not look good in print. If you look at the line that begins with `Private Sub Form1_Load`, you will notice an underscore character at the end of the line. This is a special character in Visual Basic source code that tells VB to look for the rest of the line of source code on the next line down. This lets you beautify the code and keep it from getting too messy because some lines of source code will otherwise be very long indeed!

As an example, if you look at the same generated source code on your screen, you will notice that the line actually extends beyond the edge to the right, and you must scroll the Editor window to the right in order to see the rest of the line. Visual Basic doesn't care if you use long or short lines, so the point is to make your source code easy for humans to read because most of the time either you or someone else will need to look at or modify your source code.

Check out Figure 3.10. This figure shows the very same source code that was listed before, only this time it is shown inside the Visual Basic code editor. See how I formatted that long line so that it would fit without scrolling? That's a good habit to get into because generated source code (even the minor code that is generated for a new project) is usually not formatted adequately.

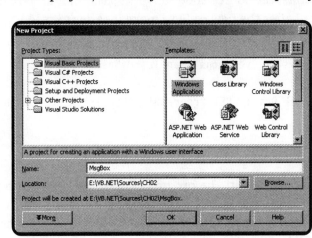

**FIGURE 3.9**

The New Project dialog box in Visual Studio is where you create new projects.

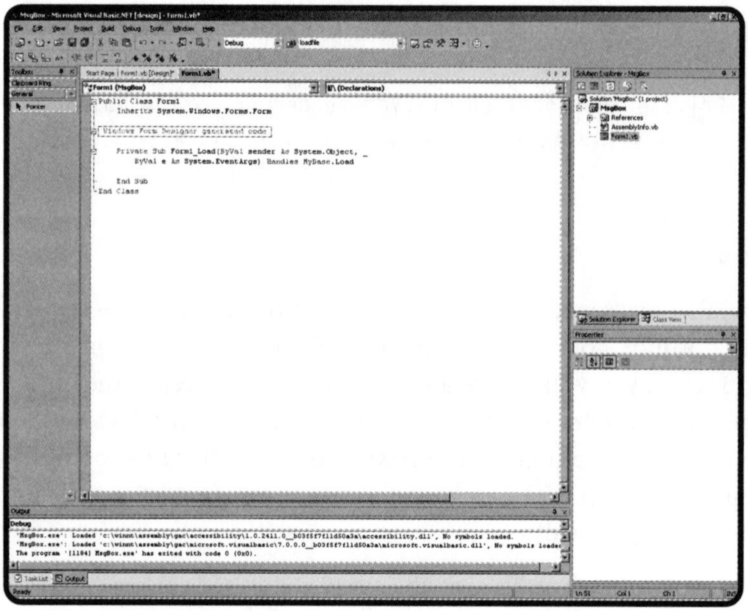

**FIGURE 3.10**

The MsgBox
project showing the
automatically
generated
source code.

If you just run the program by pressing F5 at this point, nothing special will happen because the program doesn't do anything yet. An empty form will appear on the screen, and you will need to close it. Now I'll add some functionality to the program. The subject at hand is the MsgBox function, so type in the following two lines of code into Form1_Load:

```
MsgBox("Visual Basic .NET Programming For The Absolute Beginner")
End
```

When you are done, the source code for Form1_Load should look like this. (I put spaces before and after the new code to make it easier to read.)

```
Private Sub Form1_Load(ByVal sender As System.Object, _
    ByVal e As System.EventArgs) Handles MyBase.Load

    MsgBox("Visual Basic .NET Programming For The Absolute Beginner")
    End

End Sub
```

Okay, now press F5 to run it! The program finally does something, as shown in Figure 3.11. This figure shows a MsgBox dialog with mostly default parameters. When you only pass the MsgBox function a message and no options, the function uses a default OK button and sets the title to the name of the application that called the function. In this case, it was the MsgBox program.

The standard
MsgBox pop-up
dialog using default
parameters.

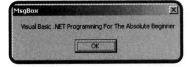

## MsgBox Button Settings

The `MsgBox` function supports a whole bunch of button options. You have probably already seen most of them from just using Windows over time because these button combinations are common. Here is the complete list of button settings supported by `MsgBox`:

1. `MsgBoxStyle.OKOnly`

2. `MsgBoxStyle.OKCancel`

3. `MsgBoxStyle.AbortRetryIgnore`

4. `MsgBoxStyle.YesNoCancel`

5. `MsgBoxStyle.YesNo`

6. `MsgBoxStyle.RetryCancel`

Let's try them all out! Just add one of the button parameters to the end of the `MsgBox` function. For example, here is how you call `MsgBox` using the `OKCancel` button setting:

```
MsgBox("Hi There!", MsgBoxStyle.OKCancel)
```

Figure 3.12 shows what that line of code looks like when you run the program.

This MsgBox dialog
was created using
the `OKCancel`
button setting.

How about another one? Try this version using the `AbortRetryIgnore` setting:

```
MsgBox("Nuclear Meltdown In Progress!", MsgBoxStyle.AbortRetryIgnore)
```

I wouldn't click the Ignore button if I were you! Here is what the `AbortRetryIgnore` version looks like (see Figure 3.13).

**FIGURE 3.13**

This version of the `MsgBox` function uses the `AbortRetry Ignore` setting.

**In prior versions of Visual Basic, the MsgBox button options were called** `vbOkOnly`, `vbOkCancel`, **and so on. The** `vb` **prefix has been replaced by the** `MsgBoxStyle` **enumeration. This is disconcerting to many long-time VB veterans, but it's actually easier to understand.**

Go ahead and try out the other button settings to gain some familiarity with the `MsgBox` options. Have you noticed that when you type in the comma after the message parameter, a drop-down list appears with all the `MsgBox` settings? This is a very cool feature, which will save you hours of time. In case you were wondering, this feature is called IntelliSense. If you are new to VB, you will love this feature. If you've seen it before, then you can probably vouch for its usefulness. After using Visual Basic with IntelliSense, it is actually painful to use other languages that do not have such a feature.

## MsgBox Icon Settings

In addition to a custom list of button settings, the `MsgBox` function allows you to add a specialized icon to the dialog. Here is the list of icon settings available:

- `MsgBoxStyle.Critical`
- `MsgBoxStyle.Question`
- `MsgBoxStyle.Exclamation`
- `MsgBoxStyle.Information`

The key to adding these icons to the message box is to add the option to one of the button settings (or alone if you want the standard OKOnly button). For example, here is how you would tell `MsgBox` to include the Critical icon:

```
MsgBox("Warning: Something Bad Happened.", MsgBoxStyle.Critical)
```

Take a look at Figure 3.14 to see the result of using `MsgBoxStyle.Critical` without a button setting. See how it automatically included the standard OK button?

This version of the
MsgBox function
includes the
Critical icon.

Now let's try another one. Modify the program again so the MsgBox function includes YesNo buttons and a Question icon. Figure 3.15 shows the result of these settings.

```
MsgBox("Do you want to format your hard drive?", _
    MsgBoxStyle.YesNo + MsgBoxStyle.Question)
```

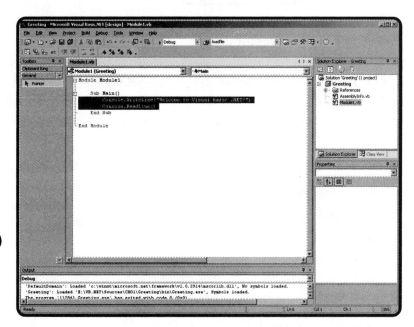

**FIGURE 3.15**

This version of the
MsgBox function
includes the
Question icon.

Feel free to try out the other icon options and use them whenever you need to emphasize the point you are trying to make with the message displayed in the message box.

## MsgBox Title

The MsgBox sample code up to this point has used the default title, which becomes the name of the application. But you can easily change the title to anything that you want. Just add another parameter after the buttons and icons and tell MsgBox what title you would like it to display. Following is an example:

```
MsgBox("Error connecting to server...", _
    MsgBoxStyle.RetryCancel + MsgBoxStyle.Exclamation, _
    "DOH!")
```

The output for this version of the MsgBox program appears in Figure 3.16. See how the title is different from all the previous runs? You can set the title to any text string that you want.

**FIGURE 3.16**

You can easily change the title displayed on the message box.

### Checking MsgBox Results

There's a feature of the MsgBox function that I have ignored up to this point, but in fact, MsgBox returns a value depending on which button you press. You can check this value by storing the return value of MsgBox in a variable. But first you have to create the variable, and it has to be declared as a MsgBoxResult.

Just like the MsgBoxStyle list, there is a list of values built into VB that contains all the results that might be returned by MsgBox. Here is the list:

- MsgBoxResult.Abort
- MsgBoxResult.Cancel
- MsgBoxResult.Ignore
- MsgBoxResult.No
- MsgBoxResult.OK
- MsgBoxResult.Retry
- MsgBoxResult.Yes

So, if you want to see if the user pressed the Yes button when you used the MsgBoxStyle.YesNo setting for the buttons, you can check what value MsgBox returns after the user presses a button. Here is some source code that shows you how to do it:

```
Dim response As MsgBoxResult
response = MsgBox("How about a game of Global Thermonuclear War?", _
    MsgBoxStyle.YesNo + MsgBoxStyle.Question, _
    "JOSHUA")
```

```
If response = MsgBoxResult.Yes Then
    MsgBox("On second thought, that's not such a good idea.")
Else
    MsgBox("Chicken!")
End If
```

This is a sizeable amount of code compared to the simplistic MsgBox examples in previous listings, but that is only because you have to check the return value passed back by the MsgBox function. Figure 3.17 shows the first MsgBox dialog.

**FIGURE 3.17**

The MsgBox function returns the value of the button that is pressed.

According to the preceding source code listing, a message box should appear no matter which button you press—either Yes or No. But depending on the button, a different message pops up. Figure 3.18 shows the result of pressing the Yes button, whereas Figure 3.19 shows the result of pressing the No button.

**FIGURE 3.18**

This message is displayed when you press the Yes button.

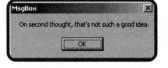

**FIGURE 3.19**

This message is displayed when you press the No button.

In addition to Yes and No, there are other button values that you can test for in your programs. If you have a hard time remembering all the options, type in **Msg-BoxResult** followed by a period, and IntelliSense should display the list of button return values for you.

## Using the InputBox Function

The second standard input dialog is invoked using the InputBox function. Input-Box is similar to MsgBox but lets you type in some text with the option of pressing OK or Cancel. When you press the OK button, InputBox returns the text string that you typed in. When you press the Cancel button, InputBox returns a blank string. InputBox is a great helper function when you need to have the user type in something, but you don't want to create a new form with controls (such as a TextBox with buttons) just to input a single value.

### Calling on InputBox

The InputBox function is a lot easier to use than MsgBox because it doesn't have as many options. You can't tell InputBox to use a different set of buttons because it only has an OK and a Cancel button. There also isn't any way to add an icon to an InputBox dialog, so it's pretty simple. Before I show you some code for the Input-Box function, you'll need to create a new project, just like you did previously for the MsgBox program. Create a new project called InputBox and then you'll be ready.

Here is some sample code that shows how to display an InputBox dialog. Remember to type this code into the Form1_Load event.

```
InputBox("Please type in your name:")
End
```

Note again that the End command just ends the program before the main form appears on the screen. Otherwise, a dorky-looking empty form will pop up after the InputBox closes, and that just will not do. If you run this program, it should look like Figure 3.20.

FIGURE 3.20

The InputBox function prompts the user to type in something.

### Checking the InputBox Return Value

Unfortunately, this program doesn't tell you what the user types in, therefore you'll need to add a variable and pass the text string into the variable. Here's the code that shows how to do that:

```
Dim input As String
input = InputBox("What do you think of Visual Basic .NET so far?")
If input = "" Then
    MsgBox("What's wrong, don't you like me?")
Else
    MsgBox("Oh, thank you very much!")
End If
```

This program checks to see if the user typed something into the input field. If the user leaves it blank or clicks the Cancel button, InputBox returns a blank string. The program displays a different message based on whether the return value is empty or not. Figure 3.21 shows the first dialog that asks the user to type something.

**FIGURE 3.21**

The InputBox function returns the text string that the user enters.

If the user types in something, the program responds politely (see Figure 3.22). However, if InputBox detects that nothing was typed in, or if the user presses the Cancel button, the program displays an annoyed message (see Figure 3.23).

**FIGURE 3.22**

The InputBox program displays a polite message if you type something into the text field.

**FIGURE 3.23**

The InputBox program complains if you don't type anything into the text field.

# Chapter Project—The Tic-Tac-Toe Game

Are you ready to put some of this new theory to good use? In the remaining part of this chapter, I am going to show you how to build a complete game based on Tic-Tac-Toe. It's such a classic, and it really is a great game to demonstrate how to create a user interface. Take a look at Figure 3.24, which shows how the game looks when first started, before a player has made a move.

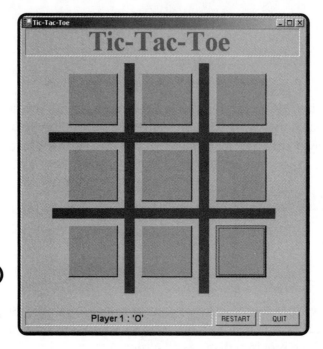

FIGURE 3.24

The Tic-Tac-Toe game as it appears when first started.

Now, Figure 3.25 is another story altogether! In this screenshot, Player O has won the game!

Figure 3.26 also shows a screenshot of the game after Player X wins.

After a player is declared the winner, you have the option of playing another game by pressing the RESTART button, or you can end the game by pressing the QUIT button. Yes, it is very simple. But as I'm sure you will agree after trying it out, this game is fun to play! I have to admit, I'm a serious gamer, and I play most of the new retail games that come out (at least the good ones, anyway). But a simple puzzle game like Tic-Tac-Toe is refreshing, don't you think? Why else is Solitaire so popular? If you know anyone who is a big Solitaire fan, for lack of any other game on their PC, perhaps it's time to replace it with Tic-Tac-Toe. After all, two players are better than one.

**FIGURE 3.25**

The Tic-Tac-Toe
game with Player O
as the winner.

**FIGURE 3.26**

The Tic-Tac-Toe
game with Player X
as the winner.

## Creating the New Project

Let's get started creating the Tic-Tac-Toe game. Start Visual Studio .NET and select New Project from either the Today Page or the File menu. The New Project dialog should appear (see Figure 3.27).

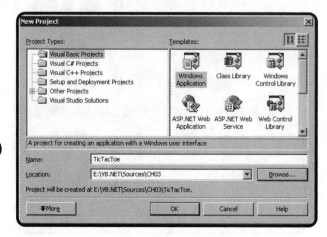

**FIGURE 3.27**

Creating a new program with the New Project dialog box.

The Tic-Tac-Toe game will be a Windows Application called "TicTacToe" and will be located in the CH03 folder for this chapter. Go ahead and create the new project now.

## The Main Form

When you create a new project like the Tic-Tac-Toe project, VB.NET adds a default form to the project called Form1. Because most Visual Basic programs need a form for one reason or another, it makes sense to generate a default form for each new project.

For the Tic-Tac-Toe game, you are going to want to resize the form. Take a look at the Properties window for Form1. It should look like Figure 3.28.

The first property for Form1 that you need to change is FormBorderStyle. If you can't find the property, I recommend setting the Properties window to Alphabetic sorting rather than Categorized. Look for a small icon at the top of the Properties window with a lowercase A and Z with a down arrow. The FormBorderStyle property is about halfway down the list. Change this property to FixedSingle as shown in Figure 3.29. The FixedSingle property setting will prevent users from resizing the form, which is a good idea in a game like this.

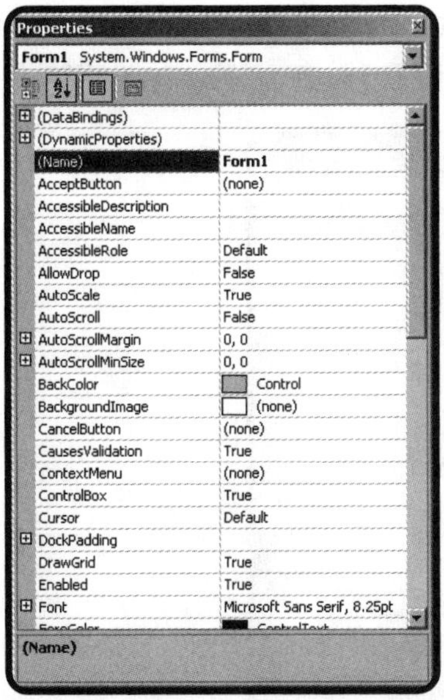

**FIGURE 3.28**

The Properties window for Form1 in the Tic-Tac-Toe project.

**FIGURE 3.29**

Changing the FormBorderStyle property for the main form of Tic-Tac-Toe.

Now scroll down the list of properties to the end of the list, and look for an item called Size. There is a little plus sign next to the property, meaning that it has more than one value. You can expand it and see the sub-values for that property. Change this property to 515, 550 (Width = 515 and Height = 550). The form should immediately resize to the dimensions you entered. As it turns out, these sub-values are the actual properties, and the parent item (Size) is just descriptive. When you need to make changes to a property using source code, you will need to refer to the actual property value, not the descriptive item (see Figure 3.30).

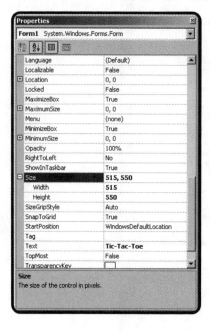

**FIGURE 3.30**

Change the Width and Height properties of the main form in the Tic-Tac-Toe project.

Next, change the property called StartPosition to the value CenterScreen so the form will be centered on the screen when it runs, as shown in Figure 3.31.

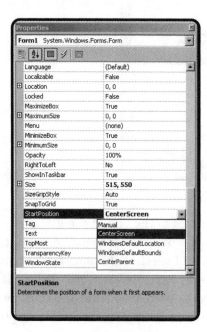

**FIGURE 3.31**

The StartPosition property determines where the form appears on the screen when run.

Finally, take a look at the Text property, which is two down on the list from StartPosition. Change the Text property to "Tic-Tac-Toe." The Text property of a form points to the caption at the top of the form. After you change this property, you should see the form title change accordingly (see Figure 3.32).

## Building the User Interface

Okay, now for the fun part. The form has been set up, so now it's ready for some controls. By the time you have finished with this section, you should have a user interface for the game that looks like Figure 3.33.

### The Program Title

The obvious place to start with this user interface (which is the most complicated one in the book thus far) is with the game title at the top. This is a Label control with a 3D border, extra-large font, and set to the color red. Locate the Label control in the Toolbox and add a new Label to the form. Position it at the top of the form and stretch it clear across the width of the form. Look at the properties for the new Label control and make the following changes:

1. BorderStyle = Fixed3D
2. Font = Times New Roman, 36pt, style=Bold
3. ForeColor = Red
4. Text = Tic-Tac-Toe
5. TextAlign = MiddleCenter

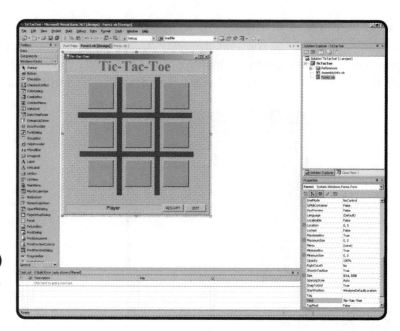

**FIGURE 3.33**

The completed user
interface for the
Tic-Tac-Toe project.

After you have added the new Label to the form and changed its properties, the
form should look like Figure 3.34.

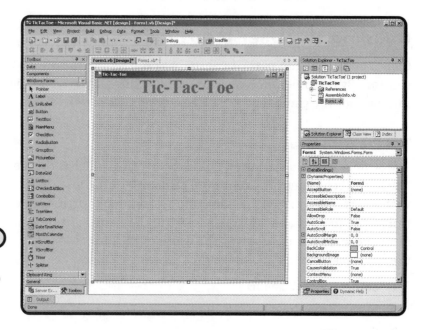

**FIGURE 3.34**

Adding the first
Label control to
the Tic-Tac-Toe
game.

## The Game Buttons

The next thing this game needs is a set of nine buttons to make up the squares that will each display "X" or "O" based on player moves. The easiest control to use for this is the Button. But rather than a plain gray button, these buttons will be green! Select the Button control and then draw nine buttons on the form, starting with the upper left, as shown in Figure 3.35. It is very important that you add the buttons in that order because the game logic is counting on these buttons being in specific places on the form to determine when there is a winner.

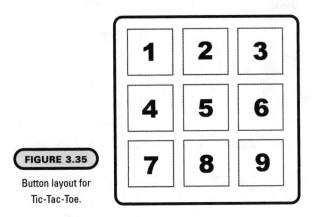

FIGURE 3.35

Button layout for
Tic-Tac-Toe.

Now for the properties—the Buttons need a green background and an extra-large font. Feel free to experiment with these properties and change the Buttons to your own preference. I chose LimeGreen for the background color, and Arial Black, 72pt for the font. After you have added all nine Button controls to the form and have set their properties, the project should look like Figure 3.36. You may need to adjust the placement of each Button to make it look just right. Precision is not very important, as long as the buttons are lined up.

## The Dividers

Now that the Buttons are in place, the game needs some classic-looking dividers to make it really look like Tic-Tac-Toe. The dividers could have been just about any control, really, as long as the background color can be changed. You could use an Image, PictureBox, Panel, Button (with no border), Label, TextBox, and so on. By simple changing border styles and background color, there are a lot of options available here. For simplicity, I decided to use the Panel control. This is actually a grouping control that can contain other controls (like the PictureBox).

First, add a new Panel control to the form and then move and resize it until it separates the first row of buttons from the other rows, as shown in Figure 3.37.

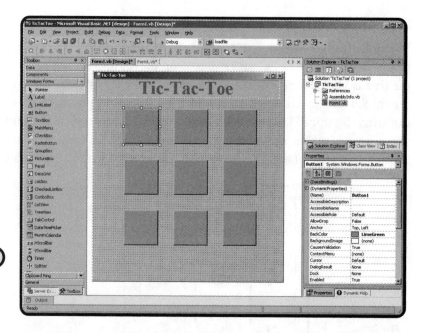

**FIGURE 3.36**

Positioning the
Button controls
for Tic-Tac-Toe.

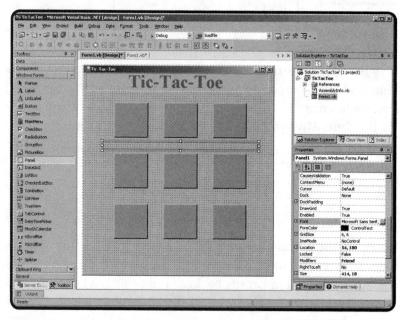

**FIGURE 3.37**

Adding the first
Panel control to
separate the rows
and columns in
Tic-Tac-Toe.

Next, change the background color of the Panel to Blue. At this point, you have a prototype Panel that you can copy and paste several times to fill in the other three spaces between the columns and rows of Buttons. Simply click the first Panel, which is called Panel1, and press Ctrl+C to copy the control into the Windows Clipboard and then press Ctrl+V to paste a copy of the control on the form.

Make two more copies of the control and then resize and reposition as necessary so that the project looks like Figure 3.38.

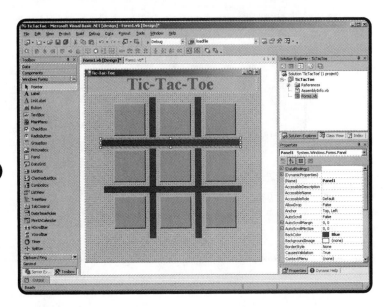

FIGURE 3.38

The placement of all four Panel controls on the form, dividing the Buttons into rows and columns for Tic-Tac-Toe.

### The Status Bar and Buttons

The final controls needed to complete the program include a Label to display status messages, a Restart button, and a Quit button. Add a new label to the form and note that it is automatically named Label2, because the program title at the top was called Label1. Change the font of Label2 to Arial, 12pt, style = Bold to help the status messages stand out amidst all the colorful controls in the game.

Next, add two buttons, and label them Restart and Quit, respectively. The Restart button should be called Button10, whereas the Quit button should be called Button11. This is important, because the source code that follows will assume that these are the names given to the buttons. After you have set up the new label and buttons, the project should look like Figure 3.39.

## Writing the Source Code

The source code for Tic-Tac-Toe is almost twice as long as the actual source code that you need to type in because, when it comes to VB.NET, all the controls that you put on a form are actually added to the source code of the form—sort of like variables. Therefore, when you add a new Button to the form, for example, VB.NET might display the button right there on the form, but it is actually parsing the newly generated source code to determine how the button should look.

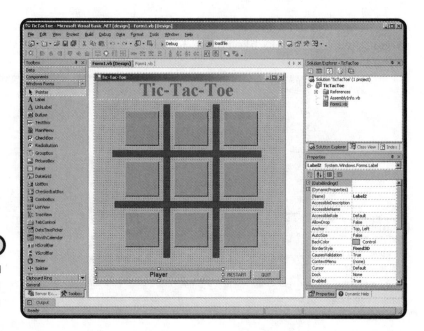

**FIGURE 3.39**

The new label and
buttons complete
the user interface
for Tic-Tac-Toe.

This code listing, as well as most of the code in this book, should be typed in immediately after the hidden region of code called "Windows Form Designer generated code." Because all this code is generated by VB.NET, there is no need to include it. Kudos to the forward-thinking designers of VB.NET who provided a means to hide blocks of code (although the default code could have been stored elsewhere).

This first section of code includes Form1_Load and the button click events for the nine buttons used in the game. Form1_Load simply calls a subroutine, RestartGame(), to reset the program variables. If you have used previous versions of Visual Basic, you might be wondering why this is called Form1_Load instead of just Form_Load. What is the "1" for? VB.NET has changed almost all the fundamental features of classic Visual Basic, including the concept of a form object. Code now refers directly to the name of a form, rather than a generic Form object. Because the main form of Tic-Tac-Toe is called Form1, the load event is called Form1_Load. As for the parameters and other new keywords (such as Handles MyBase.Load), just know that these are part of the framework, and you can ignore this extra code for the most part. It's just how VB.NET does things now. As you will discover in later chapters, these new features are extremely useful, once you learn how to take advantage of them.

The code inside each Click event is the same, except for the references to which button was pressed. You will notice a line in each event that calls a subroutine,

CheckWinner(). I will explain this subroutine later in the program listing. At this early stage, just type it in and it will make sense later.

```
Dim Token As Char
Dim Player As Integer

Private Sub Form1_Load(ByVal sender As System.Object, _
    ByVal e As System.EventArgs) Handles MyBase.Load
    RestartGame()
End Sub

Private Sub Button1_Click(ByVal sender As System.Object, _
    ByVal e As System.EventArgs) Handles Button1.Click
    Button1.Text = Token
    Button1.Enabled = False
    CheckWinner()
End Sub

Private Sub Button2_Click(ByVal sender As System.Object, _
    ByVal e As System.EventArgs) Handles Button2.Click
    Button2.Text = Token
    Button2.Enabled = False
    CheckWinner()
End Sub

Private Sub Button3_Click(ByVal sender As System.Object, _
    ByVal e As System.EventArgs) Handles Button3.Click
    Button3.Text = Token
    Button3.Enabled = False
    CheckWinner()
End Sub

Private Sub Button4_Click(ByVal sender As System.Object, _
    ByVal e As System.EventArgs) Handles Button4.Click
    Button4.Text = Token
    Button4.Enabled = False
    CheckWinner()
End Sub

Private Sub Button5_Click(ByVal sender As System.Object, _
    ByVal e As System.EventArgs) Handles Button5.Click
```

```
        Button5.Text = Token
        Button5.Enabled = False
        CheckWinner()
    End Sub

    Private Sub Button6_Click(ByVal sender As System.Object, _
        ByVal e As System.EventArgs) Handles Button6.Click
        Button6.Text = Token
        Button6.Enabled = False
        CheckWinner()
    End Sub

    Private Sub Button7_Click(ByVal sender As System.Object, _
        ByVal e As System.EventArgs) Handles Button7.Click
        Button7.Text = Token
        Button7.Enabled = False
        CheckWinner()
    End Sub

    Private Sub Button8_Click(ByVal sender As System.Object, _
        ByVal e As System.EventArgs) Handles Button8.Click
        Button8.Text = Token
        Button8.Enabled = False
        CheckWinner()
    End Sub

    Private Sub Button9_Click(ByVal sender As System.Object, _
        ByVal e As System.EventArgs) Handles Button9.Click
        Button9.Text = Token
        Button9.Enabled = False
        CheckWinner()
    End Sub
```

The next section of code that you need to type into the Tic-Tac-Toe program follows. This code listing includes events for the Restart and Quit buttons. The Restart button simply calls End to end the program, whereas the Quit button calls RestartGame() in order to reset the buttons and variables for a new game.

There are also two helper subroutines in this listing. NextPlayer(), as you might recall, was called by each of the Button_Click events in the previous listing. This subroutine checks to see who the current player is and then switches to the other player (which includes changing the Token variable to either "X" or "O"). At the end of NextPlayer() is a line that sets the status message at the bottom of the game window to display the current player.

The other helper subroutine is called DisplayWinner(). This subroutine sets the status message to display the winner and then disables all the play buttons on the form so no more moves can be made.

```
Private Sub Button10_Click(ByVal sender As System.Object, _
    ByVal e As System.EventArgs) Handles Button10.Click
    'this is called when the Restart button is pressed
    RestartGame()
End Sub

Private Sub Button11_Click(ByVal sender As System.Object, _
    ByVal e As System.EventArgs) Handles Button11.Click
    'this is called when the Quit button is pressed
    End
End Sub

Private Sub NextPlayer()
    If Player = 1 Then
        Token = "X"
        Player = 2
    ElseIf Player = 2 Then
        Token = "O"
        Player = 1
    End If
    Label2.Text = "Player " & Player & " : '" & Token & "'"
End Sub

Private Sub DisplayWinner()
    'display winner message
    Label2.Text = "Player '" & Token & "' is the winner!"

    'disable all the buttons
    Button1.Enabled = False
    Button2.Enabled = False
    Button3.Enabled = False
    Button4.Enabled = False
    Button5.Enabled = False
```

```
            Button6.Enabled = False
            Button7.Enabled = False
            Button8.Enabled = False
            Button9.Enabled = False
End Sub
```

Now for the biggest subroutine of the program! CheckWinner() is really long, but the code inside is easy to understand because it is all repetitive. This subroutine scans the game board for three "X" or "O" marks in a row—horizontally, vertically, or diagonally. If found, DisplayWinner() is called and the game is over. The players can then click the Restart button to play another game. So, basically this is the most important subroutine in the program because it contains the logic that checks to see when someone has won the game.

```
Private Sub CheckWinner()
    'check rows
    If Len(Button1.Text & Button2.Text & Button3.Text) > 0 And _
        Button1.Text = Button2.Text And Button2.Text = Button3.Text Then
        Button1.BackColor = Color.Yellow
        Button2.BackColor = Color.Yellow
        Button3.BackColor = Color.Yellow
        DisplayWinner()
    ElseIf Len(Button4.Text & Button5.Text & Button6.Text) > 0 And _
        Button4.Text = Button5.Text And Button5.Text = Button6.Text Then
        Button4.BackColor = Color.Yellow
        Button5.BackColor = Color.Yellow
        Button6.BackColor = Color.Yellow
        DisplayWinner()
    ElseIf Len(Button7.Text & Button8.Text & Button9.Text) > 0 And _
        Button7.Text = Button8.Text And Button8.Text = Button9.Text Then
        Button7.BackColor = Color.Yellow
        Button8.BackColor = Color.Yellow
        Button9.BackColor = Color.Yellow
        DisplayWinner()

    'check columns
    ElseIf Len(Button1.Text & Button4.Text & Button7.Text) > 0 And _
        Button1.Text = Button4.Text And Button4.Text = Button7.Text Then
        Button1.BackColor = Color.Yellow
        Button4.BackColor = Color.Yellow
        Button7.BackColor = Color.Yellow
```

```
            DisplayWinner()
        ElseIf Len(Button2.Text & Button5.Text & Button8.Text) > 0 And _
            Button2.Text = Button5.Text And Button5.Text = Button8.Text Then
            Button2.BackColor = Color.Yellow
            Button5.BackColor = Color.Yellow
            Button8.BackColor = Color.Yellow
            DisplayWinner()
        ElseIf Len(Button3.Text & Button6.Text & Button9.Text) > 0 And _
            Button3.Text = Button6.Text And Button6.Text = Button9.Text Then
            Button3.BackColor = Color.Yellow
            Button6.BackColor = Color.Yellow
            Button9.BackColor = Color.Yellow
            DisplayWinner()

        'check diagonals
        ElseIf Len(Button1.Text & Button5.Text & Button9.Text) > 0 And _
            Button1.Text = Button5.Text And Button5.Text = Button9.Text Then
            Button1.BackColor = Color.Yellow
            Button5.BackColor = Color.Yellow
            Button9.BackColor = Color.Yellow
            DisplayWinner()
        ElseIf Len(Button3.Text & Button5.Text & Button7.Text) > 0 And _
            Button3.Text = Button5.Text And Button5.Text = Button7.Text Then
            Button3.BackColor = Color.Yellow
            Button5.BackColor = Color.Yellow
            Button7.BackColor = Color.Yellow
            DisplayWinner()
        Else
            NextPlayer()
        End If
    End Sub
```

Finally—you've reached the last listing of the program! Are you tired of typing in source code yet? Well, don't worry because this one is only about half as long as the last one. RestartGame() basically sets up the game for a new round of play by enabling all the buttons, clearing the text on the buttons, and setting the color of the buttons back to normal. Then the subroutine starts the game by calling the NextPlayer() subroutine.

```
Private Sub RestartGame()
    're-enable the buttons
    Button1.Enabled = True
```

```
            Button2.Enabled = True
            Button3.Enabled = True
            Button4.Enabled = True
            Button5.Enabled = True
            Button6.Enabled = True
            Button7.Enabled = True
            Button8.Enabled = True
            Button9.Enabled = True

            'clear the button labels
            Button1.Text = ""
            Button2.Text = ""
            Button3.Text = ""
            Button4.Text = ""
            Button5.Text = ""
            Button6.Text = ""
            Button7.Text = ""
            Button8.Text = ""
            Button9.Text = ""

            'set the button background colors
            Button1.BackColor = Color.LimeGreen
            Button2.BackColor = Color.LimeGreen
            Button3.BackColor = Color.LimeGreen
            Button4.BackColor = Color.LimeGreen
            Button5.BackColor = Color.LimeGreen
            Button6.BackColor = Color.LimeGreen
            Button7.BackColor = Color.LimeGreen
            Button8.BackColor = Color.LimeGreen
            Button9.BackColor = Color.LimeGreen

            'set up the new game
            Player = 2
            Token = "O"
            NextPlayer()
        End Sub
```

That's the end of the program—hurray! Go ahead and save the project, then run it by pressing F5. If the program refuses to run because of a syntax error, the cause is likely a typo somewhere. Check the line of code that generated the error and make any changes needed to get it to run.

# Summary

This chapter covered the all-important subject of the Graphical User Interface, which is at the core of Visual Basic's appeal. Visual Basic .NET includes dozens of user-interface controls, and this chapter covered some of the most common controls used in Visual Basic programs. The second half of the chapter showed how to write a Tic-Tac-Toe game as a basic tutorial on programming a user interface.

## CHALLENGES

The following challenges will help to reinforce the material you have learned in this chapter.

1. Write a short program that responds to the text typed into a TextBox control using the MsgBox function. Enhance the program by adding If...Then conditional statements that respond to specific words typed into the TextBox. Check for the word "quit" in order to end the program.

2. Convert the Guessing Game program from Chapter 1 into a new version that uses the InputBox and MsgBox standard dialog functions instead of the TextBox and Button controls used in the original game.

3. Modify the Tic-Tac-Toe game so that a human player can challenge the computer by having the computer take over Player 2! Have the computer move automatically after the human player has made a move. (Hint: Add this new code in the CheckWinner() subroutine). If you are feeling especially challenged have the computer player brag about it after winning or complain after losing a game.

# CHAPTER 4

# Forms and Toolbox Controls

T he last three chapters have covered a lot of material rather quickly; there-fore, this chapter takes a step back and explains the basics of forms and controls. By the time you have finished this chapter, you should feel much more confident with these subjects, which are key to mastering Visual Basic .NET programming. Visual Basic .NET is a graphical programming language that lets you build a simple application without requiring much source code (for example, a data-base program using the built-in database controls), as you have already seen. As a visual design tool, Visual Basic .NET allows you to develop applications quickly, and this is called Rapid Application Development (RAD).

Here is a brief overview of the topics that are covered in this chapter:

- **Introduction to Windows Forms**

- **Programming basic controls**

- **Programming slider controls**

- **Programming listing controls**

- **Programming container controls**

Developing large Windows applications quickly is a trademark capability of Visual Basic. But to get the most out of the language, you need a sound understanding of how to use the user interface controls (also called Toolbox controls). This chapter explains how to customize and program the most common controls using properties, methods, and events.

## Introduction to Windows Forms

I'm sure you are eager to start mastering the controls available with Visual Basic .NET. I'll introduce you to some basic controls shortly. Right now, I think you would benefit from a little background on Windows Forms. After all, controls must have a form to contain them, therefore understanding a little about how Windows Forms works is beneficial. Visual Basic .NET also supports Web Forms, the Internet version of Windows Forms for building Web applications.

Visual Studio 6.0 included a development tool called Visual InterDev for building Active Server Pages (ASP) Web projects. Visual Studio .NET completely integrates Visual InterDev into Web Forms and ASP.NET, so that is no longer a separate tool. Figure 4.1 shows the parallelism between Windows Forms and Web Forms for building desktop and distributed applications.

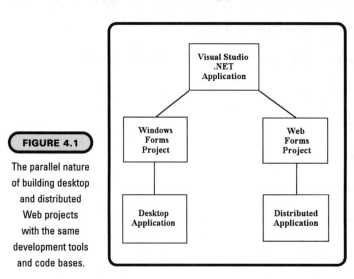

**FIGURE 4.1**

The parallel nature of building desktop and distributed Web projects with the same development tools and code bases.

## Understanding the Windows Forms Engine

In Visual Basic 6.0, the settings for controls were stored inside the form file, which had a file extension of .frm. The information in the form file doesn't really look like source code—it resembles XML (Extensible Markup Language).

In case you are not familiar with XML, it is a multi-purpose language that lets you send information over the Internet. Each piece of information—such as a person's first and last name (or even their credit card number)—can be encoded inside XML

> **Definition**
>
> A *form* is a container for controls and is the basic "window" of a Visual Basic .NET application.

using block notation. These chunks of information start with a Begin statement and end with an End statement, which might look something like this:

```
BEGIN Button Button1
    Text = "QUIT"
END Button1
```

Now remember I said that this just resembles XML but is not really XML. The basic concepts are the same, even if the syntax is not. To better illustrate the point, allow me to give you a simple example. In this example, I am going to show you the source code for a simple form with a single Button on it. First, I'll show you what this source code looks like in a Visual Basic 6.0 project, and then I'll show you what it looks like in a Visual Basic .NET project, so you can see the differences.

### Visual Basic 6.0 Form

I'll begin with the Visual Basic 6.0 source code. If you look at the following listing, you will see what I meant earlier regarding the Begin/End blocks of code. A screenshot of the project is shown in Figure 4.2.

```
VERSION 5.00
Begin VB.Form Form1
    Caption         =   "Form1"
    ClientHeight    =   3195
    ClientLeft      =   60
    ClientTop       =   345
    ClientWidth     =   4680
    LinkTopic       =   "Form1"
    ScaleHeight     =   3195
```

```
    ScaleWidth      =    4680
    StartUpPosition =    3   'Windows Default
    Begin VB.CommandButton Command1
        Caption     =    "Command1"
        Height      =    615
        Left        =    1440
        TabIndex    =    0
        Top         =    1140
        Width       =    1575
    End
End
Attribute VB_Name = "Form1"
Attribute VB_GlobalNameSpace = False
Attribute VB_Creatable = False
Attribute VB_PredeclaredId = True
Attribute VB_Exposed = False
```

**HINT**

**See the first line that shows** VERSION 5.00**? Isn't that strange because that is supposed to be a Visual Basic 6.0 project? Microsoft made changes to Visual Basic from version 5.0 to 6.0, but the actual language changed little.**

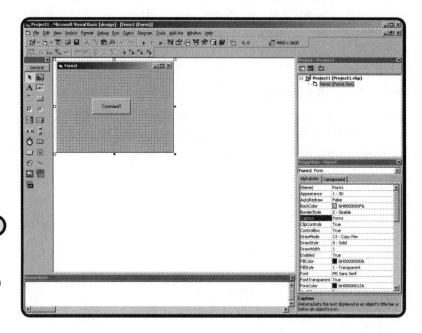

**FIGURE 4.2**

Visual Basic 6.0 project with a default form and a single button control.

## Visual Basic .NET Form

The preceding code listing for a Visual Basic 6.0 form was copied from a project with a default form called Form1. I added a single button control called `Command1` to the form. Although VB.NET forms require more code, as you can see, it is basically related to the new .NET Framework and the classes and modules. Visual Basic 6.0 and earlier didn't have the overall framework, therefore earlier form code was less complicated. The following listing shows the source code for a similar project with just a single default form and a button control. Figure 4.3 shows a screenshot of the project so that you can compare it to the previous one for Visual Basic 6.0.

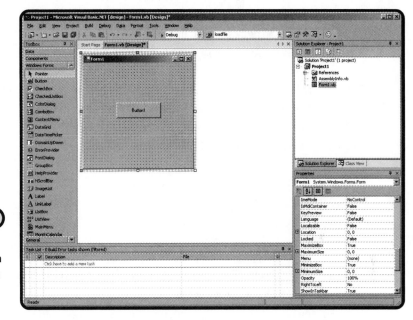

**FIGURE 4.3**

The Visual Basic .NET project with a default form and a single button control.

```
Public Class Form1
    Inherits System.Windows.Forms.Form

#Region " Windows Form Designer generated code "

    Public Sub New()
        MyBase.New()
        'This call is required by the Windows Form Designer.
        InitializeComponent()
        'Add any initialization after the InitializeComponent() call
    End Sub

    'Form overrides dispose to clean up the component list.
```

```
Protected Overloads Overrides Sub Dispose(ByVal disposing As Boolean)
    If disposing Then
        If Not (components Is Nothing) Then
            components.Dispose()
        End If
    End If
    MyBase.Dispose(disposing)
End Sub


Friend WithEvents Button1 As System.Windows.Forms.Button

'Required by the Windows Form Designer
Private components As System.ComponentModel.Container

'NOTE: The following procedure is required by the Windows Form Designer
'It can be modified using the Windows Form Designer.
'Do not modify it using the code editor.
<System.Diagnostics.DebuggerStepThrough()> _
    Private Sub InitializeComponent()
    Me.Button1 = New System.Windows.Forms.Button()
    Me.SuspendLayout()
    '
    'Button1
    '
    Me.Button1.Location = New System.Drawing.Point(88, 104)
    Me.Button1.Name = "Button1"
    Me.Button1.Size = New System.Drawing.Size(120, 40)
    Me.Button1.TabIndex = 0
    Me.Button1.Text = "Button1"
    '
    'Form1
    '
    Me.AutoScaleBaseSize = New System.Drawing.Size(5, 13)
    Me.ClientSize = New System.Drawing.Size(292, 273)
    Me.Controls.AddRange(New System.Windows.Forms.Control() {Me.Button1})
    Me.Name = "Form1"
    Me.Text = "Form1"
    Me.ResumeLayout(False)
End Sub
#End Region
End Class
```

Not very interesting, is it? The form code demonstrates how much more complicated Visual Basic .NET is over previous versions. It also shows why Microsoft added the ability to the code editor to hide sections of code—the generated code can be quite lengthy. The differences are quite significant, which is the key reason why upgrading Visual Basic 6.0 projects to Visual Basic .NET is not recommended. Because neither of these projects have any custom source code or events, other than what Visual Basic generated, it is easy to compare the two versions. Probably the most significant thing that you will notice about Visual Basic .NET is that controls are created with regular source code instead of the Begin/End blocks in the form code.

**The controls listed in the Toolbox in Visual Basic .NET are the same controls used in Visual C#, the sister language of Visual Basic .NET. In fact, the forms are used interchangeably in both languages too! If you would like to learn C#, I highly recommend *C# Programming for the Absolute Beginner*, by Andy Harris.**

## Windows Messages and Event Procedures

The engine that works behind the scenes in a VB.NET program interprets the Windows messaging system, which is how Windows tells your program when something happens to the user interface. The controls are part of the form, and therefore have access to all of the messages that the operating system sends the program. For example, when you click a button on a form, Windows sends your program a special message that includes a header pointing to the form and the control that triggered the message. Visual Basic receives this special message from the operating system and routes it to the form containing the specific button that was clicked.

What happens at this point? The form engine, which is part of the VB.NET runtime library (and also closely tied to the .NET Framework), checks to see if you have created a Click event for that button. If so, the event is called, otherwise the message is discarded. From that point, it is up to you (the programmer) to decide what happens inside that event. As the Tic-Tac-Toe program demonstrated in Chapter 3, "The Basics of a Graphical User Interface," you can do anything you want in a Button_Click event.

As you can imagine, there are thousands of different messages streaming through the Windows operating system, which are being routed to operating system processes and running applications. Visual Basic .NET handles all the details for you by breaking down the complexity into a number of events that are called automatically in your program. On the other hand, when it comes to writing

Visual C++ .NET programs, you have to handle all of the Windows messages your-self! For instance, any time a VB.NET form needs to be redrawn (such as when another window covers part of it), the form engine handles that for you. But a standard Visual C++ .NET program would have to look for the WM_PAINT message, which includes the rectangular area of the form that needs to be redrawn, and then redraw the form the hard way.

**TRICK** Although Visual C++ .NET provides the programmer with direct access to the Windows messaging system, it still supports the same Windows Forms engine that VB.NET and C#.NET use (as well as the complete .NET Framework). So, as you can imagine, Visual C++ .NET requires more work, but gives you complete control over the process.

Understanding how Windows messaging works is interesting but not necessary to write VB.NET programs (with or without a user interface). After all, VB.NET is a RAD tool that handles the messages behind the scenes, allowing you to focus entirely on solving problems. So, let's dig in and learn how to build a modern user interface.

## Programming the Toolbox Controls

This section explains how to use the most common controls available in Visual Basic .NET, including basic user-interface controls, such as Label and TextBox; slider controls, such as VScrollBar; listing controls, such as ListBox and ComboBox; and container controls, such as Panel and PictureBox.

In order to make it easier to locate controls by name, I recommend that you sort the list alphabetically. Simply right-click any-where on the Toolbox and a pop-up menu will appear. Locate an item on the pop-up menu called Sort Items Alphabetically and select it, as shown in Figure 4.4.

**Definition**

A *control* is a GUI element which resides on a form and is a basic tool for building user interfaces in Visual Basic .NET.

### Basic Controls

First, let's focus on the basic controls that are used in most programs. These con-trols are so essential that VB.NET would be utterly useless without them! Imagine trying to create a data entry application for a database without the TextBox con-trol? Yes, there is always more than one way to solve a problem, but the modern user interface that is built into Visual Basic .NET languages is truly comprehensive.

**FIGURE 4.4**

Sorting the control
Toolbox list
alphabetically.

## Button

The Button control is a key ingredient for an effective user interface. Buttons are normally found on the main form of a program and are used to perform tasks or bring up additional forms for the user. Buttons are also common on dialog boxes, such as MsgBox, InputBox, and custom dialogs. Figure 4.5 shows the Button control as it appears in the Toolbox, whereas Figure 4.6 shows the Button control on a form.

**FIGURE 4.5**

The Button
control as it
appears in the
Toolbox.

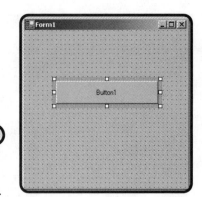

FIGURE 4.6

The Button
control as it
appears on a form.

The most common event for the Button control is the Click event. Here is an example:

```
Private Sub Button1_Click(ByVal sender As System.Object, _
    ByVal e As System.EventArgs) Handles Button1.Click

    MsgBox("Button1 was clicked")

End Sub
```

### CheckBox

The CheckBox control is a Boolean control that can be set to true or false. When the control's value is true, the check box will be filled with a small x. Figure 4.7 shows the CheckBox control as it appears in the Toolbox, whereas Figure 4.8 shows the CheckBox control on a form.

FIGURE 4.7

The CheckBox
control as it
appears in the
Toolbox.

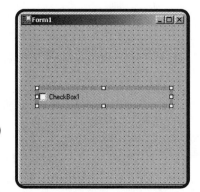

FIGURE 4.8

The CheckBox
control as it
appears on a form.

The most common event for the CheckBox control is the CheckedChanged event. Here is an example:

```
Private Sub CheckBox1_CheckedChanged(ByVal sender As System.Object, _
    ByVal e As System.EventArgs) Handles CheckBox1.CheckedChanged

    MsgBox("CheckBox1 = " & CheckBox1.Checked)

End Sub
```

### Label

The Label control is used to display static labels on a form that generally don't change while a program is running. The labels are commonly used alongside TextBox controls to describe the information stored in the TextBox (such as a database field). Labels can also be changed while the program is running, for instance, to display real-time information that changes frequently but which should not be editable by the user (as is the case with a TextBox). Figure 4.9 shows the Label control as it appears in the Toolbox, whereas Figure 4.10 shows the Label control on a form.

The most common event for the Label control is the Click event, although it is used infrequently. Here is an example.

```
Private Sub Label1_Click(ByVal sender As System.Object, _
    ByVal e As System.EventArgs) Handles Label1.Click

    MsgBox("Label1 = " & Label1.Text)

End Sub
```

**FIGURE 4.9**

The Label control
as it appears in
the Toolbox.

**FIGURE 4.10**

The Label control
as it appears
on a form.

## LinkLabel

The LinkLabel control is a specialized version of the Label control, which includes an Internet hyperlink so that when you click the label, the link is opened in the default Web browser (or e-mail program). Figure 4.11 shows the LinkLabel control as it appears in the Toolbox, whereas Figure 4.12 shows the LinkLabel control on a form.

The most common event for the LinkLabel control is the Click event. The following code illustrates how to use the LinkLabel control. Note that the Tag property is used to store the hyperlink for the LinkLabel control. You can set the Tag property during design time or run time.

```
Private Sub LinkLabel1_LinkClicked(ByVal sender As System.Object, _
    ByVal e As System.Windows.Forms.LinkLabelLinkClickedEventArgs) _
    Handles LinkLabel1.LinkClicked

    System.Diagnostics.Process.Start(LinkLabel1.Tag)

End Sub
```

**FIGURE 4.11**

The LinkLabel
control as it
appears in the
Toolbox.

**FIGURE 4.12**

The LinkLabel
control as it
appears on a form.

Setting the Tag property to http://www.premierpressbooks.com/absoluteseries.asp
will bring up the Web site shown in Figure 4.13, when the LinkLabel control is
clicked. Feel free to experiment with the Process.Start subroutine; you can open
any file or link, and Windows will invoke the default program associated with it.

## IN THE REAL WORLD

One very practical use for the LinkLabel is a link to the Software License Agreement, which is found on the About dialog that is present in most applications
(and brought up from the Help menu). Another practical use is to bring up the
default e-mail program in order to send a message to customer support for the
program. To do this, you would change the http value to an e-mail hyperlink,
with the format of mailto:user@domain.com.

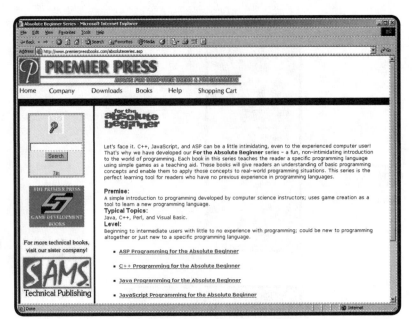

**FIGURE 4.13**

The LinkLabel control can be used to open Web sites or local files.

## ProgressBar

The ProgressBar control displays the progress of any process in the program as a graphical bar that moves across the control from left to right. Typically, the Max property is set to 100, and the Value property is a percentage, although any range of values can be used. Figure 4.14 shows the ProgressBar control as it appears in the Toolbox, whereas Figure 4.15 shows the ProgressBar control on a form.

**FIGURE 4.14**

The ProgressBar control as it appears in the Toolbox.

The most common property of the ProgressBar control is Value, which changes
the position of the graphical bar that represents the progress of an operation.
Here is an example:

```
ProgressBar1.Value = 50
```

## RadioButton

The RadioButton control is useless by itself because a mouse click can only set the
value to true, not false (as is the case with CheckBox). RadioButton controls are only
useful if two or more are placed together on a form or other container (such as a
GroupBox), because they reflect a multiple-choice value as indicated by the selected
control, not an individual true/false value. Figure 4.16 shows the RadioButton control as it appears in the Toolbox, whereas Figure 4.17 shows the RadioButton control
on a form.

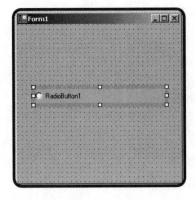

**FIGURE 4.17**

The
RadioButton
control as it
appears on a form.

The most common event for the RadioButton control is the CheckedChanged event. Here is an example:

```
Private Sub RadioButton1_CheckedChanged(ByVal sender As System.Object, _
    ByVal e As System.EventArgs) Handles RadioButton1.CheckedChanged

    MsgBox(RadioButton1.Text & " was checked.")

End Sub
```

## TextBox

The TextBox control is a multi-purpose keyboard input and text output control capable of displaying multiple lines of text with automatic word wrapping. Figure 4.18 shows the TextBox control as it appears in the Toolbox, whereas Figure 4.19 shows the TextBox control on a form.

**FIGURE 4.18**

The TextBox
control as it
appears in the
Toolbox.

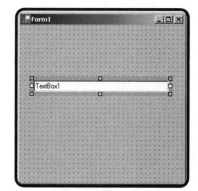

**FIGURE 4.19**

The TextBox
control as it
appears on a form.

The most common event for the TextBox control is the TextChanged event. Here is an example:

```
Private Sub TextBox1_TextChanged(ByVal sender As System.Object, _
    ByVal e As System.EventArgs) Handles TextBox1.TextChanged

    MsgBox("TextBox1 = " & TextBox1.Text)

End Sub
```

## Slider Controls

Now, I'll introduce slider controls, so named because they resemble the ProgressBar control, but feature a handle that can be manipulated with the mouse in order to change the value.

### HScrollBar

The HScrollBar control (which is shorthand for horizontal scroll bar) is most often used to scroll the main window of a program when the information contained within it is too wide to fit within the width of the window. Many applications feature this control, such as Microsoft Internet Explorer and Microsoft Word. Figure 4.20 shows the HScrollBar control as it appears in the Toolbox, whereas Figure 4.21 shows the HScrollBar control on a form.

The most common event for the HScrollBar control is the Scroll event. Here is an example:

```
Private Sub HScrollBar1_Scroll(ByVal sender As System.Object, _
    ByVal e As System.Windows.Forms.ScrollEventArgs) _
```

```
         Handles HScrollBar1.Scroll

         MsgBox("HScrollBar1 = " & HScrollBar1.Value)

End Sub
```

**FIGURE 4.20**

The `HScrollBar` control as it appears in the Toolbox.

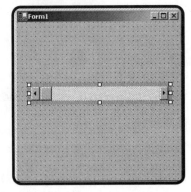

**FIGURE 4.21**

The `HScrollBar` control as it appears on a form.

## VScrollBar

The `VScrollBar` control (which is shorthand for vertical scroll bar) is similar to `HScrollBar`, most often used to scroll the main window of a program when the information contained within is too tall to fit within the height of the window. Figure 4.22 shows the `VScrollBar` control as it appears in the Toolbox, whereas Figure 4.23 shows the `VScrollBar` control on a form.

FIGURE 4.22

The VScrollBar control as it appears in the Toolbox.

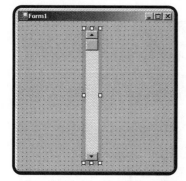

FIGURE 4.23

The VScrollBar control as it appears on a form.

The most common event for the VScrollBar control is the Scroll event. Here is an example:

```
Private Sub VScrollBar1_Scroll(ByVal sender As System.Object, _
    ByVal e As System.Windows.Forms.ScrollEventArgs) _
    Handles VScrollBar1.Scroll

    MsgBox("VScrollBar1 = " & VScrollBar1.Value)

End Sub
```

### TrackBar

The TrackBar control is useful for changing a value that falls within a specific range, and can be a useful alternative to a TextBox input field for the users of a program. Figure 4.24 shows the TrackBar control as it appears in the Toolbox, whereas Figure 4.25 shows the TrackBar control on a form.

**FIGURE 4.24**

The TrackBar control as it appears in the Toolbox.

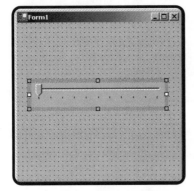

**FIGURE 4.25**

The TrackBar control as it appears on a form.

The most common event for the TrackBar control is the Scroll event. Here is an example:

```
Private Sub TrackBar1_Scroll(ByVal sender As System.Object, _
    ByVal e As System.EventArgs) Handles TrackBar1.Scroll

    MsgBox("TrackBar1 = " & TrackBar1.Value)

End Sub
```

## Listing Controls

Listing controls are extremely efficient containers that, using scrollbars and drop-downs, can display a large list of information in a small space on a form.

## ListBox and CheckedListBox

The ListBox and CheckedListBox controls display a list of information (such as a shopping list or city list in an address book program). Each individual item in the list can be checked to indicate that the item has been selected. Multiple items in the list can be selected as well. The significant difference between ListBox and CheckedListBox is that CheckedListBox includes a CheckedItems collection in addition to the SelectedItems collection that both controls include.

Figure 4.26 shows the ListBox control as it appears in the Toolbox, whereas Figure 4.27 shows the ListBox control on a form.

**FIGURE 4.26**

The ListBox control as it appears in the Toolbox.

**FIGURE 4.27**

The ListBox control as it appears on a form.

Figure 4.28 shows the CheckedListBox control as it appears in the Toolbox, whereas Figure 4.29 shows the CheckedListBox control on a form.

**FIGURE 4.28**

The CheckedList-Box control as it appears in the Toolbox.

**FIGURE 4.29**

The CheckedList-Box control as it appears on a form.

The most common event for both the ListBox and CheckedListBox controls is the SelectedIndexChanged event. Here is an example (with the initialization code in Form1_Load):

```
Private Sub Form1_Load(ByVal sender As System.Object, _
    ByVal e As System.EventArgs) Handles MyBase.Load

    ListBox1.Items.Add("List Item 1")
    ListBox1.Items.Add("List Item 2")

    CheckedListBox1.Items.Add("List Item 1")
    CheckedListBox1.Items.Add("List Item 2")

End Sub
```

```
Private Sub ListBox1_SelectedIndexChanged( _
    ByVal sender As System.Object, ByVal e As System.EventArgs) _
    Handles ListBox1.SelectedIndexChanged

    MsgBox("Selected Index = " & ListBox1.SelectedIndex)

End Sub

Private Sub CheckedListBox1_SelectedIndexChanged( _
    ByVal sender As System.Object, ByVal e As System.EventArgs) _
    Handles CheckedListBox1.SelectedIndexChanged

    MsgBox("Selected Index = " & CheckedListBox1.SelectedIndex)

End Sub
```

## ComboBox

The ComboBox control is similar to ListBox but has the added feature of supporting a drop-down list, which takes up significantly less space on the form than ListBox. Figure 4.30 shows the ComboBox control as it appears in the Toolbox, whereas Figure 4.31 shows the ComboBox control on a form.

The most common event for the ComboBox control is the SelectedIndexChanged event. Here is an example (with the initialization code in Form1_Load):

```
Private Sub Form1_Load(ByVal sender As System.Object, _
    ByVal e As System.EventArgs) Handles MyBase.Load

    ComboBox1.Items.Add("Combo Item 1")
    ComboBox1.Items.Add("Combo Item 2")

End Sub

Private Sub ComboBox1_SelectedIndexChanged( _
    ByVal sender As System.Object, ByVal e As System.EventArgs) _
    Handles ComboBox1.SelectedIndexChanged

    MsgBox("Selected Index = " & ComboBox1.SelectedIndex)

End Sub
```

**FIGURE 4.30**

The ComboBox control as it appears in the Toolbox.

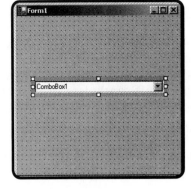

**FIGURE 4.31**

The ComboBox control as it appears on a form.

## Container Controls

Container controls are useful for grouping multiple controls together on the form so that they can be easily moved or rearranged as the application begins to take shape. The nice thing about containers is that you can move all of the sub-controls together rather than individually.

### GroupBox

The GroupBox control is the most common container and includes a border and caption. Although GroupBox has a number of events that you may use, they are not very useful and seldom needed. The primary purpose of GroupBox is to contain other controls. Figure 4.32 shows the GroupBox control as it appears in the Toolbox, whereas Figure 4.33 shows the GroupBox control on a form.

FIGURE 4.32

The GroupBox
control as it
appears in the
Toolbox.

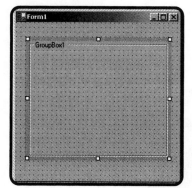

FIGURE 4.33

The GroupBox
control as it
appears on a form.

### PictureBox

The PictureBox control has a primary purpose of displaying pictures but can also contain other controls, such as the GroupBox. Figure 4.34 shows the PictureBox control as it appears in the Toolbox, whereas Figure 4.35 shows the PictureBox control on a form.

Image is the key property of the PictureBox control, which is how you load a picture into the control for display. While not used often, the key event of the PictureBox control is the Click event. The following lines of code demonstrate how to use the Click event, along with the Image property, to display a bitmap picture inside the PictureBox when it is clicked. The code assumes that a file called image.bmp is available in the current folder.

```
Private Sub PictureBox1_Click(ByVal sender As System.Object, _
    ByVal e As System.EventArgs) Handles PictureBox1.Click
```

```
PictureBox1.Image = System.Drawing.Image.FromFile( _
    Application.ExecutablePath & "\image.bmp")

End Sub
```

**FIGURE 4.34**

The PictureBox control as it appears in the Toolbox.

**FIGURE 4.35**

The PictureBox control as it appears on a form.

## Summary

By simply browsing through the Toolbox in Visual Basic .NET, you can see that there are many more controls available than I have covered in this chapter. This was meant only as an introduction to programming the most common controls found in the Toolbox. In later chapters, I will explain more of the controls and make more use of them.

What this chapter did cover, on the other hand, is the engine that powers Visual Basic .NET programs. The Windows Forms engine is a powerful new addition to

Visual Basic that was not present in previous versions. Windows Forms created with Visual Basic .NET are compatible with Visual C# and Visual C++ and vice versa. The true power of Visual Studio .NET is that Windows Forms makes it easy to build reusable forms that can be incorporated into different software projects. By learning the basics of how to program the controls that populate a form, you are taking that first step toward building powerful user interfaces.

## CHALLENGES

The following challenges will help to reinforce the material you have learned in this chapter.

1. Add controls to a form and then open the hidden section of code labeled "Windows Form Designer generated code" and see how Visual Basic .NET generated the source code that actually powers the controls.

2. Experiment with the container controls to see how groups of `RadioButton` controls work when grouped separately. Practice cutting and pasting controls into and out of containers using Ctrl+X and Ctrl+V.

3. Familiarize yourself with the properties and events for each of the controls covered in this chapter. Gain some experience by adding items to a `ListBox` and then display the text of a list item when clicked (rather than just the index).

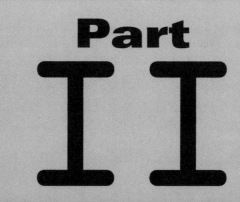

**Part**

**II**

**Programming Fundamentals in Visual Basic .NET**

Chapter 5: **Variables and Data Types**

Chapter 6: **Branching Statements and Program Logic**

Chapter 7: **Number Crunching: Mathematical and Relational Operations**

Chapter 8: **Loops, Arrays, and Structures**

# 5

# Variables and Data Types

This chapter starts a series of chapters on Visual Basic .NET programming fundamentals. The first four chapters might be thought of as a crash course on Visual Basic .NET, whereas this chapter and those that follow are more focused on teaching how the language works and how you can better use it to solve programming problems. There were many things up to this point that were not explained in depth because I wanted to give you as much exposure as possible to all that Visual Basic .NET has to offer up front. Now, you will have an opportunity to learn the nuts and bolts of the language itself.

Here are the main subjects covered in this chapter:

- **Creating and using variables**

- **Learning about data types**

- **Creating console applications**

- **Learning about variable objects**

- **Displaying variable properties**

- **Assigning values in variable declarations**

- **Creating and using strings**

Although I suspect that you will find these subjects fascinating—I know that I did!—I will try to make everything seem relevant by explaining *why* language commands were designed in a certain way and *how* those commands work together. I feel it's irrelevant to show you something new without explaining why you need to learn it. In that context, I ask that you take my word for it until you are able to grasp the "big picture"—that moment when many ideas coalesce in your mind and things begin to make sense.

The subjects of variables and data types are easy to explain but not always easy to grasp the first time around. Therefore, if you have any difficulty understanding how variables work by the end of this chapter, I recommend that you read the chapter again before moving on to the next.

## Project Preview—Typing Tutor

This chapter features a complete project—a Typing Tutor game that you will be able to build from scratch. Figure 5.1 is a screenshot of Typing Tutor.

## Variables of All Types

Here's a simple question: What is a variable? A variable is something that can change, with the connotation that it can change unexpectedly. For example, weather forecasters often speak of variable winds and variable temperatures—meaning that the wind and temperature could change without warning. In the context of computers, however, variables only change when told and cannot do anything on their own.

## What Is a Variable?

In the old days when programmers used machine language and assembly language, they would create variables by grabbing a chunk of memory and then storing a number in the newly acquired spot. This was called memory allocation and is a valid term in software today. Reserving a space in the computer's memory was a manual process that required the programmer to keep track of exactly where that space was located by creating a pointer—which is where variables came from.

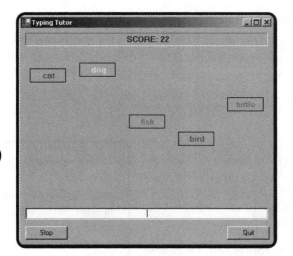

**FIGURE 5.1**

This chapter features a Typing Tutor game, which you will be able to create.

In order to make the task easier, programmers developed assembler languages that permitted the use of mnemonic words to replace the specific addresses of memory in which information is stored. Rather than keep track of the address for a pointer in memory (which in turn, points to another address in memory where actual data is located), a mnemonic was used as the pointer. Mnemonics are easier to remember than physical addresses in memory, therefore, this greatly eased the job of writing programs before more human-readable languages were invented.

> **Definition**
>
> *Assembly language* is a very low-level programming language that uses mnemonic words to represent the physical components of the computer, such as the registers in the processor. As you can imagine, it is very difficult to write programs at this level, so assembly is normally used only to write device drivers and system utility programs.

Over time, these mnemonic words came to be known as variables. So, when you hear the word "variable," just remember that it is nothing more than a pointer to an address in memory in which something is stored. VB.NET keeps track of the type of data stored in that location and does all the dirty work for you, but this process is essentially the same with all programming languages.

## Using Variables

As you might have guessed after working through the sample programs in previous chapters, the `Dim` command is used to create new variables. The syntax of `Dim` looks like this:

```
Dim Variable_Name As Data_Type
```

The As *Data_Type* part is optional. In Visual Basic 6.0, untyped variables defaulted to a special type, called Variant—sort of a catch-all type of variable that can point to any kind of data, including objects, controls, and even forms! As you might imagine, Variant variables are much slower than typed variables. As a matter of fact, Visual Basic .NET does not even support Variant. Instead, when you leave out the data type, VB.NET variables default to an *Object*. Here's an example of a real Dim statement:

```
Dim Counter As Integer
```

This statement creates an Integer variable, which is capable of holding an integer (number that has no decimal point).

In addition to the Dim command, there are two other ways to declare variables. The Public command causes a variable to be visible to other modules in the program, whereas the Private command prevents other modules from seeing a variable (and is the default when using Dim).

> **Definition**
>
> *Variables* are locations in memory in which data (such as numbers and strings) are stored. The variable itself doesn't *hold* the information, rather just the location to where the information is located.

## Learning the Data Types

A data type is the attribute of a variable, which determines what kind of data it represents. There are twelve intrinsic data types in VB.NET, as shown in Table 5.1. I have rounded off the values in order to make them easier to comprehend. In my experience, the extreme range of a data type should not be an issue; just declare variables that are certain to be large enough to hold the value.

The data types in VB.NET are drastically different from those in VB6, so when you declare a variable that you might have used in VB6, remember that the data types are not compatible. For instance, the Long type is now a 64-bit number of truly staggering range, whereas VB6 treated Longs as 32-bit numbers with a range of around four billion. For example, the new Long data type has a range of around 18,500 quadrillion. Believe it or not, you can use numbers that big with VB.NET!

> **Definition**
>
> *Data types* represent the list of possible ways to store information in a variable, whether it is an integer number, a decimal number, or a text string. The data type tells VB.NET how to store and handle the data. A special data type called Object is capable of handling any data type.

## Listing of Data Types

Now, if this is your first experience with a programming language, don't worry about data types because variables are used throughout the book, and you will get the hang of it in time. Whether you are an experienced programmer or not, the list of data types in Table 5.1 is a useful reference.

### TABLE 5.1   VARIABLE DATA TYPES

| Data Type | Bytes | Range |
|---|---|---|
| Byte | 1 | 0 to 255 |
| Boolean | 2 | True or False |
| Char | 2 | 0 to 65535 (Unicode) |
| Short | 2 | -32,768 to 32,767 |
| Integer | 4 | ~ -2,147,483,647 |
| Single | 4 | +/- 3.4028235E38 |
| Object | 4 | Any value |
| Date | 8 | Jan 1, 0001 to Dec 31, 9999 |
| Double | 8 | +/- 1.79769313486231E308 |
| Long | 8 | ~ +/- 9,223,372,036,854,775,807 |
| Decimal | 16 | +/-79,228 x $10^{24}$ |
| String | 2 x length | 0 to 2 billion (Unicode) |

### IN THE REAL WORLD

**VB.NET has significantly changed the** Short, Integer, **and** Long **data types; therefore, take care if you attempt to upgrade VB6 code to VB.NET. For instance, if you have written a program that stores data in a random-access file using your own structure format (with a** Type **statement), the VB6 code won't work! You will need to downgrade the data types in your** Type **structure because random-access files store the actual bytes used by each data type.**

The most significant difference in these data types from VB6 is the use of 64-bit and 128-bit data types (note that there are eight bits in a byte). This is a good thing, because 64-bit processors will be mainstream in only a few years. Most notably, Decimal **has replaced** Currency, **and** Object **has replaced** Variant.

## Choosing a Data Type

When deciding what data types to use in a program consider the number of bytes for each variable and select the most efficient data types. However, you must take care not to limit the variables too much, even if you think they will never exceed the data type range. This is not a license to write buggy code but simply a reminder that you can always make a program stable later on, but you can't always make it faster once you have written most of the code. Selecting the appropriate data types early on is important. Most of the time, I use the Integer, Double, and String data types. This keeps the code simple and gives programs plenty of room to breathe without sacrificing speed (as in the case with larger data types).

## The Variables Program

To help demonstrate how to use the various data types, let's write a program. If you wish, you may load the project from the CD-ROM in the folder for this chapter—the project is called Variables. This is a console application. In my opinion, there are significant advantages to using a console application when learning something new. First and foremost, console applications lack the Windows Form generated code and form event handlers. What you get with a console application is a simple Sub Main() within a simple module.

### Generated Code

Here is what the project looks like before you get started:

```
Module Module1

    Sub Main()

    End Sub

End Module
```

### Declaring Variables

After putting up with all the form code in the last few chapters, something this simple is wonderfully refreshing! Just add whatever source code you want inside Main. Now, to get this program rolling, let's create some variables:

```
Module Module1

    Dim AsciiCode As Byte
```

```
Dim Married As Boolean
Dim MiddleInitial As Char
Dim Age As Short
Dim ShoeSize As Integer
Dim AnnualIncome As Single
Dim Something As Object
Dim BirthDate As Date
Dim CarLoan As Double
Dim Weight As Long
Dim HomeLoan As Decimal
Dim Address As String

Sub Main()

End Sub

End Module
```

### Initializing Variables

Next, the variables need to be given some values in order to be useful (note the code in bold):

```
Sub Main()

    'assign values to the variables
    AsciiCode = 32
    Married = True
    MiddleInitial = "Z"
    Age = 25
    ShoeSize = 10
    AnnualIncome = 31742.56
    Something = "a text message"
    BirthDate = #1/1/2002#
    CarLoan = 18650.45
    Weight = 175
    HomeLoan = 145670.25
    Address = "1234 Bottleneck Drive"

End Sub
```

When you have finished typing in the code, the result should look like Figure 5.2.

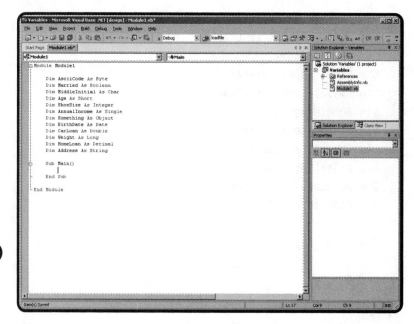

**FIGURE 5.2**

Declaring the new
variables for the
program.

## Displaying Variables

The only thing that remains is to do something with the newly assigned variables. The easiest way to show how these variables work is to display their values on the screen using the `Console.WriteLine` procedure. Here's the result of doing that (note the code in bold):

```
Sub Main()

    'assign values to the variables
    AsciiCode = 32
    Married = True
    MiddleInitial = "Z"
    Age = 25
    ShoeSize = 10
    AnnualIncome = 31742.56
    Something = "a text message"
    BirthDate = #1/1/2002#
    CarLoan = 18650.45
    Weight = 175
    HomeLoan = 145670.25
    Address = "1234 Bottleneck Drive"
```

```
'print out the variables
Console.WriteLine("THE VARIABLES PROGRAM")
Console.WriteLine("The Byte is {0}.", AsciiCode)
Console.WriteLine("The Boolean is {0}.", Married)
Console.WriteLine("The Char is {0}.", MiddleInitial)
Console.WriteLine("The Short is {0}.", Age)
Console.WriteLine("The Integer is {0}.", ShoeSize)
Console.WriteLine("The Single is {0}.", AnnualIncome)
Console.WriteLine("The Object is {0}.", Something)
Console.WriteLine("The Date is {0}.", BirthDate)
Console.WriteLine("The Double is {0}.", CarLoan)
Console.WriteLine("The Long is {0}.", Weight)
Console.WriteLine("The Decimal is {0}.", HomeLoan)
Console.WriteLine("The String is {0}.", Address)

'wait for user to press Enter
Console.WriteLine("Press Enter...")
Console.ReadLine()
End Sub
```

After typing in the source code for Sub Main, the result should look like Figure 5.3.

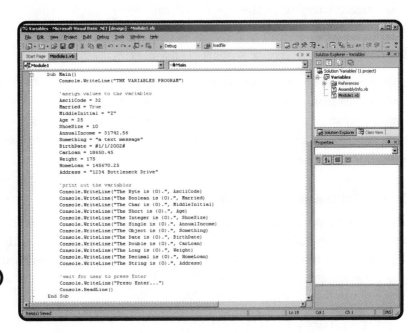

**FIGURE 5.3**

The completed
Sub Main.

### Running the Program

Well, that's about all there is to it. As I mentioned, console applications are much easier to write. Run the program by pressing F5 or click the Run icon on the tool-bar. The output from the program is shown in Figure 5.4.

```
E:\VB.NET\Sources\CH05\Variables\bin\Variables.exe
THE VARIABLES PROGRAM
The Byte is 32.
The Boolean is True.
The Char is Z.
The Short is 25.
The Integer is 10.
The Single is 31742.56.
The Object is a text message.
The Date is 1/1/2002 12:00:00 AM.
The Double is 18650.45.
The Long is 175.
The Decimal is 145670.25.
The String is 1234 Bottleneck Drive.
Press Enter...
```

**FIGURE 5.4**

Output from the
Variables program.

## Assigning Values at Declaration

One powerful new feature in VB.NET is the ability to assign values to variables as you declare them with the Dim command. For example, you can create a new string and initialize it at the same time, as follows:

```
Dim WebSiteURL As String = "http://www.premierpressbooks.com"
```

This capability has been available to other languages (such as C++) for many years and is a welcome addition to VB.NET. This can significantly cut down on the amount of source code required to set up a program. For instance, the Variables program earlier could be re-written to take advantage of variable declaration assignment.

### The VariableAssignment Program

The following program demonstrates how to assign values to variables as they are declared by rewriting the Variables program. This project is called VariableAssignment and is available on the CD-ROM in the project folder for this chapter.

```
Module Module1
    'declare and assign new variables
    Dim AsciiCode As Byte = 32
    Dim Married As Boolean = True
    Dim MiddleInitial As Char = "Z"
```

```
Dim Age As Short = 25
Dim ShoeSize As Integer = 10
Dim AnnualIncome As Single = 31742.56
Dim Something As Object = "a text message"
Dim BirthDate As Date = #1/1/2002#
Dim CarLoan As Double = 18650.45
Dim Weight As Long = 175
Dim HomeLoan As Decimal = 145670.25
Dim Address As String = "1234 Bottleneck Drive"

Sub Main()
    'print out the variables
    Console.WriteLine("THE VARIABLE ASSIGNMENT PROGRAM")
    Console.WriteLine("The Byte is {0}.", AsciiCode)
    Console.WriteLine("The Boolean is {0}.", Married)
    Console.WriteLine("The Char is {0}.", MiddleInitial)
    Console.WriteLine("The Short is {0}.", Age)
    Console.WriteLine("The Integer is {0}.", ShoeSize)
    Console.WriteLine("The Single is {0}.", AnnualIncome)
    Console.WriteLine("The Object is {0}.", Something)
    Console.WriteLine("The Date is {0}.", BirthDate)
    Console.WriteLine("The Double is {0}.", CarLoan)
    Console.WriteLine("The Long is {0}.", Weight)
    Console.WriteLine("The Decimal is {0}.", HomeLoan)
    Console.WriteLine("The String is {0}.", Address)

    'wait for user to press Enter
    Console.WriteLine("Press Enter...")
    Console.ReadLine()
End Sub

End Module
```

As you can see from Figure 5.5, the output of the VariableAssignment program is exactly the same as that from the Variables program, even though the source code is significantly shorter. Assigning values to variables as they are declared can save a lot of time and has the added benefit of ensuring that the variables start out with the correct values when the program begins. By explicitly assigning values, you have a higher measure of control over the state of the program when it starts running.

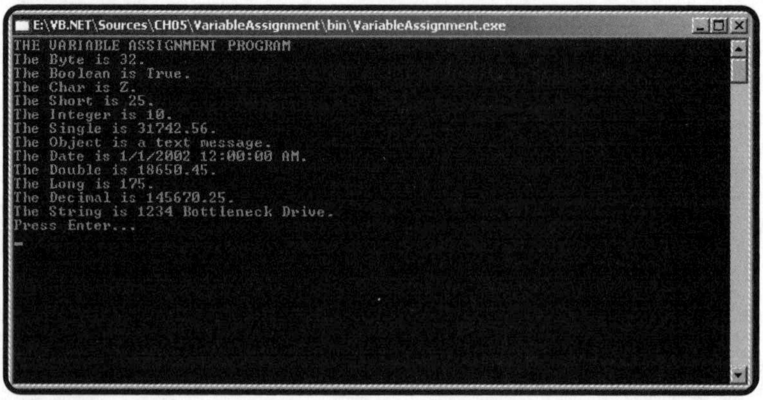

**FIGURE 5.5**

Output from the VariableAssignment program.

## Variable Objects

One of the things that I have taken for granted in the previous two programs is the automatic data conversion that VB.NET handles for you (and it does a great job at that). However, there are times when VB.NET converts a variable for output to a data type that is less than efficient or completely wrong (as in the case with rounding numbers with a decimal place). Believe it or not, all variables in VB.NET are objects. This is considerably different from VB6, in which variables were built into the language (also called intrinsic variables).

### Using Variable Objects

To demonstrate, type in the name of a variable you have declared and add a period to the end. A drop-down IntelliSense menu will appear! See Figure 5.6.

Hey, what's going on here? Variables aren't supposed to have properties and methods built in...are they? In case you were doubtful about the vast differences between VB6 and VB.NET, this single revelation alone should solidify the fact. Let's modify the Variables program again to demonstrate how variables are treated as objects by VB.NET (and other Visual Studio .NET languages). Two of the more useful properties included with numeric variables are MinValue and Max-Value. Any time you need to know the exact range of values that a variable can store, just look at MinValue and MaxValue. Another useful property is GetType, which returns a string containing the data type of the variable.

### The VariableObjects Program

Now, to really make this interesting, let's display all three of these properties for each variable. The new project is called VariableObjects and is located on the CD-ROM in

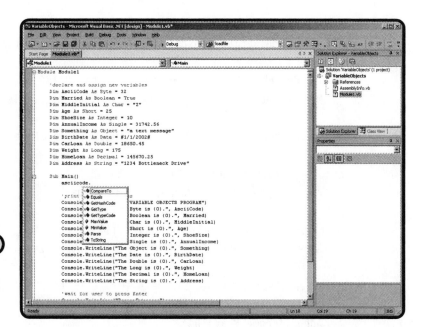

the folder for this chapter. In addition to demonstrating variable objects, this program provides more practice for displaying variables with Console.WriteLine.

```vb
Module Module1

    'declare and assign new variables
    Dim AsciiCode As Byte = 32
    Dim Married As Boolean = True
    Dim MiddleInitial As Char = "Z"
    Dim Age As Short = 25
    Dim ShoeSize As Integer = 10
    Dim AnnualIncome As Single = 31742.56
    Dim BirthDate As Date = #1/1/2002#
    Dim CarLoan As Double = 18650.45
    Dim Weight As Long = 175
    Dim HomeLoan As Decimal = 145670.25
    Dim Address As String = "1234 Bottleneck Drive"

    Sub Main()
        'print out the variables
        Console.WriteLine("THE VARIABLE OBJECTS PROGRAM")
```

```
        Console.WriteLine("AsciiCode = {0}, ({1} to {2}).", _
            AsciiCode.GetType, AsciiCode.MinValue, AsciiCode.MaxValue)

        Console.WriteLine("Married = {0}, ({1} to {2}).", _
            Married.GetType, Married.TrueString, Married.FalseString)

        Console.WriteLine("MiddleInitial = {0}.", MiddleInitial.GetType)

        Console.WriteLine("Age = {0}, ({1} to {2}).", _
            Age.GetType, Age.MinValue, Age.MaxValue)

        Console.WriteLine("ShoeSize = {0}, ({1} to {2}).", _
            ShoeSize.GetType, ShoeSize.MinValue, ShoeSize.MaxValue)

        Console.WriteLine("AnnualIncome = {0}, ({1} to {2}).", _
            AnnualIncome.GetType, AnnualIncome.MinValue, _
            AnnualIncome.MaxValue)

        Console.WriteLine("BirthDate = {0}, ({1} to {2}).", _
            BirthDate.GetType, BirthDate.MinValue, BirthDate.MaxValue)

        Console.WriteLine("CarLoan = {0}, ({1} to {2}).", _
            CarLoan.GetType, CarLoan.MinValue, CarLoan.MaxValue)

        Console.WriteLine("Weight = {0}, ({1} to {2}).", _
            Weight.GetType, Weight.MinValue, Weight.MaxValue)

        Console.WriteLine("HomeLoan = {0}, ({1} to {2}).", _
            HomeLoan.GetType, HomeLoan.MinValue, HomeLoan.MaxValue)

        Console.WriteLine("Address = {0}.", Address.GetType)

        'wait for user to press Enter
        Console.WriteLine("Press Enter...")
        Console.ReadLine()
    End Sub

End Module
```

Figure 5.7 shows the output from the VariableObjects program. The lines are not quite long enough to contain the range values for the large data types, but that's only because the values are so huge! I cheated a little with the Boolean variable because it doesn't have a MinValue or MaxValue, but it does have TrueString and FalseString properties, so no harm done. The Object variable was left out.

## What's So Special about Strings?

The String data type is the most frequently used type in VB.NET (and earlier versions as well) and deserves special recognition. The reason why strings require more explanation is that they are extremely versatile and absolutely essential for writing programs. Without strings, VB.NET would be hobbled by difficult string-handling functions, as is the case with the C++ language, which does not define a standard data type for handling strings but uses only characters. VB.NET String variables are versatile in that they can contain up to two billion characters. Although it is definitely a possibility, I have never personally seen a one gigabyte text file! Humorous as that may sound, a string could conceivably grow to that size, although I suspect that Windows would run out of memory long before the string was filled to capacity. Remember, variables are just pointers to addresses in memory. Most strings rarely exceed a few thousand characters in actual practice.

Probably the largest factor in the popularity of strings in Visual Basic (as opposed to other languages, such as Visual C++) is that Visual Basic is commonly used to build database applications, such as inventory or point of sale systems. As such, Visual Basic applications tend to deal with a lot of data entry, which is primarily textual data. Therefore, string handling is a recognized strength of the language and is highly effective. You will likely never need to write your own string-handling function because VB.NET has all the bases covered.

**IN THE REAL WORLD**

One of my biggest complaints about VB6 was the lack of a string *tokenizer*, which is a function that breaks up a string of fields separated by a character (such as a comma). String parsing comes in handy when you need to import a text file (such as a CSV file from Microsoft Excel) into a database. Without a proper string tokenizer, I have had to write my own on occasion or use a third-party software library. Fortunately, the .NET Framework includes a string tokenizer and many more similarly handy capabilities.

## Declaring and Using Strings

As you learned earlier in the chapter, the String data type requires two bytes for each character (because VB.NET strings use Unicode to store characters). To create a new String, simply use the Dim command (or the affiliated Public or Private commands):

```
Dim FirstName As String
```

In VB6 it was possible to declare a fixed-length String that contained a specified number of characters, which was deemed necessary for structured random-access files. The format for declaring a fixed-length String looked like this:

```
Dim LastName As String * 40
```

This convention is no longer allowed in VB.NET, because fixed-length strings are no longer supported. To make up for the loss, VB.NET now features the Char data type; thus, the VB.NET equivalent looks like this:

```
Dim LastName(40) As Char
```

Keep in mind that String and Char both use Unicode, therefore if you need to read a random-access or binary file, you may need to use a Byte instead.

## Modifying Strings

Simple string handling can be accomplished by setting a string equal to a value or another variable. One important thing you must remember is that you must not use the plus sign to combine strings together. That will cause problems! Instead, use the string concatenation character, the ampersand (&), as the following code demonstrates:

```
Dim String1 As String = "This is String1"
Dim String2 As String = " and this is String2."
Dim String3 As String
String3 = String1 & String2
Console.WriteLine("String3 = {0}", String3);
```

The result of this snippet of code looks like this:

```
This is String1 and this is String2.
```

## String Manipulation Functions

Concatenation is the simplest form of string manipulation. To really get a sense for the power of strings in VB.NET, you need to use some of the methods built into the String object. Following is a brief overview.

> **Definition**
>
> *Concatenation* is the process of combining two or more strings together.

**Left.** The Left function returns a specified number of characters in a string starting with the first character and moving from left to right.

**Right.** The Right function returns a specified number of characters in a string starting with the last character and moving from right to left.

**Mid.** The Mid function returns a specified number of characters in a string starting at a specified position and moving from left to right by a specified number of characters.

**Trim.** The Trim function returns a string with any whitespace removed from the left or right ends of the passed string. String objects have a built-in method of the same name.

**LTrim.** The LTrim function returns a string with any whitespace removed from the front of a passed string. String objects have a similar method called Trim-Start.

**RTrim.** The RTrim function returns a string with any whitespace removed from the end of a passed string. String objects have a similar method called TrimEnd.

**Len.** The Len function returns the number of characters in a string. Similarly, string variables have a Length property that returns the same thing.

**InStr.** The InStr function returns the position of a specified sub-string within a specified string, starting at the left and moving right.

**InStrRev.** The InStrRev function returns the position of a specified sub-string within a specified string, starting at the right and moving left.

**UCase.** The UCase function returns a string with the characters in a passed string converted to all uppercase. Similarly, string variables have a ToUpper method that performs the same thing.

**LCase.** The LCase function returns a string with the characters in a passed string converted to all lowercase. Similarly, string variables have a ToLower method that performs the same thing.

### The StringHandling Program

Let's put this collection of new functions to use in a sample program. The String-Handling program is located on the CD-ROM in the folder for this chapter.

```
Module Module1

    Dim String1 As String = "A long time ago, in a galaxy far, far away..."
    Dim First As String
    Dim Second As String
    Dim Third As String
    Dim Pos1 As Integer
    Dim Pos2 As Integer

    Sub Main()
        Console.WriteLine("THE STRING HANDLING PROGRAM")
        Console.WriteLine()
        Console.WriteLine("String1 = " & String1)
        Console.WriteLine()

        'display strings at specific locations
        Console.WriteLine("Left(String1, 16)    = " & Left(String1, 15))
        Console.WriteLine("Mid(String1, 18, 11) = " & Mid(String1, 18, 15))
        Console.WriteLine("Right(String1, 16)   = " & Right(String1, 11))
        Console.WriteLine()

        'grab strings separated by commas (tokens)
        Pos1 = InStr(String1, ",")
        Pos2 = InStrRev(String1, ",")
        First = Mid(String1, 1, Pos1 - 1)
        Second = Mid(String1, Pos1 + 1, Pos2 - Pos1 - 1)
        Third = Mid(String1, Pos2 + 1)
```

```
        'display the tokenized strings
        Console.WriteLine("First  = " & First)
        Console.WriteLine("Second = " & Second)
        Console.WriteLine("Third  = " & Third)
        Console.WriteLine()

        'display strings with whitespace trimmed
        Console.WriteLine("Trim(First)  = " & Trim(First))
        Console.WriteLine("Second.Trim  = " & Second.Trim)
        Console.WriteLine("LTrim(Third) = " & LTrim(Third))
        Console.WriteLine()

        'display upper and lower strings
        Console.WriteLine("UCase(First)    = " & UCase(First))
        Console.WriteLine("Second.ToUpper = " & Second.ToUpper)
        Console.WriteLine("Third.ToLower  = " & Third.ToLower)
        Console.WriteLine()

        'wait for user
        Console.WriteLine("Press Enter...")
        Console.ReadLine()
    End Sub

End Module
```

Figure 5.8 shows what the StringHandling program looks like when run. As you can see, VB.NET includes all of the string functions that were present in VB6 but also includes many of these functions within the String object as properties and methods.

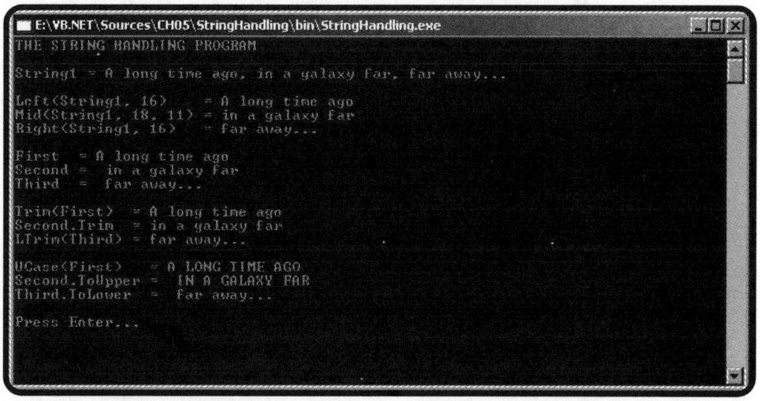

**FIGURE 5.8**

The StringHandling program.

Until you start to write programs that use strings, it is not readily apparent why they are so important. One factor that you may reasonably count on is the performance of string handling in VB.NET. Now that Variant variables are no more, string handling can be optimized to run as quickly and efficiently as possible, which was not always the case with VB6.

Confused by all these new terms, such as objects, properties, and methods? It's unavoidable at this early stage, but rest assured, you will get the full treatment in Part 3, "Object-Oriented Programming with Visual Basic .NET."

# Chapter Project— The Typing Tutor Program

The Typing Tutor program is a real-time game that uses a Timer control to move words down the screen. You must type those words to reset them before they reach the bottom of the screen. There are five words that slowly move toward the bottom at the same time, so you have to type fast! Figure 5.9 shows the state of the Typing Tutor program before the Start button has been pressed.

After the game starts, the Start button changes to a Stop button, which you can use to restart the game. For every word that you get right, you gain one point. For every word that reaches the bottom, you lose ten points! A good strategy is to knock off the easy words first and then go for more difficult words because if you make a typo and have to backspace, you could lose that word and all the others at the same time. The game was meant to be simple to understand, therefore the words start back up at the top again after you complete them. If you want to try more difficult words, feel free to change the Text property for each of the labels

**FIGURE 5.9**

The Typing Tutor program as it appears at startup.

to any word that you want. However, I recommend that you keep the words as short as possible! If the words are falling too fast for you to keep up, you can always change the timer to a higher value so the game will run slower.

## Creating the Project

Fire up Visual Studio .NET and create a new Windows Application project called TypingTutor, as shown in Figure 5.10. To bring up the New Project dialog, you will want to select New, Project from the File menu in Visual Studio .NET. Alternatively, you can press the New Project button on the Start Page.

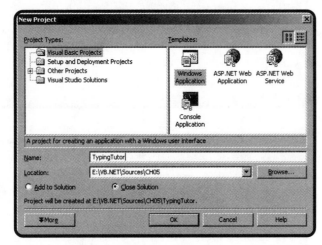

**FIGURE 5.10**

Creating the new TypingTutor project.

## Building the User Interface

Take a look at Figure 5.11 to see what the completed project looks like. Now I'll walk you through each step required to write this program.

### Creating the User Interface

**Step 1.** Let's get started! First, resize the form to 456,400 or thereabouts. Absolute precision is not important. Then rename the form by changing the Text property to **Typing Tutor**. Figure 5.12 shows the results.

**Step 2.** Add five Label controls to the form, near the top. The labels should be named Label1, Label2, Label3, Label4, and Label5. This is important because the source code refers to them by name. Change the BorderStyle property to FixedSingle. The form should look like Figure 5.13.

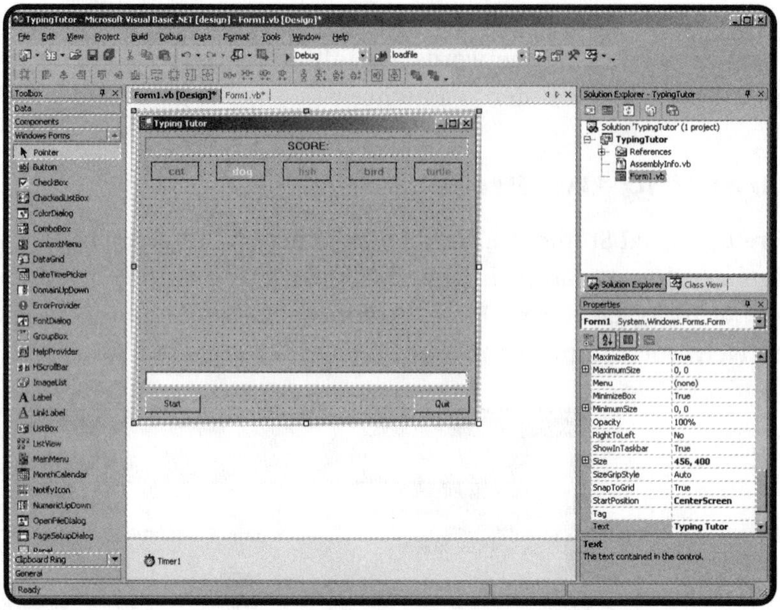

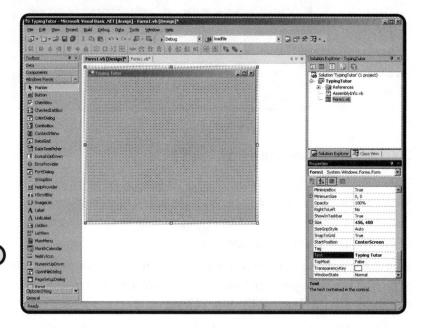

**FIGURE 5.11**

The completed TypingTutor project as it appears in the VB.NET development environment.

**FIGURE 5.12**

The TypingTutor form is ready for some controls.

**Step 3**. Let's spruce up these controls to make them more attractive. Set the Text-Align property for all five labels to MiddleCenter. Rather than setting the property for each control separately, select all five controls by holding the Ctrl key while clicking each one. The result is shown in Figure 5.14.

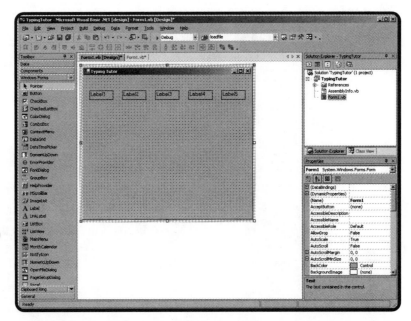

**FIGURE 5.13**

The new Label
controls have been
added to the
TypingTutor project.

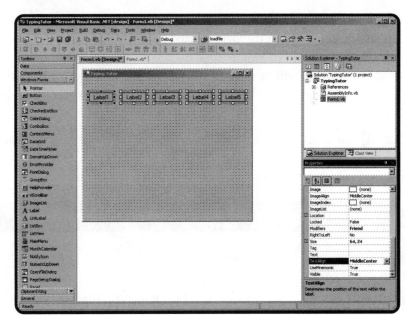

**FIGURE 5.14**

Setting the
TextAlign
property of the
Label controls to
MiddleCenter.

**Step 4**. Change the font of the Labels to Bold, as shown in Figure 5.15.

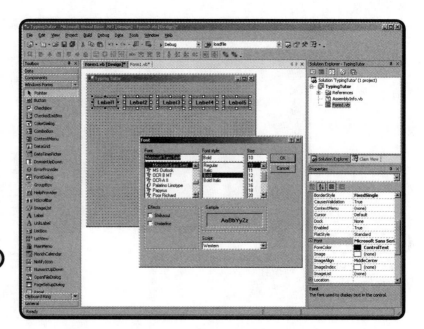

**FIGURE 5.15**

Setting the font
of each Label
to Bold.

**Step 5**. Now, let's change the ForeColor of each Label so that it is more attractive. The exact colors aren't important, just select five different colors that appeal to your sense of décor. As you change each color, change the text of each Label to a simple word that will be used in the game. You can use the words I used or make up your own—just keep them short. Figure 5.16 shows the colors and words that I chose.

**Step 6**. Add a new Label control to the top of the form and call it Label6. Change the properties of Label6 as shown in Table 5.2. Figure 5.17 shows the new Label control, which is used to display the score in the game.

## TABLE 5.2 LABEL6 PROPERTIES

| Property | Value |
|---|---|
| BorderStyle | Fixed3D |
| Font | Microsoft Sans Serif, 10pt, style=Bold |
| ForeColor | Blue |
| Location | 8, 8 |
| Size | 432, 23 |
| Text | SCORE: |
| TextAlign | MiddleCenter |

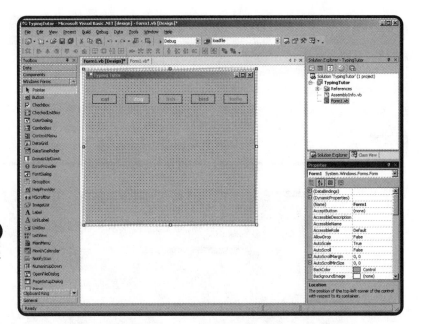

**FIGURE 5.16**

Changing the Text and ForeColor properties for the Label controls.

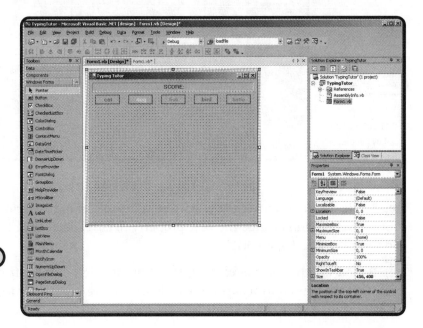

**FIGURE 5.17**

The new Label control used to display the score.

**Step 7**. Add a TextBox control near the bottom of the form. Table 5.3 shows the properties for this new control, whereas Figure 5.18 shows what the project looks like with the new TextBox.

## TABLE 5.3 TEXTBOX1 PROPERTIES

| Property | Value |
| --- | --- |
| Location | 8, 312 |
| Size | 432, 20 |
| TextAlign | Center |

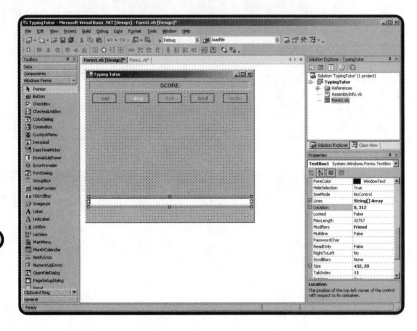

**FIGURE 5.18**

The new
TextBox control
used by the player
to type in words.

**Step 8**. Add a Button control to the bottom-right corner of the form. Call the new control Button1 and change the Text property to Quit. This is the button used to end the game (see Figure 5.19).

**Step 9**. Add another Button control, this time to the bottom-left corner of the form. Call the new control Button2 and change the Text property to Start. This is the button used to start the game (see Figure 5.20).

### Adding the Timer

To make things more interesting, this program uses a new control that has not been discussed as of yet. The new control, called Timer, generates an event for your program at pre-determined intervals and is extremely useful. To add a Timer

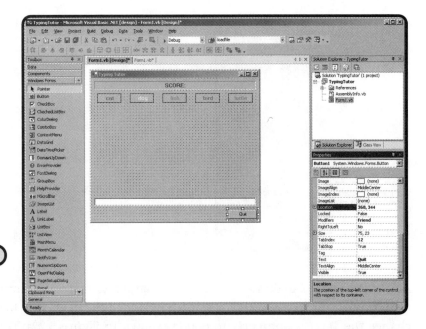

**FIGURE 5.19**

The Quit button
is used to end
the game.

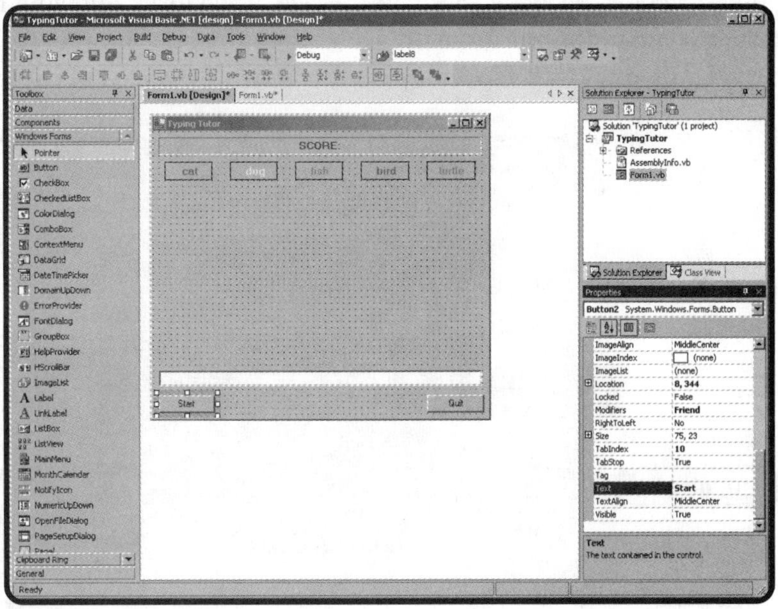

**FIGURE 5.20**

The Start button is
used to start and
stop the game.

control to the project, locate the Timer in the Toolbox, as shown in Figure 5.21,
and double-click the control to add it to your project.

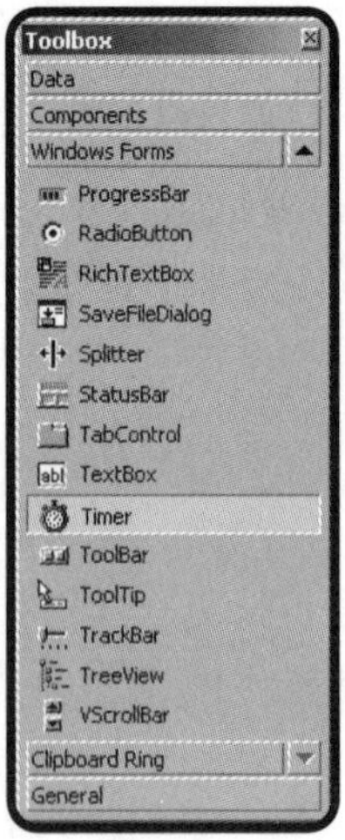

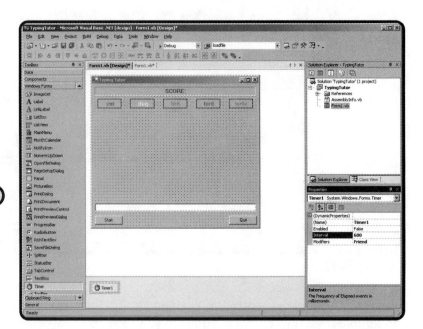

**FIGURE 5.21**

The Timer control
as it appears
in the Toolbox.

Any time you need to do something in a program with specific timing, the Timer control is the obvious choice. After you have added the new Timer to your project, change the Interval property to 600 (as shown in Figure 5.22). This is a pretty good speed for the game based on the size of the form, allowing the user enough time to type in the words before they reach the bottom. Feel free to change this number if you want to speed up or slow down the speed of the game.

**FIGURE 5.22**

Changing the
Interval
property of
Timer1 to 600
keeps the game
running at a
playable rate.

**The** Timer **control is very simple and requires very little explanation to use. Just set the interval to a millisecond value and the** Timer_Tick **event is called automatically. For example, setting the** Interval **to 600 causes the** Timer **event to be called every 600 milliseconds. Because there are 1,000 milliseconds in one second, that is just over half a second for each event.**

## Writing the Source Code

The source code for TypingTutor is comprised entirely of events for the controls (including the Timer). To bring up the default event for a control, double-click the control, and the code editor will open to the appropriate event. You can then type in the code that follows into each event. Alternatively, you can type in the code listing without double-clicking each control. Either way will work, therefore use whichever method you prefer. You can also load the project from the CD-ROM and run it directly (although I recommend creating these projects as a learning experience).

```
Dim Score As Integer = 0

Private Sub Button2_Click(ByVal sender As System.Object, _
    ByVal e As System.EventArgs) Handles Button2.Click
    If Button2.Text = "Start" Then
        Button2.Text = "Stop"
        Score = 0
        Label6.Text = "SCORE: " & Score
        Timer1.Enabled = True
        TextBox1.Focus()
    Else
        Button2.Text = "Start"
        Timer1.Enabled = False
        Label1.Top = 40
        Label2.Top = 40
        Label3.Top = 40
        Label4.Top = 40
        Label5.Top = 40
    End If
End Sub

Private Sub Timer1_Tick(ByVal sender As System.Object, _
    ByVal e As System.EventArgs) Handles Timer1.Tick
    Label1.Top = Label1.Top + 10
```

```
    If Label1.Top > 280 Then
        Label1.Top = 40
        Score = Score - 10
        Label6.Text = "SCORE: " & Score
    End If

    Label2.Top = Label2.Top + 10
    If Label2.Top > 280 Then
        Label2.Top = 40
        Score = Score - 10
        Label6.Text = "SCORE: " & Score
    End If

    Label3.Top = Label3.Top + 10
    If Label3.Top > 280 Then
        Label3.Top = 40
        Score = Score - 10
        Label6.Text = "SCORE: " & Score
    End If

    Label4.Top = Label4.Top + 10
    If Label4.Top > 280 Then
        Label4.Top = 40
        Score = Score - 10
        Label6.Text = "SCORE: " & Score
    End If

    Label5.Top = Label5.Top + 10
    If Label5.Top > 280 Then
        Label5.Top = 40
        Score = Score - 10
        Label6.Text = "SCORE: " & Score
    End If
End Sub

Private Sub TextBox1_TextChanged(ByVal sender As System.Object, _
    ByVal e As System.EventArgs) Handles TextBox1.TextChanged
    If TextBox1.Text <> "" Then
        If TextBox1.Text = Label1.Text Then
            TextBox1.Text = ""
```

```
            Label1.Top = 40
            Score = Score + 1
            Label6.Text = "SCORE: " & Score
        End If
        If TextBox1.Text = Label2.Text Then
            TextBox1.Text = ""
            Label2.Top = 40
            Score = Score + 1
            Label6.Text = "SCORE: " & Score
        End If
        If TextBox1.Text = Label3.Text Then
            TextBox1.Text = ""
            Label3.Top = 40
            Score = Score + 1
            Label6.Text = "SCORE: " & Score
        End If
        If TextBox1.Text = Label4.Text Then
            TextBox1.Text = ""
            Label4.Top = 40
            Score = Score + 1
            Label6.Text = "SCORE: " & Score
        End If
        If TextBox1.Text = Label5.Text Then
            TextBox1.Text = ""
            Label5.Top = 40
            Score = Score + 1
            Label6.Text = "SCORE: " & Score
        End If
    End If
End Sub

Private Sub Button1_Click(ByVal sender As System.Object, _
    ByVal e As System.EventArgs) Handles Button1.Click
    End
End Sub
```

## Summary

This discussion of variables and data types is probably the most important of the entire book because variable types are the core of a programming language.

Without a solid understanding of the types of variables available, it is easy to make mistakes by using them inappropriately. Although a person's age could be stored in a `Byte`, it would be wholly inadequate to store something like vehicle mileage or the price of gasoline in a `Byte` (which requires a data type with a decimal point, such as `Single`, `Double`, and `Decimal`).

This chapter also covered `String` variables, and you were introduced for the first time to variable objects—learning that the basic data types are more than they appear at first glance.

## CHALLENGES

The following challenges will help to reinforce the material you have learned in this chapter.

1. Add a slider to the Typing Tutor game, so you can adjust the speed of the game while it is running. Hint: take a look at the `Timer.Interval` property.

2. Modify the Typing Tutor game so that the words will change after they have been completed. Hint: this may require a random word generator or additional labels that are hidden on the form.

3. Add a new feature to the Typing Tutor game so that the appropriate label is highlighted when the player is typing in a word. Hint: look at the first letter of the word using the `Left` function and then highlight the appropriate `Label` control.

# Branching Statements and Program Logic

T he key to writing programs is understanding how to use program logic effectively, which means learning how branching statements work. Up to this point, you have used branching statements—perhaps without even realizing it. For instance, in the last chapter, you created a Typing Tutor program that used an `If...Then` **statement to determine when a word hit the bottom, at which point the player lost ten points. The program also checked the** `TextBox` **to see what the player was typing in, and automatically compared it to the words falling down the screen. Can you imagine how the program might have been written without the** `If...Then` **branching statement? I might go so far as to state that it would be impossible! How would you compare the words without using an** `If...Then` **branching statement? Clearly, there is more to this subject than meets the eye. Fortunately, this chapter is all about branching statements and learning about program logic—that funny thing that makes programs actually do stuff, so to speak. Specifically, this chapter covers the following topics:**

- **Learning about program logic**
- **The** `If...Then` **statement**
- **The** `Select...Case` **statement**
- **Understanding subroutines**
- **Using subs and functions**
- **Chapter project—The DiceWar Program**

## Project Preview—The DiceWar Program

This chapter features a complete project, called DiceWar, which you will learn to write from scratch. This program demonstrates how branching statements work—both If...Then and Select...Case. The project is then modified in the second half of the chapter, in which you learn about subroutines. Figure 6.1 shows a screenshot of the DiceWar program.

## Learning about Program Logic

Program logic and logical decisions are at the core of how computers work, providing a means to process data. At the highest level, programs should be designed to accomplish the following three tasks:

1. Input the data.
2. Process the data.
3. Output the result.

The goal of any programmer should be to write programs that revolve around these three basic operations: input, process, and output. When you break down any problem to its component levels, you should be able to distinctly see how these three operations apply to every program. If a program doesn't input, process, and output data or commands or information, it really isn't a program. Obviously, these operations have a wide range of application.

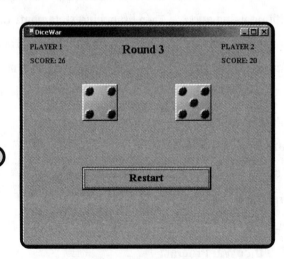

**FIGURE 6.1**

This chapter features a game called DiceWar, which you will learn to write.

Input could be the keyboard, mouse, or joystick but could also be a database, text file, serial port, or network connection. Processing might involve translating, combining, or transforming the data to suit a specific purpose. Output might be displayed data on the screen, a printed report, or possibly an output file or database. Therefore, as you can see, input, process, and output can be interpreted to mean many things. The important thing is that every program accomplishes at least this basic level of functionality.

## What Is a Branching Statement?

Branching statements are built into programming languages so that programmers (like you) can process the input and provide the output for a program. Without branching statements, the program would only be able to forward the input directly to the output, without any processing. Although this may be something that you want the program to do (such as to display a text file on the screen or print a document), it is far more likely that you will need to actually do something with input data. Branching statements allow you to create complex program logic.

 **Branching statements are synonymous with conditional statements and decision statements; therefore, when you hear any of these terms used to describe a process that occurs in a program, remember that all three refer to the same thing.**

## The If...Then Statement

The most common branching statement used in programming languages is the If...Then statement, which is often called the If...Then...Else statement. Here is the general syntax of the de-facto logic statement as it is used in Visual Basic:

```
If condition is true Then
    perform commands based on true result
Else
    perform commands based on false result
End If
```

The Else statement is equivalent to the following two individual branching statements. Note the use of End If to end each statement. This is normal for Visual Basic, but is often not used in other languages (such as C++).

```
If condition is true Then
    perform commands based on true result
End If
```

```
If condition is false Then
     perform commands based on false result
End If
```

As I mentioned, these two branching statements are equivalent to the preceding If...Then...Else statement; the Else saves a lot of time! Figure 6.2 is an example of an If...Then...Else statement and shows how input is tested for a true or false condition, whereupon program execution continues down the chosen path.

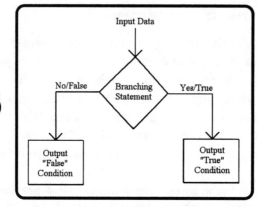

**FIGURE 6.2**

Illustration of a branching statement showing how program logic works.

## ElseIf

What happens when you need to test more than one condition at a time? In general, you should use the Select...Case statement (covered next). But there are times when it is easier to include another Else block within the If...Then statement. The answer is a new statement called ElseIf, which performs another conditional test in the event that the first one failed. Then, rather than jumping to the Else block, ElseIf commands are executed. Here is the format for the complete If...Then...ElseIf statement:

```
If condition1 is true Then
     perform condition1 commands for true
ElseIf condition2 is true Then
     perform condition2 commands for true
Else
     perform commands for false
End If
```

ElseIf forms a hierarchy of conditional tests that can become quite complex, particularly when using nested statements. Avoid creating extremely complicated branching statements because they are difficult to understand.

## Single-Line If...Then Statements

There is another format you can use with this branching statement, in which the Else and End If parts are not needed. Rather, you can code an If...Then...Else statement on a single line. Although this format is supported by Visual Basic, it is generally considered bad form, due to the lack of a closing statement—this is often a source of bugs in a program and difficult to track down. However, this form does save three lines of code. The real benefit to using this form is when you have to test many conditions in a row, and you want to keep the code listing short. Of course, such situations beg for an alternate design altogether.

```
If condition Then true statement Else false statement
```

## Using If...Then

How about a real example? Okay, here is how you might code the branching statement for a payroll program that calculates overtime pay.

```
If HoursWorked > 40 Then
    PayRate = 1.5
Else
    PayRate = 1.0
End If
```

Now, you could have just as easily written this code using two If...Then statements instead of a single If...Then...Else, and the result would have been the same. Here is what it would look like.

```
If HoursWorked > 40 Then
    PayRate = 1.5
End If

If HoursWorked <= 40 Then
    PayRate = 1.0
End If
```

**HINT**

**Chapter 7, "Number Crunching: Mathematical and Relational Operators," covers the common relational operators, such as greater than >, less than <, and equals =, along with mathematical operators, such as \*= and +=. If you don't feel confident with everything covered here, I recommend you read the next chapter and then return here for another perusal because these chapters are closely related.**

The better solution, of course, is to use the Else block instead of the second If...Then block. This allows you to add additional cases to the condition, as follows:

```
If HoursWorked > 40 Then
    MsgBox("You worked over time.")
ElseIf HoursWorked = 40 Then
    MsgBox("You worked regular time.")
Else
    MsgBox("You worked part time.")
End If
```

## The Select...Case Statement

There are times when the If...Then statement is just too unwieldy, particularly when a large number of conditions must be tested. In such circumstances, the Select...Case statement is a good alternative. In fact, you may feel free to use this branching statement instead of If...Then at any time, it's entirely up to you. Some prefer Select...Case, because it is easier to add new cases to the condition in the future. I use it any time there are more than two conditions to be tested.

### Statement Format

Here is the general format of the Select...Case statement:

```
Select Case "evaluation"
    Case value-1 [To value-2][, value-3]
        "perform condition-1 statements"
    Case value-1 [To value-2][, value-3]
        "perform condition-2 statements"
    Case value-1 [To value-2][, value-3]
        "perform condition-n statements"
    Case Else
        "perform alternate statements"
End Select
```

The Select...Case branching statement is versatile in that it is easy to add new cases (as you can see). It is also easier to read than in an If...Then statement when dealing with a lot of cases.

### Using the Select...Case Statement

To demonstrate how Select...Case works, let's rewrite the previous If...Then code as a Select...Case.

```
Select Case HoursWorked
    Case > 40
```

```
        MsgBox("You worked over time.")
    Case = 40
        MsgBox("You worked regular time.")
    Case Else
        MsgBox("You worked part time.")
End Select
```

If you type in that Select...Case statement into VB.NET, you will notice that the editor adds the word Is before each condition. For example, if you type Case > 40, the editor will fill in Case Is > 40. This is simply the syntax required in Select...Case statements for Boolean evaluations. If you need only compare a range of values or a single value, the Is isn't needed. For example:

```
Select Case Mileage
    Case Is < 10
        MsgBox("The mileage is terrible.")
    Case 11, 12, 13, 14, 15
        MsgBox("The mileage is poor.")
    Case 16, 17, 18 To 20
        MsgBox("The mileage is average.")
    Case 21 To 30
        MsgBox("The mileage is good.")
    Case 31 To 50
        MsgBox("The mileage is great.")
    Case Is > 50
        MsgBox("The mileage is amazing!")
End Select
```

 **If you don't fully understand Boolean logic at this point, don't worry, the subject is covered in some depth in Chapter 7, "Number Crunching: Mathematical and Relational Operators."**

## Understanding Subroutines

Subroutines are important for breaking up a large program into smaller, more manageable pieces, leading to better code reuse and legibility. Subroutines are also important for creating program logic. Quite often, the conditional statements in a branching statement point to a subroutine to keep the branching statement short. If each case in a branching statement includes a page of source code, it's easy to lose track of each case! Therefore, subroutines are essential parts of a programming language.

This won't be a comprehensive discussion of subroutines because every chapter from this point forward will use subroutines. You will have ample opportunity to learn all that is possible with subroutines, including how to pass multiple parameters (or as many parameters as you like), passing by value or by reference, and optional parameters. Rest assured, these advanced topics will be covered. At this point, it's more important to grasp the functional use of subroutines and how they apply to branching in a program. I will introduce you to additional features as they are needed, rather than all at once.

## Using Subs and Functions

Visual Basic supports two types of subroutines: Sub and Function. A Sub is a subroutine that does not return a value. A Function is a subroutine that does return a value. Here is the basic syntax for a Sub:

```
[Public/Private] Sub SubName([Parameters])
End Sub
```

Here is an example of a Sub that does not have a parameter:

```
Private Sub PrintHello()
    Console.WriteLine("Hello!")
End Sub
```

Here is an example of a Sub that includes a String parameter:

```
Private Sub PrintHello(Name As String)
    Console.WriteLine("Hello, " & Name & "!")
End Sub
```

 Note that the ampersand character, &, is used to tie strings together, not the plus character, +. The plus character is used to copy numbers, whereas the ampersand is used to copy characters.

## Returning Values with Functions

Functions are similar to Subs, but Functions are able to return a value. Here is the basic syntax for a Function:

```
[Public/Private] Function FunctionName([Parameters]) As DataType
End Function
```

Here is an example of a `Function` that does not have a parameter:

```
Private Function One() As Integer
     One = 1
End Function
```

Strange as it may appear, this is a legal function! Do you see how the return value is actually just set to the function itself? That is how you use the return value, as if the function name itself is a variable. Here is another example of a `Function`, only this time with a parameter:

```
Private Function TimesTen(Num As Integer) As Integer
     Triple = Num * 10
End Function
```

The `TimesTen` function is a little more interesting because you can have it return a value that is based on a parameter! The possibilities are utterly endless on what you can do with the power of subroutines. The return value of a function is determined by the data type of the function, which can be any data type that you use when creating variables, as well as custom data types that you create. Functions can also return an `Object`, which means that it can return any data type or even a user interface control (odd as that may sound).

# Chapter Project—The DiceWar Program

The DiceWar program was designed to demonstrate all of the concepts learned in this chapter, including examples of branching statements and subroutines, and more coverage of the `Timer` control.

## Running the Program

Figure 6.3 shows the DiceWar program at startup. As the figure shows, there are two dice and a button called Restart. There is also a label showing the current round, and then the score for two players.

Figure 6.4 shows the program form while the dice are being rolled by Player 1.

Figure 6.5 shows the program waiting for Player 2 to roll the dice. Note that Player 1 has already rolled, and the score has been updated.

Now, take a look at Figure 6.6, which shows the result of Player 1's dice roll. Likewise, Figure 6.7 shows the result of a dice roll by Player 2.

After three rounds of dice rolls by each player, the program announces the winner, as shown in Figure 6.8.

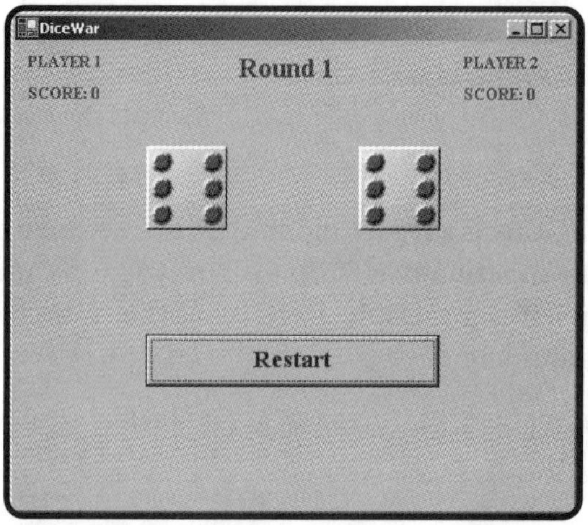

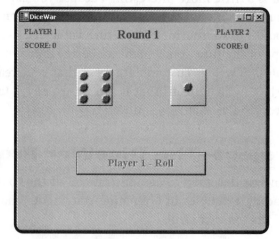

**FIGURE 6.3**

The DiceWar program at startup.

**FIGURE 6.4**

Player 1 has clicked the button, and now the dice are rolling.

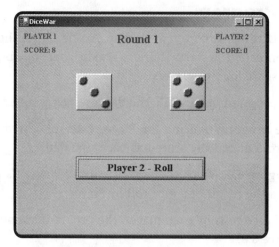

**FIGURE 6.5**

The game is now ready for Player 2 to roll the dice.

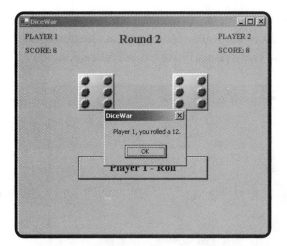

**FIGURE 6.6**

Player 1 scores a
fantastic double six.

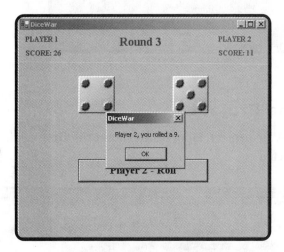

**FIGURE 6.7**

Player 2 rolls a
pretty good nine,
but is now far
behind Player 1's
score.

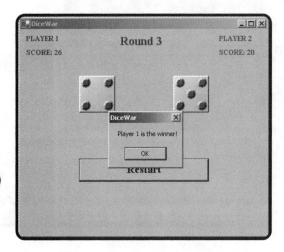

**FIGURE 6.8**

At the end of Round
3, the winner is
declared.

At the end of the third round, the program displays the results of the game and the last throw of the dice (the state of the game at the end), while waiting for the next round to start via the Restart button (see Figure 6.9).

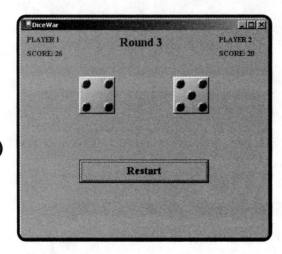

**FIGURE 6.9**

The program waits for the player to press the Restart button to start a new game.

## Designing the Project

Let's create the DiceWar project. Figure 6.10 shows the final project as it should appear when completed.

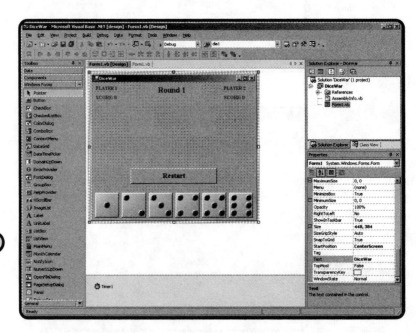

**FIGURE 6.10**

The completed DiceWar project showing the main form.

## Creating the Dice Graphics

Before you can do anything useful with the form for DiceWar, you will need some graphics for the dice. I have drawn some dice using Paint Shop Pro (see Figure 6.11) that you may copy from the CD-ROM, in the DiceWar project folder under this chapter.

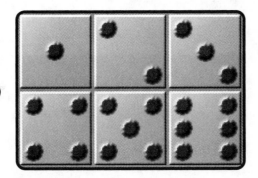

**FIGURE 6.11**

The dice images used in the game were created with Paint Shop Pro.

## Creating the New Project

First, create a new project by selecting File, New, Project, or by pressing the New Project button on the Start Page. Name the new project DiceWar, and specify a destination folder for the project (see Figure 6.12).

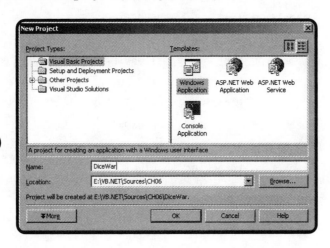

**FIGURE 6.12**

The New Project dialog, showing the new DiceWar project about to be generated.

## Creating the User Interface

Now, in the past, I have walked you step by step through the process of adding every control to the form. I suspect that you no longer need that level of help; therefore, I'm just going to list the controls that you will need in Table 6.1, along with their properties and values. Based on this simple table, you can construct the user interface for DiceWar.

## TABLE 6.1 CONTROL PROPERTIES FOR DICEWAR

| Control | Name | Property | Value |
|---|---|---|---|
| Label | Label1 | Text | PLAYER 1 |
| | | AutoSize | True |
| | | Font | Times New Roman, 10pt, style=Bold |
| | | ForeColor | 192, 0, 0 |
| | | Location | 8, 8 |
| Label | Label2 | Text | PLAYER 2 |
| | | AutoSize | True |
| | | Font | Times New Roman, 10pt, style=Bold |
| | | ForeColor | 192, 0, 0 |
| | | Location | 352, 8 |
| Label | Label3 | Text | SCORE: 0 |
| | | AutoSize | True |
| | | Font | Times New Roman, 10pt, style=Bold |
| | | ForeColor | 192, 0, 0 |
| | | Location | 352, 32 |
| Label | Label4 | Text | SCORE: 0 |
| | | AutoSize | True |
| | | Font | Times New Roman, 10pt, style=Bold |
| | | ForeColor | 192, 0, 0 |
| | | Location | 8, 32 |
| Label | Label5 | Text | ROUND 1 |
| | | Font | Times New Roman, 16pt, style=Bold |
| | | ForeColor | Blue |
| | | Location | 136, 8 |
| | | Size | 160, 32 |
| PictureBox | pb1 | Location | 104, 80 |
| | | Size | 64, 64 |
| PictureBox | pb2 | Location | 272, 80 |
| | | Size | 64, 64 |

## TABLE 6.1   CONTROL PROPERTIES FOR DICEWAR

| Control | Name | Property | Value |
|---|---|---|---|
| Button | Button1 | Text | Restart |
| | | Font | Times New Roman, 14pt, style=Bold |
| | | Location | 104, 224 |
| | | Size | 232, 40 |
| PictureBox | Die1 | Location | 8, 288 |
| | | SizeMode | AutoSize |
| | | Image | die1.bmp |
| PictureBox | Die2 | Location | 80, 288 |
| | | SizeMode | AutoSize |
| | | Image | die2.bmp |
| PictureBox | Die3 | Location | 152, 288 |
| | | SizeMode | AutoSize |
| | | Image | die3.bmp |
| PictureBox | Die4 | Location | 224, 288 |
| | | SizeMode | AutoSize |
| | | Image | die4.bmp |
| PictureBox | Die5 | Location | 296, 288 |
| | | SizeMode | AutoSize |
| | | Image | die5.bmp |
| PictureBox | Die6 | Location | 368, 288 |
| | | SizeMode | AutoSize |
| | | Image | die6.bmp |
| Timer | Timer1 | Interval | 100 |

The six PictureBox controls named Die1 to Die6 require a little more explanation, because they feature bitmap images that are actually loaded into the project at design time and used in the game directly off the form. At that point, the files on disk are no longer required, because Visual Basic stores the bitmaps inside the form binary file (the file is called Form1.resx and contains XML data).

To add the bitmaps, click the small ellipsis to the right of the Image property, as shown in Figure 6.13. The Open dialog will appear (see Figure 6.14), allowing you to select a bitmap file to load into the PictureBox. (Note that once you have loaded a picture, you no longer need the bitmap file.)

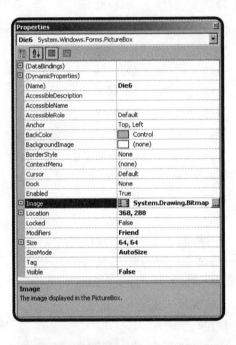

**FIGURE 6.13**

Loading a bitmap into the Image property of a PictureBox.

**FIGURE 6.14**

Selecting a bitmap file to load into the PictureBox.

## Writing the Source Code

The source code for DiceWar helps to demonstrate the topics covered in this chapter, therefore you will see quite a bit of new code in the listings that follow, including the use of subroutines. I will go over each section of code along the way so that you will be able to understand what each section accomplishes.

**Section 1.** This first block of code declares the variables used in the program, and they are all Integer variables. Note that some are initialized to starting values already. This is a feature that was discussed in Chapter 5, "Variables and Data Types."

```
Dim Player As Integer = 1
Dim Round As Integer = 1
Dim Roll1 As Integer = 1
Dim Roll2 As Integer = 3
Dim Rolls As Integer
Dim Score1 As Integer
Dim Score2 As Integer
```

**Section 2.** The next section of code includes the Form1_Load event, which is the first thing that runs when the program starts. First, the random number generator is initialized. Second, the image of a six-sided die (Die6) is copied into the two PictureBox controls, pb1 and pb2.

```
Private Sub Form1_Load(ByVal sender As System.Object, _
    ByVal e As System.EventArgs) Handles MyBase.Load
    'initialize the random number generator
    Randomize()
    'draw initial dice images
    pb1.Image = Die6.Image
    pb2.Image = Die6.Image
End Sub
```

**Section 3.** The next section of code includes the Button1_Click event, which is called when the Restart button is clicked (and subsequently renamed, as you will see shortly). The code checks the Text property of the button to determine what to do next. If the button text is Restart, the game is restarted. Otherwise, the button rolls the dice by turning on the Timer control.

```
Private Sub Button1_Click(ByVal sender As System.Object, _
    ByVal e As System.EventArgs) Handles Button1.Click
    'this event handles Restart as well as Roll
    If Button1.Text = "Restart" Then
        RestartGame()
    Else
        'disable the Roll button
        Button1.Enabled = False
```

```
            'start the rolling dice
            Timer1.Enabled = True
        End If
    End Sub
```

**Section 4.** The next section of code is the key to the whole program, the Timer1_Tick event. This event subroutine rolls the dice for three seconds, after which the value of the dice is calculated by adding the two numbers together. The timer is then disabled, the button is re-enabled, and the total is displayed in a message box. Once that processing is finished, the code checks to see if the game is over by calling a function called GameOver, which returns true or false. If the game is over, the winner is displayed—otherwise the game goes into the next round.

```
Private Sub Timer1_Tick(ByVal sender As System.Object, _
    ByVal e As System.EventArgs) Handles Timer1.Tick

    RollDie1()
    RollDie2()

    'increment the roll counter
    Rolls += 1

    'stop after 30 rolls (3 seconds)
    If RollOver() Then

        'reset roll counter
        Rolls = 0

        'disable the rolling dice
        Timer1.Enabled = False

        'disable the Roll button
        Button1.Enabled = True

        'display the dice roll for this player
        DisplayRoll(Player)

        'check for game over
        If GameOver() Then
            Button1.Text = "Restart"
            ShowWinner()
```

```
        Else
            'not end of game, go to the next round
            Label5.Text = "Round " & Round
        End If

    End If

End Sub
```

**Section 5.** The next section of code includes the `RestartGame` subroutine. The purpose of this subroutine is to reset all the variables and controls in the game to initial values so that the game can start fresh again.

```
Private Sub RestartGame()
    'reset the game settings
    Button1.Text = "Player 1 - Roll"
    Score1 = 0
    Score2 = 0
    Label4.Text = "SCORE: " & Score1
    Label3.Text = "SCORE: " & Score2
    Round = 1
    Label5.Text = "Round " & Round
    pb1.Image = Die6.Image
    pb2.Image = Die6.Image
End Sub
```

**Section 6.** This section of code includes the `RollDie1` and `RollDie2` subroutines. These two subroutines are very similar in functionality; the only difference is the controls that they update. `RollDie1` rolls the left-hand die and updates its image; `RollDie2` rolls the right-hand die and updates its image. Note the use of the `Rnd` function to generate a random number. This function will be covered in more detail in Chapter 7, "Number Crunching: Mathematical and Relational Operators." The other significant part of these subroutines is the use of a `Select...Case` statement. Note there are six cases in the branching statement corresponding to each of the six sides of a die. The statements are used to set the image of the die on the form.

```
Private Sub RollDie1()
    'generate random roll for die 1
    Roll1 = Int(Rnd() * 6) + 1

    'display the corresponding image (die 1-6)
```

```
        Select Case Roll1
            Case 1
                pb1.Image = Die1.Image
            Case 2
                pb1.Image = Die2.Image
            Case 3
                pb1.Image = Die3.Image
            Case 4
                pb1.Image = Die4.Image
            Case 5
                pb1.Image = Die5.Image
            Case 6
                pb1.Image = Die6.Image
        End Select
    End Sub

Private Sub RollDie2()
    'generate random roll for die 2
    Roll2 = Int(Rnd() * 6) + 1

    'display the corresponding image (die 1-6)
    Select Case Roll2
        Case 1
            pb2.Image = Die1.Image
        Case 2
            pb2.Image = Die2.Image
        Case 3
            pb2.Image = Die3.Image
        Case 4
            pb2.Image = Die4.Image
        Case 5
            pb2.Image = Die5.Image
        Case 6
            pb2.Image = Die6.Image
    End Select
End Sub
```

**Section 7.** The next section includes the RollOver function. This function checks to see if the dice should stop rolling based on a number. It returns a Boolean, which is a True or False value. The test number used in this case is 30. Because the timer is set to 100 milliseconds, and there are 1000 milliseconds in a second, the `Timer1_Tick` event is being called ten times per second. So, a roll counter of 30 equates to three seconds of time while the dice are randomly rolling. Each time through, `Timer1_Tick` calls the `RollOver` function to see if it is time to stop. See the `Timer1_Tick` event for more information.

```
Private Function RollOver() As Boolean
    If Rolls > 30 Then
        RollOver = True
    Else
        RollOver = False
    End If
End Function
```

**Section 8.** This section of code includes the lengthy `DisplayRoll` subroutine. This subroutine includes a parameter to help you understand how parameters can be useful in a program. Note how the subroutine includes a `Select...Case` statement, which checks the `PlayerNum` parameter. The subroutine displays a message depending on the player number. Also, if `PlayerNum = 2`, there is an additional step for Player 2, which includes incrementing the round counter. Finally, if `PlayerNum` is not a recognized number (a 1 or a 2), an error message is displayed.

```
Private Sub DisplayRoll(PlayerNum As Integer)
    'display total roll message depending on player
    Select Case PlayerNum
        Case 1
            'give player 1's score
            MsgBox("Player 1, you rolled a " & Int(Roll1 + Roll2) & ".")
            Score1 += Roll1 + Roll2
            Label4.Text = "SCORE: " & Score1

            'reset for player 2
            Button1.Text = "Player 2 - Roll"
            Player = 2
        Case 2
            'give player 2's score
            MsgBox("Player 2, you rolled a " & Int(Roll1 + Roll2) & ".")
            Score2 += Roll1 + Roll2
            Label3.Text = "SCORE: " & Score2

            'reset for player 1
            Button1.Text = "Player 1 - Roll"
            Player = 1
```

```
            'player 2 marks end of each round
            Round += 1
        Case Else
            MsgBox("PlayerNum is invalid")
    End Select
End Sub
```

**Section 9.** This section includes the GameOver function. This function is really simple; it checks to see if all three rounds have been completed, and then returns True or False.

```
Private Function GameOver() As Boolean
    If Round > 3 Then
        GameOver = True
    Else
        GameOver = False
    End If
End Function
```

**Section 10.** The last section of the program includes the ShowWinner subroutine. This is a support subroutine that uses an If...Then branching statement to determine the winner of the game. It is also smart enough to recognize when the game is a draw.

```
Private Sub ShowWinner()
    'display the winner message
    If Score1 = Score2 Then
        MsgBox("This game is a draw!")
    ElseIf Score1 > Score2 Then
        MsgBox("Player 1 is the winner!")
    ElseIf Score2 > Score1 Then
        MsgBox("Player 2 is the winner!")
    End If
End Sub
```

## Summary

Program logic is absolutely essential for computer programs to be able to do anything. Without the branching statements that make program logic possible, a program can only repeat or store information received. It is left without the ability to make any changes or decisions. Branching statements, such as If...Then and Select...Case, make program logic possible.

Procedures and functions (also called subroutines) are also very important for breaking up large sections of code into manageable parts. Repeatable sections of code can also be eliminated by putting duplicate code inside a subroutine.

## CHALLENGES

The following challenges will help to reinforce the material you have learned in this chapter.

1. Can you think of any ways to break down the source code for DiceWar into more useful subroutines? Try to further break down the program by dividing the current subroutines into even more levels of abstraction.

2. Modify the DiceWar game so that it asks each player to type in their name before the game begins, and then display the player names instead of the generic names. Hint: Use the `InputBox` function to get each player's name, and call it from `Form1_Load`.

3. Modify the DiceWar game so the computer takes control of Player 2, allowing a single player to challenge the computer. Hint: Add a branching statement at the end of `Timer1_Tick`, which automatically calls `Button1_Click` when `Player = 2`.

# Number Crunching: Mathematical and Relational Operators

**T**he last two chapters covered the very important subjects of variables and branching, which are key features of a programming language. This chapter is all about number crunching—a fun way of referring to mathematical and relational operations. These are critically important features needed to write useful programs, as you will soon see. Whereas the basic math operations of addition, subtraction, multiplication, and division are assumed, Visual Basic supports several more operations, such as modulus and exponentiation, as well as numerous statistical and financial math functions.

Here's a short list of the topics covered in this chapter:

- **Project preview—The Math Quiz Program**

- **Mathematical operators**

- **Random numbers**

- **Relational operators**

- **Chapter project—The Math Quiz Program**

Visual Basic .NET makes this rather complicated subject extraordinarily fun, believe it or not, thanks to some wonderful new ways to do math. The new short-cut operators in Visual Basic .NET offer amazing tricks that C and C++ program-mers are quite fond of using. I'll show you how to use this new feature in this chapter. Along the way, you'll learn about random numbers, reading the date and time, relational operators (greater than, equal, less than, and so on), and numerical systems.

## Project Preview—The Math Quiz Program

How much fun is all study and no play? This chapter features a complete project, called Math Quiz, which you will learn to create from scratch. The program will demonstrate all of the subjects covered in this chapter, including math opera-tors, relational operators, random numbers, as well as topics covered in earlier chapters. Figure 7.1 shows what the Math Quiz program looks like.

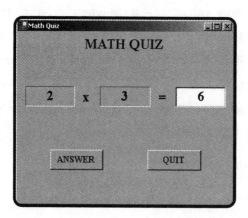

**FIGURE 7.1**

The Math Quiz program demonstrates math and relational operators.

## Mathematical Operators

Visual Basic provides a good assortment of mathematical operators that you can use in your programs. These operators are built into the language. Using num-ber conversion functions, such as CLng (for converting to a Long) and CDbl (for converting to a `Double`), you can apply mathematical operations to a variety of variables in a program. Visual Basic performs number conversion on the fly, based on the result of the operation.

## Basic Number Crunching

At the most basic level are the mathematical operations for completing addition, subtraction, multiplication, division, modulus, and exponents.

### Addition

The plus sign (+) is used to add numbers together, including numbers of different types. This includes variable assignment and formulas used in branching statements. Addition is commonly used to increment the value of a counter variable. For example:

```
Dim N As Integer = 0
N = N + 10
```

Note the use of an initializer for the variable `N`. Although Visual Basic automatically sets numbers to zero upon initialization, it is sometimes convenient to include the explicit initializer. The second line, `N = N + 10`, is called a formula because the variable is *receiving* the value of an addition operation. You could just as easily use a function (discussed in the last chapter) to return a number that is assigned to the variable. For example:

```
Private Function Twelve() As Integer
    Twelve = 12
End Function

Dim N As Integer = 0
N = 10 + Twelve()
```

Now, suppose you try to add some letters to a number; what do you think will happen? Because the number was created as an `Integer` data type, the Visual Basic compiler will complain if you try to add a `String` to it. For example, the following code

```
Dim N As Integer = 0
N = 10 + "ABC"
```

will generate a runtime error message, as shown in Figure 7.2.

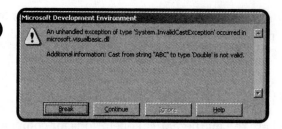

**FIGURE 7.2**

If you try to add a String to an Integer, Visual Basic will generate a runtime error.

Visual Basic .NET provides a new way to add a number to a variable, called a *shortcut operator*, which looks like this: +=. Here is an example:

```
Dim N As Integer = 0
N += 10
```

The shortcut operator only works when you need to add something to a variable. You can't add two numbers together using a shortcut operator without a variable. The shortcut operator is now built into Visual Basic, because data types are now objects with properties and methods (as you learned in Chapter 5, "Variables and Data Types"). The += operator is a special kind of method for each of the numeric data types (such as Integer, Long, Double, and so on). If you have used a previous version of Visual Basic, you will likely find shortcut operators a wonderful new feature of the language.

### Subtraction

Subtraction is also standard; it's easy to use without realizing that the subtraction operator is now built into the basic data type objects, just like the addition operator. Here is an example:

```
Dim N As Integer = 100
Dim P As Integer = 25
N = N - P
```

You may also use the shortcut operator for subtraction as well. For instance:

```
Dim N As Integer = 100
N -= 10
```

### Multiplication

Multiplication was invented to make adding and subtracting easier because it allows you to add or subtract many numbers quite easily. Like most programming languages, Visual Basic uses the asterisk (*) for multiplication. Here is an example:

```
Dim A As Integer = 9
Dim B As Integer = 6
Console.WriteLine(A & " times " & B & " = " & A * B)
```

Here is what the Console message looks like:

```
9 times 6 = 54
```

As you might have guessed, there is also a shortcut operator for multiplication, and I'll wager that you can guess what it looks like! If you guessed *=, then you were right!

```
Dim A As Integer = 12
A *= 12
```

How about a real-world example? The circumference of a circle is two times the radius times pi, or C = 2πr. Expressed in Visual Basic source code, here is how you can calculate it (note: the last line is a comment showing the result you should get by running this mini program):

```
Dim Radius As Integer = 10
Dim Circumference As Decimal
Circumference = 2 * System.Math.PI * Radius
'the answer is 62.8318530717959
```

## Division

The average human mind can handle addition, subtraction, and multiplication with ease, but for some reason, most people have trouble with division (particularly involving large numbers). Division used to be problematic for the central processors in computers because division requires a lot more work. Fortunately, modern processors are optimized to handle division quickly and efficiently. There is no longer any benefit to using integers just to speed up a program. Use whatever data type you want, and let Visual Basic worry about optimization! Here is an example of integer division:

```
Dim A As Integer = 12
Dim B As Integer = 4
Dim C As Integer
C = A \ B
```

You may want to consider using a floating-point number any time you need to divide numbers because integer division drops the remainder. There are two ways to divide numbers in Visual Basic. First, standard division uses the forward slash character (/). This is below the question mark on your keyboard. Second, the backslash character (\), which is above the Enter key on your keyboard, is designed to return just an integer as an answer, dropping any remainder. Be sure to learn the difference between these characters because the latter one doesn't work for floating-point numbers (such as Decimal, Single, and Double). Use Table 7.1 as a reference.

**TABLE 7.1 DIVISION CHARACTERS**

| Char | Name | Description |
|---|---|---|
| / | Forward slash | Floating-point division (decimal remainder) |
| \ | Backslash | Integer division (no remainder) |

Here is another example of a division operation, this time using a floating-point number:

```
Dim A As Decimal = 973.65
Dim B As Decimal = 18.50
Dim C As Decimal
C = A / B
```

 If you have a hard time remembering which division character to use, consider this analogy. The backslash is a downward slope that's quick and easy (using integers), whereas the forward slash is a hill that's difficult to climb (using decimals). You can also think of integers as a "downgrade" in precision, whereas thinking of floats as an "upgrade" in precision.

## Modulus

After talking so much about remainders in floating-point and integer division, it is fitting that the next operator is the modulus, or Mod, operator. This works similarly to the other math operators, except there is no shortcut for modulus because you must use the word *Mod*. Here is an example:

```
Dim A As Integer = 10
Dim B As Integer = 3
Dim C As Integer
C = A Mod B
```

The result of the last statement is that C = 1. Can you figure out why? When you divide 10 by 3, the answer is 3, but there is a remainder of 1. Mod ignores the answer and returns the remainder. Although this might not seem very useful to you at present, Mod is an extremely powerful math operator that can solve some uniquely difficult problems. One classic example is determining whether a number is an integer or float by looking at the remainder. You can perform that check using the following condition:

```
If A Mod B = 0 Then
```

Here is a complete example:

```
If A Mod 2 = 0 Then
    MsgBox("The variable is a whole number")
Else
    MsgBox("The variable is a floating-point number")
End If
```

## The Simple Math Program

To help demonstrate the basic math operators, I have created a program called Simple Math, located on the CD-ROM in the directory for this chapter under \SimpleMath. Rather than create the program from scratch, load the project off the CD-ROM and give it a whirl. Figure 7.3 shows what the program looks like.

The Simple Math program demonstrates how basic math operators work, while functioning as a simple calculator.

## Advanced Number Crunching

Visual Basic supports many more useful and advanced math functions than those covered to this point, including functions for trigonometry, statistics, and accounting. Table 7.2 shows a complete list of methods and properties available in the System.Math object. If you would like to see how to use these functions, type **System.Math** in the code editor, and IntelliSense will give you a drop-down list, which you can use to peruse the parameters of each math function. The next few sections highlight some of the more common advanced math functions.

## TABLE 7.2 SYSTEM.MATH PROPERTIES AND METHODS

| Name | Description |
| --- | --- |
| E | Natural logarithm |
| PI | The value of PI out to 20 digits |
| Abs | Absolute value |
| Acos | Arc cosine of an angle |
| Asin | Arc sine of an angle |
| Atan | Arc tangent of an angle |
| Atan2 | Arc tangent of an angle with two numbers |
| Ceiling | Rounding to the smallest whole number |
| Cos | Cosine of an angle |
| Cosh | Hyperbolic cosine of an angle |
| Exp | Number e raised to a power |
| Floor | Rounding to the largest whole number |
| IEEERemainder | Floating-point modulus |
| Log | Natural logarithm (e) of a number |
| Log10 | Base-10 logarithm of a number |
| Max | Larger of two numbers |
| Min | Smaller of two numbers |
| Pow | Floating-point number raised to a power |
| Round | Rounded number to a specified number of digits |
| Sign | Sign of a number |
| Sin | Sine of an angle |
| Sinh | Hyperbolic sine of an angle |
| Sqrt | Square root of a number |
| Tan | Tangent of an angle |
| Tanh | Hyperbolic tangent of an angle |

### Absolute Value

One of the most frequently needed math functions is Abs, which returns the absolute value of a number, which might be positive or negative. Abs is helpful when dealing with error-prone data that was entered manually. For example:

```
Dim PayRate As Decimal = 32.50
Dim HoursWorked As Integer = -80
Dim Income As Decimal
Income = PayRate * Abs(HoursWorked)
```

## Exponents

There is another basic math operator in Visual Basic that can be very useful: the exponent operator (^). The exponent operator is invoked by pressing Shift+6. Exponents work with powers of a number, or rather, the number multiplied by itself, for example, 9 x 9 = 81 and 9 x 9 x 9 = 729. An easier way to write this is 9 ^ 2 = 81 and 9 ^ 3 = 729. When dealing with large powers of a number, the exponent operator is very handy indeed. Here is an example:

```
Dim A As Integer = 10
Dim B As Integer = 10
Console.WriteLine("{0} ^ {1} = {2}", A, B, A ^ B)
```

The output window in Visual Basic should show this line:

```
10 ^ 10 = 10000000000
```

That's a whopping big number! Be careful when using exponents because seemingly small numbers raised to a power suddenly become enormous.

## Square Roots

The opposite of a number raised to the second power (N ^ 2) is the square root of a number. Take an earlier example, 9 x 9 = 81. The square root of 81 is 9, or rather, Sqrt(81) = 9. Remember, this differs from exponents in that square root only applies to a squared number. Here is an example:

```
Dim A As Integer = 100
Dim B As Integer
B = Sqrt(A)
'the answer is 10
```

# Random Numbers

A random number is often needed to *mix up* something, such as a deck of cards or a pair of dice, and is often applied to real-world analogies. Randomness also comes into play when dealing with data encryption and compression, as well as in simulation programs (such as business and financial simulations).

## Creating Random Numbers

Visual Basic provides an easy-to-use random number generator called Rnd, a function that returns a Single (which is similar to the Decimal and Double floating-point data types). The important thing to remember when using Rnd is that it generates decimal numbers between 0 and 1, inclusively. Here are some examples of random numbers generated with Rnd:

```
0.39239482
0.01093848
0.93827834
```

As you can see, these numbers all fall between 0 and 1. But how useful is that, after all, if you need larger numbers? Although Rnd values might be decimals, that doesn't prevent you from treating them like integers; simply multiply the Rnd value by whatever maximum value you need.

### Using Rnd

Usually you will need numbers returned as whole numbers, not floating-point numbers. To convert a float to an integer, you use the Int function, like this example that simulates rolling a six-sided die:

```
Dim A As Integer
A = Int(Rnd() * 6) + 1
```

### Using Randomize

Random numbers generated in Visual Basic are repeatable, meaning that if you stop a program and re-start it again, the same numbers will be generated in the very same order. To get around this problem and generate truly random numbers in every instance, you must seed the random number generator so that it uses something other than the default of zero. The Randomize function was created for this purpose. Any time you need to use random numbers, simply call Randomize in the Form1_Load event, and that will take care of it. The Math Quiz program later in the chapter uses this method to seed the random number generator.

## Relational Operators

The human mind is capable of seeing the differences and relationships between individual things and groups of things, such as cars in a car lot. By simply driving past a car lot, you are probably able to tell at a glance what types of cars are being offered for sale, such as pickup trucks, compact cars, vans, and sport-utility vehicles.

Computer programs are not blessed with the ability to instantly come to a conclusion with limited information. Rather, computers must evaluate differences at a highly detailed and specific level. For instance, a human might look at two cars and claim that they are absolutely identical. But a computer might examine the same two cars and find that they are made of different components, built in different years, and even point out flaws in the paint. As a result, computers are able to examine things with great precision, something humans are incapable of doing.

## Object Relationships

Relational operators deal with how values compare to each other, or rather, how they relate to each other. Relational operators are usually found within formulas that result in a Boolean (true or false) value, and are based on simple rules, such as equal, not equal, greater than, and less than. The way that objects relate to each other is determined by their data types. Variables of the same data type can relate directly without any conversion needed. But variables of different data types require some form of conversion before they can be compared using a relational operator.

Visual Basic usually converts data types automatically, but there are times when the conversion just doesn't work. For example, the section earlier in this chapter on addition showed how Visual Basic generated a runtime error because it was not able to convert "ABC" to a number in order to perform a math operation. The same applies to relational formulas that result in a Boolean. The important thing to remember is that Visual Basic may interpret a formula incorrectly when working with different data types, therefore you may want to use an explicit conversion function, as listed in Table 7.3.

## Relational Operators

The actual operators used to perform relational comparisons are covered next, with a description of how to use each one. Table 7.4 provides a quick reference.

### Equal To (=)

The *equal to* operator, (=), is used to test for the equality of two values in a formula. The equal sign is also used to assign values to a variable, but Visual Basic is smart enough to tell the difference. Here is an example of a test for an equal condition:

```
If (A = B) Then
    MsgBox("True")
Else
    MsgBox("False")
End If
```

## TABLE 7.3  DATA TYPE CONVERSION FUNCTIONS

| Name | Description |
|------|-------------|
| CBool | Convert passed value to a Boolean |
| CByte | Convert passed value to a Byte |
| CChar | Convert passed value to a Char |
| CDate | Convert passed value to a Date |
| CDbl | Convert passed value to a Double |
| CDec | Convert passed value to a Decimal |
| CInt | Convert passed value to an Integer |
| CLng | Convert passed value to a Long |
| CObj | Convert passed value to an Object |
| CShort | Convert passed value to a Short |
| CSng | Convert passed value to a Single |
| CStr | Convert passed value to a String |

## TABLE 7.4  RELATIONAL OPERATORS

| Operator | Description |
|----------|-------------|
| = | Equal to |
| <> | Not equal to |
| < | Less than |
| > | Greater than |
| <= | Less than or equal to |
| >= | Greater than or equal to |

### Not Equal To (<>)

To test for inequality use the *not equal to* operator (<>) in a formula, such as the following (note that I've surrounded formulas with parentheses for clarity):

```
If (A <> B) Then
    MsgBox("True")
Else
```

```
        MsgBox("False")
End If
```

## Less Than (<)

The *less than* operator (<) returns true when the first operand is less than the second operand in a formula. Keep in mind that this applies to any data type. You could compare two strings—if the ASCII values of the first string are less than the ASCII values of the second string, the less than comparison will return true, even though it might seem strange to compare strings in this way. Here is an example:

```
If (A < B) Then
    MsgBox("True")
Else
    MsgBox("False")
End If
```

## Greater Than (>)

The *greater than* operator (>) returns true when the first operand is greater than the second operand in a formula, as the following example demonstrates (if you would like to test this code yourself, simply fill in A and B with your own variable names):

```
If (A > B) Then
    MsgBox("True")
Else
    MsgBox("False")
End If
```

## Less Than or Equal To (<=)

The *less than or equal to* operator (<=) is a combination of two other operators: equal to (=) and less than (<). Here is an example:

```
If (A <= B) Then
    MsgBox("True")
Else
    MsgBox("False")
End If
```

Remember that combining two operators in this way is the equivalent of checking each one separately. You could accomplish the same result by creating a formula that combines both operators using the logical Or operator, as follows:

```
If (A < B) Or (A = B) Then
    MsgBox("True")
Else
    MsgBox("False")
End If
```

### Greater Than or Equal To (>=)

The last relational operator, *greater than or equal to* (>=) is also a combination of two operators: greater than (>) and equal to (=). Here is an example:

```
If (A >= B) Then
    MsgBox("True")
Else
    MsgBox("False")
End If
```

Similar to the previous example, you can accomplish the same thing by writing a compound relational formula, such as this:

```
If (A > B) Or (A = B) Then
    MsgBox("True")
Else
    MsgBox("False")
End If
```

## Chapter Project—The Math Quiz Program

The Math Quiz program was designed to demonstrate the concepts learned in this chapter, including examples of math formulas, relational operators, branching statements, and subroutines. Figure 7.4 shows a screenshot of the program asking the player to solve a math problem. Figure 7.5 shows the result of answering the math problem correctly, whereas Figure 7.6 shows the result of an incorrect answer.

### Designing the Project

Okay, let's get started creating the Math Quiz program. Create a new project in Visual Basic .NET by selecting File, New, Project, or by selecting New Project from the Start Page. Alternatively, you can load the project off the CD-ROM. The project is located in the folder for this chapter under \MathQuiz. Make sure you select a Windows Application for the project type (see Figure 7.7).

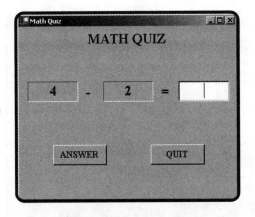

**FIGURE 7.4**

The Math Quiz
program challenges
the player with
simple math
problems.

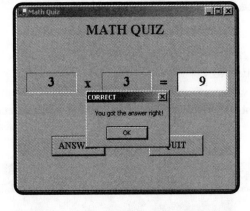

**FIGURE 7.5**

Answer the math
problem correctly,
and you will be
praised!

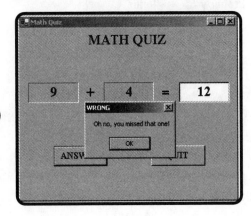

**FIGURE 7.6**

Answer the math
problem incorrectly,
and a polite
message lets the
player down gently.

By now, I'm confident that you are able to create user interfaces in Visual Basic with a good level of proficiency, therefore I'm going to list controls that you need to add to the form, along with their properties (see Table 7.4). This is the most efficient way to explain how to set up a user interface. After you are finished

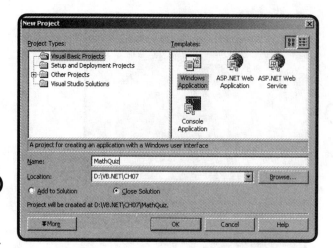

**FIGURE 7.7**

Creating the new project for the Math Quiz program.

setting up the form, the next section covers the source code behind the form that makes the program useful.

 **HINT** If you are not comfortable with adding controls to a form and setting properties, refer back to Chapter 3, "The Basics of a Graphical User Interface," for a refresher.

## TABLE 7.5 MATHQUIZ USER INTERFACE

| Object | Name | Property | Value |
|--------|------|----------|-------|
| Form | Form1 | Size | 393, 323 |
| | | Text | Math Quiz |
| Label | Label1 | Location | 10, 5 |
| | | Size | 370, 35 |
| | | Text | MATH QUIZ |
| | | Font | Times New Roman, 18pt, style=Bold |
| | | TextAlign | MiddleCenter |
| | | ForeColor | Navy |
| Label | Label2 | Location | 15, 95 |
| | | Size | 90, 35 |
| | | Text | (blank) |
| | | Font | Times New Roman, 18pt, style=Bold |
| | | TextAlign | MiddleCenter |
| | | BorderStyle | Fixed3D |

## TABLE 7.5  MATHQUIZ USER INTERFACE

| Object | Name | Property | Value |
|---|---|---|---|
| Label | Label3 | Location | 150, 95 |
| | | Size | 90, 35 |
| | | Text | (blank) |
| | | Font | Times New Roman, 18pt, style=Bold |
| | | TextAlign | MiddleCenter |
| | | BorderStyle | Fixed3D |
| Label | Label4 | Location | 115, 100 |
| | | AutoSize | True |
| | | Font | Times New Roman, 18pt, style=Bold |
| | | Text | + |
| Label | Label5 | Location | 250, 100 |
| | | AutoSize | True |
| | | Font | Times New Roman, 18pt, style=Bold |
| | | Text | = |
| TextBox | TextBox1 | Location | 285, 95 |
| | | Size | 90, 35 |
| | | Font | Times New Roman, 18pt, style=Bold |
| | | TextAlign | Center |
| | | Text | (blank) |
| Button | Button1 | Location | 60, 205 |
| | | Size | 96, 35 |
| | | Font | Times New Roman, 12pt, style=Bold |
| | | Text | ANSWER |
| | | TextAlign | MiddleCenter |
| | | ForeColor | 0, 0, 192 |
| Button | Button2 | Location | 235, 205 |
| | | Size | 96, 35 |
| | | Font | Times New Roman, 12pt, style=Bold |
| | | TextAlign | MiddleCenter |
| | | Text | QUIT |
| | | ForeColor | 0, 0, 192 |

After adding all of the controls shown in Table 7.4, the user interface for the Math Quiz program should look like the one shown in Figure 7.8.

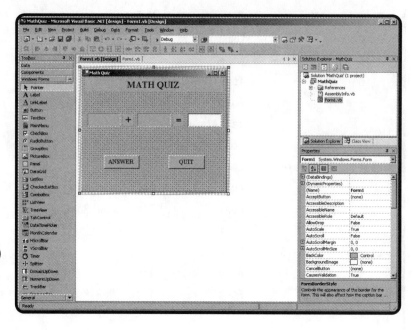

**FIGURE 7.8**

The completed user interface for the Math Quiz program.

## Writing the Source Code

The source code for Math Quiz is only about two pages in length and well commented. You should be able to follow the flow of the program and get an idea of how it works just by reading the source code. I'll break up the listing and explain each subroutine that follows. Remember to type this code in after the generated region line that hides the form code.

`Form1_Load` is the first event that you should type into the program. Again, you don't have to type all of this in that hard way! If you have finished creating the user interface, you can double-click the form and each control to bring up its default event in the code editor. `Form1_Load` is the default event that appears when you double-click a blank portion of the form. Using this method, you avoid having to type in the subroutine name and parameters.

```
Dim Answer As Integer

Private Sub Form1_Load(ByVal sender As System.Object, _
    ByVal e As System.EventArgs) Handles MyBase.Load

    'seed the random number generator
```

```
        Randomize()

        'initialize the game
        CreateMathProblem()


    End Sub
```

The first button, Button1, has a single event, Button1_Click, which runs when you click the button. The following code makes sure the user has typed a valid number into TextBox1 and then checks to see if the answer is correct, displaying the appropriate message for a correct or an incorrect answer. After that, another math problem is created, and the answer field is cleared.

```
    Private Sub Button1_Click(ByVal sender As System.Object, _
        ByVal e As System.EventArgs) Handles Button1.Click

        'make sure answer is a number
        If IsNumeric(TextBox1.Text) = False Then
            'display error message
            MsgBox("Please enter a number.")
        Else
            'check the answer
            If Val(TextBox1.Text) = Answer Then
                MsgBox("You got the answer right!", , "CORRECT")
            Else
                MsgBox("Oh no, you missed that one!", , "WRONG")
            End If
        End If

        'create a new math problem
        CreateMathProblem()

        'clear the answer field
        TextBox1.Text = ""

    End Sub
```

The second button event, Button2_Click, is used to end the program and couldn't be much simpler.

```
    Private Sub Button2_Click(ByVal sender As System.Object, _
        ByVal e As System.EventArgs) Handles Button2.Click
```

```
'quit button ends the program
End


End Sub
```

Now for the meat of the program: `CreateMathProblem`. This is a reusable subroutine (meaning that it is called from more than one place in the program), which generates two random numbers and a random math operator, filling in the values on the form (meaning, those values are inserted into the `Label` controls). To make the code as simple as possible, the answer to the math problem is pre-calculated depending on the math operator. A single line takes care of the formula and branching statement together:

```
Select Case Int(Rnd() * 3)
```

This is quite an efficient way to write the code because there is no need for a variable to generate a random math operator, which is stored in a label on the form. So in effect, this code avoids two variables that are really not needed but might have been used. If you prefer to use variables to make your programs easier to understand, by all means do so. I am simply providing some insight into the field of computer science in which there are always many ways to solve a problem.

```
Private Sub CreateMathProblem()
    Dim First As Integer
    Dim Second As Integer

    'randomize the first field
    First = Int(Rnd() * 10)
    Label2.Text = First

    'randomize the second field
    Second = Int(Rnd() * 10)
    Label3.Text = Second

    'set the math operator and answer
    Select Case Int(Rnd() * 3)
        Case 0
            'addition problem
            Label4.Text = "+"
            Answer = First + Second
        Case 1
            'subtraction problem
```

```
            Label4.Text = "-"
            Answer = First - Second
        Case 2
            'multiplication problem
            Label4.Text = "x"
            Answer = First * Second
    End Select

    End Sub
```

Now, go ahead and run the program by pressing F5. If there are any syntax errors in the program due to typos, you will need to fix the errors before the program will run.

## Summary

Well, that about sums up the math chapter (pun intended). This chapter talked about basic and advanced math operators and functions, relational operators, as well as random numbers, and included a sample game called Math Quiz, which helped strengthen your grasp of these topics.

---

### CHALLENGES

The following challenges will help to reinforce the material you have learned in this chapter.

1. Modify the Math Quiz game so that it challenges the player by using numbers larger than ten—for instance, up to twenty.

2. Modify the Math Quiz game so that it uses a Timer control to limit the amount of time the user is allowed to answer the question. Add a label that shows the timer counting down the seconds.

3. Modify the Math Quiz game so that it keeps track of the player's score by adding a point for every correct answer and deducting two points for every incorrect answer. If you are feeling ambitious, allow the game to keep track of the high score and individual players.

CHAPTER

8

# Loops, Arrays, and Structures

This chapter covers an important programming concept called *looping*, which is essential for handling large amounts of information (something at which computers excel). There are several types of loops that you can perform in Visual Basic .NET, and there are several ways to store complex data types usually associated with repetition. I will discuss the following in this chapter:

- Introduction to looping commands

- Introduction to arrays

- Introducing to structures

# Introduction to Looping Commands

Looping is a way of repeating something to accomplish a task (such as summarizing or averaging some values) or to process a long list of information. For example, it requires a loop to load a text file and display it in a TextBox because the program must load each byte of the text file in order. Another example of a repeating process is drawing a picture on the screen, one pixel at a time, as each pixel in the picture file (which might be saved as a JPG, GIF, BMP, or other format) is copied to the screen.

## What Is a Loop?

A loop is, therefore, a process of repeating or iterating through a series, from a starting point to a fixed-ending point, or upon the completion of a condition. Suppose you have a list of names, as follows:

- Bob
- Jane
- Mary
- Steve
- Andrew
- Michelle
- Laura

If you need to print out all this information, you could display each name separately, like this:

```
MsgBox("Bob is #1")
MsgBox("Jane is #2")
MsgBox("Mary is #3")
MsgBox("Steve is #4")
MsgBox("Andrew is #5")
MsgBox("Michelle is #6")
MsgBox("Laura is #7")
```

That might work for small lists, but what about lists with hundreds, thousands, or millions of entries? Computer databases could easily have millions of records, after all, and there's no way you can process each one individually. Obviously, a looping command is needed!

Suppose the list of names is stored in a `ListBox` (as shown in Figure 8.1), and you want to copy that list to a `TextBox`. A loop is a great way to accomplish this, as the Looping Names program demonstrates. If you would like to run this program, copy it off the CD-ROM for this chapter under the folder called \LoopingNames.

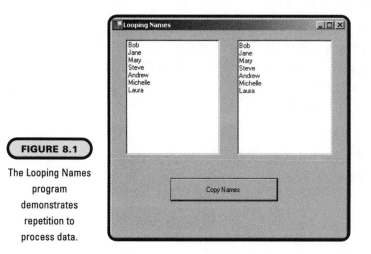

**FIGURE 8.1**

The Looping Names program demonstrates repetition to process data.

Similarly, a list of numbers can be processed with a looping command, as demonstrated in the Looping Numbers program (shown in Figure 8.2).

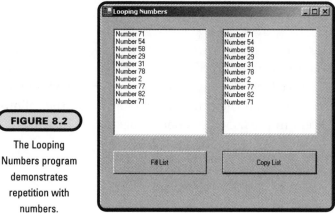

**FIGURE 8.2**

The Looping Numbers program demonstrates repetition with numbers.

## Iteration and Repetition

How might you iterate through a series of sequential numbers? First, you start with a variable that is set to one. Each time through the loop, you add one to the variable. At the end of the loop, the variable will equal some number. Here is the basic concept:

1. Start with a value.
2. Add one to the value.
3. Repeat until a condition is met.

The condition that needs to be met might be a Boolean formula, such as (Num > 100) or (A = B). The condition might also be that the counter variable has reached a certain number. This is what computer science calls a For...Next loop, odd as that may sound. The reason it is called a For...Next loop is because something happens "for every pass through the loop."

## For...Next Loop

The Visual Basic For loop looks like this:

```
For variable = start To finish
    repeating commands
Next variable
```

Here is what the loop in the Looping Names program looks like:

```
For n = 0 To ListBox1.Items.Count - 1
    TextBox1.Text &= ListBox1.Items.Item(n)
    TextBox1.Text &= vbCrLf
Next
```

Now, what kinds of problems can be solved with a For...Next loop? Plenty! Just about any situation in which you need to process a ListBox or ComboBox control, for example, calls for a For...Next loop. You might also use a For...Next loop to display things, such as the names of all the controls on a form. Add the following code to the Form1_Load event in the Looping Names program:

```
Dim n As Long
For n = 0 To Controls.Count() - 1
    Console.WriteLine("Control #" & n + 1 & " : " & _
        Controls.Item(n).Name)
Next
```

That code listing includes a For...Next loop. Do you see it? Look at the function called Controls.Count(). Controls is a collection that stores all the controls on a form, and you can loop through the controls without even knowing what they are called, thanks to the power of the For...Next loop. Here is the output from that snippet of code:

```
Control #1 : Button2
Control #2 : Button1
Control #3 : TextBox1
Control #4 : ListBox1
```

## Do Loops

The Do loop is another form of looping command built into Visual Basic. Whereas For...Next loops are adept at handling number sequences, Do loops (Do While... and Do...Until) excel when it comes to relational looping, in which a process will repeatedly loop until some Boolean condition is satisfied. There are four variations of the Do loop, and I'll cover each one individually.

### Do While...Loop

The first form of the Do loop is the Do While...Loop. This version causes the enclosed commands to repeat as long as the condition is true. You can paraphrase it like this: "While the condition is true, continue repeating the commands." Because of this wording format, it's possible that the repeating commands might never execute if the condition is false from the start. Here is the format for this version of the loop:

```
Do While condition
    repeating commands
Loop
```

The Do While...Loop command is more versatile than the For...Next loop because you can have multiple conditions applied to the loop through every iteration. For example:

```
Do While FileOpen = True and EndOfFile = False
    'process the file
Loop
```

### Do...Loop While

The Do...Loop While command is the reverse of the Do While...Loop command.

The format of the condition and the way this loop handles repetition is similar, but there is one difference.

Here is the format of the command:

```
Do
     repeating commands
Loop While condition
```

The `Do...Loop While` command will *always* run at least once through the repeatable commands because the condition is located at the bottom of the loop. Therefore, if you want to perform a loop at least once, but not necessarily more than once (unless a condition is met), you will want to use the `Do...Loop While` command. Here is an example:

```
Do
     'process the file
Loop While FileOpen = True
```

## Do Until...Loop

The third type of `Do` loop is the `Do Until...Loop` command. This one is also similar to the other `Do` loops, but this format differs from the `Do While...Loop` in that it continues to repeat *until* the condition is met, rather than *while* the condition is met. It is the negative version of the `Do` loop that continues as long as the condition is false. Here is the general format of the `Do Until...Loop` command:

```
Do Until condition
     repeating commands
Loop
```

Here is an example of the `Do Until...Loop` command. Note that the Boolean statement now looks for the variable to equal `False` before exiting the loop.

```
Do Until FileOpen = False
     'process the file
Loop
```

## Do...Loop Until

The fourth version of the `Do` loop is `Do...Loop Until`. This is the late conditional form of the `Do Until...Loop`, in which the condition is checked at the end of the loop rather than at the beginning. Therefore, this loop is guaranteed to process the repeating commands at least once.

```
Do
    repeating commands
Loop Until condition
```

Here is an example:

```
Do
    'process the file
Loop Until FileOpen = False
```

## Arrays

Looping commands really start to make sense when dealing with long lists of information, as the preceding section demonstrated. But what happens when you don't have a ListBox control handy to use as a container for the information? The answer is an array, which is a variable that has many elements.

## What Is an Array?

Suppose you have a variable called Age, declared as an Integer, which holds your age. What if you would like to keep track of the age of everyone in your family or your class? You could create many Age variables, as follows:

```
Dim Age1 As Integer
Dim Age2 As Integer
Dim Age3 As Integer
Dim Age4 As Integer
Dim Age5 As Integer
Dim Age6 As Integer
Dim Age7 As Integer
```

That is an inefficient way to handle all of the data, and there is an additional problem that arises when you add another variable to the list, such as Age8. When you do that, you will have to go back and modify the program so that Age8 is used properly. Obviously, there must be a better way.

## Declaring a Variable Array

The answer is an array. This is how you would declare the Age array:

```
Dim Ages(8) As Integer
```

Doesn't that look a lot more efficient? Not only can you iterate through an array with a looping command, you can also add new elements to an array at will, and if your program is written properly, you won't need to rewrite anything to add more elements.

## Understanding Arrays

Let's devise a hypothetical situation to help illustrate. There are eight people in your class, and you want to write a program that displays all of their ages using only a few lines of code, because you are in a hurry to get it finished. First, you need to declare an array of names to go along with the Age array:

```
Dim Names(8) As String
```

 **Arrays in Visual Basic .NET are zero-based, while arrays were one-based by default in Visual Basic 6.0 (unless the** Option Base 0 **statement was used).**

First, you need to fill the array with some data. For the sake of simplicity, let's do it the hard way. A more elegant solution would be to store the names and ages in a text file and then load that file into the array. But files are for another chapter. For now, here is how you might load the Names and Ages arrays:

```
Names(0) = "Thomas"
Ages(0) = 32
Names(1) = "James"
Ages(1) = 20
Names(2) = "Percy"
Ages(2) = 24
Names(3) = "Gordon"
Ages(3) = 38
Names(4) = "Harold"
Ages(4) = 49
Names(5) = "Terence"
Ages(5) = 17
Names(6) = "Annie"
Ages(6) = 32
Names(7) = "Clarabell"
Ages(7) = 25
```

Now that the arrays have been filled with sample data, let's write a loop to quickly display the arrays:

```
Dim n As Integer
For n = 0 To 7
```

```
        Console.WriteLine("{0} is {1} years old.", Names(n), Ages(n))
Next
```

If you would like to run the program in its entirety, you can open the NamesAges Arrays program on the CD-ROM from the folder for this chapter, under \NamesAges Arrays. The output from the program is shown in Figure 8.3.

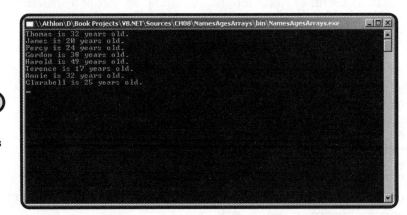

**FIGURE 8.3**

The NamesAgesArrays program fills and then displays the contents of two arrays.

Arrays are extremely useful programming *constructs* that simplify and automate the processing of sequential lists of information. But, when it comes to using multiple arrays to accomplish a task, as the NamesAgesArrays program demonstrated, there is a better way. In fact, when it comes to computer programming, it is wise to be prepared for change because there is *always* a better way to write a program, no matter how much research and effort you put into it. The science of it is what draws many people into careers as software developers.

## Structures

The preceding section demonstrated how to combine two arrays of related information in a display. That method did work, but it was inefficient. For one thing, what if the names and ages need to be sorted? Sorting one of the arrays would mess up the sequence of the other array. What happens if you need to keep track of several more pieces of information about each person in this hypothetical situation, such as height and weight? Things could become messy in a hurry with four arrays to deal with. The answer, as you might have guessed from the name of this section, is something called a *structure*.

> **Definition**
>
> A *construct* is an obnoxious and overused word in computer science, which refers to a complex statement, command, or data type. I usually refer to those things by name rather than in the abstract (with exception to the previous paragraph).

## What Is a Structure?

A structure is a programming construct (there's that word again!) that combines several variables into a group, which is then handled as a single entity. The real power of a structure, then, is the ability to create an array of that structure, rather than multiple arrays for each variable. Sound interesting? It is that, and extremely useful as well. Here is the general format of a structure:

```
Structure struct_name
    variable1 As data_type
    variable2 As data_type
    variable3 As data_type
End Structure
```

## Filling a Structure with Variables

Let's create a real structure based on the Names and Ages arrays created in the previous section. Here is how you might design the structure in order to incorporate the previous two arrays:

```
Structure Classmates
    Dim Name As String
    Dim Age As Integer
End Structure
```

As you can see, it looks very similar to the individual array declarations for Names and Ages, but I have made the variable names singular. One important point to note is that once inside a structure, variables are referred to as methods.

## Using Structure Arrays

Once you have created the structure, you can declare an array variable of the structure like this:

```
Dim people(8) As Classmates
```

Filling a structure array differs a little from filling a simple variable array. How do you get to those variables (oops, I mean methods) after you have created the structure array? Well, for starters, take a look at the variable itself, called people. There you will find the clue to accessing the methods within. As with built-in objects in Visual Basic .NET, such as System.Math (which you learned about in Chapter 7, "Number Crunching: Mathematical and Relational Operators"), Visual Basic provides the IntelliSense drop-down list any time you type in the name of an object followed by a period.

If you have Visual Basic .NET open, go ahead and create a new console application project, and type in the preceding structure definition, so you can try this out. Alternatively, you can load the Structures project from the folder for this chapter on the CD-ROM, under \Structures.

Now, move the cursor to the blank line under `Sub Main()` and type in the following:

```
people(0).
```

That's it, just `people(0)` followed by a period. Because you declared `people` to be a structure array, you should see the drop-down list showing the two methods in that structure (see Figure 8.4).

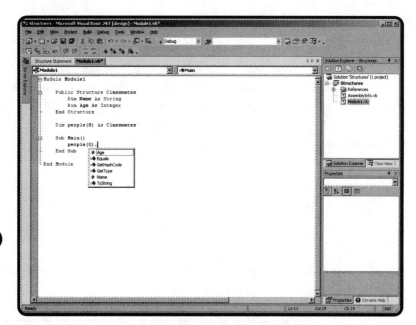

IntelliSense provides a list of the methods in the structure.

But wait, what are those other items in the drop-down list? `Equals`, `GetHashCode`, `GetType`, and `ToString` don't belong in there! After all, the structure just has two methods: `Name` and `Age`. Don't worry about those extra methods. They are just standard methods built in that Visual Basic .NET adds to the structure definition for advanced use.

Okay, now you at least have an idea of how to access the methods inside a structure. So, let's fill in the names and ages in this structure array to see how it works:

```
people(0).Name = "Thomas"
people(0).Age = 32
people(1).Name = "James"
```

```
people(1).Age = 20
people(2).Name = "Percy"
people(2).Age = 24
people(3).Name = "Gordon"
people(3).Age = 38
people(4).Name = "Harold"
people(4).Age = 49
people(5).Name = "Terence"
people(5).Age = 17
people(6).Name = "Annie"
people(6).Age = 32
people(7).Name = "Clarabell"
people(7).Age = 25
```

See how the structure name (people) now references the array index (0 to 7) instead of the method names? It makes more sense to do it this way, and it's more logical. Now you can add more methods to the structure and reference them like you did with Name and Age. Let's print out the array so you can see how that looks with a looping command.

```
Dim n As Integer
For n = 0 To 7
    Console.WriteLine("{0} is {1} years old.", _
        people(n).Name, people(n).Age)
Next
```

Figure 8.5 shows the output of the Structures program, which should look the same as the NamesAgesArrays program.

**FIGURE 8.5**

The Structures program shows how to use an array of structures.

# Summary

This chapter presented an introduction to looping statements, such as For...Next and Do While...Loop, that help to repeat commands until a condition is met. From there, the subject of arrays came up, with a discussion of how to use looping to iterate through an array, which is much easier than referencing each item in an array individually. Finally, the subject of structures was discussed as a way to make array handling easier, particularly when dealing with many variables. Structures help to reduce the number of variable arrays in a program by combining related variables in a group.

## CHALLENGES

The following challenges will help to reinforce the material you have learned in this chapter.

1. Add more methods to the Classmates structure, such as height, weight, and GPA, and then modify the Structures program to display this additional information.

2. Change the NamesAgesArrays program so that it uses 100 items rather than just eight items in the array, and note how the display changes when working with large arrays.

3. Modify the Structures program so that it uses a Do loop instead of a For...Next loop to iterate through the structure array.

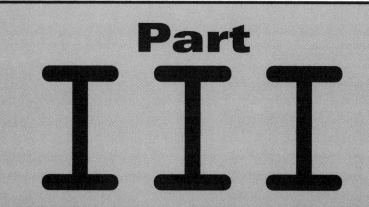

Part

III

Object-Oriented Programming with Visual Basic .NET

Chapter 9:   **The Basics of Object-Oriented Programming**

Chapter 10:  **Understanding and Using Classes**

Chapter 11:  **Namespaces and Visual Inheritance**

# The Basics of Object-Oriented Programming

Object-oriented programming is an important aspect of Visual Basic .NET, and this chapter will give you a brief introduction to the overall theory of objects and how they are created to solve real-world programming problems. By covering this information, you will gain a solid grasp of how objects work and will be prepared for more advanced Visual Basic .NET topics in later chapters, which focus heavily on object-oriented techniques.

This chapter covers the following subjects:

- Introduction to object-oriented programming

- Overview of OOP

- OOP fundamentals

- Encapsulation

- Inheritance

- Polymorphism

- Properties

- Chapter project—The Blocks Program

# Project Preview—The Blocks Program

This chapter includes a complete game called Blocks, which you will write from scratch. The project makes use of the topics covered in this chapter to create an entertaining game (see Figure 9.1).

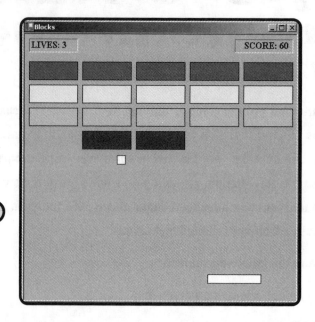

# Introduction to Object-Oriented Programming

Object-oriented programming (OOP) is a large-scale concept, which is more of a methodology than a specific way of writing programs. Applicable to many different languages, including Visual Basic .NET, OOP has been around for many years, but Visual Basic only received the full treatment with the .NET version. Visual Basic 6.0 did have rudimentary OOP features, such as properties and classes, but was not able to perform inheritance or overloading—concepts that you will be introduced to in this chapter.

# Overview of OOP

In a nutshell, OOP is a whole new way to write programs. The last great trend in computing was the structured programming model. Structured programming uses a top-down hierarchical model in which each level of the model is represented by a subroutine in the source code dependent on the calling (or parent) subroutine. The object-oriented model takes that a step further, representing those sub-levels as individual objects that are self-contained mini programs. These objects can be created for one system and then easily used again in another system because the interface to objects is generic and implementation-independent.

Okay, what does that mean, you might ask? When an object is implementation-independent, that means it is not bound to a specific application (business term for a computer program). In actual practice, object-oriented systems have not been widely adopted (or understood, for that matter). The problem is that project deadlines and a diverse workforce cause large software projects to be put together as quickly and efficiently as possible, with little regard for future projects. In many cases, OOP languages are being used to write structured code. If programmers were to sit back and first concentrate on system design, they would find that the OOP solution is faster, more robust, and more efficient. OOP is just not understood well enough by the vast majority of programmers to be put to effective use from one project to the next.

## Why Is OOP So Useful?

If this is your first exposure to OOP (or to programming, for that matter), it may not be clear how useful it is to be able to reuse source code on later projects or even share source code between projects currently in development. Try to think in the abstract: How can I write this program in such a way that when I'm finished, I can use parts of it again in another project? That way of thinking is a step in the right direction. To accomplish something like that, you need to break down a problem into manageable pieces, and then write the source code for those individual pieces separately, linking them together at the end to form a whole program.

## Changing Existing Systems

For example, suppose you are working for The Ford Motor Company, and your job as the Chief Information Officer is to reprogram all the assembly-line robots so that they work 20 percent faster, thus producing more cars per day. The only problem is that the robots are programmed with a structured design methodology, and each type of robot is controlled by a different program, written by a different programmer. Without reprogramming all the robots from scratch, how can you take structured programs and rewrite them using OOP?

There are many solutions to this hypothetic problem. But one of them might go something like this: Examine the programs controlling all of the assembly-line robots and isolate similarities among all the programs. Now, write an OOP program that encapsulates a single similar attribute of all the control programs (such as the robot startup process). Expose the attributes of the program so that you don't ruin all the other parts of the robot control programs (in other words, keep the program backward-compatible with the older software). By moving all similar code into a single OOP program and allowing other programs to gain access to the properties and methods inside the OOP program, you are able to upgrade the robot assembly control programs without rewriting the whole system. The real benefit is that once you successfully complete the first program, you can perform a similar process on other aspects of the system until you have isolated inefficiencies and possibly even eliminated bugs in the system.

### Creating New Systems

On the flipside, what if The Ford Motor Company is building a new automobile manufacturing plant, and you—as the CIO—are responsible for developing a whole new robot control system. Now is your chance to build the system using OOP from the start. First, you identify all similarities between the various types of robots and write a single OOP program that is shared among all of the robot programs. Any robots that need special programming (such as the windshield installer robot) might be programmed with OOP programs that are not reusable, due to how specific they are in nature. But any time you are required to develop a new program, you should look at the system as a whole and find any instances in which code is duplicated and attempt to eliminate it. In database circles, this is called "normalizing the database." What I'm suggesting is "normalizing the source code."

## OOP Fundamentals

If you are new to programming, you can learn how to write OOP code correctly from the start and avoid having to change your way of thinking later. Software evolves; it changes every year. Visual Basic .NET and all of the languages that make up Visual Studio .NET are radically different from Visual Basic 6.0. Although those new features are more complicated, they are in tune with OOP and help to solve programming problems more efficiently.

Now, let me give you an introduction to the components that actually make up an OOP program so you will start to get a feel for what I have been talking about up to this point. There are three aspects to OOP, as follows.

## Encapsulation

Encapsulation is the process of pulling all the data—and source code that manipulates that data—inside a self-contained entity (which is called an *object*). By keeping all the data inside the object, as well as all the subroutines and functions that work with the data, you prevent others from using the data incorrectly. In addition, encapsulation enables you to design the format of the data, as well as the processes, so that everything follows the object model—if properly designed, a blueprint for the system.

Suppose you have an apple tree in your backyard. You are a kindly neighbor, therefore you offer free apples to anyone who comes by for a visit. Soon, however, your neighbors begin to help themselves to the apples, without even bothering to knock on the door and say "hello". They have ignored you completely and helped themselves to the goodies.

In order to prevent this, what you really need to do is add a layer of control—bureaucracy—between your neighbors and your apple tree. For instance, a fence with a locked gate. But ideally, you need to pass out the apples yourself. So you do just that; every time a neighbor stops by for an apple, you select a ripe and healthy apple, and present it to your neighbor. The neighbor thanks you and goes on his way. You have interfered with the neighbor's ability to gain direct access to the source of the apples, but in doing so, you made sure the neighbor received only good apples because you threw out any bad apples beforehand.

This analogy aptly describes encapsulation of data. You want other processes in the program to have access to certain information, but you want to make sure that those processes don't do something incorrect with the information, possibly causing a bug in the program. Does encapsulation limit or slow down a program? Not really. It takes the outside process just as much time to grab the information stored in a variable as it takes for your own custom process to provide the information to that outside process. Let me give you an example to help clarify the matter.

Suppose you have an object called AppleTree, and it has an Integer variable called Apples. Here is what it might look like, hypothetically (this is not real source code):

```
Object AppleTree
    Private Apples As Integer
End Object
```

Because the Apples variable was declared as Private, no one can see it outside the AppleTree object. But you still want to be able to give away apples. To simulate this, you want to deduct one from the `Apples` variable to reflect that an apple was taken. Therefore, you must create a subroutine that is *not* `Private`:

```
Object AppleTree
    Private Apples As Integer
    Public Sub GiveApple()
        Apples -= 1
    End Sub
End Object
```

Now the `AppleTree` object can give away hypothetical apples while keeping the apples safely hidden away inside.

### Inheritance

Inheritance is another key component of an OOP program. Inheritance is the ability of one object to borrow things from another object. Inheritance is a play on words; it is more like cloning than receiving money from a departed loved one. I suspect reproduction and cloning sounded too biological, so the word inheritance was used instead. Regardless, the concept is that one object receives the attributes of another object. When the new object is used, it has a copy of the older object inside itself, which is very similar to the way genetics works. The parent passes down genes to offspring. In the computing arena, there are no mutations like there are in biological systems; however, OOP programs can inherit traits from *multiple* parents, rather than just one or two.

Let me use the analogy of the `AppleTree` object to help demonstrate how inheritance works in an OOP program. Suppose you want both green apples and red apples, and you want them to inherit from the original `AppleTree`. Call the new trees `RedAppleTree` and `GreenAppleTree`. Each of these new objects inherit from the `AppleTree` object, so they will initially look something like this:

```
Object RedAppleTree
    Inherits AppleTree
    Private Color As String = "Red"
End Object

Object GreenAppleTree
    Inherits AppleTree
    Private Color As String = "Green"
End Object
```

Now there are two new versions of the AppleTree object. See how they each inherited from the AppleTree using the Inherits statement? Each new object also declares a new variable, called Color, set to the appropriate color to differentiate them. Upon using the RedAppleTree and GreenAppleTree objects in a program, you would be able to call on the GiveApple method, which was originally located in the AppleTree object because AppleTree passed down its visible traits to its descendants.

Ah, but there's the key! I said *visible* traits. The Apples variable was declared with the Private statement, so Apples was not passed down to RedAppleTree and GreenAppleTree. Rather, these two objects received the GiveApple method. The end result is that neither of these new objects needed to include the source code for GiveApple inside their object definitions because it was already present in the parent object. Get it?

As you can imagine, this extraordinary new capability built into Visual Basic will help you to solve many problems that were very difficult to solve with earlier versions of Visual Basic. For one, you don't need to rewrite any code that doesn't perfectly suit your needs. Rather, you can just inherit the original object and make any changes that you need (assuming the parent object includes visible traits).

### Polymorphism

Polymorphism is the last of the three concepts that comprise an OOP program. Polymorphism as a word means "many shapes" and refers to the ability for the traits inside an object to change in response to different inputs or outputs. Polymorphism is probably not as important to the overall OOP scheme as encapsulation and inheritance are, but it does play an important role in aiding the other two with multi-purpose attributes that can accommodate many different situations.

The general term used to describe polymorphism in a program is *overloading*, which refers to the ability to write several versions of a subroutine using different sets of parameters. For example, suppose you want to modify the AppleTree object so that the GiveApple method accepts a parameter stating the number of apples requested. GiveApple might then deduct more than one from the Apples variable. At the same time, the original GiveApple method must be retained or else existing code might suddenly stop working. The overloaded method might look like this:

```
Object AppleTree
    Private Apples As Integer
    Public Sub GiveApple()
        Apples -= 1
```

```
        End Sub
        Public Sub GiveApple(Num As Integer)
            Apples -= Num
        End Sub
End Object
```

In this example, GiveApple has been overloaded—there are now two versions of it in the same object! That is the strength that polymorphism gives to OOP programs. New features can be added to existing objects (or descendant objects) without breaking programs that use the object.

## The Extraordinary Property

Without getting into too much detail at this point, I'd like to show you how to start using OOP. The true power of OOP comes from using *classes*, which are covered in the next two chapters. Properties have been present in Visual Basic for many years now and are the focus of the next section in this chapter.

## What Is a Property?

A *property* is a special type of method (or subroutine) that behaves like a variable, so you can assign values to a property or read the value of a property as if it were a variable. Think of a property as a *characteristic* that helps to describe the object in which it resides. But properties are definitely not variables! In practice, properties can be a very powerful form of encapsulation, enabling you to hide variables and processes behind a simple interface. You may not be able to overload a property, but you scarcely need to, because properties are already so simple to use.

## Creating Properties

Now, here is what a real property looks like (back to real code):

```
Dim decCirc As Decimal
Public Property Get Circumference() As Decimal
    Circumference = decCirc
End Property


Public Property Let Circumference(decNewValue As Decimal)
    decCirc = decNewValue
End Property
```

Note the use of the statements `Property Get` and `Property Let`. This is what allows a property to act like a simple variable when it is actually a subroutine.

## Using Properties

In your main program, you could then use the `Circumference` property like any other variable:

```
Circumference = 100
MsgBox("The circumference is " & Circumference)
Circumference = 50
Console.WriteLine("Circumference has been changed to " & _
    Circumference)
Dim Radius As Decimal
Radius = Circumference / (2 * Math.PI)
```

That last line of code using the `Radius` variable is interesting. Suppose that instead of storing the property value as the passed value, what if it performed a calculation first? That might be a good way to demonstrate the power of properties. Here is another version of the `Circumference` property, this time using a calculation to store the internal value of the property.

```
Dim decCirc As Decimal
Public Property Get Circumference() As Decimal
    Circumference = decCirc * 2 * Math.PI
End Property

Public Property Let Circumference(decNewValue As Decimal)
    decCirc = decNewValue / (2 * Math.PI)
End Property
```

This code produces the same result as the earlier `Circumference` property, but this one performs a calculation each time the property is read or set, by converting the `Circumference` into a `Radius` and back again. Wasteful, for sure, but demonstrative.

## Automatic Data Validation

The most common use for properties is to ensure that variables are set correctly within acceptable bounds. Here is a more practical example for a property using an `If...Then` branching statement to make sure the value is within the acceptable range. If the main program tries to set the `Month` property to any value outside the range of 1–12, the property isn't changed.

```
Dim intMonth As Integer
Public Property Get Month() As Integer
     Month = intMonth
End Property

Public Property Let Month (intNewValue As Integer)
     If intNewValue >= 1 And intNewValue <= 12 Then
          intMonth = intNewValue
     End If
End Property
```

## Chapter Project—The Blocks Program

The Blocks program was designed to demonstrate the concepts learned in this chapter, including OOP properties and overloaded subroutines. By walking through the source code for this game, you should have an opportunity for exposure to real-world uses for OOP techniques. Take a look at Figure 9.2, which shows the game after the player has missed the ball and lost a life.

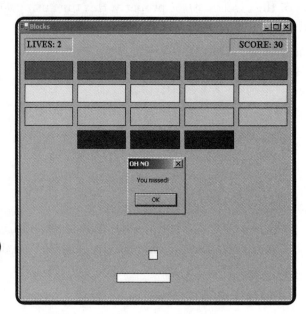

**FIGURE 9.2**

The player has missed the ball and loses a life.

Figure 9.3 shows what happens when the player loses all three lives.

Finally, look at Figure 9.4 to see what happens when the player clears all the blocks off the screen.

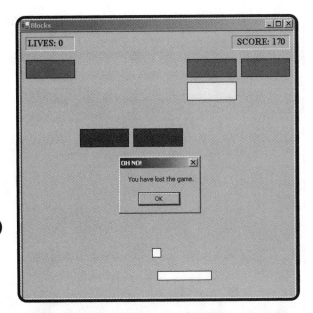

**FIGURE 9.3**

Oh no! The player has lost all three lives and loses the game!

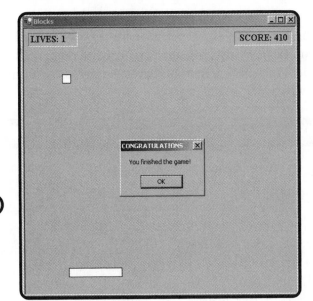

**FIGURE 9.4**

The player has cleared all the blocks from the screen and wins the game!

## Designing the Project

For starters, run Visual Studio .NET and create a new Windows Application under Visual Basic. Call the new program Blocks. Figure 9.5 shows the completed project in Visual Basic.

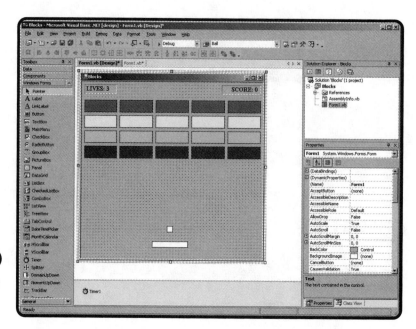

**FIGURE 9.5**

The completed user interface for the Blocks game.

Unfortunately, there are a lot of properties because each block is an individual `PictureBox` control. Table 9.1 lists the form and control properties you need to set in order to complete the game. After you have completed the form, I will go over the source code with you.

## TABLE 9.1 CONTROL PROPERTIES FOR BLOCKS

| Control | Name | Property | Value |
|---------|------|----------|-------|
| Form | Form1 | Text | Blocks |
| | | FormBorderStyle | Fixed3D |
| | | Size | 496, 490 |
| | | StartPosition | CenterScreen |
| Timer | Timer1 | Interval | 20 |
| Label | Label1 | BorderStyle | Fixed3D |
| | | Font | Times New Roman, 12pt, style=Bold |
| | | Location | 8, 8 |
| | | Size | 88, 24 |
| | | Text | LIVES: 3 |

## TABLE 9.1 CONTROL PROPERTIES FOR BLOCKS

| Control | Name | Property | Value |
|---|---|---|---|
| Label | Label2 | BorderStyle | Fixed3D |
| | | Font | Times New Roman, 12pt, style=Bold |
| | | Location | 376, 8 |
| | | Size | 104, 24 |
| | | Text | SCORE: 0 |
| | | TextAlign | TopRight |
| PictureBox | Paddle | BorderStyle | FixedSingle |
| | | Location | 192, 416 |
| | | Size | 96, 16 |
| | | BackColor | White |
| PictureBox | Ball | BorderStyle | FixedSingle |
| | | Location | 232, 376 |
| | | Size | 16, 16 |
| | | BackColor | White |
| PictureBox | Red1 | BorderStyle | FixedSingle |
| | | BackColor | Red |
| | | Location | 8, 48 |
| | | Size | 88, 32 |
| PictureBox | Red2 | BorderStyle | FixedSingle |
| | | BackColor | Red |
| | | Location | 104, 48 |
| | | Size | 88, 32 |
| PictureBox | Red3 | BorderStyle | FixedSingle |
| | | BackColor | Red |
| | | Location | 200, 48 |
| | | Size | 88, 32 |
| PictureBox | Red4 | BorderStyle | FixedSingle |
| | | BackColor | Red |
| | | Location | 296, 48 |
| | | Size | 88, 32 |

## TABLE 9.1 CONTROL PROPERTIES FOR BLOCKS

| Control | Name | Property | Value |
|---------|------|----------|-------|
| PictureBox | Red5 | BorderStyle | FixedSingle |
| | | BackColor | Red |
| | | Location | 392, 48 |
| | | Size | 88, 32 |
| PictureBox | Yellow1 | BorderStyle | FixedSingle |
| | | BackColor | Yellow |
| | | Location | 8, 88 |
| | | Size | 88, 32 |
| PictureBox | Yellow2 | BorderStyle | FixedSingle |
| | | BackColor | Yellow |
| | | Location | 104, 88 |
| | | Size | 88, 32 |
| PictureBox | Yellow3 | BorderStyle | FixedSingle |
| | | BackColor | Yellow |
| | | Location | 200, 88 |
| | | Size | 88, 32 |
| PictureBox | Yellow4 | BorderStyle | FixedSingle |
| | | BackColor | Yellow |
| | | Location | 296, 88 |
| | | Size | 88, 32 |
| PictureBox | Yellow5 | BorderStyle | FixedSingle |
| | | BackColor | Yellow |
| | | Location | 392, 88 |
| | | Size | 88, 32 |
| PictureBox | Green1 | BorderStyle | FixedSingle |
| | | BackColor | Lime |
| | | Location | 8, 128 |
| | | Size | 88, 32 |
| PictureBox | Green2 | BorderStyle | FixedSingle |
| | | BackColor | Lime |
| | | Location | 104, 128 |
| | | Size | 88, 32 |

## TABLE 9.1 CONTROL PROPERTIES FOR BLOCKS

| Control | Name | Property | Value |
|---------|------|----------|-------|
| PictureBox | Green3 | BorderStyle | FixedSingle |
| | | BackColor | Lime |
| | | Location | 200, 128 |
| | | Size | 88, 32 |
| PictureBox | Green4 | BorderStyle | FixedSingle |
| | | BackColor | Lime |
| | | Location | 296, 128 |
| | | Size | 88, 32 |
| PictureBox | Green5 | BorderStyle | FixedSingle |
| | | BackColor | Lime |
| | | Location | 392, 128 |
| | | Size | 88, 32 |
| PictureBox | Blue1 | BorderStyle | FixedSingle |
| | | BackColor | Blue |
| | | Location | 8, 168 |
| | | Size | 88, 32 |
| PictureBox | Blue2 | BorderStyle | FixedSingle |
| | | BackColor | Blue |
| | | Location | 104, 168 |
| | | Size | 88, 32 |
| PictureBox | Blue3 | BorderStyle | FixedSingle |
| | | BackColor | Blue |
| | | Location | 200, 168 |
| | | Size | 88, 32 |
| PictureBox | Blue4 | BorderStyle | FixedSingle |
| | | BackColor | Blue |
| | | Location | 296, 168 |
| | | Size | 88, 32 |
| PictureBox | Blue5 | BorderStyle | FixedSingle |
| | | BackColor | Blue |
| | | Location | 392, 168 |
| | | Size | 88, 32 |

## Writing the Source Code

The source code for Blocks is filled with interesting twists on what would other-wise be a short code listing because I have gone overboard using properties to help demonstrate how they can be used in a real program. Remember that prop-erties fall into the OOP feature called encapsulation, in which the real variables are hidden. There is also an example of polymorphism in this code listing involv-ing a subroutine that has been overloaded.

**Section 1.** Now, let's get started. The first section of code includes the property variables and the Form1_Load event. The property variables could have been used directly in the program (and I recommend that you use simple variables directly most of the time), but are instead accessed through properties, which are further down in the code listing. Now, type in this code below the Windows Form Designer generated code line. As you can see, the only thing Form1_Load accomplishes is turning on the timer.

```
Dim intSpeedX As Integer = 2
Dim intSpeedY As Integer = -2
Dim intScore As Integer
Dim intLives As Integer = 3
Dim intAllGone As Integer


Private Sub Form1_Load(ByVal sender As System.Object, _
    ByVal e As System.EventArgs) Handles MyBase.Load

    Timer1.Enabled = True
End Sub
```

**Section 2.** The next section of code includes the Timer1_Tick event, which is really the most important section of code in the whole program. This timer event checks to see if all the blocks have been cleared from the screen, at which point the player is declared the winner. After that, the ball is moved by incrementing the BallX and BallY properties (which refer to a PictureBox control named Ball). Finally, if the ball has hit the bottom of the screen, the player loses a life and the ball restarts from its original location.

```
Private Sub Timer1_Tick(ByVal sender As System.Object, _
    ByVal e As System.EventArgs) Handles Timer1.Tick

    AllGone = 0
    CheckCollisions()
    If AllGone = 1 Then
```

```
            Timer1.Enabled = False
            MsgBox("You finished the game!", , "CONGRATULATIONS")
        End If


        BallX += SpeedX
        If BallX < 3 Or BallX + Ball.Width > Me.Width - 5 Then
            SpeedX = -SpeedX
        End If
        BallY += SpeedY
        If BallY < 3 Then
            SpeedY = -SpeedY
        End If


        If BallY + Ball.Height > Me.Height - 5 Then
            Timer1.Enabled = False
            UpdateLives()
            BallX = 232
            BallY = 376
            SpeedX = 2
            SpeedY = -2
            If Lives < 1 Then
                MsgBox("You have lost the game.", , "OH NO!")
            Else
                MsgBox("You missed!", , "OH NO")
                Timer1.Enabled = True
            End If
        End If


    End Sub
```

**Section 3.** The next section of code includes the Form1_MouseMove event. This event is responsible for moving the player's paddle across the bottom of the screen. The code is really short because Visual Basic provides the mouse coordinates with this event. All the code does is set the paddle's location based on the mouse location.

```
    Private Sub Form1_MouseMove(ByVal sender As Object, _
        ByVal e As System.Windows.Forms.MouseEventArgs) _
        Handles MyBase.MouseMove

        Paddle.Left = e.X - Paddle.Width \ 2

    End Sub
```

**Section 4.** This section of code includes the CheckCollisions subroutine (which deals with all the blocks), which calls the CheckCollision subroutine (which deals with just one block at a time) for each of the blocks on the screen (as well as the player's paddle). See how the first call includes a second parameter, False? That call is using the overloaded version of CheckCollision because it is just the player's paddle that is being checked. The original CheckCollision subroutine hides the blocks when a collision occurs, but that must not happen when checking the paddle or else the player won't be able to move it any longer! The code for CheckCollision comes next.

```
Public Sub CheckCollisions()
    CheckCollision(Paddle, False)
    CheckCollision(Red1)
    CheckCollision(Red2)
    CheckCollision(Red3)
    CheckCollision(Red4)
    CheckCollision(Red5)
    CheckCollision(Yellow1)
    CheckCollision(Yellow2)
    CheckCollision(Yellow3)
    CheckCollision(Yellow4)
    CheckCollision(Yellow5)
    CheckCollision(Green1)
    CheckCollision(Green2)
    CheckCollision(Green3)
    CheckCollision(Green4)
    CheckCollision(Green5)
    CheckCollision(Blue1)
    CheckCollision(Blue2)
    CheckCollision(Blue3)
    CheckCollision(Blue4)
    CheckCollision(Blue5)
End Sub
```

**Section 5.** This section includes the original CheckCollision subroutine (the overloaded one is listed below). This code looks at the ball position and compares it to the position of the passed PictureBox control (see the src parameter). If the ball's position intersects the blocks' position, a collision has occurred! At this point, the block is erased (by setting Visible = False), and the ball is bounced away.

```
Public Sub CheckCollision(ByVal src As PictureBox, ByVal Hide As Boolean)
    If src.Visible = True Then
```

```
            If BallX > src.Location.X And _
                BallX < src.Location.X + src.Size.Width And _
                Ball.Location.Y > src.Location.Y And _
                Ball.Location.Y < src.Location.Y + src.Size.Height Then
                SpeedY = -SpeedY
                UpdateScore()
                If Hide Then
                    src.Visible = False
                End If
            End If
            AllGone += 1
        End If
    End Sub
```

**Section 6.** This section includes the overloaded version of CheckCollision. The code is really short because this code just calls the original CheckCollision sub-routine with the Hide parameter set to True. By default, then, blocks will be erased when a collision occurs (the paddle will remain after a collision). The ability to overload subroutines is extremely powerful and is a welcome feature with Visual Basic .NET over earlier versions.

```
    'declare the overloaded version of CheckCollision
    Public Sub CheckCollision(ByVal src As PictureBox)
        'call the original version
        CheckCollision(src, True)
    End Sub
```

**Section 7.** This section includes two subroutines: UpdateScore and UpdateLives. This code increments the score (or decrements the life counter) and updates the appropriate label at the top of the screen.

```
    Public Sub UpdateScore()
        Score += 10
        Label2.Text = "SCORE: " & Score
    End Sub

    Public Sub UpdateLives()
        Lives -= 1
        Label1.Text = "LIVES: " & Lives
    End Sub
```

**Section 8.** This section includes the BallX and BallY properties. These properties point to the actual Ball PictureBox control that is used to draw the ball on the screen, using the Left and Top properties of the PictureBox.

```
Public Property BallX() As Integer
    Get
        Return Ball.Left
    End Get
    Set(ByVal Value As Integer)
        Ball.Left = Value
    End Set
End Property

Public Property BallY() As Integer
    Get
        Return Ball.Top
    End Get
    Set(ByVal Value As Integer)
        Ball.Top = Value
    End Set
End Property
```

**Section 9.** This is yet another property, this time involving the life counter called Lives, used to update the label at the upper-left corner of the screen. When the ball hits the bottom, a life is taken away, and that is where this property comes into use.

```
Public Property Lives() As Integer
    Get
        Return intLives
    End Get
    Set(ByVal Value As Integer)
        intLives = Value
    End Set
End Property
```

**Section 10.** This section of code includes the SpeedX and SpeedY properties, which point to intSpeedX and intSpeedY. As a matter of day-to-day programming, I wouldn't encapsulate a simple variable like this one unless it is going to be reused in another program, or the variable needs to be exposed to other parts of the program. Normally this is overkill, but it helps to demonstrate the use of properties.

```
Public Property SpeedX() As Integer
    Get
        Return intSpeedX
    End Get
    Set(ByVal Value As Integer)
        intSpeedX = Value
    End Set
End Property

Public Property SpeedY() As Integer
    Get
        Return intSpeedY
    End Get
    Set(ByVal Value As Integer)
        intSpeedY = Value
    End Set
End Property
```

**Section 11.** This section of code includes the Score property, which points to the intScore **variable.**

```
Public Property Score() As Integer
    Get
        Return intScore
    End Get
    Set(ByVal Value As Integer)
        intScore = Value
    End Set
End Property
```

**Section 12.** This final section of code is another property called AllGone, which points to the intAllGone **variable. This couldn't be any simpler!**

```
Public Property AllGone() As Integer
    Get
        Return intAllGone
    End Get
    Set(ByVal Value As Integer)
        intAllGone = Value
    End Set
End Property
```

If you have typed in all of the code without any mistakes, you can run the program by pressing F5. The ball should start to move as soon as the program starts. If it doesn't move right away, you might want to double-check the code to make sure you didn't make any typing mistakes. As a last resort, you may want to load the Blocks project from this chapter's folder on the CD-ROM, under \Blocks.

## Summary

This chapter presented an introduction to object-oriented programming and focused on the three primary components of an OOP program: encapsulation, inheritance, and polymorphism. This chapter presented examples of how to use encapsulation through properties, and polymorphism through overloaded subroutines. The concept of inheritance is covered in the next chapter, in which you are given an introduction to the true basis for OOP in Visual Basic: classes.

### CHALLENGES

The following challenges will help to reinforce the material you have learned in this chapter.

1. The Blocks game currently has no way to restart after the game has ended. Modify the program so that it's possible to restart the game after it has ended. You might want to add a Start button that becomes visible when the game has ended.

2. The paddle in the Blocks game continues moving off the left and right edge of the screen to a certain point, which doesn't look attractive. Modify the program so that the paddle moves to the edge but doesn't go off the screen.

3. The graphics in the Blocks game are all made up of colored `PictureBox` controls. The game can be visually improved by adding real bitmaps to each `PictureBox`, including the paddle and ball. Hint: you will need a paint program, such as Paint Shop Pro or Windows Paint to save bitmap files.

# Understanding and Using Classes

**T**he last chapter introduced you to a programming methodology called *object-oriented programming* (OOP) and showed how it improved on the *structured programming* methodology that was the standard for many years. Visual Basic .NET supports all of the features of a modern OOP language, including the big three: inheritance, polymorphism, and encapsulation. You already learned how these powerful OOP techniques can vastly improve the quality of your code, reduce development time, and more closely follow the specifications of a system.

In this chapter, I will cover the following topics:

- **Introduction to Visual Basic classes**

- **The format of a class**

- **Creating Visual Basic classes**

- **Real-world example—The** Animal **class**

- **Chapter Project—The Pet Shop Program**

OOP is not extremely useful in small projects due to that extra level of overhead at the beginning of a project, in which you create the objects that go into the application before starting work on the main source code file. That overhead is well worth the time investment for medium- to large-sized projects. However, one thing I have often discovered is that seemingly simple projects often grow to become medium or large projects over time. The important thing I would like to express to you now is to get into the habit of thinking in an object-oriented way, which is what this chapter and the next chapter will help you learn to do.

## Project Preview—The Pet Shop Program

This chapter includes a complete project titled Pet Shop (shown in Figure 10.1), which you will learn to create from scratch. The Pet Shop program is full of classes and demonstrates how to use classes to solve real-world problems. The program displays a list of animals available for sale in a fictional pet shop. You can click the animals in the list to get a detailed description of each one, and you can even interact with the animals by pressing the Speak and Play buttons, which call on functions built into the animal classes.

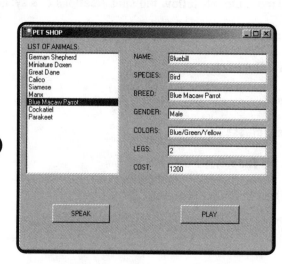

**FIGURE 10.1**

The Pet Shop program demonstrates the object-oriented topics presented in this chapter.

# Introduction to Visual Basic Classes

Okay, you are probably eager to learn more about objects, so I'll start by explaining classes. This section provides an introduction to classes, covers a little history of where classes came from, and shows how classes fit in to Visual Basic's OOP capabilities. Some of this information will sound familiar because it was covered in the last chapter. The difference is that now I am focusing on building classes, so the same topics are being revisited to show how an object-oriented program is developed with classes.

## What Is a Class?

Classes are the key ingredients of object-oriented programming and provide a basis for creating objects. An object is a self-contained, functional component in a program that accomplishes a single task, regardless of whether that task is simple or complex. A well-designed OOP program will utilize many different and versatile objects that work together to accomplish the goals of the program. The real power of this is that over time a programmer (or programming team) will be able to use these objects in more than one project. A team that simply shares code using copy and paste methods might resemble the illustration shown in Figure 10.2.

A professional programming shop will have an assortment of such objects collected over time in a *class library*. The class library may be comprised of many smaller libraries of classes (as shown in Figure 10.3).

Now, what is the difference between a class and an object? I have used the terms interchangeably, but now I will explain the difference. A class contains object-oriented source code that does something. An *object* is a *variable* that was declared to be a type of that class, like any other data type (Long, String, and so on). The data type is actually just the name of the class.

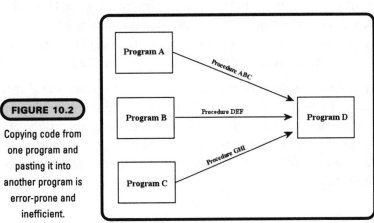

**FIGURE 10.2**

Copying code from one program and pasting it into another program is error-prone and inefficient.

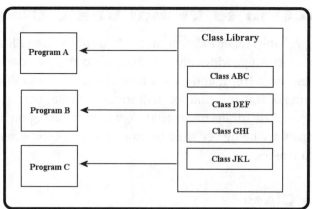

**FIGURE 10.3**

Class libraries provide commonly used source code routines as self-contained classes that become objects when used in a program.

When talking about OOP, it is often easier to describe a system using the word *object*, even though that is not technically accurate (because an object is an instance of a class). The most widely used OOP language is C++, a descendant of the C language. C++ uses the very same concepts that I have been explaining in this chapter (and the previous one), therefore what you learn here is portable. In fact, most of these concepts are directly applicable to other .NET languages, such as Visual C#.

## Understanding Classes and OOP

Objects are evolved procedures from that older methodology (see Figure 10.4). In very large systems, it is difficult for numerous programmers to work on the same system, particularly poorly documented systems (meaning those that are not easy to understand and for which there are few or no design documents).

What typically happens is that programmers will change a variable in one part of the program without realizing that another programmer was using that variable in a different part of the program. Even if those separate procedures run at different times, the fact that one changes a variable when the other procedure is expecting the variable to remain the same could cause a bug in the program.

So, what is the solution? Make sure programmers only use their own variables. But how do you claim ownership of a global variable in a program (meaning, a variable that is visible throughout the whole application)? The answer is that you *can't* keep a variable global and also prevent others from using it, inadvertently or purposefully, unless you use the OOP-based technology. Figure 10.5 illustrates the object-oriented methodology.

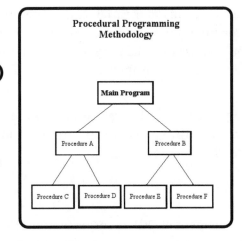

**FIGURE 10.4**

Structured
programs are
hierarchical in
nature, with low-
level code routines
below the high-
level processes
(which are usually
not reusable).

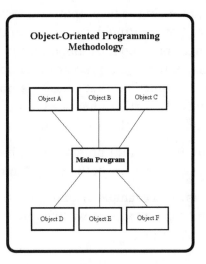

**FIGURE 10.5**

Object-oriented
programs have no
hierarchy, but are
instead made up of
numerous objects
that are each a
self-contained
entity capable of
accomplishing a
single task.

For example, suppose a program asks the user to type in a username when the program starts, and the user's name is stored in a variable called strUsername. Now suppose another programmer comes along and needs to load all of the allowed usernames from a disk file. He looks around in the program and finds that strUsername has already been created, so he uses it to read in each of the user accounts from disk. Now, without realizing that the strUsername variable has been used as a scratch pad for loading data from disk, the first programmer displays the username on the screen, and it turns out that the username is not the same one that the user typed in when the program started running!

What happens at this point? Most likely, the login programmer will pull his hair out trying to figure out what's wrong with his variable, and may resort to creating a whole new variable to solve the problem—although the problem could come up again if someone else decides to use his *new* variable, and the problem repeats itself. It is not uncommon for programmers to use existing variables in a program; after all, they may not have written the program from the start, but may have just been hired to make changes to the application. This is a common problem in structured programs.

Object-oriented programming was invented to get around these types of problems, and also to make it more intuitive to write software that more closely follows the specifications created for the program.

## Encapsulation

Arguably, the most important element of OOP is encapsulation. This was the primary reason why OOP languages were designed—to protect variables and data, and combine that data with the processing code for that data. By providing *accessor* subroutines to the data instead of granting direct access to the data, a class is able to contain the data. Furthermore, and most importantly, a class can validate changes before they are made. Because a process in an application must modify a variable using its accessor function, that process is no longer able to "mess up" the variable, even by mistake. Rather, the code built into the class verifies that the proposed changes to the variables are within acceptable limits.

Figure 10.6 shows an example of a procedural program that has full access to both the data and the logic processes, which are both exposed in the source code.

Figure 10.7, on the other hand, shows an example of an object-oriented program, which *encapsulates* the data and logic processes within the source code, preventing outside processes from interfering.

## Inheritance

Inheritance is arguably the second most important aspect of object-oriented programming (followed by polymorphism, which is covered next). Inheritance is a process in which encapsulated classes are *not* modified to solve a new problem; instead, existing classes *pass down* their data and logic processes to a new class, which can then have new data and new logic processes added to those that were passed down by the parent class.

The Pet Shop program, which you will have an opportunity to write later in this chapter, uses inheritance to show how animals are related by certain attributes. Take a look at Figure 10.8, which shows the relationship between the Animal, Dog, Cat, and Bird classes. I will explain inheritance in more detail in the next section, in which I will show you how to create these classes.

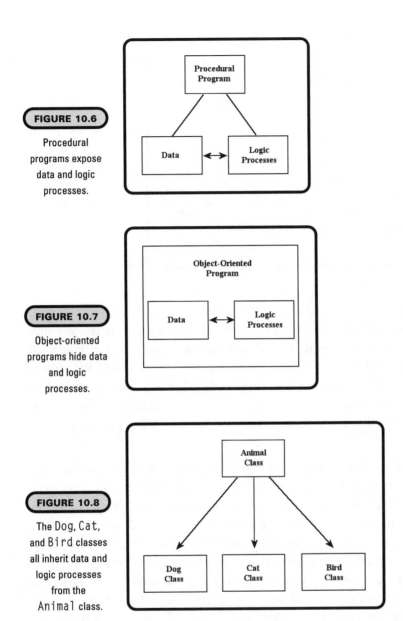

**FIGURE 10.6**

Procedural programs expose data and logic processes.

**FIGURE 10.7**

Object-oriented programs hide data and logic processes.

**FIGURE 10.8**

The Dog, Cat, and Bird classes all inherit data and logic processes from the Animal class.

## Polymorphism

Polymorphism is arguably the least important of the three major traits of an object-oriented program, but does provide a powerful and useful set of features that are difficult to go without once you have gotten used to them. Take a look at Figure 10.9 for a simplistic illustration of how polymorphism works.

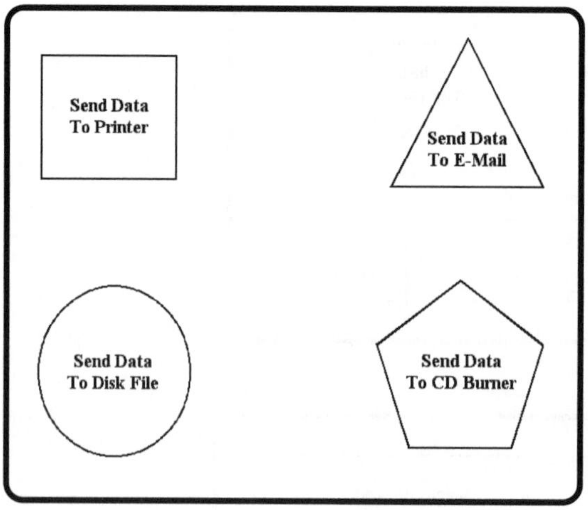

**FIGURE 10.9**

Polymorphism often involves processing data of more than one type, or processing data in more than one way.

For example, suppose you want to display the name of an animal in a pet store database, but you don't know where the name will come from; it could come from the keyboard, from a text file that describes the animal, or perhaps even from a microphone used by store employees using voice recognition. Regardless of the method of input, the pet store database needs to know the name of the animal. By using a process called *overloading*, the pet store database program can interpret these various inputs and come up with the same result regardless of the source.

The process goes the other direction as well. Suppose you are a programmer working on the pet store database program, and the owner of the store wants the program to print out sticky labels to affix to a cage for each pet. The store owner also wants the pet's name printed out on a smaller tag that is affixed to the pet's collar. The real benefit to using an overloaded procedure—which is how polymorphism is used—is that you can use the same PrintName procedure in each case, and simply change the format or the source of data used to print out the name. In addition, if you need to add new ways to print out the pet's name, you can simply overload the PrintName procedure again and thus avoid having to modify the main program to call a whole new procedure. Polymorphism, then, promotes code reuse and extensibility.

## The Format of a Class

Classes can contain any information that you want and can generally be declared Friend or Public. Private classes can also be created, but their scope must fall within another class. Friend classes are visible only within the current namespace (in previous versions of Visual Basic that would have been *current project* scope).

Generally, classes are created so that they can be used and reused in more than one application, therefore classes are almost universally declared with Public scope. I'll explain more about scope and visibility in the next chapter.

For all practical purposes, here is a sample class definition (with a single member variable) as you will see it most often:

```
Public Class MyClassName
    Private intVariable As Integer

    Sub New()
        intVariable = 0
    End Sub

    Property Variable() As Integer
        Get
            Return intVariable
        End Get
        Set(ByVal Value As Integer)
            intVariable = Value
        End Set
    End Property
End Class
```

### Class Variables

The first thing you will notice in the sample MyClassName class is the member variable called intVariable. Member variables can be declared with Public, Private, or Protected scope. You are already familiar with the first two; what, then, does Protected mean? Protected member variables are sort of in between Public and Private, accessible to descendant classes but not outside the class. Private member variables, on the other hand, are *not* visible to other classes (not even descendants). Public variables are visible all the time.

### Class Constructor

The next thing you will notice in the sample MyClassName class is a constructor called Sub New. Odd as it may appear, this is how constructors are created in VB.NET, by overloading the New operator. Remember, when you create a new object, you use New, right? Well, New is just an operator, like +, -, >, <, or =. VB.NET overloads the New operator to act as the constructor for the class. In case you are not familiar with the term, a constructor is a method that runs when the class is first instantiated (which means *created*). I'll explain constructors in more detail in the following section on creating a real-world example with the `Animal` class.

### Class Properties and Methods

The most common type of subroutine you will use in a class is a property, although you can add any `Sub` or `Function` that you want to a class and it then becomes a member method of the class. I am a big fan of properties, and I am pleased that properties now play such a big role in Visual Basic's OOP capabilities. You are free to use a property to do more than just provide access to a private variable. Any time you need to return a value, for example, it is convenient to use a property because properties are referenced just like variables in a class (and it's often difficult to tell the difference).

## Creating Visual Basic Classes

I believe that it's important to understand the theory behind a practice, but theory is often counter-productive to the learning process, especially when it comes to programming. It's so hard to imagine how things work in a computer program that often the only way to truly understand a new way of programming is to try it out—for better or for worse, mistakes and all.

So, I'm going to take you through a hands-on exercise that will support the Pet Shop program (which is the chapter project). Instead of writing the program at the end, let's first learn how to break the program down into classes, and then the main Pet Shop program will be easier to manage.

First things first. In the last chapter, I was a little misleading by calling everything (that is, data types and classes in the .NET Framework) an *object*. I wanted you to get a feel for the word and understand that programming languages often change the meaning of words (which makes things more difficult). Sure, everything is really an object when used in a program, but until then, objects don't really exist. Instead, you have a class. It's sort of like comparing the source code to a program with the compiled executable version of the program. They are both called "the program" but are mutually exclusive (you don't use the executable when writing the program, and you don't see the source code when running the executable). Of course, things get confusing when you run a program inside Visual Studio, but let's not worry about that right now.

# Real-World Example—The Animal Class

I'd like to give you a real-world example that will help solidify the subject in your mind. As I explained at the start, this chapter features a project called PetShop—a database-type program featuring a fictional pet store with animals available for sale.

The Pet Shop program needs to be able to keep track of the animals in this fictional pet shop, therefore this is a great opportunity to learn how to write a real class. What's a good way to keep track of the animals? You could create a new variable or structure for each animal, but what happens if you need to change something after the program is compiled? The whole idea is to keep things dynamic and moving along, without having to stop and redo anything. How about a class that describes the basic properties of an animal? Pets come in various shapes and sizes, so this class needs to be able to take into account that there could be dogs and birds and other types of pets, which all look and behave quite differently.

## Creating the PetShop Project

Let's start by describing the basic traits of an animal, and put them all in a class by that name. At this time, it would probably be beneficial for you to have a VB.NET project open so you can type in this source code as I explain each step of it.

 **If you are not in the typing mood, feel free to open this project from the book's CD-ROM; it is located in the folder for this chapter under \PetShop.**

Create a new VB.NET project (a regular Windows Application) and call it PetShop. Next, open the code editor for Form1, and type in the new Animal class at the very bottom of the code listing. Here's the first part of the Animal class:

```
Public Class Animal
    Private strSpecies As String
    Private strBreed As String
    Private strColor As String
    Private strName As String
    Private strGender As String
    Private intLegs As Integer
    Private intCost As Integer
End Class
```

Again, you should type this in at the bottom of the code listing for Form1. Double-click the form and then move the cursor down to the bottom—yes, even below the Form1 class! Check out Figure 10.10.

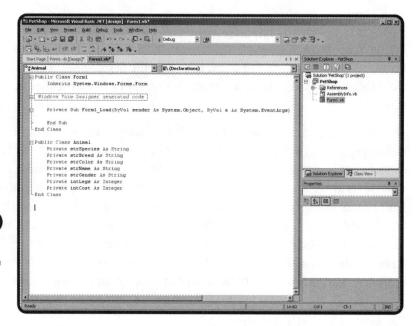

**FIGURE 10.10**

New classes can be added anywhere in VB.NET, even in the code module for a form.

If you are used to creating classes in a previous version of Visual Basic, it probably seems strange to add a class to the end of code listing for a form! VB.NET actually supports a far more powerful means of organizing classes called *namespaces*—the subject of the next chapter.

Well, that's the first part of the class! Congratulations, you have now created your first real class definition. Okay, so it doesn't do anything, but it's a start. Have you noticed that the class looks sort of like a structure definition? Classes are similar to structures, but as you saw earlier, you can add subroutines inside a class (which are called methods). In case you might not have noticed, you've been doing just that all along. See the definition of the Form1 class at the top of the code window for Form1? Yes, even the form is a class, controls are just like variables, and events like Form1_Click are the methods for a form. If the fact hasn't occurred to you yet, it seems that *everything* in VB.NET is an object. It takes quite a bit to get used to this after using earlier versions of Visual Basic! The reason is that, for all practical purposes, Visual Basic 6.0 and earlier versions were what you might call "procedural, event-driven" compilers.

## Class Constructors

A class constructor is that strange-looking subroutine that is executed when the class is first created. Now, this is where things get really bizarre (remember the MyClassName class earlier?). Instead of giving the constructor a sensible name, the designers of VB.NET decided to just call every constructor New. Yes, that's right, New. It sort of makes sense when you understand that New is a keyword in Visual Basic that you can use to create new objects in a program. Here's an example:

```
Dim var1 As New MyClassName
```

You've probably seen code that looks like that before, in which you declare a variable using the New operator. Well, that's exactly what's going on with this constructor called New: what you are doing is overloading the New operator. So without even trying, you've managed to use all three components of an object-oriented program:

1. The Pet Shop data is *encapsulated* with private variables.

2. The Animal class has *inherited* the basic functionality of an Object.

3. The New constructor has used *polymorphism* to create a constructor.

Isn't it amazing how those three things make their way into almost everything you do in an object-oriented program? If that's not clearly evident yet, it will be in time. Okay, let's add a constructor to the Animal class, just below the variables you added earlier.

```
'default constructor for Animal class
Sub New()
    Console.WriteLine("Animal default constructor")
    strSpecies = ""
    strBreed = ""
    strColor = ""
    strName = ""
    strGender = ""
    intLegs = 0
    intCost = 0
End Sub
```

Okay, now I'm really going to throw you for a loop by doing something unpleasant! The New operator is overloaded as a constructor, right? That's what the last section of code accomplished. Well, check this out: you can overload the overloaded constructor again!

Oh no, come back, it's not that bad!

Here's the part where I ask you to trust me on this one because it will all make sense when you use the class in the Pet Shop program. This is a hands-on exercise, after all, because you were tired of the theory and wanted some real-world practice creating classes (or was that my idea?). Either way, here's what's going on.

You can have as many constructors as you want in a class. That's right, as many as you want! You can overload the Sub New until you've included every possibility in your class that you can imagine. So this is really the fun part, if you think about it. You are creating something totally new in Visual Basic that wasn't built into the language.

This extra constructor has two parameters: strSpecies and intLegs. The reason is that I want to be able to add a new animal to the pet shop database without setting the Species and Legs properties every single time (it becomes repetitive when you have a lot of animals to handle). Go ahead and type it in right below the previous Sub New.

```
'overloaded constructor
Sub New(ByVal strSpecies As String, ByVal intLegs As Integer)
    Me.New()
    Species = strSpecies
    Legs = intLegs
    Console.WriteLine("Animal overloaded constructor")
End Sub
```

Now, do you see that first line of code inside the constructor that looks like this: Me.New()? That's actually calling the first constructor to initialize all the variables. See how there are no parameters in the call to Sub New()? That's the key to keeping track of your constructors—it's in the parameters. The Me part just tells VB.NET that you are talking about a constructor, and not trying to create something with the New operator (because you can't very well just call New() by itself).

## Class Properties

The rest of the code for the Animal class is just a bunch of accessor properties for the variables (you know, strSpecies, strBreed, and so on). These variables were all declared Private because a well-behaved class keeps its data hidden. So, without further ado, here's the code you'll need to add to the Animal class to make those variables accessible outside the class. If you want to save some time, type in the first property, then copy and paste it again and again for the others, just changing the data types, variable name, and so forth.

```
'accessor property for strSpecies
Property Species() As String
    Get
        Return strSpecies
    End Get
    Set(ByVal Value As String)
```

```
            strSpecies = Value
        End Set
End Property


'accessor property for strBreed
Property Breed() As String
    Get
            Return strBreed
    End Get
    Set(ByVal Value As String)
            strBreed = Value
    End Set
End Property


'accessor property for strGender
Property Gender() As String
    Get
            Return strGender
    End Get
    Set(ByVal Value As String)
            strGender = Value
    End Set
End Property


'accessor property for strColor
Property Coloration() As String
    Get
            Return strColor
    End Get
    Set(ByVal Value As String)
            strColor = Value
    End Set
End Property


'accessor property for strName
Property Name() As String
    Get
            Return strName
    End Get
    Set(ByVal Value As String)
```

```
            strName = Value
        End Set
End Property


'accessor property for intLegs
Property Legs() As Integer
    Get
            Return intLegs
    End Get
    Set(ByVal Value As Integer)
        intLegs = Value
    End Set
End Property


'accessor property for intCost
Property Cost() As Integer
    Get
            Return intCost
    End Get
    Set(ByVal Value As Integer)
        intCost = Value
    End Set
End Property
```

## Class Methods

Okay, all done with the properties. Now, how about doing something fun with the Animal class? What I'd like to do is identify each pet in the pet store by a specific trait: how does the pet *speak*, and how does the pet *play* ? Those are typical traits of any pet, whether it's a bird, a cat, or a dog. Let's give the Animal class two methods so that the animals will be able to speak and play later on. Just add this code below the properties you typed in before.

```
'base Speak function
Overridable Function Speak()
    Console.WriteLine("Animal.Speak")
    Return ""
End Function


'base Play function
Overridable Function Play() As String
```

```
        Console.WriteLine("Animal.Play")
        Return ""
    End Function
```

```
End Class
```

Okay, and that's the end of the `Animal` class! But wait, what's the deal with that word, `Overridable`? I was afraid you were going to ask that question. Just kidding!

### Overridable and Overloadable

`Overridable` is a new keyword that has to do with inheritance. Remember how one class can inherit the public and protected variables and methods in another class? Well, there's a really neat thing you can do with inherited things: you can override them in the descendant classes if they are declared with the `Overridable` keyword, and you can then replace the original method with new code. Now, the key to understanding why this is necessary is to realize that if you call an inherited method without overriding it, the method from the parent class is executed. If the original method in the parent class is sufficient to meet the needs of your new class, that's great, no changes are needed! But just remember that you *can* override the original, and type in new code for that method if you want to.

This brings up a whole new related subject: overloadable methods. Not only can you override the functionality of a inherited method, you can also change the parameters of that method (which changes the declaration itself). This is an advanced subject that I'll cover in more detail in the next chapter. For now, let's stick to overriding, because that's a complicated enough subject on its own.

## The Dog Class

Now that you've got a complete `Animal` class ready to go, I'd like to show you how it will be used to complete the Pet Shop program. What you are going to do next is inherit the functionality of `Animal` into numerous sub-classes that will represent each of the animals available for sale in the fictional pet shop. Let's start with the `Dog` class. You are familiar with the format of a class definition, right? If not, feel free to flip back a few pages any time I start to lose you because I'm going to move along more quickly now.

The `Dog` class is much shorter than the `Animal` class because it is a descendant of `Animal` and has access to all the public properties and methods in `Animal`. Type in the code listing for the `Dog` class below the `Animal` class. If this seems like a messy way to do it, hang in there, because I'll show you how to clean it up in the next chapter. It *needs* to be messy, so that I can show you how useful namespaces are!

```
Public Class Dog
    Inherits Animal

    'default constructor for Dog class
    Sub New()
        MyBase.New("Dog", 4)
        Breed = ""
        Gender = ""
        Coloration = ""
        Cost = 0
        Console.WriteLine("Dog default constructor")
    End Sub

    'overloaded constructor
    Sub New(ByVal strName As String)
        Me.New()
        Name = strName
        Console.WriteLine("Dog overloaded constructor")
    End Sub

    'overridden Play function
    Overrides Function Play() As String
        Console.WriteLine("Dog.Play")
        Return Name & " fetches the frisbie"
    End Function

End Class
```

### Inheriting from the Animal Class

Did you understand this class a little better than the last one? It is a lot easier to follow because there aren't so many properties. The most interesting part of the Dog class is the first line of code:

```
Inherits Animal
```

Leave it to Visual Basic to make some things really hard to understand, and other things ridiculously easy to understand. The Dog class inherits from the Animal class; it's that simple. The Dog class also has an overloaded constructor with a single parameter that is the name of a specific dog in the pet store.

## Overriding a Base Method

But wait, did you notice anything different about the Play function? Go back and look at the declaration of Play in the Animal class. Aside from the Console.Write-Line line (which is just used for informational purposes when running the Pet-Shop program later), the Animal.Play method returned a blank string, "", whereas the Dog.Play method returned a real message. But that's not what I'm talking about; take a look at the word Overrides. That's not the same as Overridable, as it appears in the Animal class.

You've probably already figured out what I'm going to say next! Any time you declare a base method with Overridable, inherited classes must declare the same method using the Overrides keyword. Of course, you don't have to override a method unless you need to change its functionality (for instance, returning a real message instead of an empty string).

## The GreatDane Class

Now I'm going to create yet *another* sub-class; this time inheriting from Dog, which inherits from Animal. The result is quite surprising. Any methods that Dog didn't override are available to the new class (which will be called GreatDane). The new class also has access to all of the inheritable stuff inside the Dog class! Although Dog did override the Play method, Dog didn't override the Talk method. I left it for the GreatDane class to demonstrate multiple-level inheritance. The public and protected items in a class are available to any number of descendants—not just the very next descendant! GreatDane, then, might be considered the grandchild of Animal, as shown in Figure 10.11.

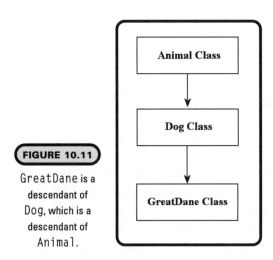

**FIGURE 10.11**

GreatDane is a descendant of Dog, which is a descendant of Animal.

Type in the code listing for the GreatDane class below the Dog class in the code window for Form1. The only significant thing about GreatDane that I would like you to notice is the Inherits Dog line. This is the key to giving GreatDane the functionality of Dog and Animal.

```
Public Class GreatDane
    Inherits Dog

    'default constructor for GreatDane class
    Sub New()
        MyBase.New()
        Breed = "Great Dane"
        Cost = 400
        Console.WriteLine("GreatDane default constructor")
    End Sub

    'overloaded constructor
    Sub New(ByVal strName As String, ByVal strColor As String)
        MyBase.New(strName)
        Breed = "Great Dane"
        Cost = 400
        Coloration = strColor
        Console.WriteLine("GreatDane overloaded constructor")
    End Sub

    'overridden Speak function
    Public Overrides Function Speak()
        Console.WriteLine("GreatDane.Speak")
        Return Name & " says 'Woof, Woof!'"
    End Function

End Class
```

### The MiniDoxen Class

To make the pet shop more interesting, I've added another dog breed—this time a Miniature Doxen. These are feisty little dogs that make great pets, so go ahead and add MiniDoxen to the code. You might notice that this is almost exactly like the GreatDane class. In fact, it is very similar. If you have other favorite types of dogs that you would like to add to the Pet Shop program, go ahead and paste a copy of the class, and then modify it with the properties for your favorite breed of dog.

```
Public Class MiniDoxen
    Inherits Dog

    'default constructor for MiniDoxen class
    Sub New()
        MyBase.New()
        Breed = "Miniature Doxen"
        Cost = 600
        Console.WriteLine("MiniDoxen default constructor")
    End Sub

    'overloaded constructor
    Sub New(ByVal strName As String, ByVal strColor As String)
        MyBase.New(strName)
        Breed = "Miniature Doxen"
        Cost = 800
        Coloration = strColor
        Console.WriteLine("MiniDoxen overloaded constructor")
    End Sub

    'overridden Speak function
    Public Overrides Function Speak()
        Console.WriteLine("MiniDoxen.Speak")
        Return Name & " says 'Boo boo boo boo!'"
    End Function

End Class
```

## The Cat Class

Now, the pet store would be pretty boring if the only animals it had available were dogs, so let's add some more animals to the pet store. I'm actually going to have you add cats and birds, but the cats will come first. Like the dog classes, the cat classes feature a main class called Cat and then two sub-classes (which happen to be called Siamese and Manx).

The main Cat class is similar to the main Dog class. There are two constructors (one overloaded with a single parameter), along with a Play method. Now here's the interesting part! The Play method that the Cat class overrides has the same format as the Play method in the Dog class. This means that when it comes time to actually use these classes in the Pet Shop program, the Dog and Cat objects will be compatible. I'll explain that more later on. For now, type in the Cat class code listing at the bottom of the source code for Form1, as you have been doing up to this point. The code listing is starting to get pretty long, isn't it? That's okay because organization comes in the next chapter, as I've mentioned already.

```
Public Class Cat
    Inherits Animal

    'default constructor for Cat class
    Sub New()
        MyBase.New("Cat", 4)
        Breed = ""
        Gender = ""
        Coloration = ""
        Cost = 0
        Console.WriteLine("Cat default constructor")
    End Sub

    'overloaded constructor
    Sub New(ByVal strName As String)
        Me.New()
        Name = strName
        Console.WriteLine("Cat overloaded constructor")
    End Sub

    'overridden Play function
    Overrides Function Play() As String
        Console.WriteLine("Cat.Play")
        Return Name & " attacks the yarn ball"
    End Function

End Class
```

### The Siamese Class

Okay, here comes the Siamese class, which inherits from Cat. See the line that accomplishes the inheritance part? This class looks exactly like the GreatDane and MiniDoxen classes, so feel free to copy and paste if you want to save yourself some typing.

```
Public Class Siamese
    Inherits Cat
```

```
'default constructor for Siamese class
Sub New()
    MyBase.New()
    Breed = "Siamese"
    Cost = 250
    Console.WriteLine("Siamese default constructor")
End Sub

'overloaded constructor
Sub New(ByVal strName As String, ByVal strColor As String)
    MyBase.New(strName)
    Breed = "Siamese"
    Cost = 250
    Coloration = strColor
    Console.WriteLine("Siamese overloaded constructor")
End Sub

'overridden Speak function
Public Overrides Function Speak()
    Console.WriteLine("Siamese.Speak")
    Return Name & " says 'Rrrrowwll!'"
End Function

End Class
```

### The Manx Class

Alright, now for the second Cat sub-class. This one is called Manx, and it is just like the Siamese class, so by all means, copy and paste whenever possible to save time. Don't worry about what all this code does at the moment. As is usually the case with object-oriented programs, there's a lot of work up front, but that work pays huge dividends later when the main program starts using classes. In fact, the code listing for the Pet Shop program later on is quite short. Now, go ahead and type in the code for the Manx class, and if you aren't crazy about Manx cats (I think they make great pets myself), feel free to give it a different name.

```
Public Class Manx
    Inherits Cat

    'default constructor for Manx class
    Sub New()
```

```
            MyBase.New()
            Breed = "Manx"
            Cost = 100
            Console.WriteLine("Manx default constructor")
        End Sub


        'overloaded constructor
        Sub New(ByVal strName As String, ByVal strColor As String)
            MyBase.New(strName)
            Breed = "Manx"
            Cost = 100
            Coloration = strColor
            Console.WriteLine("Manx overloaded constructor")
        End Sub


        'overridden Speak function
        Public Overrides Function Speak()
            Console.WriteLine("Manx.Speak")
            Return Name & " says 'Meow, ffftttt!'"
        End Function

End Class
```

## The Bird Class

Finally, we are at the home stretch with the Bird class! Do you need any additional explanation at this point? The following classes look just like those you already typed in for Dog and Cat.

```
Public Class Bird
    Inherits Animal

    'default constructor for Bird class
    Sub New()
        MyBase.New("Bird", 2)
        Breed = ""
        Gender = ""
        Coloration = ""
        Cost = 0
        Console.WriteLine("Bird default constructor")
    End Sub
```

```
'overloaded constructor
Sub New(ByVal strName As String)
    Me.New()
    Name = strName
End Sub


'overridden Play function
Overrides Function Play() As String
    Console.WriteLine("Bird.Play")
    Return Name & " bites your finger."
End Function

End Class
```

### The Cockatiel Class

The Cockatiel is a darling bird and makes a wonderful pet. I had a very cute Cockatiel for many years, named Sparky, so I'm fond of Cockatiels. If you were wondering at this point why all these similar classes couldn't have been made simpler by using a single generic class, you are right. But that is exactly what you have already done with the Dog, Cat, and Bird classes! These sub-classes (such as Cockatiel) are merely for demonstration purposes, showing how inheritance works.

You could use the Bird class to accomplish the same thing, by setting the properties of the bird to match those created in the Cockatiel sub-class. But the point is to understand how inheritance, encapsulation, and polymorphism work (and how they work in unison). Just recognize that in the real world, the Cockatiel class would be replaced with something like a database table or a user-interface form. It is also my hope that a little repetition will help you grasp these concepts. By seeing the same type of class repeated several times but with slightly different properties, I'm relying on the age-old truth that practice makes perfect.

```
Public Class Cockatiel
    Inherits Bird

    'default constructor for Cockatiel class
    Sub New()
        MyBase.New()
        Breed = "Cockatiel"
        Cost = 250
        Console.WriteLine("Cockatiel default constructor")
    End Sub
```

```
'overloaded constructor
Sub New(ByVal strName As String, ByVal strColor As String)
    MyBase.New(strName)
    Breed = "Cockatiel"
    Cost = 250
    Coloration = strColor
    Console.WriteLine("Cockatiel overloaded constructor")
End Sub


'overridden Speak function
Public Overrides Function Speak()
    Console.WriteLine("Cockatiel.Speak")
    Return Name & " says 'Squawkkk, " & Name & " want a cracker!'"
End Function

End Class
```

## The Parakeet Class

Okay, just one more and you'll be done with the pet shop classes! Just copy the Cockatiel class and paste it to the bottom of the source code listing in Form1, then make the necessary changes listed below.

```
Public Class Parakeet
    Inherits Bird

    'default constructor for Parakeet class
    Sub New()
        MyBase.New()
        Breed = "Parakeet"
        Cost = 75
        Console.WriteLine("Parakeet default constructor")
    End Sub


    'overloaded constructor
    Sub New(ByVal strName As String, ByVal strColor As String)
        MyBase.New(strName)
        Breed = "Parakeet"
        Cost = 75
        Coloration = strColor
        Console.WriteLine("Parakeet overloaded constructor")
    End Sub
```

```
'overridden Speak function
Public Overrides Function Speak()
    Console.WriteLine("Parakeet.Speak")
    Return Name & " says 'Pee-dee-deet, peet.'"
End Function

End Class
```

# Chapter Project—The Pet Shop Program

You now have a good list of classes for the Pet Shop program: the three main classes (Dog, Cat, and Bird) and then two sub-classes for each main class—all of which inherit from the base Animal class. The Pet Shop program was designed to demonstrate all of the concepts learned in this chapter, and also uses a user interface that has the look and feel of a database application.

## Running the Program

How about a quick tour of the Pet Shop program? Figure 10.12 shows the program at startup. Note that there are nine animals in the pet shop looking for loving homes.

Clicking one of the animals in the ListBox fills the TextBox fields with the particulars of that animal (Name, Species, Breed, and so on), as shown in Figure 10.13.

Figure 10.14 shows the result of clicking the Speak button, which invokes the Speak method for the object referenced in the list. Recall that Speak is an Overridable method that was originally defined in the Animal class, and passed down to the GreatDane class (by way of Dog).

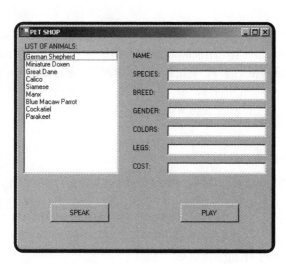

**FIGURE 10.12**

The Pet Shop
program at startup.

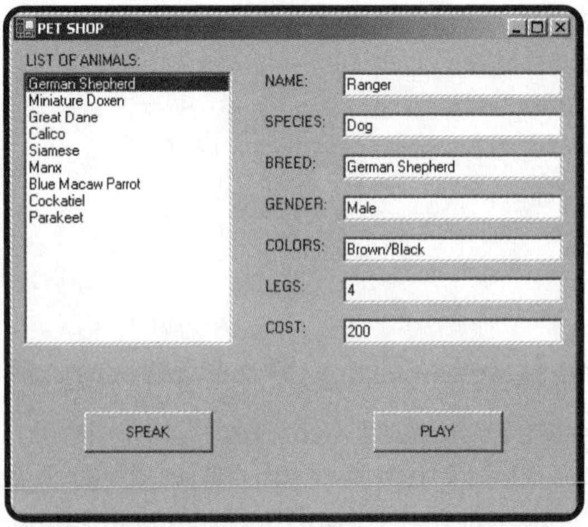

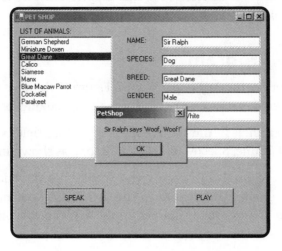

**FIGURE 10.13**

Clicking one of the items in the list fills the detail fields with information about that pet.

**FIGURE 10.14**

The Speak button calls on the Speak method for the object that is currently selected in the list.

The Play button (see Figure 10.15) displays a message by way of the Play method, overridden in the Cat class (in this example, featuring the Manx cat). Because the Manx class didn't override the Play method, VB.NET calls the method found in next highest parent class, which is Cat. Recall that Cat overrides Play but not Talk (which is overridden in Siamese and Manx).

## Revisiting the Project

You should already have the PetShop project open (after typing in the classes earlier). For reference, take a look at Figure 10.16. This figure shows the source code as it looks when you shrink sections of code with the small +/- boxes on the left edge of the Code window. I've kept the Parakeet class open for reference, although it's the last class in the listing.

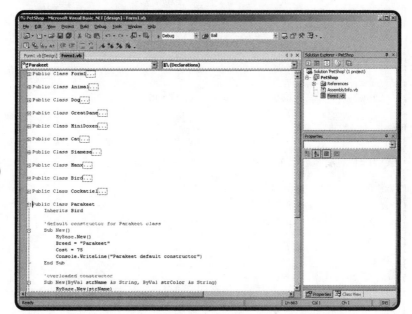

What this project needs now is a user interface. Table 10.1 lists the properties for the form and controls needed to build the PetShop project. Just add each control and set the properties as listed, or use the mouse to move and resize each control. Precision is not important, so feel free to use your own best judgment; all that matters is that the control names are correct.

## TABLE 10.1 FORM/CONTROL PROPERTIES FOR PETSHOP

| Control | Name | Property | Value |
|---------|------|----------|-------|
| Form | Form1 | Text | PET SHOP |
| | | FormBorderStyle | FixedSingle |
| | | Size | 454, 390 |
| | | StartPosition | CenterScreen |
| Label | Label1 | Location | 8, 8 |
| | | Size | 144, 16 |
| | | Text | LIST OF ANIMALS: |
| ListBox | ListBox1 | Location | 8, 24 |
| | | Size | 168, 212 |
| Label | Label2 | Location | 200, 24 |
| | | Size | 56, 16 |
| | | Text | NAME: |
| Label | Label3 | Location | 200, 56 |
| | | Size | 56, 16 |
| | | Name | SPECIES: |
| Label | Label4 | Location | 200, 88 |
| | | Size | 56, 16 |
| | | Text | BREED: |
| Label | Label5 | Location | 200, 120 |
| | | Size | 56, 16 |
| | | Text | GENDER: |
| Label | Label6 | Location | 200, 152 |
| | | Size | 56, 16 |
| | | Text | COLORS: |
| Label | Label7 | Location | 200, 184 |
| | | Size | 56, 16 |
| | | Text | LEGS: |
| Label | Label8 | Location | 200, 216 |
| | | Size | 56, 16 |
| | | Text | COST: |

**TABLE 10.1  FORM/CONTROL PROPERTIES FOR PETSHOP**

| Control | Name | Property | Value |
|---------|------|----------|-------|
| TextBox | TextBox1 | Location | 264, 24 |
|         |          | Size | 176, 20 |
|         |          | Text | (blank) |
| TextBox | TextBox2 | Location | 264, 56 |
|         |          | Size | 176, 20 |
|         |          | Text | (blank) |
| TextBox | TextBox3 | Location | 264, 88 |
|         |          | Size | 176, 20 |
|         |          | Text | (blank) |
| TextBox | TextBox4 | Location | 264, 120 |
|         |          | Size | 176, 20 |
|         |          | Text | (blank) |
| TextBox | TextBox5 | Location | 264, 152 |
|         |          | Size | 176, 20 |
|         |          | Text | (blank) |
| TextBox | TextBox6 | Location | 264, 184 |
|         |          | Size | 176, 20 |
|         |          | Text | (blank) |
| TextBox | TextBox7 | Location | 264, 216 |
|         |          | Size | 176, 20 |
|         |          | Text | (blank) |
| Button | Button1 | Location | 56, 288 |
|        |         | Size | 104, 32 |
|        |         | Text | SPEAK |
| Button | Button2 | Location | 288, 288 |
|        |         | Size | 104, 32 |
|        |         | Text | PLAY |

## Finishing the Source Code

You already have a sizeable amount of source code in this project after typing in all those classes. Now it's time to add the usual user-interface events, including the variable declarations and Form1_Load. You may want to open up the form (which should still be visible if you just finished adding the controls) and actually double-click the form itself to open up the Form1_Load event. All of the following code should go inside the Form1 class, which is located at the top of the program (recall that all the other classes were typed in below the Form1 class). In most cases, you can have VB.NET do the work for you by double-clicking each of the buttons and the ListBox (which opens the default events in the code editor).

**Section 1.** First, let's start with the variables used by this program. Often an array, which is how this program keeps track of the animals, is the best way to handle several related objects. The array is called pets and is declared with nine elements (numbered 0 to 8) as the Animal class. Now, this is the interesting part. Because Animal is the base class for Dog, Cat, and Bird, you can set the individual elements of the pets array to any of those sub-classes, and VB.NET will handle the complexities of inheritance for you. By declaring all as Animal, you are able to keep the code simple (as opposed to declaring each variable according to the specific sub-class that's needed).

```
Dim pets(9) As Animal
Dim n As Integer
```

**Section 2.** Form1_Load is first executed when the program starts running—actually, right before the form is displayed. This is where the properties for the array of animals are set. I have used the Dog, Cat, and Bird classes directly to show how to use their properties, and have also used the sub-classes (GreatDane, MiniDoxen, and so on). Note that the sub-classes require much less code than their parent classes. The reason for that is because the sub-classes set those properties in the constructor.

```
Private Sub Form1_Load(ByVal sender As System.Object, _
    ByVal e As System.EventArgs) Handles MyBase.Load

    'add the German Shepherd dog
    pets(0) = New Dog("Ranger")
    With pets(0)
        .Breed = "German Shepherd"
        .Coloration = "Brown/Black"
        .Cost = 200
        .Gender = "Male"
    End With
```

```
'add the MiniDoxen dog
pets(1) = New MiniDoxen("Cindy", "Black")
pets(1).Gender = "Female"


'add the Great Dane dog
pets(2) = New GreatDane("Sir Ralph", "Brown/White")
pets(2).Gender = "Male"
```

**Section 3.** Next comes the declaration of the Cat objects: Cat, Siamese, and Manx. Each cat has a name (Misty, Buster, and Horatio) to give them some personality.

```
'add the Calico cat
pets(3) = New Cat("Misty")
With pets(3)
    .Breed = "Calico"
    .Coloration = "Orange/Black"
    .Cost = 50
    .Gender = "Female"
End With


'add the Siamese cat
pets(4) = New Siamese("Buster", "Orange/White")
pets(4).Gender = "Male"


'add the Manx cat
pets(5) = New Manx("Horatio", "Brown")
pets(5).Gender = "Male"
```

**Section 4.** Next comes the declaration of the bird objects: Bird, Cockatiel, and Parakeet (named Bluebill, Sparky, and Sprinkles, respectively).

```
'add the Blue Macaw Parrot
pets(6) = New Bird("Bluebill")
With pets(6)
    .Breed = "Blue Macaw Parrot"
    .Coloration = "Blue/Green/Yellow"
    .Cost = 1200
    .Gender = "Male"
End With


'add the Cockatiel
pets(7) = New Cockatiel("Sparky", "Gray/Yellow")
```

```
        pets(7).Gender = "Female"

        'add the Parakeet
        pets(8) = New Parakeet("Sprinkles", "White")
        pets(8).Gender = "Male"
```

**Section 5.** The last part of Form1_Load takes the array of Animal objects and fills List-Box1 with the breed of each animal. You use this list to select a pet in the program.

```
        'add pets to the list
        For n = 0 To 8
            ListBox1.Items.Add(pets(n).Breed)
        Next
    End Sub
```

**Section 6.** This section of code includes an event for the ListBox1 control; specifically, the event that is triggered when you select one of the items in the list. This code makes a call to the Display subroutine to fill the fields with pertinent data about the selected pet.

```
    Private Sub ListBox1_SelectedIndexChanged( _
        ByVal sender As System.Object, _
        ByVal e As System.EventArgs) _
        Handles ListBox1.SelectedIndexChanged

        Display(pets(ListBox1.SelectedIndex))

    End Sub
```

**Section 7.** Next comes the Display subroutine called by the ListBox1_Selected IndexChanged event. This is a support routine that fills in the TextBox fields with the properties of a pet (passed as a parameter).

```
    Public Sub Display(ByRef pet As Animal)
        TextBox1.Text = pet.Name
        TextBox2.Text = pet.Species
        TextBox3.Text = pet.Breed
        TextBox4.Text = pet.Gender
        TextBox5.Text = pet.Coloration
        TextBox6.Text = pet.Legs
        TextBox7.Text = pet.Cost
    End Sub
```

**Section 8.** The next snippet of code involves the Button1_Click event, which is deceptively short. The single line that calls MsgBox invokes the Speak method, which is overridden by each of the lowest-level sub-classes (GreatDane, Siamese, Cockatiel, and so on). The specific object is obtained through the SelectedIndex property of ListBox1, which provides the index of the selected list item, rather than the list item itself.

```
Private Sub Button1_Click(ByVal sender As System.Object, _
    ByVal e As System.EventArgs) Handles Button1.Click

    MsgBox(pets(ListBox1.SelectedIndex).Speak)

End Sub
```

**Section 9.** The last section of code includes the Button2_Click event. Similar to Button1_Click, this event calls MsgBox to display a message returned by an overridden method located in one of the classes. In the case of the Play method, they are all found within Dog, Cat, or Bird (because the lowest-level classes do not override the Play method).

```
Private Sub Button2_Click(ByVal sender As System.Object, _
    ByVal e As System.EventArgs) Handles Button2.Click

    MsgBox(pets(ListBox1.SelectedIndex).Play)

End Sub
```

## Summary

This ends the Pet Shop program and also this chapter. Well, you have certainly had a lot to consume in this chapter on building Visual Basic classes. The Pet Shop program is the largest VB.NET program you have written so far! Although much of the code was redundant in order to build on your experience with encapsulation, inheritance, and polymorphism (the key ingredients of object-oriented programming), it provided a good example for working with classes. OOP is not an easy subject to master. If you have found this material difficult in any way, feel free to peruse key sections of the chapter again.

The following chapter covers the third part of this OOP series on namespaces and visual inheritance. In a way, these subjects are easier to understand than classes, but you will want to fully comprehend the information in this chapter and the last one before moving ahead.

# CHALLENGES

The following challenges will help to reinforce the material you have learned in this chapter.

1. The pet shop doesn't have enough animals to hold the interest of customers, so the owner would like to offer several more breeds of dogs, cats, and birds. Add new classes to the PetShop project to accommodate the owner's request. Be sure to increase the size of the array to handle the new animals.

2. The pet shop business is booming, and the owner is having a hard time keeping pets in stock due to the high demand! Increase the cost of each of the animals by 10 percent using a new variable of type `Decimal` called `decIncrease`. Hint: You might want to modify the `Display` subroutine to increase the price as it is displayed (for example, `TextBox7.Text = pet.Cost + pet.Cost * decIncrease`).

3. The owner of the pet shop is again in need of your programming expertise! The owner wants to add several new species to the pet shop. This will involve adding new classes in the same group as `Dog`, `Cat`, and `Bird`. Specifically, the owner wants to start selling fish, rabbits, turtles, and ferrets! Are you up to the challenge?

# Namespaces
# and Visual
# Inheritance

**T**he final chapter in this three-part series on object-oriented programming is geared toward organizing classes into a hierarchical structure called the *namespace*. In this chapter, I will show you how to create a namespace (or hierarchy of namespaces) to make it easier to access and share the `PetShop` classes from the previous chapter.

In this chapter, I will cover the following:

- Using namespaces

- Visual inheritance

For the purpose of demonstration, this chapter will revise the Pet Shop program from the previous chapter in order to explain how a namespace can be used to organize the classes in a program, rather than create a new program. Although I have changed the program significantly, I assume that you will be using the existing project, and I will point out specific changes that you need to make to the program.

## Using Namespaces

Namespaces allow you to organize a large number of classes into a hierarchical structure, which promotes code reuse and inheritance among classes. Without namespaces, a project quickly becomes cluttered with classes and other objects that are all on the same root namespace (the project name). Moving classes into namespaces that grow out of your own custom root namespace allows you to keep classes separate. The tutorials in this chapter demonstrate how to convert the Pet Shop program into the Pet Store program, which uses namespaces to organize the animal classes presented in the previous chapter.

### Renaming the PetShop Project

To make it easier to create the project for this chapter, I'm just going to modify the existing PetShop project from the previous chapter, even though the changes will be significant. First, let me show you how to rename that project. It will be less confusing if this new project has a different name than the one from the previous chapter (let's call it PetStore).

Open the PetShop project. (I recommend copying the whole PetShop folder to a new location, so you can keep the original intact; name the new folder PetStore). First, make sure Form1 is not open in the form designer because you can't rename a project when a form is loaded.

Now, to rename the project, select the project name in the Solution Explorer, and then highlight the Project File field in the Properties window, as shown in Figure 11.1. Rename the project file to PetStore.vbproj. This will automatically update the project name, in addition to renaming the physical file.

FIGURE 11.1

Changing the
project file is an
easy way to
rename the
entire project.

Figure 11.2 shows the result. Note that the project name in the Solution Explorer was changed to correspond to the Project File. VB.NET does this automatically for you when you rename the file.

Next, while the project name is still highlighted, open the Project menu (as shown in Figure 11.3), and select the Properties menu item.

The Project Properties dialog will appear, as shown in Figure 11.4.

Now, just change the name of the Assembly and Root namespace from PetShop to PetStore (as shown in Figure 11.5), then click the OK button.

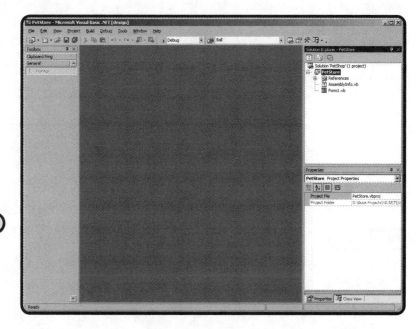

FIGURE 11.2

Changing the
Project File
automatically
updates the
project name.

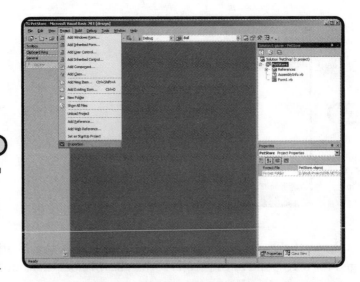

**FIGURE 11.3**

The Project menu includes the Properties menu item when the project name is selected in the Solution Explorer.

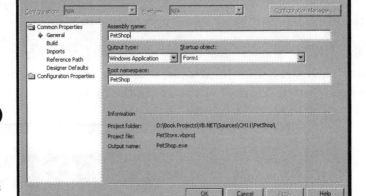

**FIGURE 11.4**

The Project Properties dialog allows you to change the settings for a project.

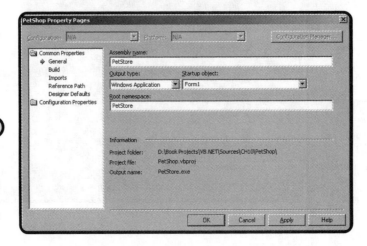

**FIGURE 11.5**

Changing the Assembly and Root namespace fields with the Project Properties dialog.

# What Is a Namespace?

A namespace is a hierarchical structure for organizing classes. You can create and use any namespace name that you want in your programs, as long as it doesn't interfere with any other namespaces that use the same name. Technically, you *can* add your own classes to existing namespaces. For example, you can add your own classes to the System or Microsoft namespaces. But I recommend against it. The flexibility is nice, but you are going to make better use of a namespace by using one of your own design.

The entire Microsoft .NET Framework—which has already become a buzz phrase in programming circles—is a huge collection of classes organized using namespaces. You have already used many of these built-in namespaces, such as System.Windows.-Forms.Form and System.Math. In those cases, System is the root namespace, whereas Windows.Forms.Form and Math are namespaces that branch off System. The .NET Framework completely encapsulates the old Windows Application Programming Interface (API). In the past, Visual Basic programmers had to use the Declare keyword to declare Windows API functions for advanced programs. Now, you have complete access to the entire Windows API using the simple .NET Framework class library, organized into a logical hierarchy of namespaces.

## Creating a Namespace

If you recall, the Pet Shop program includes a bunch of classes for the animals in the pet shop, and these classes were just added to the end of the source code for Form1. The goal of this chapter is to organize the PetShop classes, while demonstrating how to create a namespace. So, let's get started on that right now.

First, this program needs some breathing room, so let's add a new file and start moving those classes out of Form1. They just aren't manageable tacked on to the end of the Form code like that. Select Project, Add Class, as shown in Figure 11.6.

That menu command brings up the Add New Item dialog, as shown in Figure 11.7.

See the Templates window on the Add New Item dialog in Figure 11.7? That's a list of component types that you can add to your project. Make sure you select the Class template because you need a new class. Name it Pet.vb, and then click the Open button to add the new file to your project. Figure 11.8 shows what the project looks like after Pet.vb has been added.

Okay, now you get to create the new namespace! It's really easy, only involving a couple lines of code. You will be surprised at how easy and flexible the namespace feature of VB.NET really is. Add a couple blank lines above the Public Class

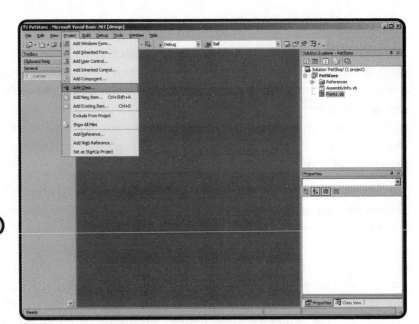

**FIGURE 11.6**

Opening the Add
New Item dialog.

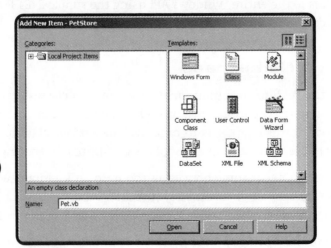

**FIGURE 11.7**

Using the Add New
Item dialog to add
a new class to
the project.

Pet line, and type in **Namespace Pets**. But don't press the Enter key after typing it in! If you do that, VB.NET will automatically add the End Namespace line, and it really needs to go below the Pet class. It is surprising how much VB.NET does automatically. The automatic filling of code block statements is a real time saver. But instead of pressing the Enter key, press the down arrow key, and watch what happens. VB.NET indents the Pet class statement! Take a look at Figure 11.9.

You might have noticed the blue squiggly line below the Namespace Pets line. This is another amazing feature of VB.NET; it compiles your program as you type, immediately finding bugs for you. Just move the mouse cursor over the squiggly line to see what VB.NET has to say about the error (see Figure 11.10).

VB.NET is just reminding you of something you already know—the End Namespace line is needed at the end. Type it in now to remove the error so that the code looks like Figure 11.11.

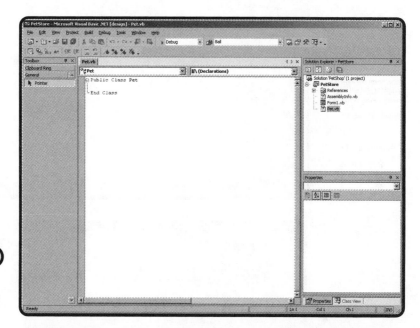

**FIGURE 11.8**

The PetStore project with a new class file added.

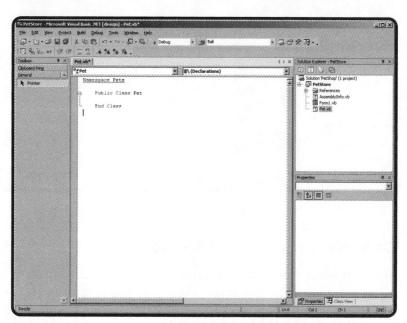

**FIGURE 11.9**

VB.NET indents blocks of code automatically, enforcing good coding standards.

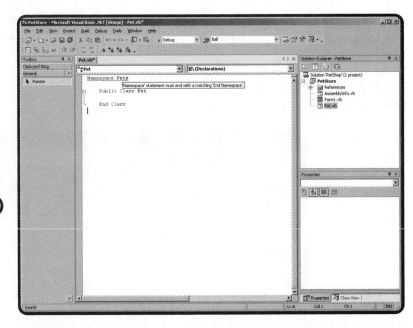

**FIGURE 11.10**

Background compilation automatically detects syntax errors in the program.

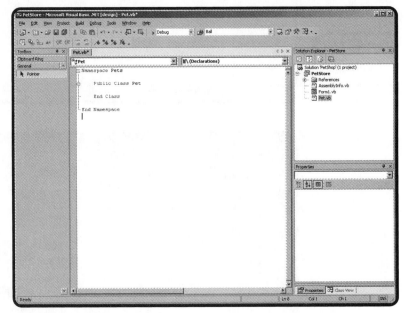

**FIGURE 11.11**

The completed Namespace block of code.

## Completing the Pet Class

Now that you have a new namespace, let's finish the Pet class. The Pet class is going to inherit from the Animal class that you created in the previous chapter. Type the following code between the Public Class Pet and End Class lines.

```
Inherits Animal

'new variables for Pet
Private strFood As String

'default constructor for Pet class
Sub New()
    MyBase.New()
    strFood = ""
End Sub

'overloaded constructor
Sub New(ByVal strSpecies As String, ByVal intLegs As Integer)
    MyBase.New(strSpecies, intLegs)
End Sub

'accessor property for strFood
Property Food() As String
    Get
        Return strFood
    End Get
    Set(ByVal Value As String)
        strFood = Value
    End Set
End Property
```

The resulting Pet class should look like Figure 11.12.

## Moving the Animal Class into the Pets Namespace

Now that you have a nice start on the Pets namespace, let's start moving code out of Form1 and into the namespace. Open the source code window for Form1, and locate the Animal class, starting with the line that shows Public Class Animal. Highlight all of the lines in the Animal class using the Shift+Arrow keys or using the mouse, and then press Ctrl+X to cut. This causes the code to be copied to the Windows Clipboard and then deleted from the source. Next, open the Pet.vb file again, move the cursor below the Namespace Pets line, and paste the text by pressing Ctrl+V. Figure 11.13 shows the result.

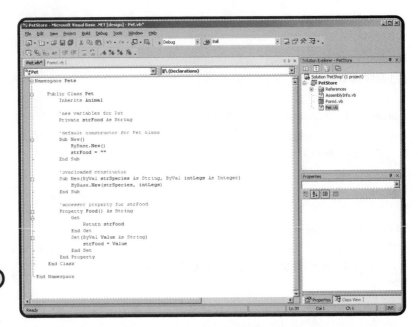

**FIGURE 11.12**

The source code
for the Pet class.

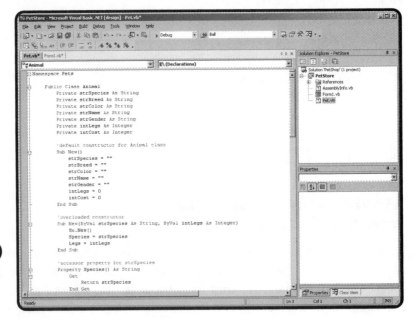

**FIGURE 11.13**

The Animal class
has been moved to
the Pet.vb file.

If you shrink the blocks of code for both the Animal and Pet classes, using the code shrink/expand symbols (which resemble the + and - symbols in Windows Explorer), the result should look like Figure 11.14. This code-hiding feature of VB.NET makes it easier to focus on sections of code while ignoring others, especially when you have a large number of classes or namespaces in a single file.

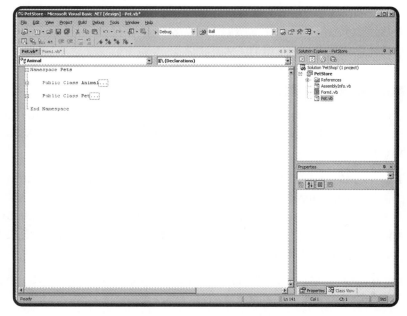

**FIGURE 11.14**

The Pet.vb file now contains both the `Animal` and `Pet` classes.

## Creating the Pets.Dogs Namespace

The next thing I'm going to do is likely to sound confusing, but with a snap of the finger, it will all make sense. What I want to do is add a level, `Dogs`, to the `Pets` namespace, and then move the `Dog` classes into this namespace. Also, the main `Dog` class will be moved into the root `Pets` namespace.

Add a new class by selecting Project, Add Class, just like you did earlier to add the Pet.vb file. Make sure you select the Class template, and name the new file Dog.vb.

First, add `Namespace Pets` around the `Dog` class, as you did earlier with the `Pet` class. Okay, now for the confusing part. Didn't you already create the `Pets` namespace in the previous step? Yes, you did! That's the magical part of namespaces. They just sort of hang out somewhere in VB.NET—compliant and flexible and willing to serve your needs. You really can do anything you want with a namespace. As I have mentioned already, namespaces are organizing structures and are not really functional as far as solving problems. You can add classes to multiple files in a project that all share the same namespace. By surrounding classes with the `Namespace name` block, those classes are part of the namespace. You can also rename the namespace at any time; just be mindful that doing so may break existing code. Because classes are *inside* a namespace, you must provide the namespace name as well as the class name when using those classes. For example, to use the `Pet` class created earlier, you would create a variable like this:

```
Dim pet1 As New Pets.Pet
```

See how the namespace and dot operator are added to the front of the class name, Pet? IntelliSense works here too, so you can see your entire namespace structure as you type in the variable declaration.

### Moving the Dog Class

Okay, now let's add the Pets and Pets.Dogs namespaces to this file. You already have the new Dog.vb file open, so just add the namespace blocks, as shown in Figure 11.15.

The GreatDane and MiniDoxen classes are going to be moved into the Pets.Dogs namespace, whereas the main Dog class is going to be moved into the Pets namespace (in this file, at least). First, let's work on Dog. Open the code for Form1 again and locate the Public Class Dog line. Cut the Dog class out of the Form1 file, and paste it into the Dog.vb file, as shown in Figure 11.16.

Important: make a single change to the Dog class so that it inherits from Pet instead of Animal. The result is shown in Figure 11.17.

Next, add two lines to the constructor:

```
'new property from Pet
Food = "doggie chow"
```

The final changes to the Dog class are shown in Figure 11.18.

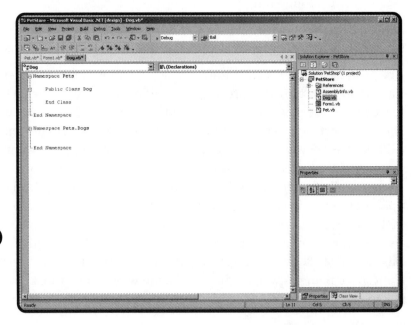

Adding a
namespace
structure to the
Dog.vb file.

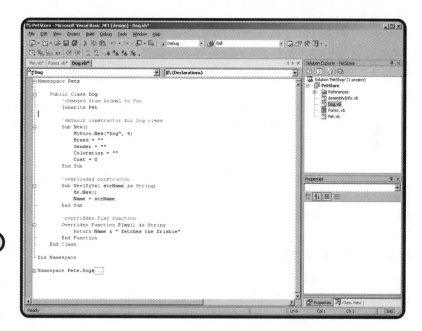

Moving the Dog
class from Form1
to Dog.vb.

Changing the
inheritance of the
Dog class from
Animal to Pet.

Why are all these changes needed, you might ask? The new Pet class that was
added to the project inherits from Animal, so none of the pets will inherit directly
from Animal any longer. Instead, they will inherit from Pet. As a result, the animals need to use a new property of the Pet class: Food. Until now, the pets have

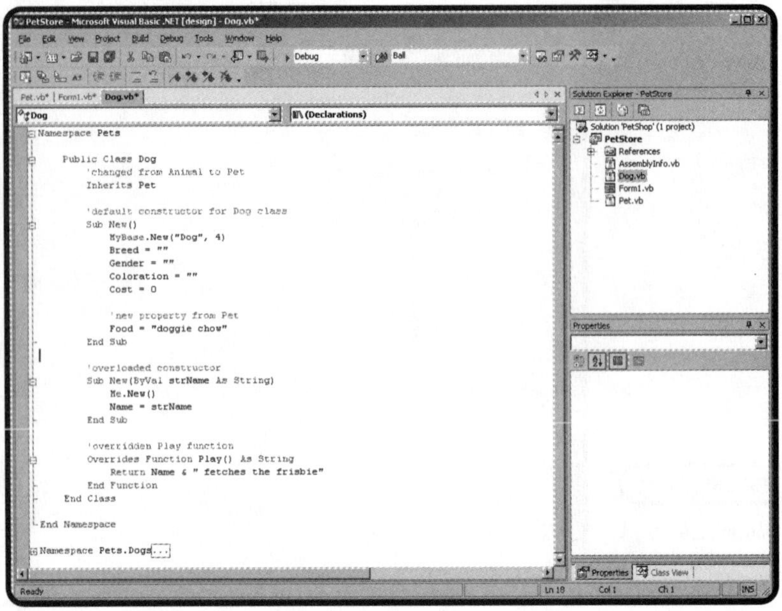

**FIGURE 11.18**

Adding two new lines to the constructor `Sub New()`.

all been eating the same generic chow, but we want to give each animal their favorite kind of food. Fortunately, this change only needs to be made to the base classes (such as `Dog`), not all the sub-classes.

> **HINT**
>
> Don't worry about errors that start showing up as squiggly blue lines in the Form1.vb file. Cutting and pasting code usually causes all kinds of problems in a project until you're finished!

Remember, you can shrink blocks of code in Form1.vb to make it easier to locate the `Dog` class. I have deleted the `Console.WriteLine` lines because they were just helpers in the previous chapter and are no longer needed.

## Moving the GreatDane and MiniDoxen Classes

You won't have to make any changes at all to `GreatDane` or `MiniDoxen`. But isn't it great just cutting and pasting code, rather than typing it all in? One thing you might be wondering is why I didn't do this in the first place in the previous chapter. In the real world, this is something that you will often have to deal with. The Pet Shop program in the previous chapter was written by the pet shop owner, and he didn't organize his project very well! So, he hired you to clean it up, and that's what you're doing now.

Open the Form1.vb file again and cut the `GreatDane` and `MiniDoxen` classes out of it. Then paste the classes into the Dog.vb file inside the `Pets.Dogs` namespace (at the bottom of the source code). Figure 11.19 shows the Dog.vb file with the classes added to `Pets.Dogs`.

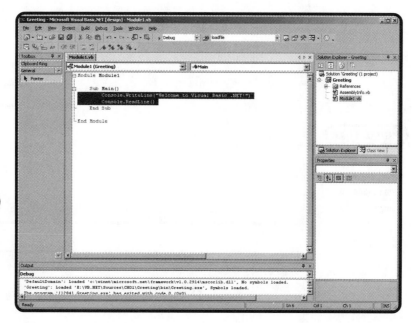

## Creating the Pets.Cats Namespace

The `Pets.Cats` namespace will resemble `Pets.Dogs` when completed, therefore I'm not going over every small detail this time. Add a new class to the project using the Project, Add Class menu item, and call it Cat.vb. Type in the `Namespace Pets` block around the new `Cat` class, and then create the `Pets.Cats` namespace below. Figure 11.20 shows the result of this first round of changes.

### Moving the Cat Class

Open the Form1.vb file and use cut and paste to move the `Cat` class into the Cat.vb file. Change `Inherits Animal` to `Inherits Pet`, and add the `Food` line to the constructor `Sub New()`, as you did with the Dog.vb file. See Figure 11.21 for the result.

### Moving the Siamese and Manx Classes

Open the Form1.vb file again and cut the `Siamese` and `Manx` classes out of it, then paste the classes into the Cat.vb file inside the `Pets.Cats` namespace (at the bottom of the source code). Figure 11.22 shows the Cat.vb file with the classes added to `Pets.Cats`.

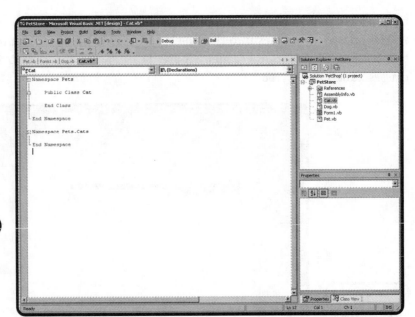

**FIGURE 11.20**

The new
`Pets.Cats`
namespace is
located in the
Cat.vb file.

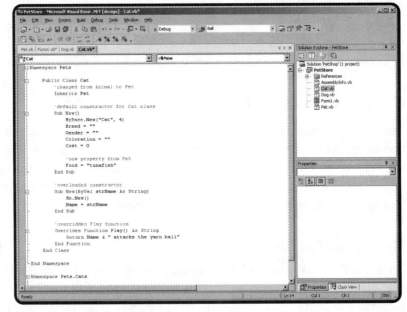

**FIGURE 11.21**

Creating the new
version of the
`Cat` class.

## Creating the Pets.Birds Namespace

Now for the final species offered in the pet store: birds. Just as you did in the preceding two instances, add a new class file to the project called Bird.vb. Add `Namespace Pets` to the top, and `Namespace Pets.Birds` to the bottom, as shown in Figure 11.23.

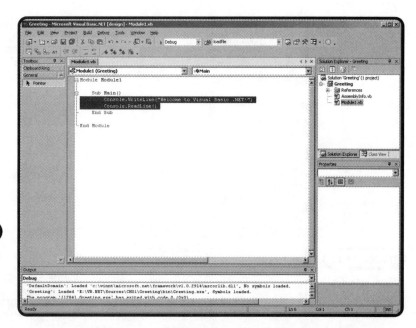

**FIGURE 11.22**

The Siamese and
Manx classes
finish off the
Cat.vb file.

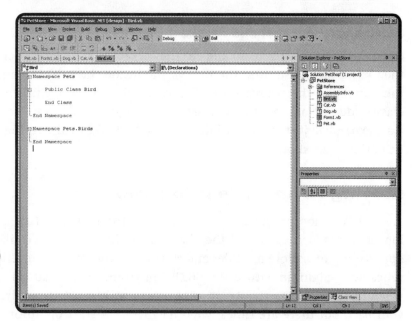

**FIGURE 11.23**

The new Bird.vb file
has been added to
the project.

## Moving the Bird Class

Open the Form1.vb file and use cut and paste to move the Bird class into the
Bird.vb file. Change the Inherits Animal line to Inherits Pet, and add the Food
line to the constructor Sub New(), as you did with the Cat.vb file. See Figure 11.24
for the result.

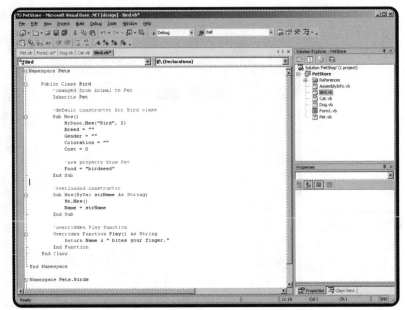

**FIGURE 11.24**

Creating the new version of the Bird class.

## Moving the Cockatiel and Parakeet Classes

Open the Form1.vb file again and cut the Cockatiel and Parakeet classes out of it, then paste the classes into the Bird.vb file inside the Pets.Birds namespace (at the bottom of the source code). Figure 11.25 shows the Bird.vb file with the classes added. Note that unlike the previous figures, this time I left the Parakeet class expanded, just to show what it should look like (while trying to get it all to fit in the screenshot).

## Moving Form Code into a Module

The old Pet Shop program is still located in the Form1.vb file, although it no longer works (because of all the changes you have made). I'd like to take this opportunity to explore modules and startup subroutines. Up to this point, I have relied on the built-in nature of a VB.NET program to automatically display Form1 when the program starts. It's an easy way to go because it requires no work on your part. But there are times when having Form1 start up automatically is not the best way to have the program run, especially when it comes to using namespaces.

The project needs a new module file to hold Sub Main, which will start up instead of Form1. (I'll show you how to change the startup object in a moment.) Select Project, Add Component to bring up the Add New Item dialog (as shown in Figure 11.26).

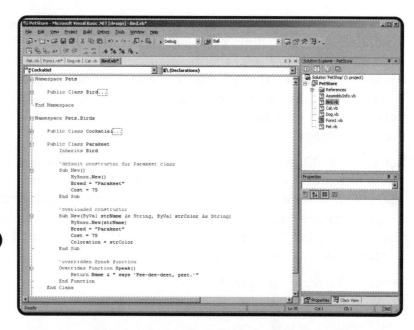

FIGURE 11.25

The Cockatiel
and Parakeet
classes finish off
the Bird.vb file.

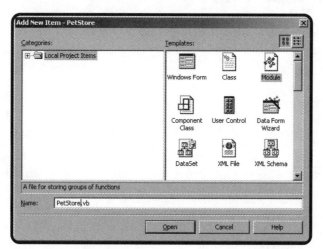

FIGURE 11.26

The new
PetStore.vb module
will include a Sub
Main startup
subroutine.

Select the Module template type and call it PetStore.vb, and then click the Open
button. Type the following code into the PetStore.vb module. The code inside
FillArray was copied out of Form1_Load, so feel free to cut and paste when possible to save time typing it in.

Note that the pets array has been renamed to petarray. Can you guess why this
was necessary? Because Pets is now the name of the namespace for this project!
Not only will duplicate names lead to confusion, they often lead to bugs in the
program. Note also the new variable called MyForm1. That's right, the form itself

is now going to be a variable instead of the main part of the program. `Sub Main` is an interesting subroutine because it has to explicitly call `MyForm1.ShowDialog`. There are two ways to display a form: using `Show` or `ShowDialog` (which actually has an overloaded version that you can ignore at this time). In previous versions of Visual Basic, you could display a form by calling `Form1.Show`. If you wanted the form to remain exclusive, as is usually the case with a dialog box, then you would use the `vbModal` parameter like this: `Form1.Show vbModal`.

Not so in VB.NET. Now, there are two versions of the `Show` method. One called `Show`, which is used mainly when you have more than one form in a project (and one of the forms is already visible), and another that displays the form as a modal form—meaning, it has the focus until closed. VB.NET programs must call `ShowDialog` to display the first form in the program. Otherwise, the form will appear and then suddenly disappear again!

Now, on with the source code for PetStore.vb.

```
'declare the form variable
Public MyForm1 As New Form1()

'declare the array variable
Public petarray(8) As Pets.Pet

Public Sub Main()
    'initialize the animals
    FillArray()

    'display the form
    MyForm1.ShowDialog()

End Sub

Private Sub FillArray()
    'add the German Shepherd dog
    petarray(0) = New Pets.Dog("Ranger")
    With petarray(0)
        .Breed = "German Shepherd"
        .Coloration = "Brown/Black"
        .Cost = 200
        .Gender = "Male"
    End With

    'add the MiniDoxen dog
```

```vbnet
    petarray(1) = New Pets.Dogs.MiniDoxen("Cindy", "Black")
    petarray(1).Gender = "Female"

    'add the Great Dane dog
    petarray(2) = New Pets.Dogs.GreatDane("Sir Ralph", "Brown/White")
    petarray(2).Gender = "Male"

    'add the Calico cat
    petarray(3) = New Pets.Cat("Misty")
    With petarray(3)
        .Breed = "Calico"
        .Coloration = "Orange/Black"
        .Cost = 50
        .Gender = "Female"
    End With

    'add the Siamese cat
    petarray(4) = New Pets.Cats.Siamese("Buster", "Orange/White")
    petarray(4).Gender = "Male"

    'add the Manx cat
    petarray(5) = New Pets.Cats.Manx("Horatio", "Brown")
    petarray(5).Gender = "Male"

    'add the Blue Macaw Parrot
    petarray(6) = New Pets.Bird("Bluebill")
    With petarray(6)
        .Breed = "Blue Macaw Parrot"
        .Coloration = "Blue/Green/Yellow"
        .Cost = 1200
        .Gender = "Male"
    End With

    'add the Cockatiel
    petarray(7) = New Pets.Birds.Cockatiel("Sparky", "Gray/Yellow")
    petarray(7).Gender = "Female"

    'add the Parakeet
    petarray(8) = New Pets.Birds.Parakeet("Sprinkles", "White")
    petarray(8).Gender = "Male"
End Sub
```

## Form1 Source Code

The code inside Form1.vb needs to be modified to accommodate all the changes that have taken place since the original Pet Shop program was written. Most of the code has now been moved to various classes and the PetStore.vb module. User-interface events remain in Form1, and they need to be modified too! Remember that the pets array was renamed, so you can't use pets any longer. Try running the program now, and you will get all kinds of errors in Form1! So, let's just rewrite Form1's source code. It's a short listing, at any rate. Just delete all the code in Form1, or modify it so that it looks like the following code listing.

```vb
Dim n As Integer

Private Sub Form1_Load(ByVal sender As System.Object, _
    ByVal e As System.EventArgs) Handles MyBase.Load

    'add pets to the list
    For n = 0 To 8
        ListBox1.Items.Add(petarray(n).Breed)
    Next
End Sub

'change this
Private Sub ListBox1_SelectedIndexChanged( _
    ByVal sender As System.Object, _
    ByVal e As System.EventArgs) _
    Handles ListBox1.SelectedIndexChanged

    Display(petarray(ListBox1.SelectedIndex))

End Sub

Public Sub Display(ByRef pet As Pets.Animal)
    TextBox1.Text = pet.Name
    TextBox2.Text = pet.Species
    TextBox3.Text = pet.Breed
    TextBox4.Text = pet.Gender
    TextBox5.Text = pet.Coloration
    TextBox6.Text = pet.Legs
    TextBox7.Text = pet.Cost
End Sub
```

```
Private Sub Button1_Click(ByVal sender As System.Object, _
    ByVal e As System.EventArgs) Handles Button1.Click

    MsgBox(petarray(ListBox1.SelectedIndex).Speak)

End Sub

Private Sub Button2_Click(ByVal sender As System.Object, _
    ByVal e As System.EventArgs) Handles Button2.Click

    MsgBox(petarray(ListBox1.SelectedIndex).Play)

End Sub
```

## Completing the PetStore Project

All that remains is changing the startup object of the PetStore project to point to Sub Main instead of Form1. If you leave it as is, you'll get an error when trying to run the program. Open the Project Properties dialog once again, and change the Startup object to Sub Main, as shown in Figure 11.27.

The conversion to PetStore is now complete! Run the program by pressing F5. The output is shown in Figure 11.28.

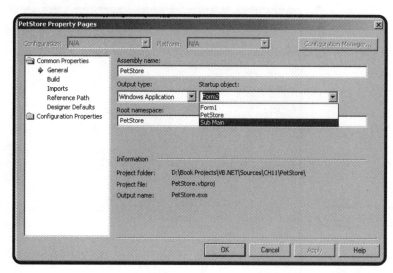

**FIGURE 11.27**

Changing the startup object to Sub Main.

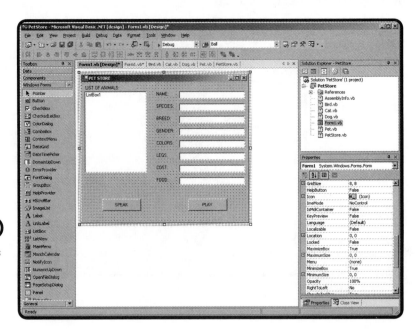

## Adding New Functionality to PetStore

Now that the program has been converted to use namespaces, I'd like to make use of the enhancements now available with the Pet class (which subclasses Animal). Actually, there's only one new feature: a property called Food, which describes the food preferred by each animal in the pet store.

First, add two new controls to Form1, Label9 and TextBox8, as shown in Figure 11.29.

**FIGURE 11.29**

The Food controls
(Label9 and
TextBox8)
have been added
to the form.

Next, the `Display` subroutine needs to be modified so that it displays the new field with the other fields for each animal. Add the following lines of code to the end of `Display`:

```
'new field available in the Pet class
TextBox8.Text = pet.Food
```

The result should look like Figure 11.30.

Great, now the Pet Store program is finished! Go ahead and run it now. The result is shown in Figure 11.31.

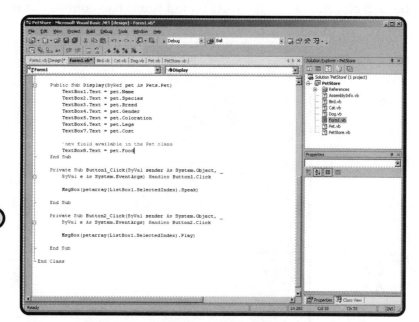

**FIGURE 11.30**

The changes to Sub Display add functionality to the new Food field.

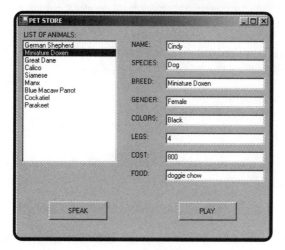

**FIGURE 11.31**

The Pet Store program now uses namespaces and features the new Food field.

# Visual Inheritance

Visual inheritance is a new feature in VB.NET, which allows you to reuse forms and controls between projects. Ideally, you would compile a form or control as a component into a .DLL file, so it could be shared. For demonstration purposes, I'll just show you how to inherit one form into another, within the same project.

## Creating a Reusable Form

Create a new Windows Application called VisualInheritance. Add four controls to the default Form1: a Label, a TextBox, and two Button controls, as shown in Figure 11.32.

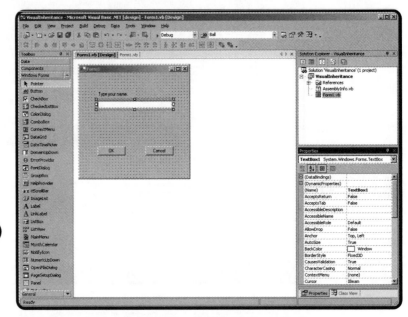

**FIGURE 11.32**

The basic dialog-style form in the VisualInheritance project.

Now, double-click the first button to open up the default event for the button. Type the following code into the Button1_Click event:

```
If TextBox1.Text.Length > 0 Then
    MsgBox("Hello, " & TextBox1.Text & "!")
End If
```

Likewise, double-click the second button and type the following code in Button2_Click:

```
End
```

Now run the program. The output should look something like Figure 11.33.

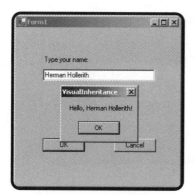

**FIGURE 11.33**

The
VisualInheritance
program running.

## Reusing the Reusable Form

Now, creating inherited forms is fairly easy, because VB.NET has a menu item
that does all the work for you. And actually, you can do it yourself because the
code that VB.NET generates is *extremely* short, as you'll see.

Select Project, Add Inherited Form. The Add New Item dialog appears, with the
Inherited Form template already selected (as shown in Figure 11.34). Accept the
default name of Form2.vb and click the Open button.

The Inheritance Picker dialog is shown (see Figure 11.35). Accept the default (in
which Form1 is selected). The new form is automatically added to the project.

Figure 11.36 shows the new form, Form2.vb, as it appears in the project. Note how
each of the controls on the new form have a small Inherited icon in the upper-
left corner.

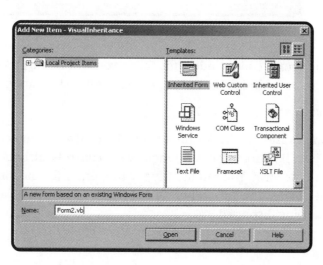

**FIGURE 11.34**

The Add New Item
dialog is used to
add an Inherited
Form to the project.

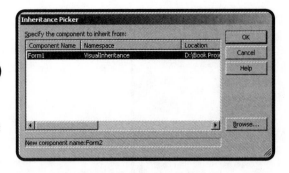

**FIGURE 11.35**

The Inheritance Picker dialog allows you to select a source for the new inherited form.

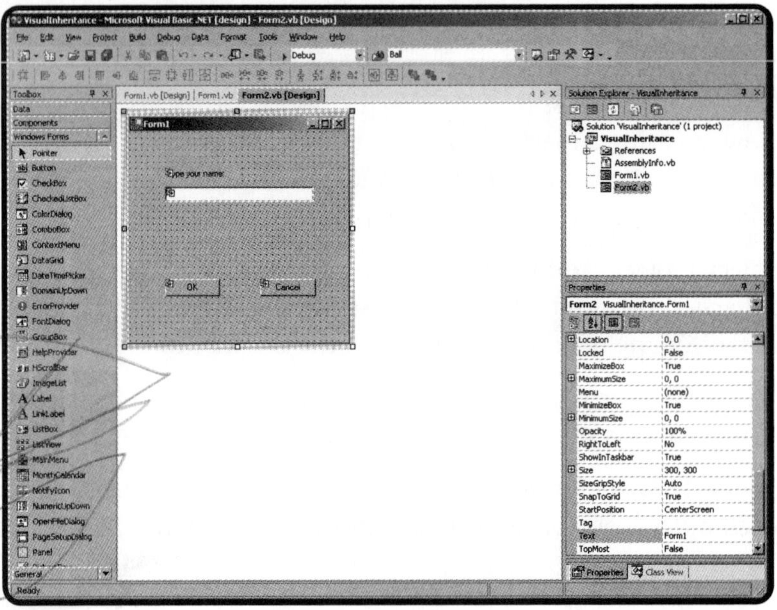

**FIGURE 11.36**

The new form is added to the project, showing all of the inherited controls.

If you open the source code window for Form2, you will be surprised to find only a single line that's significant in the project (the rest is standard generated code).

```
Inherits VisualInheritance.Form1
```

That line alone causes VB.NET to import all the controls into Form2 and causes Form2 to look just like Form1. You can't modify the controls, although you can add new controls to the form. You can modify the properties for the form, such as the Text property. Change the Text property to Form2, so you will be able to identify which form is being displayed.

## Running the VisualInheritance Program

Now let's change the `Startup` object to Form2.vb, so you can see how visual inheritance works. Right-click the project name in the Solution Explorer, and select Properties from the drop-down list that appears. The Project Properties dialog is shown in Figure 11.37.

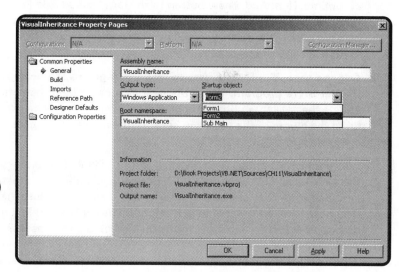

**FIGURE 11.37**

Changing the
`Startup` object
using the Project
Properties dialog.

Select `Form2` from the drop-down list of objects, and then click the OK button. Now run the program! It should operate just like it did when `Form1` was the `Startup` object. However, there's no code behind `Form2`! Amazing, isn't it? As you can imagine, you have just scratched the surface of what's possible with visual inheritance.

## Summary

Namespaces add the capability to organize classes and other things in VB.NET, such as inherited forms and controls. By organizing your classes into a hierarchy of namespaces that grows out of a root namespace of your own design, you can effectively manage large projects involving dozens or even hundreds of classes and other objects. In this chapter, you have organized the classes developed in the previous chapter into a namespace called `Pets` and found that namespaces help to group related classes. The resulting Pet Store program effectively demonstrates the power of OOP in VB.NET.

# CHALLENGES

The following challenges will help to reinforce the material you have learned in this chapter.

1. Modify the Pet Store program so that you can add new animals to the list at runtime. Hint: Add a new button to the form, called Add Pet. Then, when the user clicks this button, ask the user to select the type of animal and to give it a name. Note that you will need to increase the pet array to accommodate a larger number of entries.

2. Add the capability for the user to make changes to the fields displayed in the Pet Store program. When the user changes a field, have the program update the petarray with the appropriate value! This will be extremely useful to the owner of the pet store because the prices of the pets change on a daily basis.

3. Add another inherited form (Form3) to the VisualInheritance project, and this time have it inherit from Form2. Does VB.NET allow you to add another inherited form that subclasses a form that was already inherited? Why or why not? Can you think of how it might be possible to build a hierarchy of namespaces just for inherited forms instead of just for classes?

# Part

# IV

## Advanced Programming Topics in Visual Basic .NET

Chapter 12: **Graphics Programming**

Chapter 13: **Using Program Menus**

Chapter 14: **Sequential and Random-Access Files**

Chapter 15: **Structured Error Handling and Debugging**

CHAPTER

12

# Graphics Programming

Graphics programming is often the most rewarding and exciting part of computer programming because graphics commands don't always work the way you expect them to. And it's a great way to experiment with new programming ideas due to the immediate visual feedback that comes with learning to use graphics in a program.

In this chapter, I will cover the following:

- **Overview of graphics support**

- **The** Graphics **object**

- **The** CreateGraphics **function**

- **Drawing lines**

- **Drawing rectangles**

- **Writing a Paint program**

In previous chapters, you saw some of the graphics capabilities built into Visual Basic .NET—for example, the DiceWar game in Chapter 6, "Branching Statements and Program Logic," and the Blocks game in Chapter 9, "The Basics of Object-Oriented Programming." Whereas these games might have put regular controls to creative use, this chapter focuses on how to use *real* graphics commands for better effect.

As the DiceWar game showed, it's pretty easy to add custom artwork to a program using the PictureBox control. Although the PictureBox control is versatile, it does lack some of the features from previous versions of Visual Basic. The common commands, such as PSet, Line, and Circle have been moved to the System.Drawing namespace, and these commands (such as DrawLine and DrawRectangle) are part of what is now called the Graphics Device Interface Plus (GDI+). In actual practice, you can just think of them as Drawing methods, and I will show you that they are easy to use.

## Project Preview—The Paint Program

The complete project included in this chapter is a Paint program, which lets you draw pictures using the mouse, with several shapes, colors, and draw sizes to choose from. Figure 12.1 shows an example of the type of pictures you can create with the Paint program; this one in particular took a *long* time to draw because I wanted the American flag to look just right!

Figure 12.2 shows another screenshot of the Paint program, this time showing a drawing that was done with large filled circles.

## Graphics in Abundance!

The most basic concept in graphics programming is the pixel, which is shorthand for "picture element." Pixels make up a computer screen, and everything on the screen is defined by its dimension of width and height in pixels. For example, the most common resolution used by Windows is $1024 \times 768$, which means that the screen is 1024 pixels across and 768 pixels down, as shown in Figure 12.3.

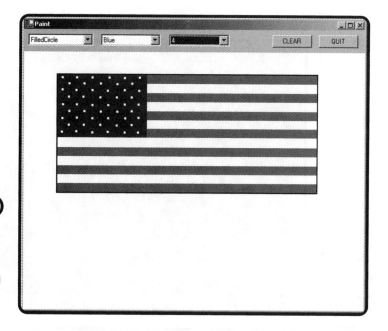

**FIGURE 12.1**

This chapter
features a Paint
program—a digital
canvas for creating
artistic
masterpieces!

**FIGURE 12.2**

It's always nice to
be greeted with a
smiling face.

Zooming into the picture by several orders of magnitude brings up the individual pixels more clearly. See Figure 12.4 for a close-up of the bottom-left corner of the figure, which shows individual pixels that make up the Start button in Windows. Because the resolution is so high in most cases, it's not always easy to see the individual pixels on the screen (especially at very high resolutions like 1600 × 1200).

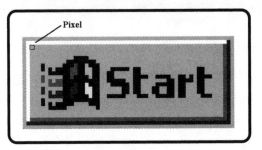

**FIGURE 12.3**

The computer screen is made up of thousands of individual pixels.

**FIGURE 12.4**

Zooming up close shows the actual pixels in a picture.

## Overview of Graphics Support

VB.NET has no built-in graphics support, which is quite a change from earlier versions of Visual Basic. Now, all graphics support is provided by the .NET Framework class library, specifically through a namespace called System.Drawing.Graphics. This namespace provides numerous methods for drawing ellipses, rectangles, arcs, lines, and other shapes.

## The Graphics Object

The System.Drawing.Graphics object is used to call most of the graphics methods you will need to use. Table 12.1 shows a list of graphics drawing routines included in this namespace.

## TABLE 12.1   SYSTEM.DRAWING.GRAPHICS DRAWING METHODS

| Method | Description |
|---|---|
| Clear | Clears the entire drawing surface using a specific color. |
| DrawArc | Draws an arc representing a portion of an ellipse. |
| DrawBezier | Draws a Bézier spline using four points. |
| DrawBeziers | Draws a series of Bézier splines from an array of points. |
| DrawClosedCurve | Draws a closed cardinal spline. |
| DrawCurve | Draws a cardinal spline. |
| DrawEllipse | Draws an ellipse defined by a bounding rectangle. |
| DrawLine | Draws a line connecting two points. |
| DrawLines | Draws multiple line segments from an array of points. |
| DrawPie | Draws a pie shape defined by an ellipse. |
| DrawPolygon | Draws a polygon defined by an array of points. |
| DrawRectangle | Draws a rectangle. |
| DrawRectangles | Draws multiple rectangles defined by an array. |

System.Drawing.Graphics also includes methods for drawing shapes filled with a brush object, which includes the fill style and fill color. Table 12.2 is a list of filled drawing routines also available in this namespace.

## TABLE 12.2   SYSTEM.DRAWING.GRAPHICS FILLED DRAWING METHODS

| Method | Description |
|---|---|
| FillClosedCurve | Draws a filled closed cardinal spline curve. |
| FillEllipse | Draws a filled ellipse. |
| FillPie | Draws a filled pie shape defined by an ellipse. |
| FillPolygon | Draws a filled polygon defined by an array of points. |
| FillRectangle | Draws a filled rectangle. |
| FillRectangles | Draws multiple filled rectangles defined by an array. |

# Basic Graphics Programming

As is usually the case with graphics programming in most languages, VB.NET requires a small amount of preparation before it will display any graphics. Previous versions of Visual Basic allowed you to call functions like PSet and Line at will because these subroutines were built in. First, you need a graphics object, so I'll show you how to create one.

## The CreateGraphics Function

Before doing any graphics programming, you need to create a variable of System.-Drawing.Graphics, like this:

```
Dim gfxobj As System.Drawing.Graphics
```

gfxobj describes that the variable points to the graphics object, although you can use any variable name you want, such as grfx or draw or any other name. Once you have declared the variable, you need to call the CreateGraphics() function to pass a pointer to the graphics object to the new variable:

```
gfxobj = CreateGraphics()
```

Once created, you are free to call on any of the methods inside gfxobj to actually draw shapes on the form.

## Drawing Lines

The Lines program (shown in Figure 12.5) fills the form with blue lines, demonstrating the basic code needed to create the graphics object and draw a line shape. There are several overloaded versions of each drawing method, allowing you to pass Point, Integer, or Single parameters, depending on need.

To write this program, create a new Windows Application, and add a Timer control, called Timer1. The Lines program starts by declaring the gfxobj variable as a System.Drawing.Graphics object, and then declares four integers: x1 and y1 represent the first point, whereas x2 and y2 represent the second point of each line that is drawn. The Timer1_Tick event sets these variables to random values, and then calls DrawLine to actually draw the line. Because Timer1.Interval is set to 10 milliseconds, the program theoretically draws 100 lines per second. (I say theoretically because not all system timers are precisely the same, depending on which version of Windows you are running.)

```
Dim gfxobj As System.Drawing.Graphics
Dim x1 As Integer
```

```
Dim y1 As Integer
Dim x2 As Integer
Dim y2 As Integer

Private Sub Form1_Load(ByVal sender As System.Object, _
    ByVal e As System.EventArgs) Handles MyBase.Load

    'create the graphics object
    gfxobj = CreateGraphics()

    'start the timer
    Timer1.Interval = 10
    Timer1.Enabled = True
End Sub

Private Sub Timer1_Tick(ByVal sender As System.Object, _
    ByVal e As System.EventArgs) Handles Timer1.Tick

    'choose random endpoints for the line
    x1 = Int(Rnd() * Me.Width)
    y1 = Int(Rnd() * Me.Height)
    x2 = Int(Rnd() * Me.Width)
    y2 = Int(Rnd() * Me.Height)

    'draw the line
    gfxobj.DrawLine(Pens.RoyalBlue, x1, y1, x2, y2)
End Sub
```

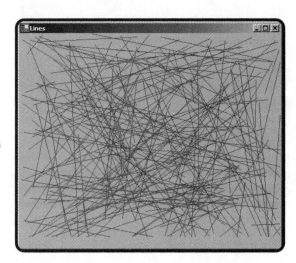

**FIGURE 12.5**

The Lines program demonstrates how to create a graphics object and draw lines on the form.

## Drawing Rectangles

The Rectangles program (shown in Figure 12.6) fills the form with red rectangles, and is similar to the Lines program except for the single line that actually draws the shape.

To see the program in action, modify the Lines program, replacing the old Timer1_Tick event with this new one. Alternatively, you can create a new project, called Rectangles, copy the source code from the Lines program into the new project, and then replace Timer1_Tick as follows. Do you see how there are also four points that define the two opposing corners of a rectangle, like there are for drawing a line?

```
Private Sub Timer1_Tick(ByVal sender As System.Object, _
    ByVal e As System.EventArgs) Handles Timer1.Tick

    'choose random endpoints for the line
    x1 = Int(Rnd() * (Me.Width - 100))
    y1 = Int(Rnd() * (Me.Height - 100))
    x2 = Int(Rnd() * 100)
    y2 = Int(Rnd() * 100)

    'draw the rectangle
    gfxobj.DrawRectangle(Pens.Red, x1, y1, x2, y2)
End Sub
```

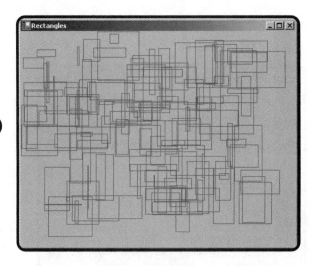

**FIGURE 12.6**

The Rectangles program fills the form with rectangles using the DrawRectangle method.

## Colors, Pens, and Brushes

Colors are extremely easy to use in VB.NET, thanks to a plethora of pre-defined color constants built into the `Color`, `Pen`, and `Brush` objects. To see for yourself, type **Colors.** (that's a period), and you should see an IntelliSense list appear with all the colors available. A similar list will appear for the `Pens` and `Brushes` objects, which are used for drawing outline and filled shapes (respectively).

Feel free to use `Pens.Color` or `Brushes.Color` directly as a parameter any time you need to use these constants. For example, here is how the Lines program filled the pen parameter (assuming x1, y1, x2, and y2 are `Integer` variables):

```
DrawLine(Pens.RoyalBlue, x1, y1, x2, y2)
```

Likewise, when calling a method that needs a `Brush` object as a parameter, you can use a brush constant (assuming x, y, width, and height are `Integer` variables):

```
FillRectangle(Brushes.Aqua, x, y, width, height)
```

## Chapter Project—The Paint Program

The Paint program is not a lengthy project, but I want to explain each step for you to make sure you understand how the graphics commands are used. Let me first show you examples of what you can do with the program (although I already showed you my best work at the beginning of the chapter; now, how much will you pay for the canvas shown in Figure 12.1?). Of course, there is a lot of room for improvement here, as outlined in the Challenges at the end of the chapter. But this is a good start because the program is very functional, even with such a small list of features and drawing modes.

The first screenshot (Figure 12.7) shows the output when `Circle` mode is selected.

The next screenshot, shown in Figure 12.8, shows the result when `Square` mode is selected (although I'm sure you could come up with a better drawing!).

Figure 12.9 shows the output when `Pie` mode is selected.

Selecting a filled drawing mode, such as `FilledCircle`, results in a more attractive display, as shown in Figure 12.10.

The `FilledRectangle` mode (see Figure 12.11) also allows you to do some more interesting things, such as a mock-up of the Blocks program from Chapter 9, "The Basics of Object-Oriented Programming." You can use the Paint program to design screens for your own programs.

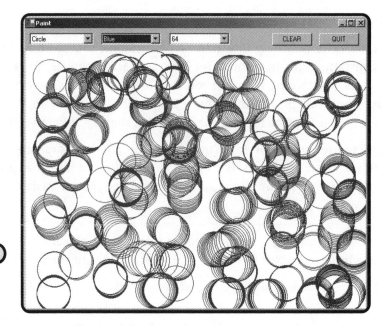

**FIGURE 12.7**

Drawing big blue
circles with the
Paint program.

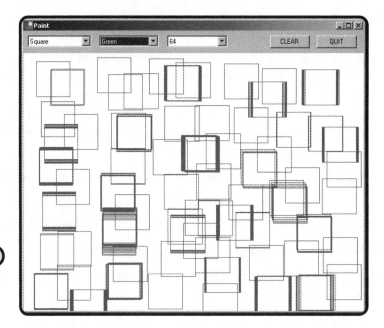

**FIGURE 12.8**

Drawing big green
squares with the
Paint program.

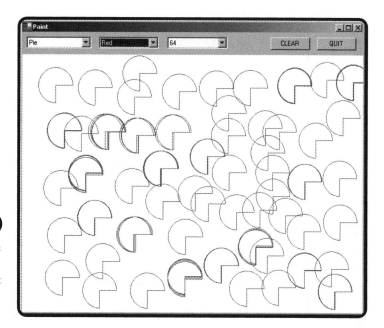

**FIGURE 12.9**

Drawing pie shapes
with the Paint
program—or is that
a familiar arcade
game character?

**FIGURE 12.10**

Drawing filled
circles is a snap
with the Paint
program.

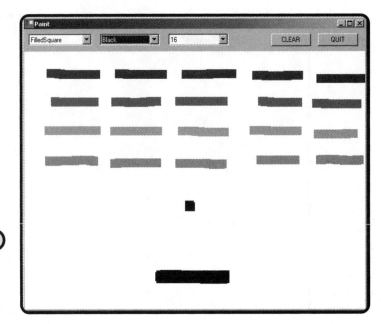

Drawing filled
rectangles—or
is that the
Blocks game?

Finally, Figure 12.12 shows the FilledPie mode used to draw filled pie shapes.

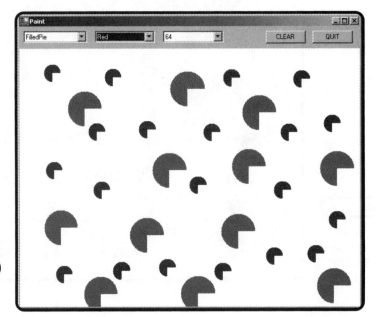

It's raining blue and
red pies!

## Creating the Project

The Paint project includes several ComboBox controls and two buttons atop a Panel control, which is fixed to the top of the form. The completed project is shown in Figure 12.13.

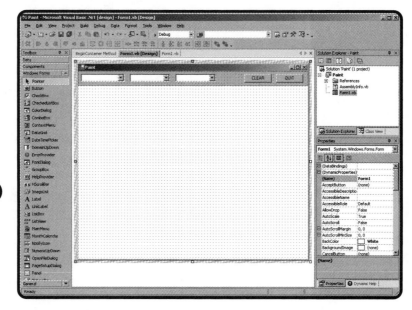

The completed Paint project showing how Form1 should look in the VB.NET form designer.

**Section 1.** First, create a new Windows Application called Paint. There should be a default form added to the project called Form1. Table 12.3 describes how to set up the user interface on the form.

### TABLE 12.3   FORM/CONTROL PROPERTIES FOR PAINT

| Control | Name | Property | Value |
|---|---|---|---|
| Form | Form1 | Text | Paint |
| | | BackColor | White |
| | | Size | 648, 536 |
| | | StartPosition | CenterScreen |
| Panel | Panel1 | Dock | Top |
| | | BackColor | Control |
| | | Size | 640, 40 |

## TABLE 12.3  FORM/CONTROL PROPERTIES FOR PAINT

| Control | Name | Property | Value |
|---------|------|----------|-------|
| ComboBox | ComboBox1 | DropDownStyle | DropDownList |
| | | Location | 8, 8 (inside Panel1) |
| | | Size | 121, 21 |
| ComboBox | ComboBox2 | DropDownStyle | DropDownList |
| | | Location | 144, 8 (inside Panel1) |
| | | Size | 121, 21 |
| ComboBox | ComboBox3 | DropDownStyle | DropDownList |
| | | Location | 144, 8 (inside Panel1) |
| | | Size | 121, 21 |
| Button | Button1 | Location | 464, 8 (inside Panel1) |
| | | Text | CLEAR |
| Button | Button2 | Location | 552, 8 (inside Panel1) |
| | | Text | QUIT |

## Writing the Source Code

The source code for Paint primarily consists of user-interface control events and filling the combo boxes with values when the program starts. I'll go over each section of code step by step.

**Section 2.** The first few lines of code should be added (as usual) right below the Windows Form Designer generated code line. These are variable declarations for the pen, brush, and drawsize variables.

```
Dim pen As System.Drawing.Pen = Pens.Black
Dim brush As System.Drawing.Brush = Brushes.Black
Dim drawsize As Integer
```

**Section 3.** The first event of the program is Form1_Load, which runs right before the form is displayed. Form1_Load just fills each of the three combo boxes with relevant values. For instance, ComboBox1 contains the drawing styles (Circle, Square, and so on), ComboBox2 contains colors, and ComboBox3 contains integer drawing sizes.

```
Private Sub Form1_Load(ByVal sender As System.Object, _
    ByVal e As System.EventArgs) Handles MyBase.Load

    'fill the style list
    ComboBox1.Items.Add("Circle")
    ComboBox1.Items.Add("Square")
    ComboBox1.Items.Add("Pie")
    ComboBox1.Items.Add("FilledCircle")
    ComboBox1.Items.Add("FilledSquare")
    ComboBox1.Items.Add("FilledPie")
    ComboBox1.SelectedIndex = 0

    'fill the color list
    ComboBox2.Items.Add("Black")
    ComboBox2.Items.Add("Blue")
    ComboBox2.Items.Add("Violet")
    ComboBox2.Items.Add("Green")
    ComboBox2.Items.Add("Red")
    ComboBox2.Items.Add("Orange")
    ComboBox2.Items.Add("Yellow")
    ComboBox2.Items.Add("White")
    ComboBox2.SelectedIndex = 0

    'fill the size list
    ComboBox3.Items.Add("2")
    ComboBox3.Items.Add("4")
    ComboBox3.Items.Add("8")
    ComboBox3.Items.Add("16")
    ComboBox3.Items.Add("32")
    ComboBox3.Items.Add("64")
    ComboBox3.SelectedIndex = 0
End Sub
```

**Section 4.** Now for the real meat of the program. Form1_MouseMove is an event that is triggered any time you hold down a mouse button while moving the mouse over the form. In this case, the Paint program only cares about the left mouse button, so a check is made to draw only when the left button is being pressed.

Depending on the draw style selected in ComboBox1, one of six shapes is added to the form at the position of the mouse when the button is pressed: circle, square, pie, filled circle, filled square, or filled pie.

```
Private Sub Form1_MouseMove(ByVal sender As Object, _
    ByVal e As System.Windows.Forms.MouseEventArgs) _
    Handles MyBase.MouseMove

    'see if the left mouse button was pressed
    If e.Button <> MouseButtons.Left Then Exit Sub

    'create the graphics object
    Dim gfxobj As System.Drawing.Graphics = CreateGraphics()

    'draw mode based directly on ComboBox1 value
    Select Case ComboBox1.Text
        Case "Circle"
            'draw a circle
            gfxobj.DrawEllipse(pen, e.X, e.Y, drawsize, drawsize)

        Case "Square"
            'draw a square
            gfxobj.DrawRectangle(pen, e.X, e.Y, drawsize, drawsize)

        Case "Pie"
            'draw a pie
            gfxobj.DrawPie(pen, e.X, e.Y, drawsize, drawsize, 90, 270)

        Case "FilledCircle"
            'draw a filled circle
            gfxobj.FillEllipse(brush, e.X, e.Y, drawsize, drawsize)

        Case "FilledSquare"
            'draw a filled square
            gfxobj.FillRectangle(brush, e.X, e.Y, drawsize, drawsize)

        Case "FilledPie"
            'draw a filled pie
            gfxobj.FillPie(brush, e.X, e.Y, drawsize, drawsize, 90, 270)
    End Select
End Sub
```

**Section 5.** The Form1_MouseDown event is also included for those cases in which the user just presses the mouse button. Form1_MouseMove is only executed when the mouse is moving, so a single mouse click isn't registered without MouseDown. To keep the code simple, this event simply calls MouseMove, passing on the parameters directly.

```
Private Sub Form1_MouseDown(ByVal sender As Object, _
    ByVal e As System.Windows.Forms.MouseEventArgs) _
    Handles MyBase.MouseDown

    'make single click also draw
    If e.Button = MouseButtons.Left Then
        Form1_MouseMove(sender, e)
    End If
End Sub
```

**Section 6.** The second ComboBox includes a list of colors in textual form, which isn't usable by the drawing methods, so these colors must be converted to actual pen and brush values. A single Select...Case statement takes care of that.

```
Private Sub ComboBox2_SelectedIndexChanged( _
    ByVal sender As System.Object, ByVal e As System.EventArgs) _
    Handles ComboBox2.SelectedIndexChanged

    'change the pen and brush color
    Select Case ComboBox2.Text
        Case "Black"
            pen = Pens.Black
            brush = Brushes.Black
        Case "Blue"
            pen = Pens.Blue
            brush = Brushes.Blue
        Case "Violet"
            pen = Pens.Violet
            brush = Brushes.Violet
        Case "Green"
            pen = Pens.Green
            brush = Brushes.Green
        Case "Red"
            pen = Pens.Red
            brush = Brushes.Red
        Case "Orange"
            pen = Pens.Orange
            brush = Brushes.Orange
```

```
                Case "Yellow"
                     pen = Pens.Yellow
                     brush = Brushes.Yellow
                Case "White"
                     pen = Pens.White
                     brush = Brushes.White
          End Select
    End Sub
```

**Section 7.** Selecting a draw size from `ComboBox3` causes that combo's `Text` property to equal the actual number, therefore it's an easy matter to grab that value and convert it to an `Integer` using the `Int` function.

```
Private Sub ComboBox3_SelectedIndexChanged( _
    ByVal sender As System.Object, ByVal e As System.EventArgs) _
    Handles ComboBox3.SelectedIndexChanged

    'change the draw size based on combobox value
    drawsize = Int(ComboBox3.Text)
End Sub
```

**Section 8.** Clicking the CLEAR button (`Button1`) should cause the form's drawing area to be cleared, wiping it clean for a fresh round of artistic expression. To accomplish this seemingly simple task, you need to create a new `gfxobj` variable because the one used in `Form1_MouseMove` is a local variable and not visible in `Button1_Click`. After the object is created, a call to `Clear` solves the problem.

```
Private Sub Button1_Click(ByVal sender As System.Object, _
    ByVal e As System.EventArgs) Handles Button1.Click

    'create a temporary graphics object
    Dim gfxobj As System.Drawing.Graphics = CreateGraphics()

    'clear the form
    gfxobj.Clear(ActiveForm.BackColor)
End Sub
```

**Section 9.** The last section of code for the Paint program handles the click event for the QUIT button (`Button2`). A simple call to `End` takes care of it.

```
Private Sub Button2_Click(ByVal sender As System.Object, _
    ByVal e As System.EventArgs) Handles Button2.Click
```

```
        'end program
        End
End Sub
```

## Summary

This chapter presented a brief overview of the graphics capabilities of VB.NET. Although there are many more advanced graphics commands available, you now have a good start to writing graphical programs and games, and you should be able to spruce up regular applications with some interesting graphics here and there. I highly recommend adding that little extra touch to your development projects!

### CHALLENGES

The following challenges will help to reinforce the material you have learned in this chapter.

1. Modify the Lines program to test some of the other drawing commands, such as DrawPolygon and DrawBezier. These methods produce some interesting results and are worth investigating.

2. Enhance the Paint program by adding new commands to ComboBox1, such as Arc and FilledArc, among others.

3. Add more colors to ComboBox2 in the Paint program so the user will have a larger palette for making more interesting drawings.

# Using Program Menus

T his chapter will teach you how to create and use menus in VB.NET. You can create two types of menus: main menus and context menus. I'll go over each type of menu, showing you how to edit the menu structures and how to use menus in your programs. The main menu is the most common type of menu, found at the top of most Windows applications. Context menus are often called pop-up menus because they appear when the user right-clicks an item on the screen (for instance, the list of files in Windows Explorer).

In this chapter, I will cover the following topics:

- Creating a main menu
- Creating a context menu

# Creating a Main Menu

Visual Basic 6.0 used a special Menu Editor for constructing both drop-down and main menus for applications. The Menu Editor wasn't the easiest thing in the world to use—for one thing, it was located inside a dialog box instead of directly on the form. Microsoft took another approach for creating menus in VB.NET. Now menus take shape as controls that you add to a form.

Let's try creating menus with the Menu Designer. Create a new Windows Application project, called MainMenu. Resize the form to make it a little bigger than the default, so there's room for menus at the top.

## The MainMenu Control

The main menu for a program is now the MainMenu control (see Figure 13.1). In Visual Basic 6.0, menus were created with the Menu Editor. Now, the MainMenu control adds a visual designer to the form, allowing you to design and edit menus right on the form—which is much easier than the previous Menu Editor.

Double-click the MainMenu control, or drag the control from the Toolbox to your form. Did you notice what happened? Instead of adding the control to your form, the control moved down to the Component tray, as shown in Figure 13.2.

**FIGURE 13.1**

The MainMenu control provides a main menu to an application.

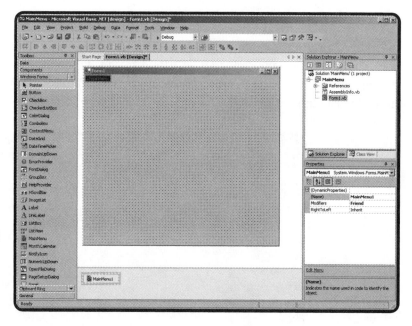

**FIGURE 13.2**

The MainMenu
control is added to
the Component tray
instead of the form.

Take notice of the fledgling new menu that appears on the form when the Main-
Menu1 control is selected. There is now a small menu bar at the top of the form with
a single item labeled Type Here. Click that label, and the Menu Designer will kick
in allowing you to edit the main menu for the program, as shown in Figure 13.3.

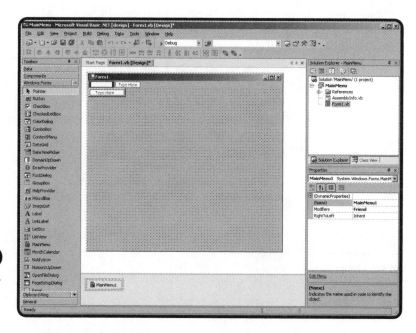

**FIGURE 13.3**

The Menu Designer
is used to edit
menus.

## Customizing the Main Menu

The Menu Designer is extremely easy to use. Each time you click on a `Type Here` label, the Menu Designer adds an edit field to that label and expands it, adding another menu item to the right and below. Type `Apples` in the first menu field, then click the label directly below `Apples`, as shown in Figure 13.4.

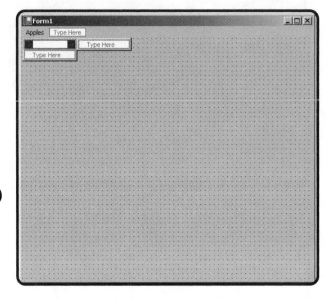

**FIGURE 13.4**

Editing menu names and adding menu items are easy tasks with the Menu Designer.

Add two menu items under `Apples`: `Red Apple` and `Green Apple`. The result should look like Figure 13.5.

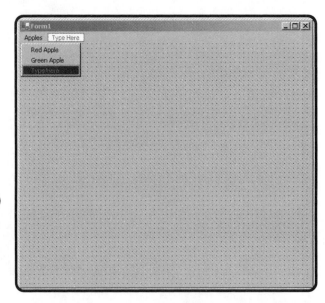

**FIGURE 13.5**

The `Apples` menu now includes two menu items: `Red Apple` and `Green Apple`.

Now, click the `Type Here` label to the right of the `Green Apple` menu item. This will create a sub-menu, which branches from `Green Apple`. Add two menu items: `Regular` and `Caramel`, as shown in Figure 13.6.

Now that `Apples` has a few menu items to make it interesting, let's add another top-level menu. Click the `Apples` menu again to bring up the `Type Here` label. Click the label and type **Grapes**, as shown in Figure 13.7.

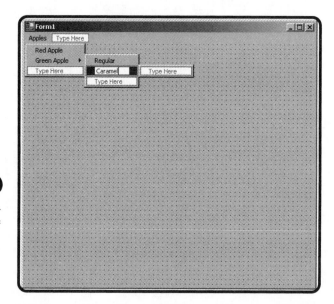

**FIGURE 13.6**

There is now a sub-menu to the right of `Green Apple` with two menu items: `Regular` and `Caramel`.

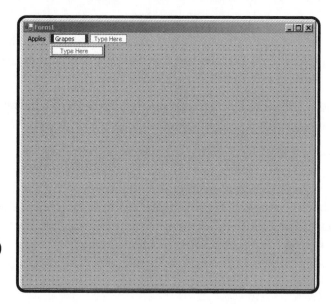

**FIGURE 13.7**

Adding the `Grapes` menu.

The top-level main menu now has two menus: Apples and Grapes. Click the Type Here label below Grapes to add items to the menu. Add Red Grapes and Green Grapes to the Grapes menu, as shown in Figure 13.8.

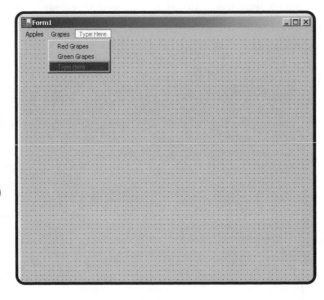

**FIGURE 13.8**

The Grapes menu now has two menu items: Red Grapes and Green Grapes.

You have probably already noticed that you can change the properties for each menu item by clicking the item and then looking at the Properties window. There are several special features you can apply to your menus, such as adding a check mark beside a menu item, disabling menu items, or even making menu items invisible.

Try setting a few properties now to see the results. Change the Checked property for Red Grapes to True, and then set the Green Grapes menu item Enabled property to False. The result is shown in Figure 13.9.

Now let's try out the menus you've just created. Press F5 to run the program. Figure 13.10 shows the output of the program.

Oh no, the menu doesn't show up. Why do you suppose it doesn't work? In Visual Basic 6.0, the main menu was a permanent resident on a form. But in VB.NET, you can create several different menus and plug each one into a form at any time to accommodate the current state of the application. To fix the problem, double-click the form to bring up the code editor and the Form1_Load event. Type the following line into the Form1_Load event:

```
Me.Menu = MainMenu1
```

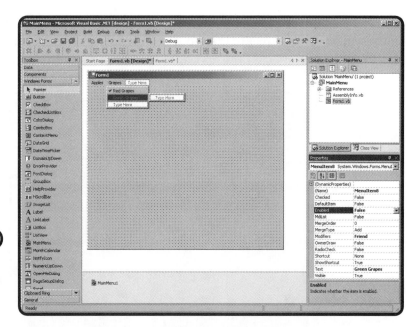

FIGURE 13.9

Menu items have properties that can be set at design time or runtime.

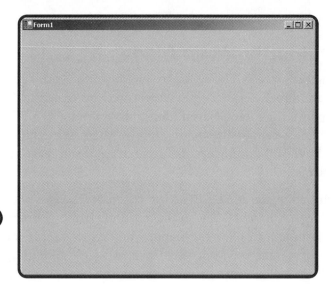

FIGURE 13.10

The Main Menu program's first trial run.

HINT

The Me **object points to the current** form **class, which is usually** Form1 **in your project (unless you have renamed the form).**

Run the program again by pressing F5, and you should see the menu appear this time, as shown in Figure 13.11. Try out the menus, and see how the Checked and Enabled properties affected the appearance and functionality of the menu items.

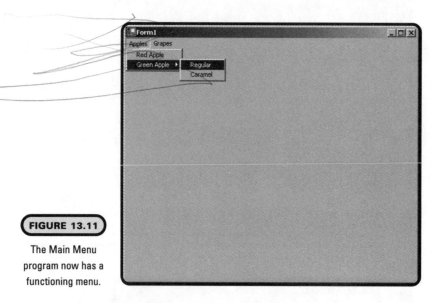

**FIGURE 13.11**

The Main Menu program now has a functioning menu.

## Programming the Main Menu

The Main Menu program might be functional, but it has not been programmed to trigger any events yet. Because you just learned how to create the menus from a visual standpoint, the menus haven't been programmed yet. I'll show you how to add functionality behind the menus to give them something to do. As you might expect, in VB.NET adding events to a menu is just as easy as adding events to regular controls.

Bring up the form designer in VB.NET so you can make changes to the menu. If the form doesn't show Apples and Grapes at the top, don't panic, the menus haven't disappeared. The form only displays the menus when the MainMenu1 control—down in the Component tray—has been selected. Click MainMenu1 to highlight it, and the menu on the form will appear again. Select the Red Apple menu item, as shown in Figure 13.12.

**HINT** If the menus disappear from the form, click the MainMenu1 **control in the Component tray to make the menus visible again.**

Now, double-click the Red Apple menu item. The code editor will open to the MenuItem2_Click event, as shown in Figure 13.13.

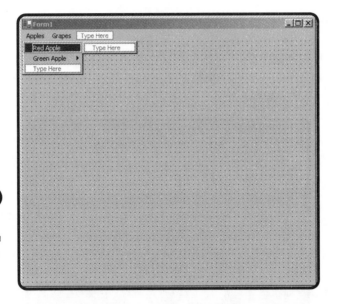

**FIGURE 13.12**

Selecting the
Red Apple menu
item in preparation
for creating a
click event.

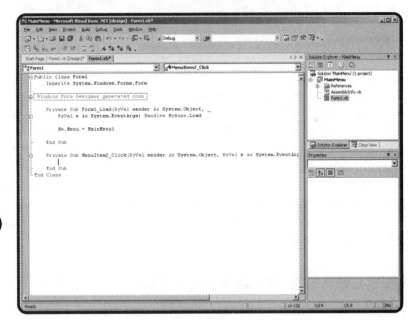

**FIGURE 13.13**

The MenuItem-
2_Click event is
the default event
for the Red
Apple menu item.

Although I didn't have you change the name of the menu items, you are certainly free to give them more descriptive names so that the events are more easily identified. For example, you might give the Red Apple menu item the name of mnuRedApple. For now, I'll just continue to refer to the menus by their default names.

Now, type in the following line of code inside the MenuItem2_Click event:

```
MsgBox("You clicked " & MenuItem2.Text)
```

Now, run the program again; open the Apples menu, and select Red Apple. The result is shown in Figure 13.14.

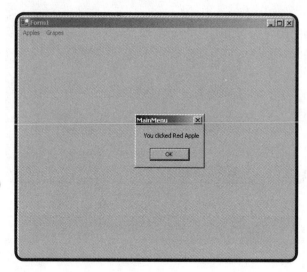

**FIGURE 13.14**

Adding functionality to program menus is extremely easy to do.

 **HINT** Whereas it's possible to add an event for top-level menus, it is generally considered poor program design. Top-level menus should *always* have at least one menu item that drops down to keep the user interface consistent. For example, it is better to have a Help, About menu rather than just leaving About at the top level.

You can add similar events to the other menu items to gain more experience programming menu events. Double-click each menu item in the Menu Designer to bring up the default click event for each, and then display the name or any other information that you want.

## Creating a Context Menu

Context menus (also referred to as pop-up menus) are common in the Windows user interface—typically invoked by right-clicking some object on the screen. In fact, context menus are often more useful and intuitive than main menus because context menus offer functionality for a specific object in an application. On the contrary, main menus usually accommodate top-level program functionality, such as saving and loading files. For an example of a context menu, right-click anywhere in the Form Designer window of VB.NET (for example, on the form itself), and the context menu shown in Figure 13.15 will appear.

FIGURE 13.15

Context menus
usually appear
when the right
mouse button is
clicked on an
object.

## The ContextMenu Control

A large application may have dozens of context menus for manipulating objects on the screen, although many applications could benefit by using more of them. To add a context menu to a VB.NET program, select the ContextMenu control in the Toolbox (shown in Figure 13.16), and drag it to the form (or more specifically, to the Component tray).

After adding the ContextMenu control, VB.NET gives the new control the default name of ContextMenu1 and adds a label to the top of the form called Context Menu (see Figure 13.17).

## Customizing the Context Menu

After the new control has been added to the form, the Menu Designer for a context menu allows you to design the new context menu in a manner that is very similar to main menus. Click the top-level menu, and an item will appear beneath. Click that item, type a name into the edit field, and then add additional menu items as necessary.

FIGURE 13.16

The
ContextMenu
control has the
functionality
needed to add pop-
up menus to an
application.

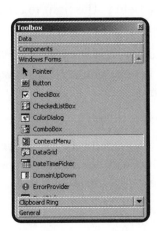

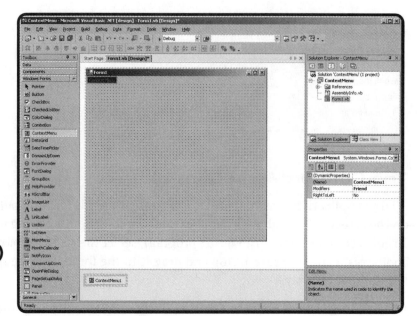

FIGURE 13.17

Adding a new
ContextMenu
control to the form.

The difference with context menus, however, is that you can't change the top-level name. The default name, Context Menu, is not modifiable because context menus do not have a top level—just a single level, which appears when the menu is displayed. However, you can set the properties for each of the menu items.

Let's add some menu items to ContextMenu1. Click the top-level Context Menu label to make the first menu item appear with the label of Type Here. Now, you don't exactly want to double-click this label. Rather, you want to click it once to select it, pause a second, then click it again to open the field for editing. Type Insert into the field, and then click the Type Here field to the right to create a sub-menu for Insert.

What I'd like to do is show you how to modify a Label control at runtime by having ContextMenu1 pop up when you right-click the control. I'll show you how to do that after the context menu has been completed.

Add two menu items next to Insert, called Date and Time (see Figure 13.18).

Now, add another menu item below Insert, and call it Color. This menu item will also bring up a sub-menu with colors that will change the appearance of the label. Add four items to the sub-menu next to Color: Black, Blue, Green, and Red (as shown in Figure 13.19).

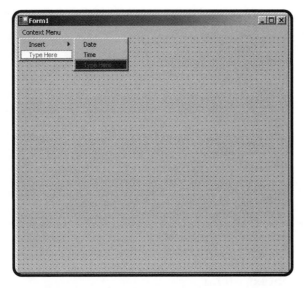

**FIGURE 13.18**

The context menu
now includes a
sub-menu with
two items.

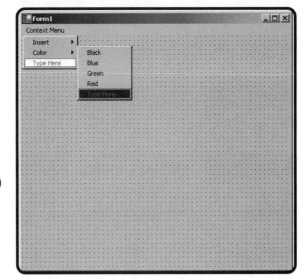

**FIGURE 13.19**

The context menu
now includes a
second sub-menu,
called Color, with
several items.

## Programming Context Menus

Great, now you've created your first context menu. Let's do something interesting
to show off the capabilities of context menus. The program needs a big Label control in the middle of the form. Double-click the Label control from the Toolbox, or
select it and then draw the control on the form. The new control is called Label1.
Table 13.1 shows the properties that need to be set for this control. You may need
to resize the form to accommodate the large label, if you haven't already.

## TABLE 13.1 LABEL1 PROPERTIES

| Control | Name | Property | Value |
|---------|--------|-------------|----------------------|
| Label | Label1 | BorderStyle | Fixed3D |
| | | Font | Arial, 16pt, style=Bold |
| | | Location | 112, 112 |
| | | Size | 256, 48 |
| | | Text | (blank) |
| | | TextAlign | MiddleCenter |

### Displaying the Context Menu

The next part is easy because all you need is for the MouseDown event to call on the context menu. For starters, double-click Label1 to bring up the code editor. You don't want the Label1_Click event because there's no easy way to check for the right mouse button using this event. What you need is MouseDown. Select Label1 from the class browser combo box, shown in Figure 13.20.

Once you have Label1 selected, look in the second combo box for the MouseDown event (see Figure 13.21).

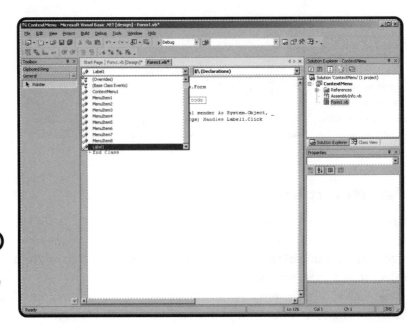

**FIGURE 13.20**

Browsing for Label1 using the class browser combo box.

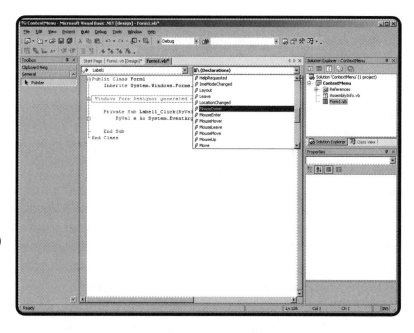

**FIGURE 13.21**

Browsing for
`MouseDown` using
the event browser
combo box.

Once you have it, click the event to add it to the Code Editor window, as shown
in Figure 13.22.

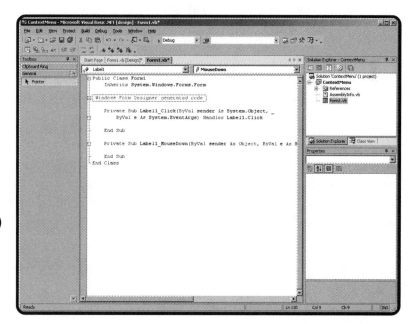

**FIGURE 13.22**

The
`Label1_Mouse
Down` event has
been added to
the project.

Type the following code into the `Label1_MouseDown` event:

```
If e.Button = MouseButtons.Right Then
    ContextMenu1.Show(Label1, New Point(e.X, e.Y))
End If
```

This snippet of code first checks to see if the right mouse button was clicked. If so, the next line then displays the pop-up menu using `ContextMenu1.Show`. The first parameter is the control name (`Label1`), which isn't really used in this program, but is interesting because `ContextMenu1` sends that name through to the menu click events. Anyway, the second parameter is the interesting one. The `Show` method requires a `Point` instead of two integers, which would have been more convenient, because `e.X` and `e.Y` hold the mouse position. But that's not a problem because you can just create a new `Point` on the fly, as shown.

### Adding Functionality to the Context Menu Items

All that remains now is to add functionality to the context menu items. First, let's do the `Date` and `Time` items. You can double-click the menu items directly to have VB.NET add the default event to the code editor, or you can type it in as follows:

```
Private Sub MenuItem2_Click(ByVal sender As System.Object, _
    ByVal e As System.EventArgs) Handles MenuItem2.Click
    'set the label to the current date
    Label1.Text = System.DateTime.Now.ToShortDateString
End Sub


Private Sub MenuItem3_Click(ByVal sender As System.Object, _
    ByVal e As System.EventArgs) Handles MenuItem3.Click
    'set the label to the current time
    Label1.Text = System.DateTime.Now.ToShortTimeString
End Sub
```

The code for the `Color` menu items is very straightforward. In each case, the `Label1.ForeColor` property is set to the appropriate color. Here's the code that accomplishes that:

```
Private Sub MenuItem5_Click(ByVal sender As System.Object, _
    ByVal e As System.EventArgs) Handles MenuItem5.Click

    Label1.ForeColor = Color.Black
End Sub
```

```
Private Sub MenuItem6_Click(ByVal sender As System.Object, _
    ByVal e As System.EventArgs) Handles MenuItem6.Click

    Label1.ForeColor = Color.Blue
End Sub

Private Sub MenuItem7_Click(ByVal sender As System.Object, _
    ByVal e As System.EventArgs) Handles MenuItem7.Click

    Label1.ForeColor = Color.Green
End Sub

Private Sub MenuItem8_Click(ByVal sender As System.Object, _
    ByVal e As System.EventArgs) Handles MenuItem8.Click

    Label1.ForeColor = Color.Red
End Sub
```

That's all there is to it! Now go ahead and press F5 to run the program. Right-click the label and insert the date or time, and then change the text color using the Color menu (see Figure 13.23).

**FIGURE 13.23**

The Context Menu program features a functional pop-up menu!

# Summary

This chapter explained how to create and program your own main menus and context (pop-up) menus using the Menu Designer and source code. Most applications feature at least a main menu, but often include one or more context menus as well for customizing the user interface or performing actions on specific controls on the form. VB.NET allows you to attach any MainMenu control to a form to change the menu structure based on the processes going on in the program.

## CHALLENGES

The following challenges will help to reinforce the material you have learned in this chapter.

1. Gain some additional experience with the Main Menu program by adding several more top-level food menus (such as Bananas, Oranges, and Watermelon), each with menu items and sub-menus that allow the user to select a specific type of fruit using the menus.

2. The Context Menu program is a simple example of an otherwise powerful feature for customizing a program to user tastes. Add several more properties to the menu so that the user can make even more changes to the Label control to suit his or her preferences. For example, add more colors to the Color menu, and perhaps even add a BackColor sub-menu, which changes the background color of the label.

# Sequential and Random-Access Files

This chapter covers file input and output using sequential and random-access files, which I'll explain shortly. File access is an important subject that is often ignored in graphical languages, such as VB.NET, because the language handles so much of the "behind the scenes" work for you. Understanding how to read and write files is an important skill that this chapter helps to develop. File access has changed significantly since Visual Basic 6.0 (like so many other features).

I cover the following topics in this chapter:

- **Introduction to file processing**

- **Using sequential files**

- **Sequential file i/o—The ReadWrite program**

- **Create a rich text editor—The ScratchPad program**

- **Using random-access files**

- **Random-access file i/o—The RandomTest program**

- **Chapter project—The Trivia program**

## Project Preview—The Trivia Program

The complete project included in this chapter is a trivia program, which asks a series of general educational questions, thus demonstrating how to use the file access routines presented in this chapter. See Figure 14.1 for a screenshot of the Trivia program.

## Introduction to File Processing

You are probably already aware of files because they permeate the Windows operating system, and it's difficult to use a computer without thinking in terms of storing data with files. This very book was written using Microsoft Word 2000 and each chapter was stored in its own file. But what is a file, really? The term "file" was borrowed from the method of organization inherent in a file cabinet, where there are drawers filled with open-end folders containing paper, usually standard or legal in size.

A computer file system is similar to a file cabinet, but far more versatile and expandable. The file cabinet itself might be thought of as the physical hard drive in your computer. File cabinets have drawers that are represented in a computer's file system as partitions (or just a single partition if you have one large hard drive, denoted by a C:\ label). Opening a file cabinet drawer is analogous to accessing a hard-drive partition (also called a logical drive when more than one partition is being used). Refer to Figure 14.2 for an illustration of this analogy.

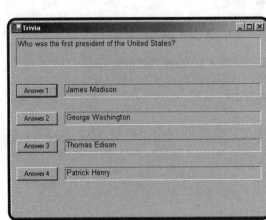

**FIGURE 14.1**

The Trivia program demonstrates how to use the file access routines in this chapter.

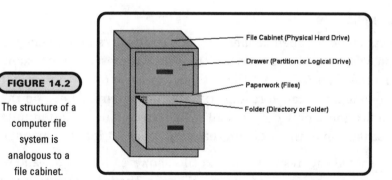

**FIGURE 14.2**

The structure of a computer file system is analogous to a file cabinet.

Now, there are all kinds of different file systems in use, such as NTFS, FAT32, CDFS, UDF, and HPFS, to name just a few. Then there are truly weird operating systems, such as UNIX and Linux, that treat everything as a file—from hard drives to modems. That's just strange, if you ask me.

Now here's a fun idea if you are interested in learning to use Linux. Did you know you can install it on your Windows PC, and then choose which OS to run when your computer starts up? It's all explained in the book, *Add Red Hat Linux 7 to Your Windows Desktop In a Weekend*, by Brian Proffitt (Premier Press).

## Reading and Writing Files

Reading a file is sort of like pulling paperwork from a folder in the file cabinet and literally reading it, as the phrase implies. When you open a file using a program like Microsoft Word or Excel, the program goes to the directory (folder) that you specify and looks for the file you want to open. The program then loads that file into memory and displays it on the screen.

You might think of writing to a file as similar to opening a folder and stuffing a piece of paper in. Or, you might think of writing to a file as actually writing with pen and paper, or with a typewriter, or even with a word processor and printer. I prefer the first analogy myself because it seems to reflect more closely what is happening in the physical file system when a file is saved.

## File Access Modes

There are two basic ways to read and write files, and these two methods will be the same for every computer system in the world because it is a core concept to computing.

### Sequential (Text) Files

The first file access mode is called *sequential* because it works in a single-file, sequential fashion, whether reading or writing to a file. The most common example of a sequential file is an ASCII text file with an extension of .txt. You might have seen a common text file called readme.txt, which is often included on the CD-ROM with applications, providing installation instructions or last-minute changes to the distribution of the program that didn't make it into the manual.

Sequential files are not always restricted to text files, however. It's just as valid to read a file one byte at a time and call it sequential access. That's how Wave sound files are loaded—a byte at a time in a sequential manner. The computer might load the file so fast that it seems to read it in a single block.

### Random-Access (Structured) Files

The second type of file access mode is called random access, in an odd twist of words. There is really nothing *random* about random-access files. They can be read from and written to in a sequential manner as well, but this type of access mode has additional capabilities. Also called *structured* file access, this method provides a file pointer that can jump to any record in the file without having to start from the beginning to read each record individually to locate the desired position.

The ability to jump to any location in the file gives the structured random-access file a great deal of flexibility. This method was used to create databases before relational database management systems (RDBMS) were invented—with products like Oracle and dBase leading the PC database market in the early years of the IBM PC. You might have heard the term "flat-file database." That essentially describes a random-access file that stores database records.

## Using Sequential Files

VB.NET makes it easy to read and write a sequential file, with several useful methods built into the language for this purpose. In this section, I'll go over the file routines that you will need to read and write sequential files. This won't be a comprehensive reference for accessing sequential files, just the essentials.

## Understanding Sequential Files

Sequential files store data in a linear, or sequential, manner in a disk file. Think about the way you type letters and words into a word processor or e-mail program—one keystroke at a time. Those individual characters are stored in the document or message as a `byte` array in sequential order. To read or write the message to or from a file, these bytes are transferred one at a time.

## Reading and Writing Sequential Files

There are four primary methods for reading and writing sequential files, as the following sections explain.

### The FileOpen Method

The first method that you need to learn about is `FileOpen`, which opens a file using one of several available file access modes and sharing options. If the concept of "opening" a file seems foreign to you, consider what it takes to load Web pages in a Web browser.

First, you type in a uniform resource locator (URL) into the location box, indicating the Web site that you want to "visit." The whole concept of "visiting" a Web site is misleading because you are not a visitor at all. You are just a client who is downloading the content from the Web site to your PC and browsing the information before discarding it and moving on to another Web page. In fact, your computer doesn't even communicate *directly* with the Web server computer. What actually happens is that both computers send messages back and forth, without any guarantee or receipt of delivery either way. If the Web server is particularly busy, you may not even get a response from it.

At any rate, opening a file using the `FileOpen` method is precisely the same sort of functionality that a Web browser uses to read a Web page; each Web page is downloaded and stored in a temporary folder on your hard drive, where it is then loaded into the Web browser and displayed. Similarly, any graphics that are needed by the Web page are downloaded individually and displayed on the Web page. Each of these file access routines involves reading a file sequentially.

### The WriteLine Method

The `WriteLine` method writes a single line of text to a sequential file. Actually, the method is somewhat misleading because it doesn't write a "line" so much as it writes an array of bytes out to the file. It's up to you, the programmer, to tell `WriteLine` to actually add a newline character to the end of each line (denoted with the `vbCrLf` constant). If you fail to use `vbCrLf` at the end of a `WriteLine` command, the next line of text will be tacked on to the current line, and the result will be messy. I'll show you how this works in the ReadWrite program later in this section.

### The LineInput Method

The `LineInput` method does the opposite of the `WriteLine` method; that is, it reads a line of text from a sequential file into memory. Fortunately, `ReadLine` is a little smarter than its close sibling, `WriteLine` because it knows how to use the newline character, reading it and stripping it out of the text for you.

### The FileClose Method

The `FileClose` method closes a file that was previously opened with the `FileOpen` method, and is based on a specific file number that is passed as a parameter.

## Sequential File I/O— The ReadWrite Program

The ReadWrite program (shown in Figure 14.3) is a simple demonstration of the sequential file handling commands that I just covered. First, the program writes out several lines of text to a text file called `ReadWrite.txt`. The program than loads the text file and displays it in a `TextBox` control.

## Building the ReadWrite Program

Start by creating a new Windows Application called ReadWrite. Alternatively, you can load this project off the CD-ROM under the folder \Sources\CH14\ReadWrite.

All you need for this program is a single `TextBox` control on the form, called `TextBox1`. After adding the `TextBox`, you'll need to set the `MultiLine` property to `True` in order to resize `TextBox1`. Once completed, your project should resemble Figure 14.4.

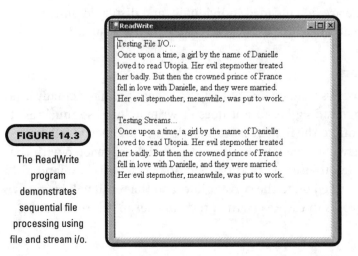

**FIGURE 14.3**

The ReadWrite program demonstrates sequential file processing using file and stream i/o.

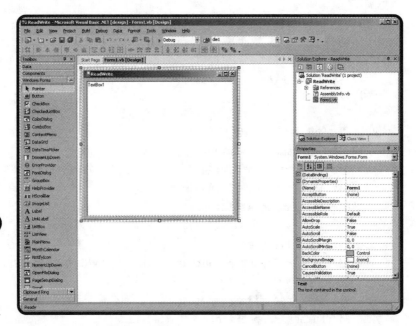

**FIGURE 14.4**

The form for the
ReadWrite
program, loaded
into the Forms
Designer in VB.NET.

## Writing the Source Code

That's all there is to the user interface, because ReadWrite is just a demonstration program that shows how to read and write a sequential file using standard file routines and streams. So, open the source code window by pressing F7. The first thing you will need to add is an Imports statement to the very top of the source code file, like this:

```
Imports System.IO
```

There are three subroutines in this program: Form1_Load, TestFileIO, and Test-Streams. Form1_Load calls the other two subroutines, which help break up the program and make it easier to understand (rather than just leaving all the code directly inside Form1_Load). One important thing to remember when working with files is that each open file is assigned a file number. As you will see in the code listing that follows (namely, the TestFileIO subroutine), you must request an available file number before attempting to open a file for reading or writing. You may use a specific number (such as 1, 2, or 3) for the file number, but doing so may conflict with other open files.

Type in the following code below the Windows Form Designer generated code line.

```
Private Sub Form1_Load(ByVal sender As System.Object, _
    ByVal e As System.EventArgs) Handles MyBase.Load
```

```vb
        Me.Show()
        TextBox1.Font = New Font("Times New Roman", 12)
        TestFileIO()
        TestStreams()
    End Sub

    Private Sub TestFileIO()
        Dim Filename As String
        Dim InputText As String
        Dim InputLine As String
        Dim FileNumber As Integer

        'set the filename
        Filename = Directory.GetCurrentDirectory() & "\ReadWrite.txt"

        'find a free file number
        FileNumber = FreeFile()

        'open the text file for output
        FileOpen(FileNumber, Filename, OpenMode.Output, OpenAccess.Write)

        'write some lines of text to the file
        WriteLine(FileNumber, _
            "Once upon a time, a girl by the name of Danielle")
        WriteLine(FileNumber, _
            "loved to read Utopia. Her evil stepmother treated")
        WriteLine(FileNumber, _
            "her badly. But then the crowned prince of France")
        WriteLine(FileNumber, _
            "fell in love with Danielle, and they were married.")
        WriteLine(FileNumber, _
            "Her evil stepmother, meanwhile, was put to work.")

        'close the file
        FileClose(FileNumber)

        'find a free file number
        FileNumber = FreeFile()
```

```
    'open the text file for input
    FileOpen(FileNumber, Filename, OpenMode.Input, OpenAccess.Read)

    'read the file into a temporary variable
    Do Until EOF(FileNumber)
        InputLine = LineInput(FileNumber)
        InputText &= InputLine.Substring(1, _
            InputLine.Length - 2) & vbCrLf
    Loop

    'close the file
    FileClose(FileNumber)

    'display the contents of the file
    TextBox1.Text = "Testing File I/O..." & vbCrLf
    TextBox1.Text &= InputText & vbCrLf

    'remove the default text selection
    TextBox1.Select(0, 0)

End Sub

Private Sub TestStreams()
    Dim infile As StreamReader
    Dim outfile As StreamWriter
    Dim Filename As String
    Dim InputText As String

    Filename = Directory.GetCurrentDirectory() & "\ReadWrite.txt"

    outfile = New StreamWriter(Filename)
    outfile.WriteLine( _
        "Once upon a time, a girl by the name of Danielle")
    outfile.WriteLine( _
        "loved to read Utopia. Her evil stepmother treated")
    outfile.WriteLine( _
        "her badly. But then the crowned prince of France")
    outfile.WriteLine( _
        "fell in love with Danielle, and they were married.")
    outfile.WriteLine( _
```

```
            "Her evil stepmother, meanwhile, was put to work.")
        outfile.Close()

        infile = New StreamReader(Filename)
        InputText = infile.ReadToEnd()
        TextBox1.Text &= "Testing Streams..." & vbCrLf
        TextBox1.Text &= InputText
        infile.Close()

        'remove the default text selection
        TextBox1.Select(0, 0)
    End Sub
```

# Creating a Rich Text Editor—
# The ScratchPad Program

The ScratchPad program (shown in Figure 14.5) is a simple text editor, which barely taps the features of the RichTextBox control, but uses just enough of those features to load and save rich text or plain text files.

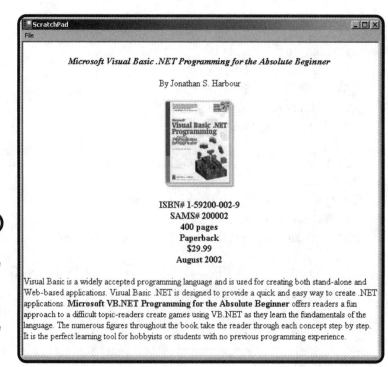

**FIGURE 14.5**

The ScratchPad program is capable of reading rich text files (with embedded images) that are compatible with Microsoft Word.

Because ScratchPad doesn't have much functionality, you will have to add special effects to a rich text document using Microsoft Word or Windows WordPad. Save the file as an .rtf file, and then you can load it into ScratchPad. You can even edit the file in ScratchPad. For instance, you can copy and paste text and images to and from other applications using ScratchPad.

## Opening and Saving RichText Files

The functionality for loading and saving rich text or plain text files is built into the RichTextBox control, so that somewhat invalidates the learning potential of this section. However, RichTextBox is an incredibly powerful control, which is capable of being used as a full-function word processor, given some effort. The ScratchPad doesn't include any functionality for changing the font, but the Rich-TextBox control supports it! In fact, you can even have embedded images in a rich text document.

Figure 14.6 shows a screenshot of the OpenFileDialog, which appears when you select Open from the File menu in ScratchPad. You can select rich text or plain text files to load.

Figure 14.7 shows a screenshot of the SaveFileDialog, which appears when you select Save from the File menu in ScratchPad. You can select to save the contents of the RichTextBox as either a rich text file or a plain text file. When you save as plain text, the formatting and images are stripped before being saved.

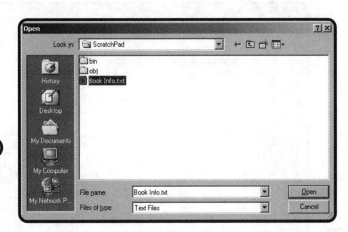

**FIGURE 14.6**

The OpenFileDialog lets you choose a rich text or plain text file to load.

**FIGURE 14.7**

The SaveFileDialog lets you save a rich text or plain text file.

## Writing the Source Code

The ScratchPad project is like all the other programs in this book—simple. It's actually surprising how simple it is, considering how much functionality is built into it. As you have learned already, that functionality is completely contained inside the RichTextBox control—a wonderful control that you should keep in mind when working on your own applications.

The ScratchPad project is a standard Windows Application with a single form, as shown in Figure 14.8.

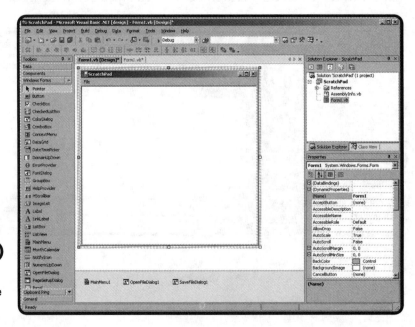

**FIGURE 14.8**

The ScratchPad project showing the main form.

For this project, you will need to first add the RichTextBox control to the form. Resize the control so that it fills the entire form, as shown in the figure. Then add three more controls to the project by double-clicking their names in the Toolbox, or by dragging them to the form:

- MainMenu
- OpenFileDialog
- SaveFileDialog

Now open the Code window by selecting View, Code, or by pressing F7. As usual, look for the region comment line Windows Form Designer generated code, and type in the following code below that line. If you want to save yourself some typing, you can return to the Form Designer (Shift+F7) and double-click each of the menu items to bring up the default Click event for each one, then look at the following code listing and type in the relevant code for each menu item.

```
Private Sub Form1_Resize(ByVal sender As Object, _
    ByVal e As System.EventArgs) Handles MyBase.Resize

    'resize the RichTextBox control to fill the form
    RichTextBox1.Width = Me.Width - 10
    RichTextBox1.Height = Me.Height - 50
End Sub

Private Sub MenuItem2_Click(ByVal sender As System.Object, _
    ByVal e As System.EventArgs) Handles MenuItem2.Click

    'clear the contents of the RichTextBox control
    RichTextBox1.Clear()
End Sub

Private Sub MenuItem3_Click(ByVal sender As System.Object, _
    ByVal e As System.EventArgs) Handles MenuItem3.Click

    Dim filename As String
    Dim substr As String
    Dim filetype As Integer

    'display the OpenFileDialog
    OpenFileDialog1.DefaultExt = "*.rtf"
    OpenFileDialog1.Filter = "RichText Files|*.rtf|Text Files|*.txt"
```

```vbnet
        OpenFileDialog1.ShowDialog()

    'save the filename
    filename = OpenFileDialog1.FileName
    If filename.Length > 0 Then
        'determine file type: rich text or plain text
        substr = filename.Substring(filename.Length - 4, 4)
        If substr.ToUpper() = ".TXT" Then
            filetype = RichTextBoxStreamType.PlainText
        Else
            filetype = RichTextBoxStreamType.RichText
        End If
    End If
    'load the file
    RichTextBox1.LoadFile(filename, filetype)
End Sub

Private Sub MenuItem4_Click(ByVal sender As System.Object, _
    ByVal e As System.EventArgs) Handles MenuItem4.Click

    Dim filename As String
    Dim substr As String
    Dim filetype As Integer

    'display the SaveFileDialog
    SaveFileDialog1.DefaultExt = "*.rtf"
    SaveFileDialog1.Filter = "RichText Files|*.rtf|Text Files|*.txt"
    SaveFileDialog1.ShowDialog()

    'save the filename
    filename = SaveFileDialog1.FileName
    If filename.Length > 0 Then
        'determine the file type: rich text or plain text
        substr = filename.Substring(filename.Length - 4, 4)
        If substr.ToUpper() = ".TXT" Then
            filetype = RichTextBoxStreamType.PlainText
        Else
            filetype = RichTextBoxStreamType.RichText
        End If
    End If
```

```
     'save the file
     RichTextBox1.SaveFile(filename, filetype)
End Sub

Private Sub MenuItem6_Click(ByVal sender As System.Object, _
     ByVal e As System.EventArgs) Handles MenuItem6.Click

     'quit menu item ends the program
     End
End Sub
```

# Using Random-Access Files

Random-access (or structured) files are faster than sequential files, and, unlike sequential files, you can read or write a record at any position in the file. VB.NET keeps track of a file pointer at the current position in which read/write operations are performed. You can read and write records at any time, and you can seek through the file for a specific record.

Based on these features, doesn't it seem like you could write your own database program using random-access files? In fact, that's definitely possible, and not even particularly difficult to pull off. Based on the code I demonstrate in this section and the code for the Trivia game at the end of the chapter, you will have all the tools you need to write an address book database, a grocery list database, or any other type of flat-file database program.

## Understanding Random-Access Files

Random-access file input and output doesn't work the same way that sequential file i/o works because random-access files are based on a structure, or record format, whereas sequential files just look at bytes (such as the bytes that make up a text file). However, random-access files share many of the same methods that sequential files use. What you need before being able to use random-access files is an introduction to structures.

## Structures—User-Defined Types

A structure in VB.NET is a group of variables that are treated as a whole and make up a new type of object (although structures are not strictly considered object-oriented). For example, suppose you want to keep track of an employee database for your company. Imagine the amount of work required to track just a handful of employee records, much less hundreds or thousands of them. Using simple variables and perhaps arrays, the task would be completely daunting.

Fortunately, structures were invented to solve problems like these more elegantly. Instead of a huge array of names, another array for addresses, and another array for phone numbers, what you end up with is an array of structures, each of which has all the information you need for an employee (such as name, address, and phone number), all built in.

## Creating Custom Structures

You create a new structure using the `Structure` keyword. Here is a sample structure:

```
Structure Employee_Data
    Dim Name As String
    Dim Salary As Decimal
End Structure
```

Note how the structure contains normal-looking variables, complete with the `Dim` keyword.

## Using the <VBFixedString> Attribute

Structures used in a program for organizational reasons need not worry about the structure in a file, but programs that read and write records in a random-access file need to be more precise in the definition of a structure, because when it comes to structures files, every byte counts. Normal string declarations are treated as variable-length strings, as it should be in VB.NET, which has dropped the use of slow and error-prone fixed-length strings. However, random-access files need a precise byte count. Therefore, VB.NET provides the `<VBFixedString>` property to structures, allowing you to give a specific fixed length for strings. This allows random-access files to read and write structures filled with strings of a specific size.

Here is an example of how you would declare the structure using a fixed-length `Name` variable:

```
Structure Employee_Data
    <VBFixedString(20)> Dim Name As String
    Dim Salary As Decimal
End Structure
```

Note the `<VBFixedString>` parameter (the number in parentheses). This tells the attribute how many bytes need to be reserved in the structure for the string that follows.

## The Seek Method

Possibly the most common method you will find in use with random-access files (aside from FileOpen and FileClose) is Seek. This method jumps to a specific position in the file, based on the size of a record. You can then easily jump to any record in a file and read or write a structure record to that position.

The Seek method has a somewhat unfortunate name because there is no "searching" involved in this process. It really just involves moving the file pointer from one location to another in the file. To actually search through a random-access file, you would need to read each record in turn, as in a sequential manner, and examine the fields inside the record for the data you are looking for.

# Random-Access File I/O— The RandomTest Program

The RandomTest program (shown in Figure 14.9) is a simple demonstration of random-access file-handling commands. First, the program creates a structure to hold information about employees, then writes a record to a test file, called Employee.dat. The program then closes and re-opens the file, loads the employee record, and then displays it in a TextBox control.

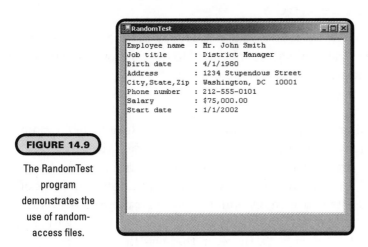

**FIGURE 14.9**

The RandomTest program demonstrates the use of random-access files.

## Building the RandomTest Program

Start by creating a new Windows Application, called RandomTest. Alternatively, you can load this project off the CD-ROM under the folder \Sources\CH14\RandomTest.

All you need for this program is a single TextBox control on the form, called TextBox1. After adding the TextBox, you'll need to set the MultiLine property to

True in order to resize TextBox1. Once finished, your project should resemble Figure 14.10.

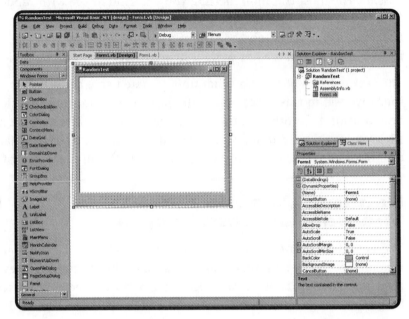

**FIGURE 14.10**

The RandomTest
program
demonstrates
how to read and
write to a random-
access file.

## Writing the Source Code

After adding TextBox1, open the source code window by pressing F7. The first thing you will need to do is add an Imports statement to the very top of the source code file, just like you did with the ReadWrite program:

```
Imports System.IO
```

The source code for RandomTest is actually simpler than the ReadWrite program because there's only one way to read and write random-access files. The most complicated part of the program is the definition for the Employee_Data structure. It's kind of intimidating because of the VBFixedString attributes in front of the string variables in the structure. In my opinion, that's far more difficult and less intuitive than the way fixed-length strings were handled in Visual Basic 6.0 (for example, Dim Title As String * 3). However, that was the structured way, and this is now the object-oriented way. As you learned back in the OOP chapters, OOP requires a little more effort, but produces better results in the end.

Here is the source code for the RandomTest program.

```
Structure Employee_Data
    Dim BirthDate As Date
    <VBFixedString(3)> Dim Title As String
```

```vb
        <VBFixedString(20)> Dim LastName As String
        <VBFixedString(20)> Dim FirstName As String
        <VBFixedString(40)> Dim Address As String
        <VBFixedString(20)> Dim City As String
        <VBFixedString(2)> Dim State As String
        <VBFixedString(10)> Dim ZIP As String
        <VBFixedString(20)> Dim Phone As String
        <VBFixedString(20)> Dim JobTitle As String
        Dim Salary As Decimal
        Dim StartDate As Date
    End Structure

    Private Sub Form1_Load(ByVal sender As System.Object, _
        ByVal e As System.EventArgs) Handles MyBase.Load

        Dim employee As Employee_Data
        Dim filenum As Integer
        Dim filename As String
        Dim temp As String

        'set the textbox font to fixed
        Me.Font = New Font("Courier New", 10)

        'find a free file number
        filenum = FreeFile()

        'set the filename
        filename = Directory.GetCurrentDirectory() & "\Employee.dat"

        'open the file
        FileOpen(filenum, filename, OpenMode.Random, OpenAccess.ReadWrite, _
            OpenShare.Default, Len(employee))

        'fill the employee record
        With employee
            .Title = "Mr."
            .LastName = "Smith"
            .FirstName = "John"
            .BirthDate = CDate("04/01/1980")
            .Address = "1234 Stupendous Street"
```

```vbnet
        .City = "Washington"
        .State = "DC"
        .ZIP = 10001
        .Phone = "212-555-0101"
        .JobTitle = "District Manager"
        .Salary = 75000
        .StartDate = CDate("01/01/2002")
End With

'write the record
FilePut(filenum, employee, 1)

'close the file
FileClose(filenum)

'open the file again
FileOpen(filenum, filename, OpenMode.Random, _
    OpenAccess.ReadWrite, OpenShare.Default, Len(employee))

'read the first record
FileGet(filenum, employee)

'display the record
With employee
    'employee name
    temp = "Employee name".PadRight(15) & ": "
    temp &= .Title.Trim() & " " & .FirstName.Trim()
    temp &= " " & .LastName.Trim() & vbCrLf
    'job title
    temp &= "Job title".PadRight(15) & ": "
    temp &= .JobTitle.Trim() & vbCrLf
    'birth date
    temp &= "Birth date".PadRight(15) & ": "
    temp &= .BirthDate & vbCrLf
    'address
    temp &= "Address".PadRight(15) & ": "
    temp &= .Address.Trim() & vbCrLf
    'city,state,zip
    temp &= "City,State,Zip".PadRight(15) & ": "
    temp &= .City.Trim() & ", " & .State.Trim()
```

```
            temp &= "   " & .ZIP.Trim() & vbCrLf
            'phone
            temp &= "Phone number".PadRight(15) & ": "
            temp &= .Phone.Trim() & vbCrLf
            'salary
            temp &= "Salary".PadRight(15) & ": "
            temp &= Format(.Salary, "Currency") & vbCrLf
            'start date
            temp &= "Start date".PadRight(15) & ": "
            temp &= .StartDate
        End With
        TextBox1.Text = temp

        'remove the text selection
        TextBox1.Select(0, 0)

        'close the file
        FileClose(filenum)
    End Sub
```

## Chapter Project—The Trivia Program

The ScratchPad program was neat, but I sort of cheated by using the RichTextBox control and avoided using any code to work with files directly. Plus, the Random Test program did not show enough about random-access files to give you real exposure to actual code. To remedy the situation, I'd like to show you the Trivia game I wrote for this chapter. This program will demonstrate how to use structured random-access files. Figure 14.11 shows what the Trivia program looks like.

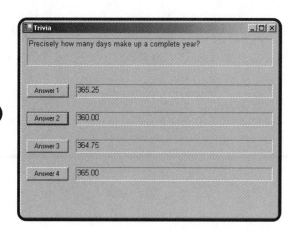

**FIGURE 14.11**

The Trivia program includes several questions that test the player's knowledge of the world.

## Creating the Project

The Trivia project includes several Label and Button controls. The completed project is shown in Figure 14.12.

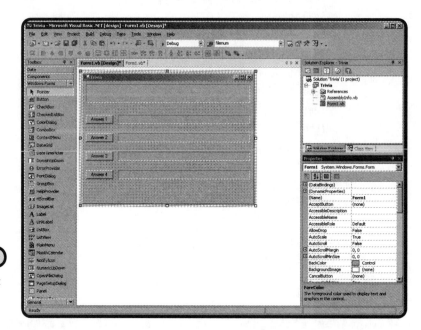

**FIGURE 14.12**

The Trivia project with the main form visible.

## TABLE 14.1  PROPERTIES FOR TRIVIA PROGRAM

| Control | Name | Property | Value |
|---------|------|----------|-------|
| Form | Form1 | Text | Trivia |
| | | Size | 464, 344 |
| | | StartupPosition | CenterScreen |
| Label | lblQuestion | BorderStyle | Fixed3D |
| | | Font | Arial, 10pt |
| | | Location | 8, 8 |
| | | Size | 440, 48 |

## TABLE 14.1 PROPERTIES FOR TRIVIA PROGRAM

| Control | Name | Property | Value |
|---------|------|----------|-------|
| Label | lblAnswer1 | BorderStyle | Fixed3D |
| | | Font | Arial, 10pt |
| | | Location | 96, 88 |
| | | Size | 352, 23 |
| Label | lblAnswer2 | BorderStyle | Fixed3D |
| | | Font | Arial, 10pt |
| | | Location | 96, 136 |
| | | Size | 352, 23 |
| Label | lblAnswer3 | BorderStyle | Fixed3D |
| | | Font | Arial, 10pt |
| | | Location | 96, 184 |
| | | Size | 352, 23 |
| Label | lblAnswer4 | BorderStyle | Fixed3D |
| | | Font | Arial, 10pt |
| | | Location | 96, 232 |
| | | Size | 352, 23 |
| Button | Button1 | Text | Answer 1 |
| | | Location | 8, 88 |
| | | Size | 75, 23 |
| Button | Button2 | Text | Answer 2 |
| | | Location | 8, 136 |
| | | Size | 75, 23 |
| Button | Button3 | Text | Answer 3 |
| | | Location | 8, 184 |
| | | Size | 75, 23 |
| Button | Button4 | Text | Answer 4 |
| | | Location | 8, 232 |
| | | Size | 75, 23 |

## Writing the Source Code

The source code for Trivia consists primarily of user-interface control events and file read/write routines.

```
Structure Trivia_Data
    <VBFixedString(80)> Dim Question As String
    <VBFixedString(30)> Dim Answer1 As String
    <VBFixedString(30)> Dim Answer2 As String
    <VBFixedString(30)> Dim Answer3 As String
    <VBFixedString(30)> Dim Answer4 As String
    Dim CorrectAnswer As Integer
End Structure


Dim trivia As Trivia_Data
Dim FileNumber As Integer
Dim TotalQuestions As Integer
Dim CurrentRecord As Integer
Dim filename As String


Private Sub Form1_Load(ByVal sender As System.Object, _
    ByVal e As System.EventArgs) Handles MyBase.Load

    CreateDatabase()
    CurrentRecord = 1
    GetNextQuestion()
End Sub


Private Sub Button1_Click(ByVal sender As System.Object, _
    ByVal e As System.EventArgs) Handles Button1.Click

    CheckAnswer(1)
End Sub


Private Sub Button2_Click(ByVal sender As System.Object, _
    ByVal e As System.EventArgs) Handles Button2.Click

    CheckAnswer(2)
End Sub
```

```
Private Sub Button3_Click(ByVal sender As System.Object, _
    ByVal e As System.EventArgs) Handles Button3.Click

    CheckAnswer(3)
End Sub

Private Sub Button4_Click(ByVal sender As System.Object, _
    ByVal e As System.EventArgs) Handles Button4.Click

    CheckAnswer(4)
End Sub

Private Sub CreateDatabase()
    FileNumber = FreeFile()
    filename = Directory.GetCurrentDirectory() & "\Trivia.dat"
    FileOpen(FileNumber, filename, OpenMode.Random, _
        OpenAccess.ReadWrite, OpenShare.Default, Len(trivia))

    'create the first record
    trivia.Question = "Who was the first president of the " & _
        United States?"
    trivia.Answer1 = "James Madison"
    trivia.Answer2 = "George Washington"
    trivia.Answer3 = "Thomas Edison"
    trivia.Answer4 = "Patrick Henry"
    trivia.CorrectAnswer = 2
    TotalQuestions = 1
    FilePut(FileNumber, trivia, TotalQuestions)

    'create the second record
    trivia.Question = "Who was the first person to fly across " & _
        "the Atlantic Ocean?"
    trivia.Answer1 = "Roscoe Tuner"
    trivia.Answer2 = "Steve Wittman"
    trivia.Answer3 = "Charles Lindbergh"
    trivia.Answer4 = "George Lucas"
    trivia.CorrectAnswer = 3
    TotalQuestions += 1
    FilePut(FileNumber, trivia, TotalQuestions)
```

```
        'create the third record
        trivia.Question = "Precisely how many days make up a " & _
            "complete year?"
        trivia.Answer1 = "365.25"
        trivia.Answer2 = "360.00"
        trivia.Answer3 = "364.75"
        trivia.Answer4 = "365.00"
        trivia.CorrectAnswer = 1
        TotalQuestions += 1
        FilePut(FileNumber, trivia, TotalQuestions)

        'create the fourth record
        trivia.Question = "What is the speed of light in " & _
            "kilometers per second?"
        trivia.Answer1 = "50,000 km"
        trivia.Answer2 = "186,000 km"
        trivia.Answer3 = "4,890,000 km"
        trivia.Answer4 = "100,000 km"
        trivia.CorrectAnswer = 4
        TotalQuestions += 1
        FilePut(FileNumber, trivia, TotalQuestions)

        FileClose(FileNumber)
    End Sub

    Private Sub GetNextQuestion()
        'read the record and display it
        FileOpen(FileNumber, filename, OpenMode.Random, _
            OpenAccess.ReadWrite, OpenShare.Default, Len(trivia))

        'locate the current record
        Seek(FileNumber, CurrentRecord)

        'read the record
        FileGet(FileNumber, trivia)

        'display the question
        lblQuestion.Text = trivia.Question
        lblAnswer1.Text = trivia.Answer1
```

```
        lblAnswer2.Text = trivia.Answer2
        lblAnswer3.Text = trivia.Answer3
        lblAnswer4.Text = trivia.Answer4

        'close the file
        FileClose(FileNumber)
    End Sub

    Private Sub CheckAnswer(ByVal ans As Integer)
        'check the answer
        If trivia.CorrectAnswer = ans Then
            MsgBox("That's correct!")
        Else
            MsgBox("I'm sorry, the correct answer is " & _
                trivia.CorrectAnswer & ".")
        End If

        'increment the record number
        CurrentRecord += 1
        If CurrentRecord <= TotalQuestions Then
            GetNextQuestion()
        Else
            MsgBox("Game over!")
        End If
    End Sub
```

## Summary

This chapter covered the important and practical subject of file input and output.
There are two primary file access modes: sequential and random-access. Sequential files are accessed from beginning to end, one byte at a time. Random-access
files may be accessed from any position in the file for read/write operations, and
may be used for small flat-file databases. Several sample programs were demonstrated in this chapter that explained how to use the file access routines built into
VB.NET and the Framework.

# CHALLENGES

The following challenges will help to reinforce the material you have learned in this chapter.

1. The ScratchPad program supports opening and displaying rich text files, including those with embedded graphics and formatting, and supports copy-and-paste operations. Enhance the editor by allowing the user to highlight sections of text and change the font.

2. The Trivia program has all the core functionality needed to develop either an educational program or a game. By adding additional features, you can adapt the program for your own purposes. First, enhance the Trivia program with the functionality for keeping track of the score.

3. To make the Trivia program truly reusable and adaptable for multiple subjects, you will need a trivia editor program. Use the source code presented in the Trivia program for reading and writing random-access files, and develop an editor program that lets users add, edit, and delete questions in the trivia database.

# Structured Error Handling and Debugging

VB.NET introduces a different way to handle errors than Visual Basic 6.0. Structured error handling provides a way to intelligently deal with errors when they occur, rather than leaving the issue somewhat mishandled, as was the case in previous versions of Visual Basic. Structured and nested error handling using Try...Catch...Finally blocks provides a great deal of power over potential errors that may occur in your programs. Along with the new error handler, VB.NET features an intuitive and easy-to-use debugger, which helps to prevent bugs from working their way into programs.

This chapter covers the following topics:

- Introduction to error handling

- Writing an error handler

- Debugging in VB.NET

# Introduction to Error Handling

In Visual Basic 6.0, error handling was prone to failure. It was unable to efficiently handle every potential error condition while using the archaic and unfortunate On Error Goto statement to trap errors. The fact that a language as recent as Visual Basic 6.0 still relied on the Goto statement is surprising enough, but when you take into account the amount of work that goes into each new version of Visual Basic, the fact is nothing short of shocking. I had high hopes for VB6 after using VB5 for over a year. Alas, VB6 was lacking in more than just error-handling features (such as class inheritance). Nevertheless, it was the most popular development tool in the world—eclipsed, perhaps, only by VB.NET.

## Avoid the Dreaded Exception Error!

In previous versions of Visual Basic, a typical subroutine with error handling looked like this:

```
Private Sub Form_Load()
    On Error GoTo Sub_Error
    'do something here
    Exit Sub
Sub_Error:
    MsgBox("Error " & Err.Number & ": " & Err.Description)
End Sub
```

The Form_Load routine above included a typical error handler in VB6. Note the use of the On Error Goto Sub_Error statement, which jumps to the Sub_Error label when an error occurs. Without this rudimentary form of error handling, the Visual Basic program will terminate on an exception error or program error.

## Trapping Program Errors

The problem with error handling is that you never know exactly where an error might occur. Therefore, the tendency is to add an error handler to every routine in the program, just in case (especially in an important or critical application).

**TRICK** In commercial applications, the error-handling code can account for as much as half of the total source code!

Regardless of the language or features, there really is no escaping this reality, unless your main routine is tasked with processing all errors. That's actually a viable alternative, but you may not be able to get specific error messages in such a case. The only way to show explicitly where an error occurs is to add error handlers to each routine individually.

# Writing an Error Handler

Suppose you are writing a database program that will be used by hundreds of users—perhaps more. Given that it is inescapable to write a large application without bugs, do you want that large of a user base encountering mysterious error messages and running into frequent problems with the program? Obviously not. The answer is to carefully consider the error-handling requirements of the application and add the appropriate error-handling code.

## Try...Catch...Finally

Here is the VB.NET version of the sample code presented earlier. Instead of Form_Load, this one uses Form1_Load, as is the case with VB.NET.

```
Private Sub Form1_Load(ByVal sender As System.Object, _
    ByVal e As System.EventArgs) Handles MyBase.Load

    Try
        'do something here
    Catch
        MsgBox("Error " & Err.Number & ": " & Err.Description)
    End Try
End Sub
```

Look at how well structured and easy to understand this error handler is compared to the VB6 handler. First, and most importantly, there is no Goto statement. Second, it's obvious exactly what will happen if an error occurs: "Try this," and then if something bad happens, "catch the error."

There's another keyword available to a VB.NET error handler, Finally. Given that the code below the Catch statement is executed if there *is* an error, what about cleanup code regardless of an error? That's what the Finally statement does—

allows you to add code to the bottom of the `Try` block that is executed whether an error occurs or not. Here's what it looks like:

```
Private Sub Form1_Load(ByVal sender As System.Object, _
    ByVal e As System.EventArgs) Handles MyBase.Load

    Try
        'do something here
    Catch
        MsgBox("Error " & Err.Number & ": " & Err.Description)
    Finally
        'this is executed whether or not an error is trapped
    End Try
End Sub
```

## Improved Error Handling

Using this structured method of handling errors, it's now possible to provide more accurate error messages to the end-user of your applications. For general use, you will want to wrap your normal lines of code in a method with a `Try...Catch...End Try` block. This replaces the old `On Error Goto` statement, which is essential for catching errors.

Just get into the habit of adding the `Try` statement to the top of each sub or function you write (or those provided by VB.NET, such as events), followed by a `Catch` and `End Try` statement at the bottom of the routine. Below the `Catch` statement, add a call to `MsgBox`, as shown in the previous sample code, which displays the error.

**Note that VB.NET still supports** `On Error Goto`, **but you may not combine this with** `Try...Catch` **in a single subroutine.**

## Debugging in VB.NET

Debugging is a crucial aspect of software development, particularly when a project is nearing completion, and testing has begun. I often insert breakpoints in key areas of the program and watch it run, noting the value of variables when the program breaks, before allowing the program to continue running. But the real benefit to debugging is when there is a legitimate bug in the program that is causing it to do something incorrectly.

# The ErrorTest Program

To demonstrate error handling and debugging, you'll need a program to experiment on. Create a new Windows Application called ErrorTest, or load the project off the CD-ROM from \Sources\CH15\ErrorTest. Here's the source code for the program:

```
Dim ClickCount As Integer
Dim first As Decimal = 1
Dim second As Decimal = 0
Dim third As Decimal

Private Sub Form1_Load(ByVal sender As System.Object, _
    ByVal e As System.EventArgs) Handles MyBase.Load

    Try
        MsgBox("Preparing to divide by zero...")
        third = first / second
    Catch
        MsgBox("Error " & Err.Number & ": " & Err.Description)
    Finally
        MsgBox("Whew, that was a close one!")
    End Try
End Sub

Private Sub Form1_Click(ByVal sender As Object, _
    ByVal e As System.EventArgs) Handles MyBase.Click

    ClickCount += 1
    MsgBox("Click count: " & ClickCount)
End Sub
```

## Running the ErrorTest Program

After typing in the code, run the program to see what happens, and then I'll go over some debugging tips with you. First, a message box will appear with the message, "Preparing to divide by zero..." as shown in Figure 15.1.

**FIGURE 15.1**

The ErrorTest program first warns you that it's about to commit an error.

Clicking the OK button then results in another message box appearing, this time bearing bad news (see Figure 15.2).

The ErrorTest program creates a "division by zero" error to demonstrate error handling.

Clicking OK the second time brings up the final message box displayed by the error handler in Form1_Load, as shown in Figure 15.3.

The third message box is called by the code inside Finally.

A blank form will then appear, which you can close. This demonstration program doesn't use the form for anything other than built-in events.

### Inserting and Removing Breakpoints

Now, let's stop the program before it reaches the error. Let me show you how to do that. Referring to Figure 15.4, you want to highlight the line third = first / second. Click anywhere in the line, or highlight the whole line, and press F9 to toggle a breakpoint. Note that you can also click the left margin of a line to toggle a breakpoint.

### Running the Program in Debug Mode

Run the program by pressing F5. The first message box, "Preparing to divide by zero..." should appear. When you click the OK button, the program will halt at the breakpoint, as shown in Figure 15.5.

### Keeping an Eye on Variables

Now, here's the fascinating part of debugging with Visual Basic. While the program is paused at the breakpoint, you can move the mouse cursor over variables and objects in the source code to bring up a ToolTip that shows the contents.

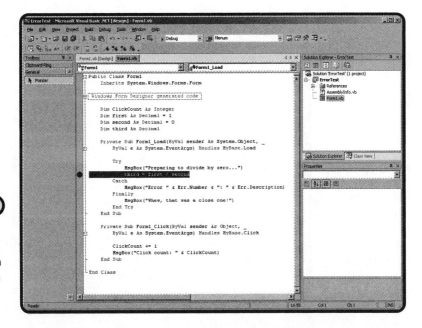

**FIGURE 15.4**

Breakpoints allow you to pause the program execution to check variables or the state of the program.

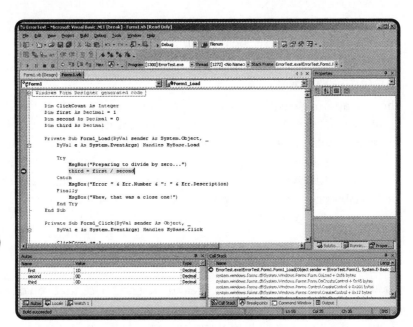

**FIGURE 15.5**

Breakpoints cause the program to pause execution at a line of code.

Check out Figure 15.6, which shows the value of the variable, first. The value 1D shows that the variable is a Decimal type.

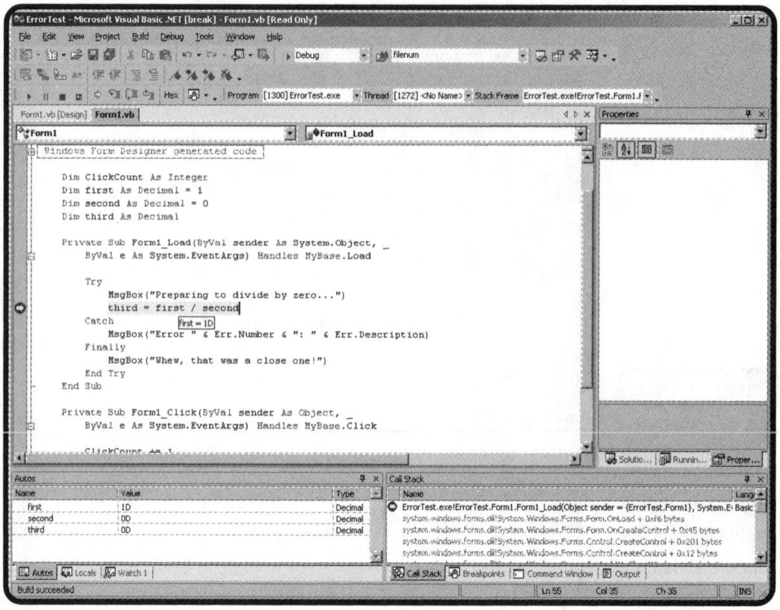

**FIGURE 15.6**

While paused, you can reveal the contents of variables and objects in a program by hovering the mouse over words.

Okay, press F5 to let the program continue running. Click through the next two message boxes and close the form to end the program.

## The Autos Window

There is another easy way to keep track of the value of variables near a breakpoint (that is, variables in the currently executing routine). Refer to Figure 15.6 again and look at the bottom-left corner to the Autos window. See how it shows the three variables used to generate the "division by zero" error: first, second, and third? This convenient window is automatically updated with the values of any variables currently in scope—that is, variables in the current subroutine (sub, function, and so on).

## Changing Variables at Runtime

Now I'd like to show you another great debugging trick that you can use in VB.NET: changing variables at runtime. Return to the Code window for the ErrorTest program, and remove the existing breakpoint that you created earlier. Add a new breakpoint in the Form1_Click event, as shown in Figure 15.7.

Go ahead and run the program now, by pressing F5. Click the OK button on each of the three message boxes until the blank form appears again. Now, click the form. The Form1_Click event is fired, and the program will pause at your breakpoint, as shown in Figure 15.8.

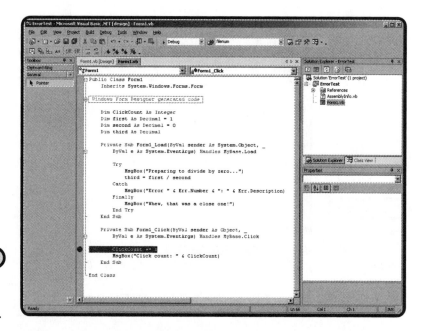

FIGURE 15.7

Adding a new
breakpoint to the
ErrorTest program.

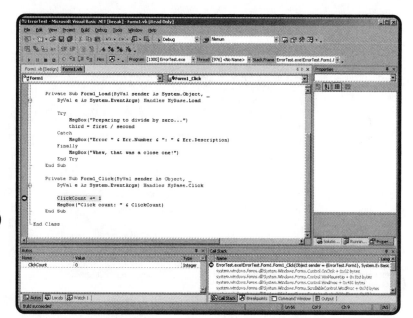

FIGURE 15.8

The ErrorTest
program has
paused at the
breakpoint inside
`Form1_Click`.

Okay, now for the fun part. You can change the value of variables by simply modifying the value displayed in the Autos window. Figure 15.9 shows how I have changed the value of the variable `ClickCount`, to 100 (look down in the lower-left corner for the updated value).

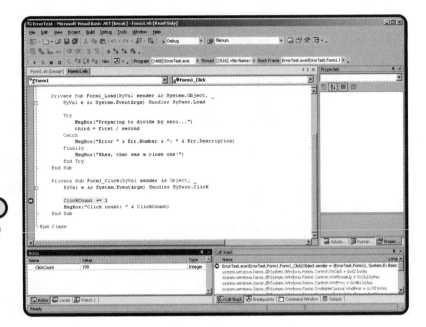

FIGURE 15.9

The new value of
ClickCount
was manually
changed while
the program
was paused.

Press F5 to allow the program to continue. A message box will appear, showing the new value of ClickCount (see Figure 15.10).

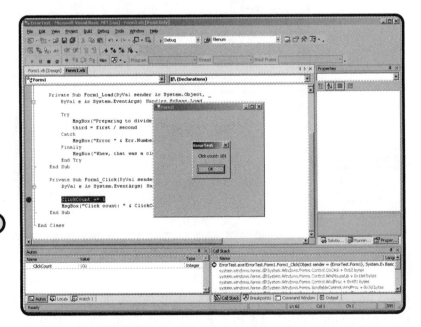

FIGURE 15.10

The value of the
ClickCount
variable is
displayed in the
message box.

# Summary

The subjects of error handling and debugging go hand-in-hand, therefore it was appropriate that they were both covered in this chapter and shared the same sample program, ErrorTest. This chapter introduced the new error-handling mechanism available in VB.NET, the `Try...Catch...Finally` block, which allows for structured handling and more robust and informative trapping of errors. VB.NET still has the excellent debugging facilities that were present in VB6, but includes additional features, such as the Autos window.

## CHALLENGES

The following challenges will help to reinforce the material you have learned in this chapter.

1. The ErrorTest program was fairly simple, but did provide a basis for testing an error handler and debugging features of VB.NET. See if you can break the program in other ways by introducing commands that might generate an exception error, and see what happens when you fail to handle the error properly in a `Try...Catch` block.

2. The Trivia program from Chapter 14, "Sequential and Random-Access Files," as well as all the sample programs throughout the book, could benefit significantly from error-handling code. If you are up to the task, open your favorites among the sample programs in this book and add error handling to them. This will make the programs more robust and usable because error handling code was purposely left out to keep these programs simple.

3. Learning to properly debug a program involves carefully tracking the values of variables and objects in the program. Try adding several more variables of various data types (such as `String` and `Date` variables) to the ErrorTest program, and gain more experience debugging a program with various data types.

**Part**

**V**

**Appendices**

Appendix A: **Recommended Reading**

Appendix B: **Using the Book's CD-ROM**

# Recommended Reading

**F**ollowing is a list of books that you will find useful in your quest to master the subject of computer programming. This list includes books that I personally own and recommend. They are excellent resources for beginning and intermediate programmers, covering various subjects and languages.

**Adams, Jim**. *Programming Role-Playing Games with DirectX.*
Premier Press. ISBN 0-7615-3521-7. February 2002.
This book is a fascinating journey into the art of programming role-playing games, with an intuitive presentation of the genre and enough theory and code to develop a 3D RPG with multiplayer capabilities.

**Barron, Todd**. *Multiplayer Game Programming.*
Premier Press. ISBN 0-7615-3298-6. June 2001.
This book delves into the details of writing multiplayer programs using Windows Sockets API and also Microsoft DirectPlay. It includes two sample games that show how to create game servers and 3D game clients.

**Engel, Wolfgang F., et al**. *Beginning Direct3D Game Programming.*
Premier Press. ISBN 0-7615-3191-2. April 2001.
This book is an easy introduction to programming Microsoft Direct3D. If you are interested in writing 3D programs with DirectX, but don't have a lot of experience with the C language, you will find this book useful.

**Foxall, James D**. *Practical Standards for Microsoft Visual Basic .NET.*
Microsoft Press. ISBN 0735613567. June 2002.
This book is a detailed discussion of programming standards for VB.NET and was mainly written for experienced programmers and programming teams that need to share source code. I find this book useful as a resource for VB.NET coding tricks and for pointers on writing correctly formatted code.

**Gosney, John**. *ASP Programming for the Absolute Beginner.*
Premier Press. ISBN 1-931841-01-2. November 2001.
This book provides a basic introduction to Active Server Pages, what this technology is, and what you can do with it. Combined with a scripting language like JavaScript or VBScript, ASP is a powerful Web development language, and this book will show you how it works.

**Halvorson, Michael**. *Microsoft Visual Basic .NET Step by Step.*
Microsoft Press. ISBN 0735613745. January 2002.
This is a thorough book for intermediate VB.NET programmers who would like to use some of the more complicated features of the language, and yet it is also useful as a resource for Visual Basic 6.0 programmers who are learning VB.NET.

**Harbour, Jonathan S**. *Pocket PC Game Programming:*
*Using the Windows CE Game API.*
Premier Press. ISBN 0-7615-3057-6. May 2001.
This book will teach you how to write programs for Pocket PC devices such as the Cassiopeia, Jornada, and iPAQ. Using simple games, this book starts with basic Windows programming and progresses to writing a complete multiplayer game.

**Harbour, Jonathan S**. *Visual Basic Game Programming with DirectX.*
Premier Press. ISBN 1-931841-25-X. February 2002.
This book is a comprehensive guide to writing games with Visual Basic 6.0, with coverage of Windows API graphics using the GDI, as well as complete tutorials and sample games using DirectX 8.0, including multiplayer DirectPlay and Direct3D games.

**Harris, Andy**. *Microsoft C# Programming for the Absolute Beginner.*

Premier Press. ISBN 1-931841-16-0. May 2002.

This book provides an easy-to-follow discussion of Visual C# .NET, from basic concepts to advanced program logic and the .NET Framework.

**Harris, Andy**. *Palm Programming for the Absolute Beginner.*

Premier Press. ISBN 0-7615-3524-1. August 2001.

This book provides the reader with all the tools and source code needed to write programs for the Palm PDA platform using the PocketC compiler and related Palm libraries.

**Henkemans, Dirk, et al**. *C++ Programming for the Absolute Beginner.*

Premier Press. ISBN 1-931841-43-8. August 2001.

This book starts with the basics of writing Visual C++ programs, covering the basic aspects of the language and development environment, and then progresses to more advanced subjects, such as DirectX, with numerous easy-to-follow source code listings for sample games.

**LaMothe, André**. *Tricks of the Windows Game Programming Gurus.*

Sams Publishing. ISBN 0-672-31361-8. September 1999.

This book is the standard by which game programming books must follow, covering Windows programming and all aspects of DirectX in a single volume, with comprehensive coverage of physics, artificial intelligence, collision, and advanced gaming techniques.

**McManus, Jeffrey P**. *Jeffrey McManus' Database Access with Visual Basic 6.*

Sams Publishing. ISBN 0672314223. January 1999.

This is a terrific book for beginning database programmers because the author makes no assumptions about the experience level of the reader, providing simple tutorials and explanations for connecting to data sources, such as Access and SQL Server, with additional coverage of ASP and data reporting.

**Russell, Joseph P**. *Java Programming for the Absolute Beginner.*

Premier Press. ISBN 0-7615-3522-5. August 2001.

This book teaches the fundamentals of the Java 2 language, with numerous sample games to demonstrate the topics covered in each chapter.

**Stephens, Rod**. *Visual Basic Graphics Programming*.

Wiley Computer Publishing. ISBN 0-471-35599-2. October 1999.

This book is for experienced Visual Basic programmers who would like to tap into advanced mathematical and simulation programming, including terrain rendering, ray tracing, fractals, custom graphs, and visual representations of data.

**Vine, Michael**. *C Programming for the Absolute Beginner*.

Premier Press. ISBN 1-931841-52-7. July 2002.

This book provides a thorough introduction to the C language, which is the language upon which C++ was built. By writing simple games, the reader will learn the techniques needed to master the C language.

**Vine, Michael**. *Visual Basic Programming for the Absolute Beginner*.

Premier Press. ISBN 0-7615-3553-5. July 2001.

This book is a beginner's guide to Visual Basic 6.0 programming, providing a simple tutorial style that is readable by anyone, even non-programmers. Sample games help to reinforce the material presented in each chapter.

**Walsh, Peter**. *The Zen of Direct3D Game Programming*.

Premier Press. ISBN 0-7615-3429-6. June 2001.

This book is a solid reference for programming Direct3D and several other aspects of DirectX 8.0 using Visual C++. The author assumes that the reader has at least some experience with C++ and DirectX and quickly jumps into advanced Direct3D programming techniques.

# Using the Book's CD-ROM

he CD-ROM disc that comes with this book contains important files that you will want to use when working through the source code and sample projects in the book. The CD comes pre-loaded with a very cool Autorun program, which fires up the default Web browser. This allows you to browse the contents of the CD using a menu of various links for installing the programs and files on your hard drive. Simply insert the CD into your CD-ROM drive, and it should begin running automatically.

## Project Source Code Files

The most important files on the CD are the project files, which include the source code for the sample programs in the book. The projects are stored in folders, which are laid out by chapter from the \Source Code directory. For instance, the source code for the program in Chapter 3 is located in \Source Code\Chapter 3.

When a chapter includes more than one program (as is often the case), the individual programs are located in sub-folders under each chapter. For instance, the Trivia program from Chapter 14 is located in \Source Code\Chapter 14\Trivia.

Be sure to turn off the read-only status of the files when you copy them from the CD-ROM to your hard drive. To turn off the read-only attribute, highlight all of the files and folders that need to be changed within Windows Explorer, then select File, Properties to bring up the Properties dialog. From there, you can turn off the read-only property. This read-only setting is due to the way files are stored on the CD-ROM. If you would like to directly run the programs right on the CD-ROM, you may feel free to do so.

A self-extracting archive file called Sources.exe is also available. When you run this program, it will allow you to install the source code for the book to your hard drive.

## Ready-to-Run Sample Programs

The projects from the book have all been compiled into executable programs that you can run directly without compiling them first. If you would like to browse all of the sample programs in the book, simply look in each chapter folder for project executables, which are located under the \bin folder. For example, the aforementioned Trivia program from Chapter 14 can be run directly from the folder \Source Code\Chapter 14\Trivia\bin. The \bin folder is where executables are automatically created upon being compiled.

# Index

## A

About dialog box, LinkLabel control use, 123
Abs (absolute value) function, 204–205
Active Server Pages.NET (ASP.NET), 47–48
ActiveX Data Objects.NET (ADO.NET), 47
Add New Item dialog box
    adding inherited forms, 319
    adding new class to a project, 297–298
*Add Red Hat Linux 7 to Your Windows Desktop
    in a Weekend* (Brian Proffitt), 365
addition (+) operator, 199–200
Align property, 162
AllGone property, 255
ampersand (&) character, string concatenation,
    156–157
Animal class, 267–273, 301–302
AppleTree object, 239–242
arrays
    declaring, 225–226
    described, 225
    one-based, 226
    structures, 228–230
    uses, 226–227
    zero-based, 226
assembly language, 143
asterisk (*) character, multiplication operator,
    200–201
AutoDock, Visual Studio.NET, 63–65
automatic data validation, properties, 243–244
Autos window, variable tracking, 398

## B

back-end programs, 73
background processes, multi-tasking, 73
backslash (\) character, division operator, 202
Ball PictureBox control, 250, 254
BallX property, 250, 254
BallY property, 250, 254
Begin statement, 113
binary files, editing, 61
Bird class, 280–283, 309–310
bitmaps, adding to DiceWar project, 188
block notation, XML (Extensible Markup
    Language), 113

Blocks project
    AllGone property, 255
    Ball PictureBox control, 250, 254
    ball position checking, 252–253
    BallX property, 250, 254
    BallY property, 250, 254
    CheckCollisions subroutine, 252–253
    design elements, 245–249
    enabling the timer, 250–251
    Form_1Load event, 250
    Form1_MouseMove event, 251
    intAllGone variable, 255
    intScore variable, 255
    intSpeedX variable, 254–255
    intSpeedY variable, 254–255
    life counter, 254
    Lives property, 254
    paddle positioning, 251
    Score property, 255
    screen elements, 236, 244–245
    source code, 250–256
    SpeedX property, 254–255
    SpeedY property, 254–255
    Timer1_Tick event, 250–251
    UpdateLives subroutine, 253
    UpdateScore subroutine, 253
    updating score, 253, 255
boldface text, Label controls, 163–164
books, recommended list, 405–408
Boolean controls, CheckBox, 120–121
Boolean variable, 155
borders, GroupBox control, 134–135
BorderStyle property, 161
branching statements. *See also* statements
    described, 175
    Else, 175–176
    ElseIf, 176
    End If, 175–176
    If, 175–176
    If...Then, 37, 175–178
    If...Then...Else, 175–178
    If...Then...ElseIf, 176
    Select...Case, 178–179
    single-line If...Then, 177
breakpoints, inserting/removing, 396

Brush object, 333
Build menu, Visual Studio.NET, 53
Button control, 27–30, 72, 78–79, 99, 119–120, 166
button settings, MsgBox() function, 85–86
Button_Click event, 30–32, 117
Button1_Click event, 189–190, 215
Button2_Click event, 215–216

## C

*C# Programming for the Absolute Beginner*
        (Andy Harris), 117
C++ language, OOP methodology, 260
captions
    forms, 97
    GroupBox control, 134–135
caret (^) character, exponent operator, 205
Cat class, 277–280, 307–308
CDbl function, 198–199
CDFS, file system type, 365
CD-ROM
    sample programs, 410
    source code files, 410
CenterScreen property, 96
central processing unit (CPU), multi-processing
        computers, 72, 74
Char data type, 156
CheckBox control, 120–121
CheckCollisions subroutine, 252–253
CheckedChanged event, 121, 126
CheckedListBox control, 131–133
Checked property, 350
CheckWinner() subroutine, 103, 106–107
Circle command, 326
Circle mode, Paint project, 333–334
Circumference property, 243
class library, 259–260
class list, source code editor window display,
        33–34
class property, 266, 270–272
classes
    Animal, 267–273, 301–302
    Bird, 280–283, 309–310
    Cat, 277–280, 307–308
    Cockatiel, 281–282, 310
    constructors, 265–266, 268–270
    described, 259–260
    Dog, 273–277, 303–306
    encapsulation, 262
    format of, 264–266
    GreatDane, 275–276, 306–307
    hierarchy, 261
    inheritance, 262–263
    Manx, 279–280, 307
    methods, 266, 272–273

MiniDoxen, 276–277, 306–307
MyClassName, 265
namespaces, 268
Parakeet, 282–283, 310
Pet, 300–301
polymorphism, 263–264
properties, 266
Siamese, 278–279, 307
variables, 265
versus objects, 259
CLEAR button, Paint project, 342
Click event, 117, 120–121, 135–136
client programs
    business environment type, 72
    defined, 72
    foreground processes, 73
CLng function, 198
Cockatiel class, 281–282, 310
code editor window
    binary file editing, 61
    code entry conventions, 15–19
    HTML file editing, 59–60
    IntelliSense support, 59–60
    switching between source-code/user-interface
        view, 59
code errors, squiggly line display, 299
code reuse concept, 8, 49
code, writing conventions, 7–9, 15–19
Color object, 333
colors
    Label controls, 164
    pre-defined, 333
ComboBox control, 133–134, 337–338
comma (,) character, variable separator, 18
Command Prompt window, running programs
        from, 13–14, 19–20
commands
    Circle, 326
    Dim, 143–144, 150
    DrawLine, 326
    DrawRectangle, 326
    End, 90
    File, New, Project, 20
    File, Save All, 17, 38
    Line, 326
    looping, 220–225
    Private, 144
    Project, Add Class, 297
    Project, Add Inherited Form, 319
    PSet, 326
    Public, 144
    ReadLine(), 15–16
    WriteLine(), 17–18
Common Language Runtime (CLR), Visual
        Studio.NET, 44

components, 8
computers
    dedicated, 73
    mainframe, 74
    multi-processing systems, 74
    server clusters, 74
    server farms, 74
concatenation
    ampersand (&) character, 156–157
    defined, 157
    string manipulation functions, 157–158
conditional statements. *See* branching
        statements
Console Application template, selecting, 11
constructors, class, 265–266, 268–270
constructs
    arrays, 225–227
    defined, 227
    structures, 227–230
containers
    grouping controls, 134–136
    listing controls, 130–134
context menus
    Color items, 360–361
    Date item, 360
    default naming conventions, 356
    displaying, 358–360
    editing in Menu Designer, 355–357
    item additions, 355–356
    Label1 control, 357–358
    MouseDown event, 358–360
    properties, 358
    Time item, 360
    top-level non-support, 356
ContextMenu control, 355
Control Toolbox
    Guessing Game project, 23–30
    Visual Studio.NET element, 62–65
controls
    adding to Component tray, 346–347
    adding/removing, 76–79
    Ball PictureBox, 250, 254
    basic, 119–127
    Boolean, 120–121
    Button, 27–30, 72, 78–79, 99, 119–120, 166
    CheckBox, 120–121
    CheckedListBox, 131–133
    ComboBox, 133–134, 337–338
    containers, 134–136
    ContextMenu, 355
    defined, 72, 118
    DiceWar project, 186–187
    Font property, 25–26
    form placement methods, 24
    GroupBox, 134–135

HScrollBar, 127–128
intrinsic, 76
Label, 24–27, 72, 77, 97–98, 121–122, 161–165,
        357–358
LinkLabel, 122–124
ListBox, 131–133
listing, 130–134
MainMenu, 346–347
moving, 80
naming conventions, 79–80
Panel, 72, 99–101
PictureBox, 72, 135–136, 187
ProgressBar, 124–125
property setting methods, 80–81
RadioButton, 125–126
resize blocks, 24
resizing, 80
RichTextBox, 372
sliders, 127–130
sorting alphabetically, 118
Text property, 24
TextAlign property, 26–27
TextBox, 27–30, 72, 77–79, 126–127, 165–166
Timer, 72, 160, 166–169
TrackBar, 129–130
VScrollBar, 128–129
conventions, code writing, 7–9, 15–19
conversion functions, data type, 208
counters, life, 254
CreateGraphics function, 330
CreateMathProblem subroutine, 216–217
creating property, 242–243
Ctrl key, setting multiple control properties, 162
curly braces { and } characters, variables, 17–18
Currency data type, 145
customer support, LinkLabel control use, 123

**D**

data, encapsulation, 239–240
data input, program logic task, 174
Data menu, Visual Studio.NET, 54
data processing, program logic task, 174
data types
    Char, 156
    conversion functions, 208
    Currency, 145
    Decimal, 145
    defined, 144
    Double, 146
    Integer, 146
    Long, 144–145
    Object, 144
    selection guidelines, 146
    Short, 145

data types *(continued...)*
    String, 146, 155–160
    variable attributes, 144–146
    Variant, 145
database administrator (DBA), 75
database design methodology, 5–6
Database Management System (DBMS), 75
databases, Visual Basic.NET development, 5–6
Debug menu, Visual Studio.NET, 53
Debug mode, ErrorTest program, 396
Debug.WriteLine function, 62
debugging
    breakpoint insertion/removal, 396
    changing variables at runtime, 398–400
    ErrorTest program, 395–398
    variable tooltips, 396–398
Decimal data type, 145
decision statements. *See* branching statements
declarations
    arrays, 225–226
    assigning variable values, 150–152
    Paint project variables, 338
    strings, 156
    variable methods, 143–144
dedicated computer, server program advantages, 73
defined property, 242
described subroutine, 179–180
design time, 77
dialog boxes
    described, 82
    InputBox() function, 90–91
    MsgBox() function, 82–90
DiceWar project
    bitmap addition, 188
    Button1_Click event, 189–190
    controls, 186–187
    creating, 184–188
    dice graphics, 185
    DisplayRoll subroutine, 193–194
    Form1_Load event, 189
    GameOver function, 194
    Integer variables, 189
    PictureBox controls, 187
    RestartGame subroutine, 191
    RollDie1 subroutine, 191–192
    RollDie2 subroutine, 191–192
    RollOver function, 192–193
    screen elements, 174, 182–184
    ShowWinner subroutine, 194
    source code, 188–194
    Timer1_Tick event, 190–191
    user interface, 185–188
Dim (dimension) keyword, 17
Dim command, 143–144, 150

DisplayRoll subroutine, 193–194
DisplayWinner() subroutine, 105
dividers, Panel control, 99–101
division (/ or \) operator, 201–202
Do loop, 223
Do Until...Loop, 224
Do While...Loop, 223
Do...Loop Until loop, 224–225
Do...Loop While loop, 223–224
Dog class, 273–277, 303–306
DOS Prompt. *See* Command Prompt, 13
Double data type, 146
Drawing method, 326
drawing
    lines, 330–331
    rectangles, 332
DrawLine command, 326
DrawRectangle command, 326
drop-down lists, ComboBox control use, 133–134

**E**

edit fields, Menu Designer, 348
Edit menu, Visual Studio.NET, 51
Editor window, IDE section, 23
electromyography (EMG) science, Telemyo device,
    71
Else statement, 175–176
ElseIf statement, 176
e-mail, LinkLabel control use, 123
Enabled property, 350
encapsulation, object-oriented programming
    (OOP) element, 239–240, 262
End command, 90
End If statement, 175–176
End statement, 113
equal sign (=), equal to operator, 207–208
equal to (=) operator, 207–208
error handling
    error trapping, 392–393
    exception error avoidance, 392
    Finally keyword, 393–394
    On Error Goto Sub_Error statement, 392
    Try...Catch statement, 393–394
    Try...Catch...End statement, 394
error messages, MsgBox() function use, 82
error trapping, 392–393
ErrorTest program, 395–398
escape characters, Trivia project, 385
event notification, Button control, 78–79
event procedures, form engine interpretation,
    117–118
events
    adding to a form, 34
    Button_Click, 30–32, 117

Button1_Click, 189–190, 215
Button2_Click, 215–216
CheckedChanged, 121, 126
Click, 117, 120–121, 135–136
defined, 30
Form_Load, 32–36
Form1_Load, 102, 189, 214, 250, 338
Form1_MouseDown, 340–341
Form1_MouseEvent, 339–340
Form1_MouseMove, 251
MouseDown, 358–360
Scroll, 127–130
SelectedIndexChanged, 132–133
selecting from source code editor window, 33–34
TextChanged, 127
Timer_Tick, 169
Timer1_Tick, 190–191, 250–251
exponent (^) operator, 205
Extensible Markup Language (XML), block
    notation, 113

## F

FalseString property, 155
FAT32, file system type, 365
file extensions
    frm (form file), 76, 113
    rtf (rich text), 373
    sln (solution), 7
file systems, 364–365
File, New, Project command, 20
File, Save All command, 17, 38
FileClose method, 368
FileOpen method, 367
files
    access modes, 365–366
    binary, editing, 61
    defined, 364
    HTML, editing, 59–60
    project storage path selections, 12
    random-access (structured), 366, 377–383
    reading/writing, 365
    rich text, 372–377
    sequential (text), 366–377
FilledCircle mode, Paint project, 333, 335
FilledPie mode, Paint project, 336
FilledRectangle mode, Paint project, 333, 336
Finally keyword, 393–394
FixedSingle property, 94, 161
folders
    automatic creation upon starting a new
        project, 13
    project storage path selections, 12
Font property, 25–26

Font selection dialog box, 25–26
fonts
    boldface text, 163–164
    controls, 25–26
Food property, 316
For...Next loop, 222–223
ForeColor property, 164
foreground processes, multi-tasking, 73
form file (frm) file extension, 76
Form_Load event, 32–36
Form1_Load event, 102, 189, 214, 250, 338
Form1_Load subroutine, 369
Form1_MouseDown event, 340–341
Form1_MouseEvent event, 339–340
Form1_MouseMove event, 251
Format menu, Visual Studio.NET, 54
FormBorderStyle property, 94
forms
    adding events to, 34
    captions, 97
    defined, 113
    horizontal scroll bars, 127–128
    main, 94–97
    multiple-choice value display w/RadioButton
        control, 125
    resizing, 94–96
    reusable, 318–321
    static label display, 121
    vertical scroll bars, 128–129
    Web Forms, 112
    Windows Forms, 112–118
formulas, addition (+) operator, 199
forward slash (/) character, division operator,
    201–202
frm (form file) file extension, 113
front-end programs, 73
Function type subroutine, 180
functions
    Abs (absolute value), 204–205
    CDbl, 198–199
    CLng, 198
    CreateGraphics, 330
    data type conversion, 208
    Debug.WriteLine, 62
    GameOver, 194
    InputBox(), 90–91
    InStr, 157
    InStrRev, 157
    LCase, 158
    Left, 157
    Len, 157
    LTrim, 157
    Mid, 157
    MsgBox(), 82–90

functions *(continued...)*
  Randomize, 206
  Right, 157
  Rnd (random number), 206
  RollOver, 192–193
  RTrim, 157
  standard dialogs, 81–91
  string manipulation, 157–158
  string tokenizer, 156
  Trim, 157
  UCase, 158
  value returns, 180–181
  WinMain, 44
  WndProc, 44

**G**

game buttons, Button control, 99
GameOver function, 194
GetType property, 152
gfxobj variable, 342
GiveApple method, 241–242
global variables, declaring, 36
Globally Unique Identifier (GUID), 76
graphical user interface (GUI)
  adding/removing controls, 76–79
  background processes, 73
  defined, 70–71
  development history, 6–7
  foreground processes, 73
  moving/resizing controls, 80
  multi-processing, 72, 74
  multi-tasking, 72–73
  server clusters, 74
  server farms, 74
  standard dialogs, 81–91
  Tic-Tac-Toe project, 92–108
  user interface controls, 72
  user interface device types, 71
Graphics Device Interface Plus (GDI+), 326
Graphics object, 328–329
graphics
  bitmaps, 188
  CreateGraphics function, 330
  dice, 185
  filled drawing methods, 329
  line drawing, 330–331
  Lines program, 330–331
  Paint project, 333–343
  pixels, 326–328
  pre-defined colors, 333
  Rectangles program, 332
  System.Drawing.Graphics namespace, 328–329
  Windows resolutions, 326, 328

GreatDane class, 275–276, 306–307
greater than (>) operator, 209
greater than or equal to (>=) operator, 210
GreenAppleTree object, 240–241
GroupBox control, 134–135
Guessing Game project
  Button control, 27–30
  Button_Click event, 30–31
  control Toolbox, 23–30
  creating new project, 20–23
  event selections, 33–34
  Form_Load event, 32–36
  game logic, 37–38
  Label control, 24–27
  naming conventions, 21
  Project Type selection, 21
  random number generation, 32–37
  saving, 38
  screen elements, 4–5
  source code entry, 30–32
  storage folder path selections, 22
  TextBox control (input field), 27–30
  validation code, 30, 32
  Windows Application template, 21–23

**H**

Harris, Andy (*C# Programming for the Absolute Beginner*), 117
Help menu, Visual Studio.NET, 56
horizontal scroll bars, 127–128
HPFS, file system type, 365
HScrollBar control, 127–128
HTML files, editing, 59–60
Hungarian Notation, variable naming convention, 80
hyperlinks, LinkLabel control, 122–124

**I**

icon settings, MsgBox() function, 86–87
IDE, control Toolbox, 23–30
If statement, 175–176
If...Then statement, 37, 175–178
If...Then...Else statement, 175–178
If...Then...ElseIf statement, 176
Image property, 135, 188
inheritance, (OOP) element, 240–241, 262–263
Inheritance Picker dialog box, adding inherited forms, 319–320
Inherited Form template, 319
input fields, TextBox control, 77–78
InputBox() function
  return values, 91
  user input use, 82

InStr function, 157
InStrRev function, 157
intAllGone variable, 255
Integer data type, 146
Integer variable, 144–145, 189
integrated development environment (IDE),
        common screen elements, 23
IntelliSense, .NET support, 59–60
Intermediate Language (IL), 44
Interval property, 168
intrinsic controls, 76
intScore variable, 255
intSpeedX variable, 254–255
intSpeedY variable, 254–255
intVariable variable, 265
iteration, sequential numbers, 222

**J**

joysticks, GUI user-interface device, 71

**K**

keyboards
    GUI user-interface device, 71
    text input/output w/TextBox control, 126–127
keywords
    Dim (dimension), 17
    Finally, 393–394
    Overloadable, 273
    Overridable, 273

**L**

Label control
    alignments, 26–27
    context menus, 357–358
    described, 72, 77
    font selections, 25–26
    form placement methods, 24
    Guessing Game project, 24–27
    program title, 97–98
    programming, 121–122
    properties, 161–165
    text entry, 24
labels
    boldface text, 163–164
    static, 121
LAN technicians, hardware oriented, 75
Large Icons button, New Project dialog box, 11
LCase function, 158
Left function, 157
Len function, 157
less than (<) operator, 209

less than or equal to (<=) operator, 209–210
life counter, Blocks project, 254
Line command, 326
LineInput method, 368
lines, drawing, 330–331
Lines program, drawing lines, 330–331
LinkLabel control, 122–124
Linux, operating system type, 365
list boxes, listing controls, 130–134
ListBox control, 131–133
lists, drop-down, 133–134
Lives property, 254
Location field, New Project dialog box, 12
Long data type, 144–145
loops
    described, 220–221
    Do, 223
    Do Until...Loop, 224
    Do While...Loop, 223
    Do...Loop Until, 224–225
    Do...Loop While, 223–224
    For...Next, 222–223
    iteration, 222
    repetition, 222
low-level code, 48
LTrim function, 157

**M**

main form, Tic-Tac-Toe project, 94–97
main menu, Visual Studio.NET, 50–51
mainframe computers, 74
MainMenu control, 346–347
MainMenu project
    Checked property, 350
    edit fields, 348
    editing in Menu Designer, 348–352
    Enabled property, 350
    event triggers, 352–354
    item additions, 348–350
    MainMenu control, 346–347
    property editing, 350
    sub-menus, 349
    top-level menu addition, 349–350
Manx class, 279–280, 307
Math Quiz project
    Button1_Click event, 215
    Button2_Click event, 215–216
    CreateMathProblem subroutine, 216–217
    Form1_Load event, 214
    screen elements, 198, 211
    source code, 214–217
    user interface, 212–214

mathematical operators. *See also* operators
addition (+), 199–200
division (\ or /), 201–202
exponent (^), 205
modulus (Mod), 202–203
multiplication (*), 200–201
square root (Sqrt), 205
subtraction (-), 200
Max property, 124
MaxValue property, 152
Menu Designer
context menu editing, 355–357
edit fields, 348
item additions, 348–350
main menu editing, 348–352
property editing, 350
sub-menus, 349
top-level menu addition, 349–350
Type Here labels, 348
Menu Editor, Visual Basic 6.0, 346
menus
context, 354–361
main, 346–354
top-level, 349–350
Visual Studio.NET, 50–56
method list, source code editor window display,
33–34
methods
class, 266, 272–273
Drawing, 326
FileClose, 368
FileOpen, 367
filled drawing, 329
GiveApple, 241–242
LineInput, 368
Play, 277
Seek, 379
System.Math object, 204
WriteLine, 367
Microsoft SQL Server 2000
dedicated computer advantages, 73
GUID as primary key, 76
Microsoft.NET, COM (Component Object Model)
replacement, 42
Microsoft.NET Framework, built-in namespaces, 297
Mid function, 157
MiddleCenter property, 162
MiniDoxen class, 276–277, 306–307
minus sign (-) character, subtraction operator, 200
MinValue property, 152
Module template, moving form code to, 311–313
modules, moving form code to, 310–313
modulus (Mod) operator, 202–203
Month property, 243–244

More button, New Project dialog box, 13
mouse, GUI user-interface device, 71
MouseDown event, 358–360
MsgBox() function
button settings, 85–86
default parameters, 82–85
definition, 82
icon settings, 86–87
MsgBoxStyle enumeration, 86
pop-up window message display, 82
result values, 88–90
titles, 87–88
MsgBoxStyle enumeration, vb prefix
replacement, 86
multiplication (*) operator, 200–201
multi-processing systems, 74
multi-processing, 72, 74
multi-tasking, 72–73
MyClassName class, 265

## N

Name field, New Project dialog box, 12
NamesAges Arrays program, 227
namespaces
class, 268
creating, 297–300
described, 296–297
hierarchy, 297
Microsoft.NET Framework built-in, 297
moving classes to, 301–303
moving form code into a module, 310–313
Pets.Birds, 308–310
Pets.Cats, 307–308
Pets.Dogs, 303–307
System.Drawing, 326
System.Drawing.Graphics, 328–329
System.Math, 297
System.Windows, 297
uses, 294
Windows.Forms.Form, 297
.NET Framework
defined, 43
emerging technologies, 48–49
IntelliSense support, 59–60
low-level code, 48
object-oriented standards, 49–50
reusable code, 49
software standards, 48
New Project dialog box
automatic folder creation, 13
file/folder path selections, 12
large/small icon display, 11
Location field, 12

More button, 13
Name field, 12
new project creation, 20–23
opening from the File menu, 20
programming languages, multiple language
    support, 8
Project Types list, 9–10. 21
storage folder pat selections, 22
Templates list, 10–11
Windows Application template, 21–23
NextPlayer() subroutine, 104–105, 107–108
not equal to (<>) operator, 208–209
Notepad program, TextBox control example, 78
NTFS, file system type, 365
numbers
    copying with plus (+) character, 180
    random, 205–206
    shortcut operators, 200–201

## O

Object data type, 144
object relationships, relational operators, 207
object-oriented programming (OOP)
    Block project, 244–255
    C++ language, 260
    class methodology, 260–262
    described, 9, 236–238
    element property, 242–244
    encapsulation, 239–240, 262
    inheritance, 240–241, 262–263
    overloading programs, 241–242
    polymorphism, 241–242, 263–264
    properties, 242–244
    uses, 237
objects
    AppleTree, 239–242
    Brush, 333
    Color, 333
    defined, 239, 259
    encapsulation, 239–240
    Graphics, 328–329
    GreenAppleTree, 240–241
    Pen, 333
    RedAppleTree, 240–241
    System.Math, 203–204
    variables, 152–155
    versus classes, 259
On Error Goto Sub_Error statement, 392
one-based arrays, Visual Basic 6.0, 226
Open File dialog box, adding bitmap files, 188
OpenFileDialog box, ScratchPad project, 373
operating systems, 365

operators
    mathematical, 198–203
    relational, 206–210
    shortcut, 200–201
Output window, Visual Studio.NET element,
    62–63
Overloadable keyword, 273
overloading, 241–242
Overridable keyword, 273

## P

Paint project
    Circle mode, 333–334
    CLEAR button, 342
    ComboBox controls, 337–338
    FilledCircle mode, 333, 335
    FilledPie mode, 336
    FilledRectangle mode, 333, 336
    Form1_Load event, 338
    Form1_MouseDown event, 340–341
    Form1_MouseMove event, 339–340
    gfxobj variable, 342
    Pie mode, 333, 335
    properties, 337–338
    QUIT button, 342–343
    screen elements, 326–328, 333–336
    Select...Case statement, 341–342
    source code, 338–343
    Square mode, 333–334
    Text property, 342
    variable declarations, 338
    variables, 338
Paint Shop Pro, dice graphics, 185
Panel control, 72, 99–101
Parakeet class, 282–283, 310
parameters, MsgBox() function button settings,
    85–86
Pen object, 333
Pet class, 300–301
Pet Shop project
    Animal class, 267–274
    Bird class, 280–283
    Cat class, 277–280
    class constructors, 268–270
    class methods, 272–273
    class properties, 270–272
    Cockatiel class, 281–282
    Dog class, 273–277
    GreatDane class, 275–276
    Manx class, 279–280
    MiniDoxen class, 276–277
    Overloadable keyword, 273
    Overridable keyword, 273

Pet Shop project *(continued...)*
    overriding a base method, 275
    Parakeet class, 282–283
    renaming, 294–295
    screen elements, 258, 283–284
    Siamese class, 278–279
    source code, 288–291
    user interface, 285–287
Pets.Birds namespace, 308–310
Pets.Cats namespace, 307–308
Pets.Dogs namespace, 303–307
PetStore project
    adding new class to, 297–298
    Animal class, 301–302
    Bird class, 309–310
    Cat class, 307–308
    Cockatiel class, 310
    compiling programs as you type, 299
    Dog class, 303–306
    enhancements, 316–317
    Food property, 316
    Form1.vb source code, 314–315
    GreatDane class, 306–307
    Manx class, 307
    MiniDoxen class, 306–307
    moving Animal class into Pets namespace,
        301–303
    moving form code into a module template,
        310–313
    Parakeet class, 310
    Pet class, 300–301
    Pets.Birds namespace, 308–310
    Pets.Cats namespace, 307–308
    Pets.Dogs namespace, 303–307
    PetStore.vb source code, 312–313
    screen elements, 294–295
    Siamese class, 307
    startup object modification, 315–316
PictureBox control, 72, 135–136, 187
pictures, PictureBox control use, 135–136
Pie mode, Paint project, 333, 335
pixels, graphics display element, 326–328
Play method, 277
plus (+) character, number copying, 180
plus sign (+) character, addition operator, 199–200
polymorphism, OOP element, 241–242, 263–264
pop-up menus. *See* context menus
pop-up windows, message display with MsgBox()
    function, 82
PowerBuilder, application design tool, 75
primary keys, GUID uses, 76
Private command, 144
Private scope, variables, 265
procedures, Console.WriteLine, 148–149, 153–154

process progress, ProgressBar control use, 124
productivity, 70
Proffitt, Brian (*Add Red Hat Linux 7 to Your
    Windows Desktop in a Weekend*), 365
profiles, Start Page customization, 66–67
program logic
    branching statements, 175–179
    returning values w/functions, 180–181
    subroutines, 179–181
    tasks, 174–175
programmers, software oriented, 75
programming languages
    assembly, 143
    C++, 260
    project templates, 10–11
    Visual Basic.NET described as, 5
    Visual C#, 6
    Visual C#.NET, 46
    Visual C++, 6
    Visual C++.NET, 47
    Visual J#.NET, 47
    Visual Studio.NET elements, 42–48
programs. *See also* projects and Windows
    Applications
    back-end, 73
    background processes, 73
    client, 72
    compiling as you type, 299
    ErrorTest, 395–398
    foreground processes, 73
    front-end, 73
    Lines, 330–331
    multi-processing, 72, 74
    multi-tasking, 72–73
    NamesAges Arrays, 227
    overloading, 241–242
    process progress display, 124
    RandomTest, 379–383
    ReadWrite, 368–372
    Rectangles, 332
    run time, 77
    running (F5 key), 15
    running from the Command Prompt, 13–14,
        19–20
    sample on CD-ROM, 410
    server, 70, 72
    Simple Math, 203
    StringHandling, 158–160
    VariableAssignment, 150–152
    VariableObjects, 152–155
    Variables, 146–150
ProgressBar control, 124–125
Project, Add Class command, 297
Project, Add Inherited Form command, 319

Project Explorer. *See* Solution Explorer
Project menu, Visual Studio.NET, 52
Project Properties dialog box, renaming a project, 295–296
Project Types list, New Project dialog box, 21
Project Types, New Project dialog box element, 9–10
projects. *See also* programs and Windows Applications
 Blocks, 236, 244–255
 creating a new folder automatically, 13
 creating new, 20–23
 cross-version development, 45–46
 design time, 77
 DiceWar, 174, 181–194
 file/folder storage path selections, 12
 Guessing Game, 4
 Math Quiz, 198, 210–217
 naming conventions, 12, 21
 Paint, 326–328, 333–343
 Pet Shop, 258
 PetStore, 294–295
 Project Types selection, 9–10
 renaming, 294–295
 saving, 38
 ScratchPad, 372–377
 starting new, 9
 storage folder path selections, 22
 template selection, 10–11
 Tic-Tac-Toe, 70–71, 92–108
 Trivia, 364
 Typing Tutor, 142–143, 160–171
 Visual Basic 6.0 porting, 45
 VisualInheritance, 318–321
properties
 Align, 162
 AllGone, 255
 automatic data validation, 243–244
 BallX, 250, 254
 BallY, 250, 254
 BorderStyle, 161
 CenterScreen, 96
 Checked, 350
 Circumference, 243
 class, 266, 270–272
 context menu Label control, 358
 creating, 242–243
 defined, 242
 Enabled, 350
 FalseString, 155
 FixedSingle, 94, 161
 Font, 25–26
 Food, 316
 ForeColor, 164

 FormBorderStyle, 94
 GetType, 152
 Image, 135, 188
 Interval, 168
 label control, 161–165
 Lives, 254
 Max, 124
 MaxValue, 152
 MiddleCenter, 162
 MinValue, 152
 Month, 243–244
 object-oriented programming (OOP) element, 242–244
 Paint project, 337–338
 Score, 255
 Size, 95
 SpeedX, 254–255
 SpeedY, 254–255
 StartPosition, 96
 System.Math object, 204
 Tag, 121–122
 Text, 24, 97, 160, 162, 342
 TextAlign, 26–27
 Trivia project, 384
 TrueString, 155
 uses, 243
 Value, 124–125
 <VBFixedString>, 378
Properties window
 IDE section, 23
 setting control properties, 80–81
 Visual Studio.NET element, 62
Property Get statement, 243
Property Let statement, 243
Protected scope, variables, 265
PSet command, 326
Public command, 144
Public scope, variables, 265

## Q

QUIT button
 Paint project, 342–343
 Tic-Tac-Toe project, 92, 101

## R

RAD, 69
RadioButton control, 125–126
random numbers
 creating, 205–206
 Globally Unique Identifier (GUID), 76
 Guessing Game project generation, 32–37

random numbers *(continued...)*
   Randomize function, 206
   Rnd (random number) function, 206
random-access files
   custom structures, 378
   described, 377
   RandomTest program, 379–383
   Seek method, 379
   user-defined types, 377–378
   <VBFixedString> attribute, 378
Randomize function, 206
RandomTest program, random-access files, 380–383
Rapid Application Development (RAD) tool,
     Visual Basic.NET, 4–5
ReadLine() command, 15–16
ReadWrite program, sequential files, 368–372
Rectangles program, drawing rectangles, 332
RedAppleTree object, 240–241
relational databases, RDBMSs, 75
relational operators
   equal to (=), 207–208
   greater than (>), 209
   greater than or equal to (>=), 210
   less than (<), 209
   less than or equal to (<=), 209–210
   not equal to (<>), 208–209
   object relationships, 207
repetition, sequential numbers, 222
resize blocks, controls, 24
resolutions, common Windows, 326, 328
resources, books, 405–408
RESTART button, Tic-Tac-Toe project, 92, 101
RestartGame() subroutine, 102, 104, 107–108, 191
result values, MsgBox() function, 88–90
results output, program logic task, 174
return values, InputBox() function, 91
reusable code, .NET Framework, 49
rich text files, ScratchPad project, 372–377
RichTextBox control, 372
Right function, 157
Rnd (random number) function, 206
RollDie1 subroutine, 191–192
RollDie2 subroutine, 191–192
RollOver function, 192–193
rtf (rich text) file extension, 373
RTrim function, 157
run time
   described, 77
   variable editing, 398–400

## S

SaveFileDialog box, ScratchPad project, 373–374
Score property, 255

ScratchPad project
   OpenFileDialog box, 373
   opening/saving files, 373–374
   RichTextBox control, 372
   rtf (rich text) file extension, 373
   SaveFileDialog box, 373–374
   screen elements, 372–373
   source code, 374–377
scroll bars
   horizontal, 127–128
   listing controls, 130–134
   vertical, 128–129
Scroll event, 127–130
Seek method, 379
Select...Case statement, 178–179, 341–342
SelectedIndexChanged event, 132–133
sequential files
   described, 366
   FileClose method, 368
   FileOpen method, 367
   LineInput method, 368
   reading/writing, 367–368
   ReadWrite program, 368–372
   WriteLine method, 367
sequential numbers, iteration/repetition, 222
server administrators, hardware oriented, 75
server clusters, 74
server farms, 74
server programs
   background processes, 73
   business environment type, 72
   Database Management System (DBMS), 75–76
   dedicated computer advantages, 73
   defined, 70
Short data type, 145
shortcut operators
   addition (+=), 200
   multiplication (*=), 201
   subtraction (-=), 200
ShowWinner subroutine, 194
Siamese class, 278–279, 307
Simple Math program, 203
single-line If...Then statement, 177
Size property, 95
Small Icons button, New Project dialog box, 11
software developers, software oriented, 75
Software License Agreement, LinkLabel control
     use, 123
Solution explorer
   IDE section, 23
   Project Explorer replacement, 61
   renaming projects, 294–295
solution (sln) file extension, 7
sorts, Toolbox controls alphabetically, 118

source code
    "beneath" the form concept, 30
    block notation, 113
    Blocks project, 250–256
    DiceWar project, 188–194
    ErrorTest program, 395
    Guessing Game project, 30–32
    Lines program, 330–331
    low-level code, 48
    Math Quiz project, 214–217
    Paint project, 338–343
    Pet Shop project, 288–291
    PetStore.vb, 312–313
    RandomTest program, 380–383
    ReadWrite program, 369–372
    ScratchPad project, 374–377
    squiggly line (error) display, 299
    StringHandling program, 158–159
    Tic-Tac-Toe project, 101–108
    Trivia project, 386–389
    Typing Tutor project, 169–171
    underscore (_) character, 83
    VariableAssignment program, 150–151
    VariableObjects program, 153–154
    Variables program, 146–150
    Visual Basic 6.0 form, 113–114
    Visual Basic.NET form, 115–117
source code editor window, 33–34
source code files, CD-ROM, 410
special characters, underscore (_), 83
SpeedX property, 254–255
SpeedY property, 254–255
Square mode, Paint project, 333–334
square root (Sqrt) operator, 205
Start Page
    starting a new project, 9
    user interface customization, 66–67
StartPosition property, 96
statements. *See also* branching statements
    Begin, 113
    branching, 175–179
    conditional, 37
    End, 113
    If...Then, 37
    On Error Goto Sub_Error, 392
    Property Get, 243
    Property Let, 243
    Select...Case, 341–342
    Try...Catch, 393–394
    Try...Catch...End, 394
    Try...Catch...Finally, 393–394
    Type, 145
static labels, form display, 121
status bar, Tic-Tac-Toe project, 101

String data type, 146, 155–160
StringHandling program, 158–160
strings
    ampersand (&) character, 156–157
    declaring, 156
    defined, 16
    manipulation functions, 157–158
    modifying, 156–160
    tokenizer, 156
    uses, 156
structured files. *See* random-access files
structures
    arrays, 228–230
    defined, 228
    variables, 228
Sub type subroutine, 180
subroutines
    CheckCollisions, 252–253
    CheckWinner(), 103, 106–107
    CreateMathProblem, 216–217
    described, 179–180
    DisplayRoll, 193–194
    DisplayWinner(), 105
    Form1_Load, 369
    Function type, 180
    NextPlayer(), 104–105, 107–108
    RestartGame(), 102, 104, 107–108, 191
    RollDie1, 191–192
    RollDie2, 191–192
    ShowWinner, 194
    Sub type, 180
    TestFileIO, 369–371
    TestStreams, 369, 371–372
    types, 180
    UpdateLives, 253
    UpdateScore, 253
subtraction (-) operator, 200
support libraries, Visual Studio.NET, 43, 47–48
syntax errors
    curvy line display, 35–36
    defined, 36
System.Drawing namespace, 326
System.Drawing.Graphics namespace, 328–329
System.Math namespace, 297
System.Math object, 203–204
System.Windows namespace, 297

**T**

Tag property, 121–122
tasks, program logic, 174–175
Telemyo device, electromyography (EMG) science,
    71

templates
    Console Application, 11–13
    Inherited Form, 319
    large/small icon display, 11
    Visual Basic, 11
    Windows Application, 21–23
Templates list, New Project dialog box, 10–11
TestFileIO subroutine, 369–371
TestStreams subroutine, 369, 371–372
text files. *See* sequential files
Text property, 24, 97, 160, 162, 342
text strings, Label control, 77
TextAlign property, 26–27
TextBox control, 27–30, 72, 77–79, 126–127,
        165–166
TextChanged event, 127
Tic-Tac-Toe project
    Button control, 99
    centering main form, 96
    CheckWinner() subroutine, 103, 106–107
    DisplayWinner() subroutine, 105
    dividers, 99–101
    form captions, 97
    form sizing, 94–96
    Form1_Load event, 102
    game buttons, 99
    game title, 97–98
    Label control, 97–98
    main form, 94–97
    NextPlayer() subroutine, 104–105, 107–108
    Panel control, 99–101
    RestartGame() subroutine, 102, 104, 107–108
    restarting, 92, 101
    screen elements, 71, 92–93
    source code, 101–108
    status bar, 101
    user interface building, 97–101
Timer control, 72, 160, 166–169
Timer_Tick event, 169
Timer1_Tick event, 190–191, 250–251
timers
    adding to Typing Tutor project, 166–169
    enabling, 250–251
titles
    form captions, 97
    Label control, 97–98
    MsgBox() function, 87–88
    Tic-Tac-Toe project, 97–98
tokenizer, strings, 156
toolbars, 56
Toolbox
    controls, 23–30
    IDE section, 23
    sorting controls alphabetically, 118

Toolbox window, user-interface control display,
        76–77
Tools menu, Visual Studio.NET, 55
tooltips, debugging, 396–398
TrackBar control, 129–130
Trim function, 157
Trivia project
    escape characters, 385
    properties, 384
    screen elements, 364, 383
    source code, 386–389
    Try...Catch...Finally statement, 393–394
true/false values, Boolean controls, 120–121
TrueString property, 155
Try...Catch statement, 393–394
Try...Catch...End statement, 394
Try...Catch...Finally statement, 393–394
Type statement, 145
types subroutine, 180
Typing Tutor project
    Button control, 166
    creating, 161
    form sizing, 161–162
    Label control properties, 161–165
    screen elements, 142–143, 160
    source code, 169–171
    TextBox control, 165–166
    timer addition, 166–169
    Timer control, 160, 166–169
    user interface, 161–171

U

UCase function, 158
UDF, file system type, 365
underscore (_) character, source code
        continuation use, 83
Unicode, String/Char data type requirement, 156
UNIX, operating system type, 365
untyped variables, 144
UpdateLives subroutine, 253
UpdateScore subroutine, 253
user input, InputBox() function, 82, 90–91
user interfaces
    Button control, 119–120
    DiceWar project, 185–188
    Math Quiz project, 212–214
    Pet Shop project, 285–287
    Tic-Tac-Toe project, 97–101
    Typing Tutor project, 161–171
users, preventing form resizing, 94

# V

validation, Guessing Game project, 30, 32
Value property, 124–125
values
    assigning to variables at declaration, 150–152
    Boolean control true/false, 120–121
    MsgBox() function results, 88–90
    multiple-choice, 125
    range changes, 129–130
    returning w/functions, 180–181
variable attributes data type, 144–146
variable scope, 36
VariableAssignment program, 150–152
variables
    64-bit versus 128-bit, 145
    assigning values at declaration, 150–152
    Boolean, 155
    brush, 338
    changing at runtime, 398–400
    class, 265
    comma (,) character as separator, 18
    creating w/Dim command, 143–144
    curly braces { and } characters, 17–18
    data types, 144–146
    debugging tooltips, 396–398
    declaration methods, 143–144
    declaring, 17, 146–147
    defined, 16, 144
    development history, 142–143
    Dim (dimension) keyword, 17
    displaying, 148–149
    drawsize, 338
    gfxobj, 342
    global declarations, 36
    Hungarian Notation, 80
    initializing, 147–148
    intAllGone, 255
    Integer, 144–145, 189
    intScore, 255
    intSpeedX, 254–255
    intSpeedY, 254–255
    intVariable, 265
    Long data type, 144–145
    mnemonic words, 143
    numeric, 152
    Object data type, 144
    objects, 152–155
    Paint project, 338
    pen, 338
    Private scope, 265
    Protected scope, 265
    Public scope, 265

Short data type, 145
shortcut operators, 200–201
String data type, 155–160
structures, 228
tracking in Auto window, 398
untyped, 144
uses, 143–144
variable scope, 36
Variant, 144
Variables program
    displaying variables, 148–150
    initializing variables, 147–148
    output display, 150
    running, 150
    variable declarations, 146–147
Variant data type, 145
Variant variable, 144
vb prefix, replaced by MsgBoxStyle enumeration,
    86
<VBFixedString> property, 378
versions, Visual Studio.NET, 44
vertical scroll bars, 128–129
View menu, Visual Studio.NET, 52
Visual Basic 6.0
    Menu Editor, 346
    one-based arrays, 226
    sample form source code, 113–114
    upgrade path, 44–45
    Variant variable, 144
Visual Basic .NET
    code reuse concept, 8, 49
    code writing conventions, 7–9, 15–19
    cross-version development, 45–46
    database design methodology, 5–6
    debugging, 394–399
    graphical programming language, 4
    graphical user interface (GUI), 6–7
    graphics support issues, 328
    integrated development environment (IDE), 23
    intrinsic controls, 76
    multiple language support, 8
    porting Visual Basic 6.0 projects, 45
    pre-defined colors, 333
    Professional versus Standard version, 10
    RAD (Rapid Application Development) tool, 4–5
    sample form source code, 115–117
    starting, 9
    templates, 11
    Visual Basic 6.0 upgrade path, 44–45
    Visual C# Toolbox control similarities, 117
    Visual Studio.NET element, 42, 44–46
    Windows Form engine sharing, 6
    zero-based arrays, 226

Visual C# language
  Visual Basic.NET compatibility, 6
  Visual Basic.NET Toolbox control similarities,
    117
Visual C#.NET language, 46
Visual C++ language, Visual Basic.NET
    compatibility, 6
Visual C++.NET language
  described, 47
  Windows Forms engine, 118
visual inheritance, reusable forms, 318–321
Visual InterDev, Visual Studio.NET integration, 112
Visual J#.NET language, 47
Visual Studio 6.0, Visual InterDev, 112
Visual Studio.NET
  Active Server Pages.NET (ASP.NET), 47–48
  ActiveX Data Objects.NET (ADO.NET), 47
  AutoDock feature, 63–65
  Build menu, 53
  code editor window, 58–61
  Common Language Runtime (CLR), 44
  Control Toolbox, 62–65
  cross-version development, 45–46
  Data menu, 54
  Debug menu, 53
  development environment, 50–67
  Edit menu, 51
  enterprise architect, 43
  Format menu, 54
  Help menu, 56
  IntelliSense support, 59–60
  Intermediate Language (IL), 44
  languages, 42–48
  main menu, 50–51
  menus, 50–56
  .NET Framework, 48–50
  Output window, 62–63
  porting Visual Basic 6.0 projects, 45
  profiles, 66–67
  Project menu, 52
  Properties window, 62
  Solution Explorer, 61
  support libraries, 43, 47–48
  toolbars, 56
  Tools menu, 55
  user interface elements, 50–65
  versions, 44
  View menu, 52
  Visual Basic.NET, 42, 44–46
  Visual C#.NET, 46
  Visual C++.NET, 47
  Visual InterDev integration, 112
  Visual J#.NET, 47

Window menu, 55
Windows Forms Designer, 56–58
VisualInheritance project
  adding inherited forms, 319–320
  control addition, 318
  reusable forms, 318–321
  running, 321
  Startup object, 321
voice recognition, user interface form, 71
VScrollBar control, 128–129

W

Web Forms, Windows Forms similarities, 112
Web sites
  eBay, 73
  Visual Studio.NET versions, 44
Window menu, Visual Studio.NET, 55
Windows Applications. See also programs and
    projects
  ErrorTest, 395–398
  MainMenu, 346–354
  RandomTest program, 379–383
  ReadWrite program, 368–372
  VisualInheritance, 318–321
Windows Application template, Guessing Game
    project, 21–23
Windows Form engine, Visual Basic.NET
    compatibility, 6
Windows Forms
  block notation, 113
  described, 23
  event procedures, 117–118
  Visual Basic 6.0 form source code, 113–114
  Visual Basic.NET form source code, 115–117
  Visual InterDev integration, 112
  Web Forms similarities, 112
  Windows messaging system, 117–118
Windows Forms Designer, Visual Studio.NET,
    56–58
Windows messaging system, form engine
    interpretation, 117–118
Windows versions, common screen resolutions,
    326, 328
Windows.Forms.Form namespace, 297
WinMain function, 44
WndProc function, 44
workspace, sln (solution) file extension, 7
WriteLine() command, 17–18
WriteLine method, 367

Z

zero-based arrays, Visual Basic.NET, 226